Standard Contract Terms in Cross-Border Business Transactions

Studien zum europäischen

Privat- und Prozessrecht

Herausgegeben von Marina Wellenhofer

Begründet von Manfred Wolf

Band 14

PETER LANG

Frankfurt am Main · Berlin · Bern · Bruxelles · New York · Oxford · Wien

Gintautas Šulija

Standard Contract Terms in Cross-Border Business Transactions

A Comparative Study from the Perspective of European Union Law

PETER LANG
Internationaler Verlag der Wissenschaften

Bibliographic Information published by the Deutsche Nationalbibliothek
The Deutsche Nationalbibliothek lists this publication in the Deutsche Nationalbibliografie; detailed bibliographic data is available in the internet at http://dnb.d-nb.de.

Zugl.: Frankfurt (Main), Univ., Diss., 2010

D 30
ISSN 1434-2405
ISBN 978-3-631-60343-7

www.peterlang.de

Vorwort der Herausgeberin

Die vorliegende Schriftenreihe zum europäischen Privat- und Prozessrecht wurde von Herrn Prof. Dr. Manfred Wolf begründet. Der erste Band der Reihe erschien 1999. Nach seinem Tod im Juni 2007 habe ich als seine Lehrstuhlnachfolgerin an der Universität Frankfurt am Main die Herausgeberschaft übernommen.

Die Schriftenreihe wird sich weiterhin sowohl dem materiellen Recht als auch dem Verfahrensrecht widmen. Bevorzugt werden wirtschaftsrechtliche Themen unter Berücksichtigung der europäischen und internationalen Zusammenhänge präsentiert werden. Der Begriff des Wirtschaftsrechts wird in einem weiten Sinne verstanden und auch bürgerlich-rechtliche Abhandlungen umfassen, soweit sie einen Bezug zum Wirtschaftsleben aufweisen. Beiträge hierzu sind willkommen.

Marina Wellenhofer

PREFACE

The title '*Standard Contract Terms in Cross-Border Business Transactions: a Comparative Study from the Perspective of European Union Law*' implies that this paper will offer research into European contract law and the law of the Union. The book is conventionally divided into two major parts. Part I presents an insight into the theory of European contract law, while Part II explains the possible influence of Union law on the further development of European civil law.

Part I presents an overview of regulation of standard form contracts in the selected jurisdictions of the Union. Generally, the term 'regulation of standard form contracts' refers to the techniques and procedures that are established by the government and case law to control the fairness and reasonableness of contracting or contractual arrangements. At the beginning, Chapter I of Part I deals with the theoretical justification for interfering in the freedom of contract. The necessity of regulating standard form contracts is explained by arguing that absolute freedom of contract does not contribute enough to the welfare of society, even if we assume that such freedom exists in reality. The issue of regulating freedom of contract is very complex in nature, and the rationale of such regulation often depends on the angle from which it is observed. It is commonplace in the modern law of contract that businesses are ordinarily considered as having stronger bargaining power and more experience than consumers in fixing their contractual relations as they choose. Chapter II goes further into details by explaining the regulation of unfair trade practices in the selected jurisdictions of the Union. Four jurisdictions of the Union – Germany, France, England, and Lithuania – have been selected for closer examination in order to build up a comprehensive view in the three major jurisdictions of the Union as well as in the 'new Europe'[1]. Chapter III deals specifically with the regulation of exemption and limitation terms as they are mostly misused in standard form contracts. Accordingly, English and German legal systems are considered more closely by comparing the regulations on exemption and limitation terms and discussing the forthcoming reforms. Finally, peculiarities of international business-to-business contracts are observed in Chapter IV. This chapter deals with the issues of choice of law in order to ascertain what actual freedom the contracting parties have in choosing the preferred legal order and such national regulations with regard to standard contract terms.

Part II elucidates the links between national contract laws and the Union law. In particular, the paper discusses the on-going 'Europeanisation' of the

[1] This term became famous after the Donald Rumsfield's speech on 22 January 2003 who answering *Charles Groenhuijsen's* question broadly referred to the Eastern European countries liberated from the Soviet rule.

contract laws of the Member States. The legitimacy of national regulations on standard form contracts is observed in the light of the provisions of the Union law pertaining to the free movement of economic factors. Since 2001, the Union has made several significant steps toward unification of private law systems in Europe. Thus, Chapter I of Part II observes the implications of market freedoms on national private laws. It seems that the Court of Justice plays an important role not only by setting aside the rules not in line with the TFEU but by actually introducing new rules determining which trade obstacles in the internal market should be abolished. In this way, this book reflects the case law of the Court of Justice, interpreting and developing the concept of the free and unhindered movement of economic factors. Chapter II provides a somewhat more detailed insight into the interaction of national laws of contract with market freedoms. In view of the obstacles a trader may face in abiding by unknown foreign regulations, the national regulations are assessed in the light of so-called 'indistinctly applicable measures' that are prohibited under the Union law. Further, the research examines whether or not regulations on standard form contracts have an appreciable effect on trade among Member States and what kind of rules may be invoked to justify the application of such national regulations. Finally, Chapter III contemplates different options aimed at eliminating trade restrictions created by foreign regulations on standard form contracts.

I would like to express my sincere gratitude to Dr. Manfred Wolf, a Professor of Johann Wolfgang Goethe University (Frankfurt am Main), who inspired me to pursue research into the European contract law and advised on the preparation of this paper until the summer of 2007. Moreover, my warm thanks are due to Prof. Dr. Marina Wellenhofer who took over the supervision of the paper after the Professor suddenly passed away. I also thank Prof. Dr. Joachim Zekoll for his important insights into the area of European private law and corporate law. Finally, my grateful acknowledgements go to all my family, and friends, colleagues from Vilnius University and the University of Cambridge with whom I discussed the topics of European private law and the recent developments in European Union law. I am also greatly indebted to the DAAD (German Academic Exchange Service) for providing funding for this research project.

The main work was completed in October 2009; later developments, incorporating the consolidated version of the Treaty on European Union and the Treaty on the Functioning of the European Union together with some other statutory and case law developments up to April 2010 were considered at the proof-reading stage.

Gintautas Šulija

TABLE OF CONTENTS

PART 2: THE INTERACTION OF UNION LAW AND NATIONAL REGULATIONS ON STANDARD CONTRACT TERMS

TABLE OF CASES

Cases are listed in alphabetical order

THE COURT OF JUSTICE OF THE EUROPEAN UNION

NATIONAL COURTS

UNITED KINGDOM

GERMANY

LITHUANIA

ABBREVIATIONS

AC	Appeal Cases (Law Reports)
AcP	Archive for Civil Practice (Archiv für die civilistische Praxis)
AG	Advocate General
AGBG	Law Governing General Terms of Business 1977 (Gesetz zur Regelung des Rechts der Allgemeinen Geschäftsbedingungen vom 9.12.1976)
All ER	All English Law Reports
Am. J. Com. L.	American Journal of Comparative Law
App Cas.	Law Reports, Appeal Cases, House of Lords
BB	Business Consultant (Betriebs-Berater)
BGB	German Civil Code (Bürgerliches Gesetzbuch)
BGBl.	Federal Law Gazette (Bundesgesetzblatt)
BGH	German Federal Court of Justice (Bundesgerichtshof)
BGHZ	Collection of the Decisions of German Federal Court in Civil Law Matters
Brussels I Regulation	Council Regulation (EC) No. 44/2001 of 22 December 2000 on Jurisdiction and the Recognition and Enforcement of Judgements in Civil and Commercial Matters
BVerfG	German Federal Constitutional Court (Bundesverfassungsgericht)
BVerfGE	Decisions of the German Federal Constitutional Court (Entscheidungen des Bundesverfassungsgerichts)
BW	Burgerlijk Wetboek (Civil Code, The Netherlands)
C. L. P.	Current Legal Problems
C.M.L. Rev.	Common Market Law Review
Cal. L. R.	California Law Review
Cambridge L.J.	Cambridge Law Journal
Cass. Comm.	Cour de Cassation, chamber commerciale (France)
cf.	compare (Latin confer)
CFR	Common Frame of Reference
CISG	United Nations Convention on Contracts for the International Sale of Goods (Vienna, 1980)
Code Civil	French Civil Code
Codice civile	Italian Civil Code
Col.	Column
Colum. L. Rev.	Columbia Law Review
Commission	European Commission

Comp. Law	Company Lawyer
Cornell L.R.	Cornell Law Review
Cornell LQ	Cornell Law Quarterly
CYELS	Cambridge Yearbook of European Legal Studies
DGFT	Director General of Fair Trading
Draft Bill	Unfair Contract Terms Bill 2005
DZWir	German Magazine for Economy (Deutsche Zeitschrift für Wirtschaft)
ed., eds	editor(s)
E.L. Rev.	European Law Review
EBLR	European Business Law Review
EC Treaty	Consolidated Version of the Treaty Establishing the European Community as amended in accordance with the Treaty of Nice Consolidated Version (OJ 2002 C 325/1-184)
EC	European Community
EEC	European Economic Community
EGBGB	Introductory Law to the German Civil Code (Einführungsgesetz zum Bürgerlichen Gesetzbuch)
ER	English Reports
ERCL	European Review of Contract Law
ERPL	European Review of Private Law
et al.	and others (Latin et alii)
et seq.	and following (Latin et sequentes)
EU	European Union
EU Treaty	Treaty on European Union (OJ 2010/C 83/01)
EuZW	European Journal for Commercial Law (Europäische Zeitschrift für Wirtschaftsrecht)
Hague Convention	Hague Convention on the International Sale of Goods (Hague, 1964)
Hanse LR	Hanse Law Review
Harv. L. Rev.	Harvard Law Review
HGB	German Trade Code (Handelsgesetzbuch)
HL	House of Lords
ibid.	in the same work (Latin ibidem)
I.C.C.L.R.	International Company and Commercial Law Review
ICLQ	International Comparative Law Quarterly
J. B. L.	Journal of Business Law
J. Leg. Stud.	Journal of Legal Studies
JA	Legal Working-Sheets (Juristische Arbeitsblätter)
JCP	Journal of Consumer Policy

JR	Legal Review (Juristische Rundschau)
JuS	Legal Training (Juristische Schulung)
JW	Legal Weekly (Juristische Wochenschrift)
JZ	Lawyers' Journal (Jurististenzeitung)
L.Q. R.	Law Quarterly Review
Law Com	Law Commission
LCC	Civil Code of the Republic of Lithuania
LG	German District Court (Landgericht)
LJ	Lord Justice
Lloyd's Rep	Lloyd's Law Reports
Loi Scrivener	Loi 78-23 du 10 janvier 1978 sur la protection et l'information des consommateurs de produits et de services
Ltd.	Limited
Market freedoms	Market freedoms referring to the free movement of goods, persons, services and capital in the internal market
M.L.R.	Modern Law Review
MDR	Monthly Script of German Law (Monatschrift für Deutsches Recht)
MEEs	Measures having equivalent effect
Member State	Member State of the European Union
MünchKomm	Munich Commentary (Münchener Kommentar)
N. L. J.	New Law Journal
NJW	New Legal Journal (Neue Juristische Zeitschrift)
O. J. L. S.	Oxford Journal of Legal Studies
ÖABG	Austrian Civil Code (Österreichisches Allgemeines Bürgerliches Gesetzbuch)
OJ	Official Journal of European Communities
OLG	Higher Regional Court in Germany (Oberlandesgericht)
ORGALIME	European Group of the mechanical, electrical, electronic and metalworking industries
Para (paras)	Paragraph (paragraphs)
Parliament	European Parliament
PECL	The Principles of European Contract Law (sometimes referred to as Lando-Principles)
QB	Queen's Bench Division, Law Reports
RabelsZ	Rabel's Journal for Foreign and International Law (Rabels Zeitschrift für ausländisches und internationales Recht)

Regulations 1994	Unfair Terms in Consumer Contracts Regulations 1994
Report	Joint Report 'Unfair Terms in Contract' English and Scottish Law Commissions (Law Com No 292, Scot Law Com No 199, 2005)
RG	The Supreme Court of the German Reich (Reichsgerich)
RIW	Law of International Business (Recht der Internationalen Wirtschaft)
Rome Convention	EC Convention on the Law Applicable to the Contractual Obligations (Rome, 1980)
Rome Treaty	Treaty Establishing the European Economic Community (Rome, 1957)
Rome I Regulation	The Regulation No. 593/2008 of the European Parliament and of the Council on the Law Applicable to Contractual Obligations
Rome II Regulation	Regulation No. 864/2007 of the European Parliament and the Council of 11 July 2007 on the Law Applicable to Non-Contractual Obligations
Scot Law Com	Scottish Law Commission
SCT	Standard contract terms
SEA	Single European Act of 1 July 1987
sec.	Section
SMEs	Small and medium sized enterprises
SMG	The Law on the Modernization of the Law of Obligations (Gesetz zur Modernisierung des Schuldrechts)
The Commissions	The Law Commission and the Scottish Law Commission
Treaty of Lisbon	Treaty of Lisbon amending the Treaty on European Union and the Treaty establishing the European Community (OJ 2007 C 306/01)
TEU	Treaty on European Union (OJ 2010/C 83/01)
TFEU	Treaty on the Functioning of the European Union (OJ 2010/C 83/01)
trans.	translated
Tul. L. Rev.	Tulane Law Review
U. Chicago L.Rev.	University of Chicago Law Review
U. Pa. L.R.	University of Pennsylvania Law Review
UCC	Uniform Commercial Code
UCTA	Unfair Contract Terms Act 1977

UNIDROIT	International Institute for the Unification of Private Law
UNIDROIT Principles	UNIDROIT Principles of International Commercial Contracts
Union	European Union
UTCCR	Unfair Terms in Consumer Contracts Regulations 1999, SI 1999 No. 2083 (replacing SI 1994 No. 3159)
Va. L. Rev	Virginia Law Review
vol., vols.	Volume(s)
Wisconsin L.R.	Wisconsin Law Review
WLR	Weekly Law Reports
Yale L. J.	Yale Law Journal
ZEuP	Journal for European Private Law (Zeitschrift für Europäisches Privatrecht)
ZfRV	Journal for Comparative Law (Zeitschrift für Rechtsvergleichung)
ZHR	Journal of the Total Trade Law (Zeitschrift für die gesamte Handelsrecht)
ZIP	Journal of Commercial Law and the Practice of Insolvency (Zeitschrift für Wirtschaftsrecht und Insolvenspraxis)
ZvglRWiss	Journal for Comparative Jurisprudence (Zeitschrift für vergleichende Rechtswissenschaft)
ZWirtR	Journal for Commercial Law (Zeitschrift für Wirtschaftsrecht)

INTRODUCTION

> 'Reasons for choosing the law of contract lie not only in its importance in any modern system. It is, moreover, a field in which lawyers are increasingly having to look beyond the confines of their own systems, particularly within the European Economic Community, and in which the movement for harmonisation and unification is likely to gain momentum. But before there can be harmonisation or unification there must be mutual understanding'.
>
> *Barry Nicholas*, December 1981,
> The French Law of Contract (Clarendon Press Oxford 1992) vii

RELEVANCE

In recent decades European economic integration has developed in tandem with the internal market[2]. In theory, the creation of the internal market requires enabling a supplier to sell his goods or provide services unrestricted in the internal market. However, owing to various trade barriers created by Member States, it is still difficult to fully enjoy the benefits created by the Union market freedoms. Thus harmonised rules seem to encompass more and more areas; and since the Union has now acquired competence over these areas through secondary legislation, national regulators no longer have the exclusive right to act autonomously. The expanding - sometimes also negatively referred to as 'encroaching' - competences of the Union raise doubts as to what common rules are really indispensable for the proper functioning of the internal market, and where the Union has overstepped its competences[3].

It seems that there is no unambiguous answer to the question of where European integration should halt and what further areas of private law will be harmonised. Will the creation of the internal market mean a gradual and full merger of national legal systems within the borders of the Union, and if so, what would this new European contract law look like in future? Even if there were no obstacles to the Union attaining competence over the adoption of a unified private law, it is not easy to identify clearly what actual inter-state repercussions

2 The development of the common market is sometimes defined as the third stage of economic integration. *See e.g.* Barnard C. *The Substantive Law of the EU. The Four Freedoms* (Oxford: Oxford University Press 2004) 9; Mortelmans K. 'The Common Market, the Internal Market and the Single Market, What's in a Market?' 35 *C.M.L. Rev.* (1998) 107 *et seq*

3 In this regard, see also: 'Lugano' Opinion 1/03 of 7 February 2006; cf. 'Tobacco Advertising' C-376/98

the enactment of harmonised rules would eliminate[4]. Indeed, how can we set aside trade obstacles in inter-state trade if we don't know what exactly these trade obstacles are? The unification of European private law creates many dilemmas that are difficult to resolve: first, is it really necessary to enact a unified civil code or special trade code in Europe?; second, should this hypothetical civil or trade code or European guidelines be mandatory or merely optional?; third, do the institutions and bodies of the Union have sufficient competence to do this. The numerous reactions to these issues would suggest that one can hardly expect the Member States to develop a sound and unanimous approach in the foreseeable future[5].

In the meantime, both academic writers and practitioners offer different scenarios on the elimination of trade barriers in the area of private law. Some academics support the creation of a common European law of contract[6]; some of them, however, back only initiatives directed towards the creation of common rules of contract law that are confined to cross-border European transactions[7]; some of them advocate enacting more directives aimed towards achieving a

---

4 In this context, probably the most striking example was the Draft Directive on Services in the Internal Market. *See*: Directive 2006/123/EC of the European Parliament and of the Council of 12 December 2006 on services in the internal market, L376/36 27.12.2006)

5 For example, Davies persuasively argues: '*What kind of rules might be necessary in operating an internal common market? Shared criminal law, at least concerning fraud? Common tax rule? A Common Contract Code? Harmonised Education System to Ease Migration of Persons? A single language? All are arguable'*. *See*: Davies G. 'Subsidiarity: the Wrong Idea in Wrong Place, at the Wrong Time' 43 *C.M.L. Rev.* (2006) 65

6 For instance, one of the most prominent advocates for the unification of private law in Europe Prof. Lando contends that the Principles of European Contract Law could be a first step towards a European Code of Contracts. *See*: Lando O. 'Principles of European Contract Law: An Alternative to or a Precursor of European Legislation?' 40(3) *Am. J. Com. L* (1992) 577; Lando O. 'Optional or Mandatory Europeanisation of Contract Law' 1 *ERPL* (2000) 59 *et seq*; Basedow J. 'Codification of Private Law in the European Union: the making of a Hybrid' 1 *ERPL* (2001) 35 *et seq*; Mattei U. 'A Transaction Costs Approach to the European Code' 5 *ERPL* (1997) 537 *et seq;* Meyer J. 'BB - Europareport: Auf dem Weg zu einem Europäischen Zivilgesetzbuch' *BB* (2004) 1285 *et seq*

7 *For different approaches on enhancing harmonisation of European contract law compare:* Grundmann S., Stuyck J. 'An Academic Green Paper on European Contract Law – Scope, Common Ground and Debated Issues', in: *An Academic Green Paper on European Contract Law* (The Hague: Kluwer Law International, 2002) 21 *et seq;* von Bar Ch., Lando O., Swan S. 'Communication on European Contract Law: Joint Response of the Commission on European Contract Law and the Study Group on a European Civil Code' 2 *ERPL* (2002) 235-236; van den Bergh V. L. 'The Principles of European Tort Law: The Right Path to Harmonisation?' 4 *ERPL* (2006) 514 *et seq*; Franzen M. *Privatrechtsangleichung durch die Europäische Gemeinschaft* (Berlin New York 1999)

higher degree of common private law elements[8], preparing an optional code for the contracting parties[9], or simply generally support further developments of European contract law[10]. Generally speaking, the initiatives to approximate European civil laws are assessed positively by most stakeholders; however, there is no unanimous position on the best methods and approaches on implementing ideas for the approximation civil laws in Europe.

At the same time, sceptical views are popular among academic writers as well. Beyond the content of the proposed Union legislation, it may be doubted whether mechanism of making laws 'from above' via the supra-national institutions of the Union suits the needs of Europe's peoples best. Perhaps paternalistic interventions aimed at safeguarding public interests diminishes the very credibility of the Union and contributes to 'the lack of democracy', which is so criticised in the Union. Nevertheless, realistically speaking, one can hardly expect that the current agreement between twenty-seven Member States would be possible without supranational interference[11]. An intensive discussion regarding the so–called 'europeanisation' of national private law systems at the Union level commenced after 2001, though some extensive research projects on this issue had begun several decades ago[12]. In 2001, the Commission launched a debate on whether the absence of common rules on European contract law directly or indirectly obstructs the internal market and, if so, to what extent[13]. Interestingly, after presenting 'On European Contract Law', a Communication from the Commission to the Council and the Parliament, the Commission has become less ambitious in adopting uniform private law in the whole of the

---

8 *See*: Müller–Graf P.-Ch. 'EC Directives as a Means of Private Law Unification', in: Towards a European Civil Code. (ed.) Hartkamp A. Hesselink M. *et. al.* (Ars Aequi Libri – Nijmegen Kluwer Law International 2004) 77 *et seq*

9 Gerven W. van 'Harmonisation of Private Law: do we need it?' 41(1) *C.M.L. Rev.* (2004) 531

10 See, *e.g.*, Möllers T. 'European Directives on Civil Law. The German Approach: Towards the Re-codification and New Foundation of Civil Law Principles' 6 *ERPL* (2002) 795 *et seq*

11 It should be noted that there are some suggestions that only interested countries could participate in the preparation of the European Civil Code (by drawing parallels with the Economic and Monetary Union of the European Union). Later every interested Member State would be able to opt-in. *See*: Koopmans T. 'Towards a European Civil Code?' 5 *ERPL* (1997) 542

12 *See*: Ciacchi A. C. 'An Optional Instrument for Consumer Contracts in the EU: Conflict of Laws and Conflict of Policies', in: *The Politics of the Draft Common Frame of Reference*, Somma A. ed. (Wolters Kluwer Law and Business, The Netherlands 2009) 3 *et seq*

13 Communication from the Commission to the Council and the European Parliament 'On European Contract Law', Brussels 11.07.2001 Com (2001) 398 Final, para 23

Union[14]. In 2007, for example, the Commission stated that there are currently no plans to propose a European Civil Code[15].

It can be contended that a unified European law of contract is neither necessary nor possible at least at this stage[16]. Moreover, perhaps a realistic solution would be simply to accept that trade distortions arising from divergent legal systems is a lesser evil while the 'European machine is accelerating, producing an ever more confusing amount of supranational rules and thereby extensively affecting the deeper structures of our legal systems'[17]. It is true that there are many arguments in favour of the view that private law should now grow organically without radical interventions from the Union. Even if one agrees that significant obstacles to trade – *e.g.* trade externalities, reduction of transactional, informational asymmetries - created by the rules of private law *de facto* exist, the costs of such approximations seem to be enormous in comparison to the gains of eliminating trade distortions (which are often merely hypothetical) in the Union. Moreover, apart from the issue of legal efficiency, many national governments treat national private law and its terminology as a part of their cultural heritage, which should be saved unchanged no matter what economic or legal gains are achieved by approximating laws[18].

---

14 It would probably be right to assert that any plans to elaborate the mandatory European Civil Code are no longer on the Commission's agenda since publishing the Action Plan 'On a more Coherent European Contract Law' of 12 February 2003. This idea has mostly been endorsed by legal academics, but not by practitioners or businesses.

15 *See*: Report from the Commission. Second Progress Report on the Common Frame of Reference, Brussels 25.7.2007 COM (2007) 447 final. *Cf.* Council of the European Union. Press release 2863rd Counsel meeting Justice and Home Affairs, Luxembourg, 18 April 2008; European Parliament Resolution of 3 September 2008 on the CFR for European contract law, reference B6-0374/2008.

16 *See*: Remien O. *Zwingendes Vertragsrecht und Grundfreiheiten des EG-Vertrages* (Tübingen: Mohr Siebeck 2003) 84-7; Wagner G. 'The Economics of Harmonisation: the Case of Contract Law' 39 *C.M.L. Rev.* (2002); Weatherill S. 'Why object to the Harmonisation of Private Law by the EC?' 12 *ERPL* (2004) 633; Legrand P. 'Against a European Civil Code' 60 *M.L.R.* (1997) 44 (for a commentary and criticism of Legrand's arguments see: Zeno-Zencovich V. 'The European Civil Code', European Legal traditions and neo-positivism' 4 *ERPL* (1998) 351 *et seq*); Weir T. 'All or Nothing' 78 *Tul. L. Rev.* (2004) 511; Van Den Bergh V. L. 'The Principles of European Tort Law: The Right Path to Harmonisation?' 4 *ERPL* (2006) 514 *et seq*; Markesinis B. 'Why a Code is not the Best Way to advance the Cause of European Legal Unity' 5 *ERPL* (1997) 519 *et seq*

17 Rield K. 'The Work of the Lando Commission from an Alternative Viewpoint' 1 *ERPL* (2000) 75

18 For example, the French Civil Code (Napoleonic Code) is often regarded as the cultural heritage of the French Revolution. This argument is relevant for England as well. *Cf.* Lando O. 'On Legislative Style and Structure' 4 *ERPL* (2006) 476; Basedow J. 'Das BGB im künftigen europäischen Privatrecht, der hybride Kodex – Systemsuche zwischen nationaler Kodifikation und Rechtsvergleichung', 200 *AcP* (2000) 445 *et seq*

On the other hand, I would suggest that a unified private law in Europe – no matter what content it would accrue - would create more legal certainty and transparency, which is of paramount importance for many small market participants. Moreover, even though many scholars, practitioners, and businesses remain sceptical about the necessity of developing a European civil code, it would be right to contend that there is a broad consensus that in favour of further discussions leading to the evolutionary approximation of national systems or at least to the identification of relevant legal differences that lead to trade distortions in the first place.

Currently, it is mostly matters of consumer protection where the law of contract is harmonised in the Member States. However, in real life consumers are not always the only party to be disadvantaged in contractual arrangements. It is difficult to answer whether small and medium sized enterprises should be treated equally with other businesses or whether some kind of special protectionist regime across Europe should be created for them[19]. Though finding a general answer is hardly possible, it is the case that many small and medium sized enterprises do not possess strong bargaining power, and therefore they may have no other choice than to accept harsh contractual terms similar to other consumers if they want to enter into a contract at all. Moreover, small and medium sized enterprises are not usually familiar with the principles of foreign legal systems, but they may also wish to expand and do business in other jurisdictions of the Union[20]. In particular, this is relevant for small but highly specialised manufacturers from small jurisdictions that are looking for new clients in some larger jurisdiction. For these reasons, it would probably be reasonable to surmise that the multiplicity of little-known regulations makes

---

[19] *Positively see*: Sefton-Green, R. 'The DCFR: A Technical or Political Toolbox?', in: *The Politics of the Draft Common Frame of Reference*, Somma A. ed. (Wolters Kluwer Law and Business, The Netherlands 2009) 45; Hesselink M. 'The CFR and Social Justice', in: *The Politics of the Draft Common Frame of Reference*, Somma A. ed. (Wolters Kluwer Law and Business, The Netherlands 2009) 109-110

[20] As *Staudenmayer* notes, 'unless the enterprise consults lawyers with training and experience, it can be never sure that the legal advice is completely accurate and covers all necessary aspects and suggests what is economically the most favourable solution. For small and medium size entities, such problems can even create a threshold effectively preventing the conclusion of cross border transactions'. *See*: Staudenmayer D. 'The Commission Communication on European Contract Law: What Future for European Contract Law?' 2 *ERPL* (2002) 255 *et seq*; Smits J. *The Need for a European Contract Law. Empirical and Legal Perspectives.* ed. Smits J. (Groningen: Europa Law Publishing 2005) 17 *et seq*; Bonell M. J. 'The Need and Possibilities of a Codified European Contract Law' 5 *ERPL* (1997) 505 *et seq*. It should be noted that the necessity to protect SMEs was recognised by the Union too. This protection is covered *inter alia* by Directive 86/653/EEC on self-employed commercial agents and Directive 2000/35/EC on combating late payment in commercial transactions.

doing business in the other jurisdictions of the Union less attractive than in the home jurisdiction. One can assume that even if small and medium sized enterprises are familiar with foreign legal systems they may be concerned about possible legal surprises or face a competitive disadvantage in comparison with local suppliers[21]. Finally, sometimes just the adherence to different domestic regulations may also mean that companies would not be able to adopt uniform marketing and trade practices throughout the Union. These issues are especially relevant if we encounter national regulations dealing with standard contract terms. It is likely that a company would be reluctant to do business in an unfamiliar foreign legal system or to enter into export contracts at all, if as *Collins* explains, the company's normal standard contract forms would be struck out, or its standard contract terms offered inadequate protection against unexpected liabilities[22]. Moreover, the uncertainty and vagueness of contractual relations can deter exporters from trading in these jurisdictions, and therefore such national regulations may be seen as limiting inter-state trade[23]. It is, therefore, submitted that the Union should at least endeavour to minimise the legal risks for companies that decide to engage in cross-border business transactions. In light of this, the present paper is mostly confined to an analysis and comparison of the effect of national laws on standard form contracts in

---

21 *See also*: Joint Response of the Commission on European Contract Law and the Study Group on a European Civil Code (Osnabrück 2001)

22 Collins H. 'Good Faith in European Contract Law' 14(2) *O.J.L.S.* (1994) 230. *See also:* Lando O., 'Principles of European Contract Law: An Alternative to or a Precursor of European Legislation?' 40(3) *Am. J. Com. L.* (1992) 573; Wolf M. 'Harmonisation of Protection against Unfair Contract Terms in Private European Law', in: 'European Legal Traditions and Israel', Rabello A. M., *ed.* (Jerusalem: The Harry and Michael Sacher Institute for Legislative Research and Comparative Law 1994) 379

23 *See selected bibliography of the ongoing debate:* Collins H. 'Good Faith in European Contract Law' 14(2) *O.J.L.S.* (1994) 230; Lando O. 'Principles of European Contract Law: An Alternative to or a Precursor of European Legislation?' 40(3) *Am. J. Com. L.* (1992) 573; Wolf M. *Harmonisation of Protection against unfair Contract Terms in Private European Law*, in: *European Legal Traditions and Israel*, Rabello A.M. ed. (Jerusalem: The Harry and Michael Sacher Institute for Legislative Research and Comparative Law 1994) 379; Tillmann W. 'Towards a European Civil Code' *ZEuP* (1997) 595 *et seq*; Armbrüster Ch. 'Ein Schuldvertragsrecht für Europa? Bemerkungen zur Privatrechtsangleichung in der Europäischen Union nach „Maastricht" und „Keck"' 60 *RabelsZ* (1996) 72 *et seq*; Beale H. 'The Development of European Private Law and European Commission's Action Plan on Contract Law' X *Juridica International* (2005) 7; Hommelhoff P. 'Zivilrecht unter dem europäischer Rechtsangleichung' 192 *AcP* (1992) 71 *et seq*; von Bar Ch., Lando O., Swan S. 'Communication on European Contract Law: Joint Response of the Commission on European Contract Law and the Study Group on a European Civil Code' 2 *ERPL* (2002) 194 *et seq,* Michaels R., Jansen N. 'Private Law beyond the State? Europeanisation, Globalisation, Privatisation' 54 *Am. J. of Com. L.* (2006) 843

commercial contracts. Furthermore, the question of how businesses can possibly be affected by these foreign regulations, should they decide to be engage in commercial activity in other jurisdictions within the European Union, will be examined.

It must be noted that rigid rule as to the enforceability of contracts collides with a state's right to intervene to protect more vulnerable parties in the market. One could tentatively advocate the retention of social justice in Europe as it fosters solidarity among its citizens, and thus suggest that the creation of equal levels of protection for weaker commercial parties across Europe should outweigh the rigid rule ensuring the stability of contractual relations. It must also be conceded that a quick unification or even approximation of national laws regulating unfair trade practices in business-to-business contracts is scarcely to be expected in the foreseeable future. Though there are some undeniable merits to having unified legislation in the laws of contract, similar goals – *inter alia* protecting a more vulnerable commercial party against unfair disadvantage – can be achieved via different alternative means (*e.g.* consistent interpretation of functionally similar legal rules, general guidelines, *etc.*). For instance, the convergence of case law can be a viable alternative to the harmonisation of the law of contract[24]. Finally, it must be stressed that the Court of Justice has never explicitly required a full approximation of laws within the Union to achieve the functioning of the internal market:

> 'The concept of a common market ... involves the elimination of all obstacles to intra-Community trade in order to merge the national markets into a single market'[25].

This does not, however, mean that there have been no attempts to approximate the law of contract in the Member States. In 1989 the Parliament officially called on the Commission to prepare a common European Code of Private Law[26]. In the event, this was not achieved; indeed, one may find many

---

24 *See*: Ciacchi A. C. 'Non-Legislative Harmonisation: Protection from unfair Suretyships', in: *The Harmonisation of European Contract Law. Implications for European Private Laws, Business and Legal Practic*e ed. Vogenauer S., Weatherill S. (Oxford and Portland, Oregon: Hart Publishing 2006) 197 *et seq*

25 Gaton Schul C-15/81, para 33. *Cf.* Weatherill S. 'Free Movement of Goods' 52(4) *ICLQ* (2003) 1021 *et seq*; Oliver P. 'Some Further Reflections on the Scope of Articles 28-30 (*ex* 30-36)' 36(4) *C.M.L. Rev.* (1999) 784-5

26 European Parliament 'Resolution on Action to Bring into Line the Private Law of the Member States', 26 May 1989, OJ, C 158/401, reiterated in: European Parliament 'Resolution on the Harmonisation of Certain Sectors of the Private Law of the Member States' 6 May 1994, OJ C 205/518

rationales for retaining the diversity[27] of regulation on standard form contract in Europe:

First, in some cases default autonomous contract law systems can create better environments for parties to shape their relations in accordance with their preferences[28]. In some cases, national regulators end up competing among themselves by offering the best legal environment for businesses and contractual arrangements. Some commentators argue that the elimination of diversity in European civil laws would reduce innovation and experimentation and the possibility of finding the best rules for contractual relations; furthermore, national government would have fewer capacities to react to local voters' needs, while the law of contract would lose its national character, *etc*[29]. These arguments are rather controversial because of the impossibility of proving these advantages empirically. One may argue that it is difficult for local businesses to take advantage of legal diversity. To have it otherwise, one should have exact knowledge of different laws, their application practices and the effect on inter-state business patterns. For example, even where intelligent lawyers are involved in cross-border contract negotiations, they may sometimes be wrong in assessing

---

27 Interestingly, according to Article I-8 of the Treaty establishing Constitution for Europe, the motto of the European Union shall be 'united in diversity' (*see*: OJ C 310/01)

28 *For more in-depth discussions on this issue see:* Beale H. 'The European Civil Code Movement and the European Union's common frame of reference', *Legal Information Management, Legal Information Management* (2006) 7; Gerven W. van 'Harmonisation of Private Law: do we need it?' 41(2) *C.M.L. Rev.* (2004) 508; Grundman S., Stuyck J. (ed.) *An Academic Green Paper on European Contract Law* (The Hague: Kluwer Law International 2002); Chamboredon A. 'The Debate on a European Civil Code: for an "Open Texture,"' in: *The Harmonisation of European Private Law*, van Hoecke M., Ost F. (Oxford and Portland, Oregon: Hart Publishing 2000); Hesselink M. 'Non-Mandatory Rules in European Contract Law, European Review of Contract law' 1 *ERCL* (2005) 44 *et seq*, Hesselink M. (ed.) *The Politics of a European Civil Code* (The Hague: Kluwer Law International 2006); Bussani M., Mattei U. 'The Common Approach of to European Private Law' 3 *Col. L.R.* (1997) 339; Alpa G. 'European Community Resolutions and the Codification of "Private Law"' 2 *ERPL* (2000) 321; Drexl J. 'Community Legislation Continued: Complete Harmonisation, Framework Legislation or Non-Binding Measures – Alternative Approaches to European Contract Law, Consumer Protection and Unfair Trade Practices?' 13 *EBLR* (2002) 557

29 Smits J. 'Diversity of Contract Law and the European Internal Market', in: *The Need of a European Contract Law. Empirical and Legal Perspectives*, Smits J. ed. (Groningen: Europa Law Publishing 2005) 177-8. *Cf.* Smits J. *The Making of European Private Law. Towards ius Commune Europeum as a a mixed legal system* (Intersentia 2002) 66 *et seq.* Grundmann S. The Role of Competition in the European Codification Process, in: European Private Law after the Common Frame of Reference, Micklitz H.-W., Cafaggi F. eds. (Edward Elgar 2010) 36 *et seq.* However, the benefits of retaining legal diversity are sometimes over-estimated, and there is a lack of relevant empirical justification 'for' and 'against' unification of private laws in Europe. *See*: Basedow J. 'A Common Contract Law for the Common Market' 33 *C.M.L. Rev.* (1996) 1185

the merits of foreign laws. Finally, competition in offering the best legal environment leads to more general considerations as to whether the Union is interested in promoting processes that are commonly referred as the 'race to the bottom'. A Member State may refuse to enact strict but reasonable rules on standard form contracts in the hope that the absence of such strict regulations would attract more businesses to choose its law as well as the jurisdiction in general as the place of dispute resolution.

Second, it would be quite controversial if institutions of the Union centrally or the Member States separately were to take action to regulate the effectiveness of standard form contracts. There is no explicit legal basis in the TFEU for the Union to issue a Common Civil Code for Europe. Pursuant to Articles 115 and 114 TFEU [*ex* 94 and 95 EC], the institutions of the Union can merely enact rules that contribute to the accomplishment of the internal market. After some successful attempts at challenging the validity of Directives, the Court of Justice has made it clear that the Union does not possess general competence to regulate the internal market. In this regard, it has been much discussed whether legislation on European contract law would be consistent with the TFEU [*ex* EC Treaty] at all[30].

Third, political resistance can be of paramount importance even where theory proves that adopting unified rules would otherwise be of undeniable merit for the whole Union. Member States have no obligation to move towards the harmonisation of national legal systems in general and the approximation of regulations on standard contract terms for business-to-business transactions. Research indicates that some Member States, as well as powerful business associations (*e.g.* German *Verband Deutscher Maschinen- und Anlagenbau*), have also explicitly objected to attempts to enact any general legislation in the areas aimed at harmonising the law of contract in Europe[31]. Interestingly, responses from continental Europe about the prospective harmonisation of civil

---

30 These issues will be discussed in the subsequent chapters further. *For more see:* 'Tobacco Advertising' C-376/98, para 83; British American Tobacco C-491/01, para 179; Weatherill S. 'Reflections on the EC's competence to develop "European contract law"' 13(3) *ERPL* (2005) 415

31 *See:* British Communication on European Contract Law. A Position on behalf of the Law Reform Committee of the General Bar Council of England and Wales. 21 October 2001. Baroness Ashton of Upholland 'Harmonisation of European Contract Law – The United Kingdom Governement's Thinking', in: *The Harmonisation of European Contract Law. Implications for European Private Laws, Business and Legal* Publishing 2006) 245 *et seq.*; Mance, Lord Jonathan 'Is Europe Aiming to Civilise the Common Law?' *EBRD* (2007) 77 *et seq*; McKendrick E. 'Harmonisation of European Contract Law: The State we are' in: *The Harmonisation of European Contract Law. Implications for European Private Laws, Business and Legal* Publishing 2006) 19 *et seq.*; Smits J. (ed.) *The Need for a European Contract Law. Empirical and Legal Perspectives* (Groningen: Europa Law Publishing 2005) 7 *et seq*

laws are much more positive than those from England and Wales[32]. Most of the objections stemming from England in relation to its reluctance to europeanise its civil laws owes to the traditional adherence and belief in strengths of the common law. Furthermore, there are some practical arguments. It is probably right to argue that many English lawyers believe that any approximation of laws would result in a possible loss of the revenue generated in the legal and financial sector where English law is chosen as a governing law for international contracts. For example, the ISDA (the International Swaps and Derivatives Association) Master Agreement is usually governed either by English or New York law, according to the choice of the parties[33]. Thus, it is also clear that any European interference could adversely influence financial markets in the City of London. For example, most aviation contracts are customarily regulated by English or New York law, and the choice of these jurisdictions is justified by the alleged lack of relevant case law in other European jurisdictions. It is often believed that the German law - in particular, that relating to the regulation of standard form contracts – is one of the most restrictive in Europe[34], and therefore international business participants tend to avoid systems that are overly restrictive[35]. In the event that common law and continental law were approximated, English law might lose its advantages, such as that of rendering more security to parties that their contracts would not be invalidated where standard contract terms were surprising, disproportionate or otherwise unfair[36].

In light of this political climate, it is submitted that voluntary harmonisation of private law systems via inter-governmental cooperation by all

---

[32] See the responses to the Communication on European Contract Law COM (2001) 398. The author shares Hondius' ideas that Germany remains 'one the strongholds of the movement towards harmonisation of private law in Europe', the French and Italian scholars are also interested in the harmonisation processes, while the Netherlands remains one of the leading countries in the law debate on possible harmonisation of private law in Europe. *For more see*: Hondius E. 'European Private Law – Survey 2002-2004' 6 *ERPL* (2004) 882-7

[33] Combar response to the Commission's Communication of 12 October 2001.

[34] For so-called 'hidden traps' in German law see, *e.g.*, Graf von Westphalen F. 'Fallstricke bei Verträgen und Prozessen mit Auslandsberührung' *NJW* (1994) 2113

[35] *Cf.* Workshop on Standard Terms and Conditions (STCs) Brussels, 19 January 2004, Summary of Proceedings

[36] Interestingly, the Nordic countries remain sceptical about the harmonisation of the law of contract as well. The major reason for this is so-called 'welfarist thinking' (in contrast to the traditional English adherence to freedom of contract), which is widely embedded in Scandinavian countries. Thus a possible approximation of the law of contract throughout continental Europe would probably mean that the level of protection of a weaker party would be weakened in these countries. *For more arguments see:* Wilhelmsson T. 'The Legal, the Cultural and the Political – Conclusions from Different Perspectives on Harmonisation of European Contract Law' 13 *EBLR* (2002) 544 *et seq*

Member States is hardly to be expected. In addition, it is easy to comprehend the attitude of practitioners. In the event that regulations on standard form contracts changed significantly, they would have to learn a whole new contract law from scratch, and would lose the competitive advantage they have gained through long years of studying at national universities and practising in one of the jurisdictions of the Union. Finally, it is sometimes reported that continental lawyers may be reluctant to learn common law, as it is difficult for them to comprehend[37].

Fourth, as mentioned above, there are undeniable differences in legal culture and traditions between private law systems in the Member States. It is probably true that European common law jurisdictions (England and Wales; Ireland) have experienced greater difficulties in transposing directives, as in common law countries statutes - the same as contracts - must be interpreted word for word without the possibility of judicial interpretation, which runs contrary to the practice in continental law[38]. Without a doubt, countries of different legal traditions should begin an approximation of legal terminology by identifying fundamental concepts (*e.g.* hardship, consideration, good faith, penalties included into a contract) that are widely accepted in common law or continental law. For example, the English judiciary does not permit the enforcement of penalty clauses[39], which is justified on the grounds that terms of a contract cannot be used for parties to profit from a breach of a contract. Thus, a company incorporated in a foreign jurisdiction inevitably faces the problem of knowing how to interpret little known legal regulations. It is submitted that these different concepts of common and continental law cannot be eliminated as a matter of formalism; they underlie different policies and values and are therefore stipulated differently in law.

Nonetheless, it seems that the question of a possible approximation of standard form contracts and other private laws is not completely irrelevant. It

---

[37] Legrand P. 'Against a European Civil Code' 60 *M.L.R.* (1997) 52

[38] Hesselink M. 'Special Issue on Critical Legal Theory and European Private Law' 3 *ERPL* (2002) 216. *See also*: Lando O. 'On Legislative Style and Structure' 4 *ERPL* (2006) 476-7; Mülhans Ch. *Die Umsetzung der Klausel-Richtlinie und ihre Auswirkung auf den Binnenmarkt. Eine Untersuchung anhand der Umsetzungsgesetze zur Richtlinie 93/13 EWG in Deutschland, Frankreich und im Vereinigten Königreich* (Frankfurt am Main 2004). There is a wide debate on how to reconcile UCTA 1977 and Directive 93/13/EEC on Unfair Terms in Consumer Contracts in England. UCTA goes beyond the Directive, as it includes business-to-business contracts as well as some issues of non-contractual liability, whereas the Directive goes beyond UCTA as it regulates almost all contractual terms and not only the exclusion clauses. *Weatherill* noted that 'the law is frankly rather messy'. *See*: Weatherill S. 'Harmonisation: how much, how little? 16 *EBLR* (2005) 540

[39] Dunlope Pneumatic Tyre Co Ltd v. New Garage Co Ltd. [1915] AC 79. Cf., however, with Golden Bay Realty Pte Ltd. v. Orchard Twelve Investments Pte Ltd. [1991] 1 W.L.R. 981

has been acknowledged that the discrepancies in different areas of legal regulations can adversely affect cross-border business transactions in the internal market. For these reasons, the Commission has explicitly backed the elaboration of Union-wide standard contract terms in the Communication of 2003. The Commission has said that it:

> '... is aware ... of initiatives in which *standard contract terms* have been developed for international transactions ... This demonstrates the usefulness of standard terms developed for use in various Member States and, in particular, in cross-border transactions'[40].

However, the practical implementation of these ideas later appeared to be much less ambitious.

The Commission positioned itself rather as a facilitator in setting up a website on which information relating to the validity of standard contracts would be shared[41]. Considered from today's perspective, it is clear that these limited goals were not achieved either. In recent years, the Commission has become even more reticent, arguing, for example, that it would be difficult to see how standard terms drafted for one sector could be of use to another sector. Moreover, if standard contract terms posted on the website are not checked for their validity and enforceability in all jurisdictions of the Union, or their compatibility with the laws of the Union, this would greatly reduce the value of such exchange[42]. Whereas the Commission was hesitant in submitting any further proposals on the elaboration of common standard terms, the European Parliament in its Resolution of 23 March 2006 repeatedly stressed the necessity of making further steps towards a harmonisation of civil laws. It has, *inter alia,* highlighted the vulnerability of small businesses that often sign contracts not tailored to their needs:

> '...the term 'business' covers more than just large corporations and includes *small – even one-person – undertakings* which will often requires

40 Communication from the Commission to the European Parliament and the Council '*A more Coherent European Contract Law: An Action Plan*', COM (2003) 68 final, OJ, 2003 C 63/01, paras 84-5

41 Weatherill S. 'Reflections on the EC's competence to develop "European contract law"' 13(3) *ERPL* (2005) 410. *See also:* Schultze R. 'European Private Law and the Existing EC Law' 1 *ERPL* (2005) *3 et seq*. This proposal was also criticised as it was sometimes noted that law firms would be reluctant to publish the templates of their standard clauses and reveal their best practices and legal know-how. Hesselink M. The European Commission's Action Plan: Towards a More Coherent European Contract Law? 4 *ERPL* (2004) 418

42 Report from the Commission first annul progress report on European Contract Law and the Acquis Review COM (2005) 456 final, para 4.1

contracts that are specially tailored for their needs and take account of their relative vulnerability when contracting with large corporations'[43].

What would be the future legislative and judicial ramifications of this resolution? The answer is far from clear. It seems that the resolution shows at least a political will to carry on work aimed at the preparation of guidelines for establishing similar protection of small enterprises throughout the Union. In the author's view, the particular legal outcome in the form of new regulations would be highly dependent on a political consensus, and not on the efforts of scholars. As long as the Member States expressly or tacitly deny the idea of a comprehensive civil code at the political level, it is unlikely that any relevant documents drafted by scientific associations or *ad hoc* groups would come to life. Nevertheless, less ambitious developments leading to the actual convergence of private law systems throughout the Union are not completely out of the question.

In this regard, this book now turns to the role of the Court of Justice. It is submitted here that the Court of Justice may also contribute to the abolition of trade barriers hindering free movement of goods and services in future[44]. However, it should also be borne in mind that in its rulings the Court of Justice has dealt mostly with public law regulations (*e.g.* administrative factors)[45] in relation to products and prohibited trade barriers in intra–Union trade under the TFEU. On the other hand, ordinarily the Court of Justice has not dismissed applications purely on the grounds that potential restrictions derived from private law regulations, and examines all kind of potential intra-Union trade restrictions. Thus, further contribution to the abolition of trade restrictions and approximation of civil laws might be expected from the Court of Justice as well.

Indeed, the growing scope of interventions in favour of market freedoms suggests that the Court of Justice is ready to analyse seriously all kinds of national rules that may impede foreign participants' access to markets or rules that otherwise adversely affect fair competition in the internal market, no matter to which area of law they belong[46]. In recent jurisprudence of the Court of Justice, Article 34 TFEU [*ex* 28 EC] is interpreted not only as a pure non-discrimination prohibition, but as a provision prohibiting all kinds of unjustified

[43] European Parliament '*Resolution on European Contract Law and the Revision of the Acquis: the Way Forward*' of 23 March 2006, 2005/2022 (INI) para 1, 4

[44] *For a general comment see:* van Gerven W. 'The ECJ Case-Law as a Means of Unification of Private Law?', in: *Towards a European Civil Code.* Hartkamp A. Hesselink M. *et. al.*, eds. (Ars Aequi Libri – Nijmegen Kluwer Law International 2004) 101 *et seq*

[45] *For an interesting contribution see*: Gkoutzinis A. 'Free Movement of Services in the EC Treaty and the Law of Contractual Obligations relating to Banking and Financial Services' 41 *C.M.L. Rev.* (2004) 119 *et seq*

[46] *See*: De Agostini C-34/95-36/95, Gourmet C-405/98, Morellato C-416/00, *etc.*

restrictions impeding the free flow of economic factors. In light of some interesting rulings[47], it would seem that legal boundaries of market freedoms stretch far further than was initially expected at the time the Rome Treaty was signed. In practice, traders often seek to challenge national rules that limit their economic activity before courts just because the other Member States have somewhat less strict rules[48], and therefore they assert that these strict rules are impeding free access to the market[49]. However, these arguments have not been endorsed by the Court of Justice. As AG *Tesauro* in the *Hünermund* case explained, Article 34 TFEU [*ex* 28 EC] does not provide the right to the unhindered pursuit of one's commercial activities[50]. For the sake of completeness, this research paper pays some attention to the negative integration of private law systems in the Union. Thus, general developments in the case law of the Court of Justice[51] as well as the interaction of the market freedoms with private law will be investigated further.

Finally, even if a substantive political consensus is achieved with regard to the approximation of regulations on standard form contracts in business-to-business transactions, the question remains as to the most effective legal mechanism for regulating contractual relations between European companies. The phrase 'the devil is in the detail' applies perfectly if one compares the common law and continental law of contract. These systems still have different notions of contractual relations, such as the concept of freedom of contract and good faith. Having regard to these discrepancies, analysis of possible convergence of the legal systems of the Union and elaboration of the most effective model for tackling unfair business practices leads to a more fundamental and profound dilemma about the public regulator's intervention in contractual relations in the 21st century.

---

47 About relevance of service provider's family life to the market freedoms see: Carpenter C-60/00; *also:* Editorial 40 *C.M.L. Rev.* (2003) 537 *et seq. For some valuable comments and critisism*: Acierno S. 'The Carpenter Judgement: Fundamental Rights and Limits of the Community Legal Order' 28 *E.L. Rev.* (2003) 398; Harbacevica S., Reich N. 'Citizenship and Family on Trial: A Fairly Optimistic Overview of Recent ECJ Practice with regard to Free Movement of Persons' 39 *C.M.L. Rev.* (2002) 628

48 The Court of Justice has however rejected this argumentation. See *e.g.* Alpine Investments C-384/93

49 *See also*: Criminal Proceedings v. Harry Franzén C-189/95, Parfums Christian Dior SA C-337/95

50 AG Tesauro in: Hünermund C-292/92, para 22

51 It must be noted that the Court of Justice has adopted hundreds of rulings on the market freedoms in recent decades. Furthermore, the institutions of the Union produced a number of documents on the completion of the internal market. In this regard, the paper deals only the with most renowned cases which, as commonly acknowledged, changed the direction of the Court of Justice's case law and which are most meaningful to the analysis of the interaction of Union law and private law.

PURPOSES

Since *Voltaire* said of pre-revolutionary France that it was 'an absurd and terrible thing that what is true in one village is false in another'[52] there have been innumerable endeavours to compare different legal systems in order to discover the best solution. It seems that the enlarged Union is struggling with similar challenges to pre-revolutionary France: every market participant of the Union working or doing business in another Member State must abide by the foreign laws of that jurisdiction, which are often unknown to him or her. In light of this political background, the main purpose of this paper is to evaluate selected European (English, German, Lithuanian, and French) laws on the regulation of standard form contracts in business-to-business transactions. In particular, the book examines whether the multiplicity of contract law clauses analysed herein may be regarded as a non-tariff barrier to trade between Member States, and what should be done to eliminate the prohibited, and under certain circumstances tolerated, trade restrictions in the Union.

The selection of these four jurisdictions is based on the fact that most of the world's jurisdictions are conventionally divided into the Anglo-American common law, the Napoleonic, and the Roman–Germanic group[53]. Thus, one can extrapolate major trends from these jurisdictions to the Union and, to a certain extent, for the rest of the world[54]. Moreover, much attention in this study will be devoted to those new jurisdictions from central and northern Europe that joined the Union in 2004. During the fifty years of Soviet occupation that started just before or after The Second World War, these countries were deprived of the chance to develop their own legal systems. Only in the 1990s did they finally revert to the legal families to which they belonged before the Soviet occupation took place. For example, the Baltic countries carried out a reform of private law by re-implementing legal terminology of the Roman – German legal system, together with some contributions from the Netherlands[55] and Scandinavian countries. It must also be noted that it was relatively easy for new Member States to re-shape their private law systems in comparison with Western

[52] Voltaire *Oeuvres de Voltaire. Dialogues*. Backquenois, éditeur (Paris 1838) 5

[53] For the purposes of simplicity, in some parts of this book the Napoleonic and the Roman–German groups are defined as belonging to the continental or civil law system

[54] For the classification of legal systems worldwide *see, e.g.*, <www.cia.gov/library/publications/the-world-factbook/fields/2100.html>. For a general comment about jurisdictions of the world and criteria see, *e.g.*, Wood P. *Law and Practice of International Finance* (London: Sweet & Maxwell 2008) 15-28; René D., Brierley J. *Major Legal Systems in the World Today. An Introduction to the Comparative Study of Law* (London: Stevens 1985)

[55] Notably, the new Dutch *Burgerlijk Wetboek* (Civil Code) was a source of inspiration for many private law reforms carried out in Central and Northern Europe after the 1990s.

European countries. Old Soviet case law was mostly irrelevant and undeveloped for the free market conditions that emerged in these countries after the 1990s. Hence, any radical amendments to private law could have been made a bit easier in these countries as these changes did not have a big impact on the other areas of law reformed at the same time.

Generally speaking, most legal systems permit private parties to decide on the terms on which they deal with each other. Still, none of the legal systems is completely liberal and leaves everything to private agreement between the parties. Naturally, every legal system provides for some regulations that apply to contracts of a certain nature, and will not allow parties to contract out of these rules by agreement. Thus parties may be subject to mandatory provisions of national law contrary to their intentions, which means that even if the whole legal system was voluntary chosen not all of its rules may be desired by both contracting parties.

Indeed, the idea of regulating contractual relations comes from a more general assumption that unregulated markets cannot secure a reasonable balance of contractual rights and obligations. The objectives of regulation of standard form contracts are very similar to the general objectives of mandatory laws. It is often believed that unregulated contracts can be detrimental to the weaker contracting party and even third parties as the latter can carry the costs of flawed contractual relations. In particular, this monograph considers whether or not common rules can be created at the Union level for business-to-business contracts pertaining to the control of unfair standard terms. It is submitted that the PECL and UNIDROIT Principles may provide some useful guidance on the regulation of standard form contracts as the scope of these principles is not confined merely to consumer contracts. It is a fact of European law that while laws on unfair trade practices were harmonised in 1993 for consumer protection reasons by virtue of Directive 93/13/EEC on Unfair Terms in Consumer Contracts, regulation of business-to-business contracts has been left out of the scope of Union competence, except in some areas (*e.g.* franchising, late payments in commercial transactions, security settlement systems). The idea of expanding the scope of the Directive in favour of protection of 'small' professionals (*e.g.* farmers, fishermans, shopkeepers, artisans) was endorsed by some scholars also[56]. The Economic and Social Committee recommended that the Commission consider the possibility of affording similar protection not only to consumers, but also to SMEs,[57] but these recommendations did not gain sufficient support among other institutions. In the light of these developments, consumer-related matters remain outside the scope of this research.

---

[56] See, *e.g.*, Lando O. 'Liberal, social and "ethical" justice in European Contract Law' 43 *C.M.L. Rev.* (2006) 829

[57] *See*: ECOSOC Opinion OJ 1991 C159

Nonetheless, the whole regulation of standard contract terms is an undeniably wide area. Such regulation covers many issues starting from the effectiveness of incorporation of terms to the interpretation of these terms. A judge starts by examining the issue of incorporation of contract terms, and only if they are incorporated effectively is the term examined in the light of other statutory rules as well as common law principles of construction[58]. However, in many jurisdictions statutory law is not always sufficiently clear on what is actually prohibited or what is tolerated under certain circumstances. In view of this fact, the Commission has convincingly concluded that it is not easy to determine which contract rules may privately be agreed and which not[59]. Because of the variety of mandatory rules among Member States and the resulting ambiguity, on the whole research focuses mostly on a comparison of regulations with regard to control over exclusion or limitation clauses, as they are mostly misused in commercial arrangements. Broadly speaking, these are terms in a contract or in a notice that purport to restrict, exclude or modify a liability, duty or remedy that would otherwise arise from the legally recognised relationship between parties[60]. Though most of the prohibitions relating to exclusion or limitation clauses derive from general principles - *e.g.* good faith, equal bargaining power, fair commercial practice - many jurisdictions have some explicit statutory regulations on what is permitted and what liabilities parties cannot contract out of.

The comparison of different prohibitions on exclusion clauses is a good opportunity to reconsider general principles of intervention in the freedom of contract. Indeed, to what extent should parties be permitted to shape their contractual relations? Should special protection be granted only to consumers or also extended to businesses? Moreover, is this protection relevant only to small businesses or also to huge corporations? Finally, one may question whether national mandatory contract law regulations of should cover only domestic business dealings or international business transactions as well. It seems that

---

58 *For some relevant case law see:* Wight v. British Railways Board [1983] C.L.Y. 424; Bingham L.J. in Interfoto Library v. Stilleto Ltd [1988] 1 All E.R. 348. In German law, the doctrine of interpretation (construction) of standard contract terms is often considered as a third (final) stage of the examination thereof. *Cf.* Fehl N. 'Systematik des Rechts der Allgemeinen Geschäftsbedingungen' *ZIP* (1987) 690 *et seq*

59 *See:* Communication from the Commission to the European Parliament and the Council 'A more Coherent European Contract Law: An Action Plan', COM (2003) 68 final, OJ, 2003 C 63/01, para 32; Storme M. *Freedom of Contract: Mandatory and Non-Mandatory Rules in European Contract Law* (Conference European Legal Harmony: Goals and Milestones, Tartu, December 6th, 2005); Hesselink M. 'Non-Mandatory Rules in European Contract Law 1 *ERCL* (2005) 60

60 Yates D., Hawkins A. J. *Standard Business Contracts: Exclusion and Related Devices* (London: Sweet & Maxwell 1986) 4-6

these considerations relate to the whole concept of civil law. Quite often regulators' or even judges' choices (though this is ordinarily denied) depend on their political views, historical development of the country, legal and cultural diversity, dominant ideologies (*e.g.* social-democratic, liberal, conservative[61]), dominant public opinion in a country, as well as many other factors that at first sight sometimes seem irrational. For example, the approach of the English law of contract was traditionally much more liberal and conservative than those in continental Europe. To a certain extent, these tendencies currently correlate with the enforcement of standard contracts.

It is suggested that national legislators should take a realistic approach and intervene in contractual arrangements only if such new regulation would contribute more to the interests of both parties and society in general. This interference is especially problematic if one considers the regulation of business-to-business contracts, where the needs of various enterprises may differ substantially from each other and, therefore, it is difficult to draw unanimous conclusions about what regulation is useful for most of them. Moreover, the small company in question may be not just a small artisan or family business, but rather a special purpose company, which is *de facto* supported by a large corporation, and therefore has much stronger bargaining power than the contract counterpart. Finally, any empirical experiments regarding the regulation of standard form contracts - and possibly in the other areas of private law - are almost undoable. Indeed, such questions as whether or not foreign regulations may act as a deterrent can be answered differently by different enterprises, particularly depending on their location in the Union, size, capital and many other factors.

Comparative Methodology

The following research is based on the functionalist method of comparative law[62]. The methodology aims to present an integrated view on how European laws deal with similar problems - in particular this book compares different approaches to the question of how exclusion and limitation clauses incorporated in standard form contracts are regulated in different jurisdictions. Having compared different European legal orders, this research will be completed by

---

61 For an interesting contribution on European values in private law see: Lando O. 'Liberal, Social and 'Ethical' Justice in European Contract Law' 43 *C.M.L. Rev.* (2006) 817 *et seq*

62 Collins H. 'Methods and Aims of Comparative Contract Law' 11(3) *O. J. L. S.* (1991) 398; Sacco R. 'Legal Formants: A Dynamic Approach to Comparative Law' 39 *Am. J. Com. L.* 1991) 1-34; Schnitzer A. *Vergleichende Rechtslehre* Bd. I (Basel 1961); Graziadei M. 'The Functional Heritage', in: *Comparative Legal Studies: Traditions and Transitions*, Legrand P., Munday R. eds. (Cambridge: Cambridge University Press 2003); Schmitthoff M. 'The Science of Comparative Law' 7 *Cambridge L.J.* (1939) 94-110, *etc.*

assessing the implications of Union law for the private law systems of the Member States.

From a more general perspective, the functional method deals with different issues by hypothesising different legal consequences arising from similar factual circumstances. A utilitarian approach is applied in this book, whereby comparing legal rules and techniques from different jurisdictions aims to find the best legal solutions to the problems tackled. Furthermore, it should be borne in mind that this monograph gives a general theoretical insight rather than a practical memorandum on the regulation of standard form contracts in business-to-business transactions. In short, the assessment of different legal systems is two-fold: first, the analysis will be focused on the comparison of different legal regulations; then, legal rules will be evaluated for their importance for case law.

It is widely acknowledged that a detailed comparison of different legal systems is highly complex. That is why it is often difficult to implement directives in different Member States in a similar fashion. For example, the absence of similar rules in other jurisdictions can be explained not by a gap in social regulation, but simply by the fact that similar controls do exist, but in other legal instruments or social dimensions. The non-existence of certain regulations does not necessarily imply that these rules should be transplanted from one country to another. Applying this to the regulation of standard contracts, some jurisdictions have stricter rules with respect to the incorporation of standard terms into a contract, while other jurisdictions put more weight on assessing the content of contracts (or so-called direct substantive control).

As a consequence, the same standard contract terms would not be enforceable in both jurisdictions, though the particular legal grounds for invalidating them are different. Furthermore, certain generalisations may not be accurate, given the difficulty of collecting relevant similar data from different jurisdictions. In my view, one should probably also rely on common sense in approaching these matters, as well as considering the regulations from a more general perspective. Interestingly, the functionalist approach has been severely criticized by legal post-modernists. For example, *Peters* and *Schenke* must be right in their assessment of the limits of our cognitive abilities:

> 'At all stages of comparative research […] the problems are not moral and cultural blindness, ethnocentricity and legal imperialism, but the lack of full knowledge and understanding of foreign legal rules and culture'[63].

---

[63] Peters A., Schwenke H. 'Comparative beyond Post-Modernism' 49 *ICLQ* (2000) 800

Some other commentators are even more sceptical about the reliability of this approach, given that is hardly possible to comprehend the specifics of foreign law. *Watson*, in defining the perils of comparative law, draws a more radical conclusion:

> 'To begin with, comparative law is superficial [...]. The explanation is patent: it is hard enough to know in detail one branch of the law of one system, but to know the history of that branch and its relationship with that of some other system is well-night impossible'[64].

It would go well beyond the objectives of this book to discuss what advantages accrue to comparative studies. Indeed, this research aims more at the acquisition of knowledge (which is sometimes defined as the aim of comparative law[65]), and unveiling internal connections among different legal systems, rather than solving concrete practical problems by applying different foreign laws. It appears that even if the same words or expressions appear to be linguistically synonymous with equivalent words (e.g. *contracts - contrats – Verträge – sutartys*) in other legal systems, the underlying concepts differ substantially[66]. Therefore, sometimes it does not suffice merely to have good foreign language skills to get a full insight into a foreign legal system[67]. One has to understand at least the basic principles according to which a legal system operates, as well as specific legal terminology. However, it cannot be said that the comparison of legal norms is completely impossible and therefore makes no sense. In fact, there are many lawyers who are qualified in several jurisdictions and successfully deliver detailed memoranda on the merits and shortcomings of concluding transactions under different legal systems. In many cases, contracts used in an international transaction (*e.g.* aircraft lease agreements) are analysed for their enforceability under different legal systems. On the other hand, some of the legal post-modernists' criticisms seem to be justified, as in practice lawyers tend to ignore

---

64 Watson A. *Legal Transplants: an Approach to Comparative Law* 2nd ed. (Athens and London: The University of Georgia Press 1993) 10. *For the comparative legal theory and the convergence of the systems see*: Menski W. *Comparative Law in a Global Context* (Cambridge: Cambridge University Press 2006) 50-54

65 *Cf.* Sacco R. 'Legal Formants: A Dynamic Approach to Comparative Law' 39 *Am. J. Com. L.* (1991) 4

66 For example, the agreement to manage an estate would fall under French 'contrats', but they are 'trusts' and not 'contracts' under English law. Moreover, the English notion of a contract includes gratuitous contracts. *For more examples see, e.g.*, Sacco R. 'Legal Formants: A Dynamic Approach to Comparative Law' 39 *Am. J. Com. L.* (1991) 12-4

67 Legrand P. 'European Legal Systems are not Converging' 45(1) *ICLQ* (1996) 52. The problems of application of foreign law were also stressed in the Joint Response of the Commission on European Contract Law and the Study Group on a European Civil Code (Osnabrück 2001)

those legal systems with which they are less familiar[68]. It is probably true to say that the more a lawyer is knowledgeable about legal practice in his own country, the more he favours it over the law of other jurisdictions.

Furthermore, it should also be borne in mind that the differences in legal practice are not only to be explained by differences in regulation. For instance, even if we consider such harmonised areas of private law as consumer protection from unfair contract terms[69], the volume of case law is different in England and Germany. Unfair standard form contracts are contested much more often before German courts than English courts. If both jurisdictions provide more or less similar minimal protection for consumers, how can this be explained? Does this mean that English law provides better protection and there is no necessity to contest the terms before court or does it means that no companies want to be a defendant before the English courts? One possible answer is that successful preventive control by the British FTO contributes to low litigation rates in England, while German litigants are more likely to contest the validity of standard terms in contracts before courts because of the widespread existence of litigation insurance and relatively lower litigation costs in that country. However, one should also consider that the peculiarities of the English Civil Procedure Rules – rules on disclosure, case management conferences, obligatory communication between solicitors, *etc.* - makes any litigation substantially more expensive in England. All in all, a common sense approach to the general legal environment of a country should also be considered when assessing the case law of different jurisdictions.

In order to assimilate these inter-cultural differences as well as to overcome the scepticism associated with comparative research, the functional method is combined with the following further legal research methods: systematic analysis, historical analysis, and meta-analysis. This research considers every legal system as a unity – in *Leppaule's* words 'the whole of which expresses itself in each part'[70] - with its own social, political, and historical differences. While comparing different regulations, much attention is paid to the policies underlying them. In this regard, economic and social rationales will be also observed in this book.

As a methodological starting point for this analysis, the position taken was first formulated by *Zweigert* and *Kötz*, who contend that practical results of

68 As *Basedow* rightly contends, legal advisers recommended choice of law almost invariably settles on domestic law, and this advice is usually due to pure ignorance of the alternative options offered by foreign legislations. Basedow J. 'A Common Contract Law for the Common Market' 33 *C.M.L. Rev.* (1996) 1182

69 *See:* Directive 93/13/EEC (OJ 21 April 1993 L95 /29)

70 Leppaule P. 'The Function of Comparative Law. With a Critique of Sociological Jurisprudence' XXXV *Harv. L. Rev.* (1922) 853

different legal systems are similar (*praesumptio similitudinis*)[71]. It is submitted that legal differences between different Member States lie mainly not in legal outcomes, but rather in the origin of their laws. Furthermore, I would suggest that most jurisdictions in the Union face more or less similar problems (*inter alia*, protection of a weaker party from detrimental contract terms). Thus, this book seeks to scrutinise how different legal systems deal with the issue of exclusion or limitation of liability in contractual relations by eliminating unfairness in contractual relations. Needless to say, not all the countries examined here have similar concepts of contract law. Likewise, the comparison of different regulation models for standard form contracts can be criticised on the grounds that the approaches are simply incomparable. One may also contend that the Union's different legal systems often have no common denominator that ensures 'the possibility of neutral and objective meaning and value'[72].

Nonetheless, the argument that the regulation of standard form contracts can be treated as a commonly accepted European phenomenon seems more convincing. That is why, in the author's view, regulations on standard contract terms can be compared across different European jurisdictions. The Principles of European Contract Law (the 'PECL'), that are sometimes referred to as Lando-Principles (Art. 2.104, 4.110, 4.118), referred to 'not individually negotiated contract terms', while the regulations of standard contract terms are also included in the UNIDROIT Principles (Art. 2.1.19-2.1.22). As mentioned, Directive 93/13/EEC on Unfair Terms in Consumer Contracts (similar to the PECL) covers all 'individually non-negotiated contract terms' in the scope of the regulation[73], which is a somewhat broader concept than 'standard contract terms'.

Pursuant to Article 2.1.19(2) of UNIDROIT Principles standard terms are the 'provisions which are prepared in advance for general and repeated use by one party and which are actually used without negotiation with the other party'.

---

71 Zweigert K., Kötz H. *Introduction to Comparative Law.* Trans. by Weird T. (3rd ed.) (Oxford: Clarendon Press 1998) 40. *For further theoretical in-depth analysis see*: Legrand P. 'The same and the different', in: *Comparative Legal Studies: Traditions and Transitions*, Legrand P., Munday R. eds. (Cambridge: Cambridge University Press 2003) 245-247; Örücü E. *The Enigma of Comparative Law. Variations on a Theme for the Twenty-first Century* (Martinus Nijhoff Publishers: Leiden/Boston 20004) 19-27; Hesselink W. M. *The New European Private Law. Essays on the Future of Private Law in Europe* (The Hague, London New York: Kluwer Law International 2002) 48-9

72 Peters A., Schwenke H. 'Comparative beyond Post-Modernism' 49(4) *ICLQ* (2000) 811. As to the supporters and opponents of the functionalist approach, *see:* Michaels R. *The Functional Method of Comparative Law* 2005 (the working paper downloaded from http://ssrn.com/abstract=839826 on 1 November 2007) 3-5

73 *See*: Article 3 of the Directive 93/13/EEC. *Compare:* Dean M. 'Unfair Contract Terms: the European Approach' 4 *M.L.R.* (1993); Duffy P. 'Unfair Contract Terms and the EC Directive' *J.B.L.* (1993)

Thus individually non-negotiated terms can also include terms tailored for a single transaction[74].

These European and international developments would suggest that the regulation or, conversely, possible non-regulation of standard contract terms should be required reading in all jurisdictions of the Union and should be discussed further in detail.

---

[74] This approach could have been found to contradict the notion of the free market as well as the freedom of contract because it prevents parties from choosing contract terms they desire. However, the view that even individually negotiated terms could be unfair and detrimental to the weaker party owing to imbalances in bargaining power is widely supported in the Nordic countries. Wilhelmsson T. 'Standard Form Conditions', in: *Towards a European Civil Code*. Hartkamp A., Hesselink M. *et. al.* eds. (Ars Aequi Libri – Nijmegen Kluwer Law International 2004) 441

Part 1:

Regulation of Standard Form Contracts in the Jurisdictions of Selected European Union Member States

1. MYTHS AND REALITY ABOUT THE FREEDOM OF CONTRACT

'Indeed, no reasonable man believes in unrestricted freedom of person, property or contract. If the life of the community is to function at all, freedom must not become licence, its use not abuse'
Prausnitz O. *The Standardisation of Commercial Contracts in English and Continental Law* (London: Sweet & Maxwell 1937) 30

1.1 TRUE AND DISGUISED PURPOSES OF THE STANDARDISATION OF CONTRACTS

Rapid technical development in the 19th century significantly increased the volumes of commodities and goods produced. At the same time, the trade in mass-produced objects accelerated the spread of standard form contracts that could be used whenever the same goods, commodities or services were involved. Thus, the historical genesis, or to be more precise - the genesis of the wide application of standard form contracts, is often linked to global industrialisation[75]. The same contract terms were offered to a large number of business partners or ordinary consumers. Gradually, standard form contracts were applied not only to mass transactions and mass merchandising work, but also for ordinary trade in goods and later for trade in services. The popularity of standard form contracts first became apparent in transport, insurance and banking practices, and quickly spread to other fields of business.

Indeed, it is difficult to envisage how many types of contracts - *e.g.*, e-commerce, banking, and software contracts - could be concluded without recourse to standard contract terms[76]. In such cases, the party that signs contracts

[75] *For some historical in-depth analysis see:* Miloš V. *Recht und Normierung in der Industriellen Revolution. Neue Strukturen der Normsetzung in Völkerrecht, staatlicher Gesetzgebung und gesellschaftlicher Selbstnormierung* (Frankfurt am Main: Vittorio Klostermann 2006) 110; Hellwege P. *Allgemeine Geschäftsbedingungen, einseitig gestellte Vetragsbedingungen und die allgemeine Rechtsgeschäftslehre* (Tübingen: Mohr Siebeck 2010) 19-196; Zweigert K., Kötz H. *Introduction to Comparative Law.* Trans. by Weird T. 3rd ed. (Oxford: Clarendon Press 1998) 333; Basedow in: MünchKomm, before § 305, para 1; Raiser L. *Das Recht der Allgemeinen Geschäftsbedingungen* (Gentner, Nachdruck Bad Homburg 1961); Heinrichs, in: Paland, Überbl. v § 305, § 305, para 4; Kötz H., Ulmer in: Ulmer/Brandnen/ Hensen, Einl., para 3; Kotz H., Flessner A. *Europäisches Vertragsrecht Band I.* (Tübingen: Mohr Siebeck 1996) 210.

[76] *Cf.* Adams J. N. 'Unconscionability and the Standard Form Contract', in: *Welfarism in Contract Law* Brownsword R., Howells G. and Wilhelmsson T. eds. (Darthmouth Publishing Company Limited, 1994) 233; Munz M. *Allgemeine Geschäftsbedingungen in den USA und Deutschland im Handelsverkehr* (Heidelberg 1992) 25; Prinz zu Löwenstein M. 'AGB–Probleme beim Ein- und Verkauf von Computersoftware' *BB* (1985) 1696

often just clicks an 'accept the terms' button online without opening the standard terms or reading them through (partly because they are often printed in small letters or partly because the user finds it irrelevant or boring to read the complex legal language)[77]. Some commentators argue that standard form contracts amount to more than 99% of all contracts made nowadays[78]. In fact, many daily services - *e.g.* public transport, parking, purchasing groceries, dry-cleaning - are also offered on the basis of general terms. As the Commission outlined, there are two types of transaction that are *not* generally concluded on standard terms: (i) atypical transactions, where the standard terms would be inappropriate, and (ii) where the transaction does not involve substantial risk for the supplier (so-called on-the-spot transactions)[79]. All other transactions could well be concluded on standard terms, or at least using contracts where some of the terms are standard.

Standard form contracts may be defined as contracts drafted for a number of transactions concerning the same product or service and accepted by the other party in whole without negotiation. In real life it is, however, not always easy to qualify a contract as a standard contracts. *Yates* and *Hawkings* have elegantly defined standard form contracts, as being like elephants, which may be easily recognized, but it is devilish to describe them[80]. Various concepts emphasize either the form of appearance of these contract terms, or economic purposes, or multiple application or some other characteristics of standard contracts[81]. For example, the French doctrine of the *contrat d'adhésion* (the contract of adhesion) used to define standard form contracts where terms are not intended to be amended by the other party[82]. The LCC uses an expression 'standard contract terms' (Art 6.185 LCC). This definition implies that the contract terms were first formulated by the *proferens* (*i.e.* the party in whose favour contract terms were drafted) for multiple application. Therefore these terms are included in a contract without negotiation. Practically speaking, standard contract terms include clauses that govern non-payment, exclusion and limitation clauses, penalty clauses, clauses on governing law and arbitration, modification of a

---

77 Probably for these reasons the Electronic Commerce Directive 2000/31/EC provides that contract terms and general conditions must be made available in a way that allows the recipient to store and reproduce them (Art. 10(3))

78 Slawson W. D. 'Standard Form Contracts and Democratic Control of Lawmaking Power' 84 *Harv. L. Rev.* (1971) 529

79 Commission Communication presented to the Council on 14 February 1984 (based on COM (84) 55 final) Unfair Terms in Contracts Concluded with Consumers. Bulletin of the Communities Communities Supplement 1/84

80 Yates D., Hawkins A. J. *Standard Business Contracts: Exclusion and Related Devices* (London: Sweet & Maxwell 1986) v

81 *Cf.* Brunner A. *Allgemeine Geschäftsbedingungen im internationalen Privatrecht* (Grüsch 1985) 20-1

82 Gardette J. M. Die Behandlung der „unangemessenen" Klauseln nach dem französischen „AGB" – Gesetz (Verlag Versicherungswirtschaft GmbH Karlsruhe 2005) 38 *et seq*

contract, *etc*. The incorporation of such terms into a contract permits the parties to avoid uncertainties where the essential commercial duties are not performed as agreed.

In general, the ratio underlying the application of standard form contracts is to speed-up and simplify a growing number of business dealings[83]. However, one may also find many other arguments that would justify the use of such terms. It is a commonplace that the standardisation of contracts makes it easier to organise business and assess risks, and probably the most important issue is that this should enable businesses to save costs by means of simplified contracting (the *so-called* rationalisation of business)[84]. Furthermore, it is evident that a product sold with each contract drafted separately would make the price of a product much higher, or perhaps such products would not be competitive in the market at all. Contracting on the basis of standard terms usually requires no additional legal costs; moreover, an organisation can also remove discretion from its employees from negotiating contract terms where this is not desired or makes no economic sense[85]. In practice, account managers often stress to business partners that standard terms represent corporate policy and that they are, therefore, not permitted to make any alterations or otherwise deviate from these terms without approval from their legal department. In short, it is often more economically efficient to do business on the basis of standard form contracts.

From a more general perspective, standardisation of contract terms has not only economic, but also legal significance. Standard form contracts contribute to the development of legal doctrines. For example, many standard terms were first invented by private market participants and later used by the regulator to draft typical contracts. Many typical terms of franchising, netting, leaseback as well as other modern banking contracts (*e.g.* bank loans, syndicated loans, futures, forwards, options, swaps) were first drafted on the basis of permanently used standard contract terms, but not by academic writers. Historically, the idea of incorporated typical contract terms (*'lois supplétives'* in

---

83 Ratz in: Staub, § 346, note 168. *See also*: Heinrichs in: Paland, before § 305, § 305, para 4; Brunner A. *Allgemeine Geschäftsbedingungen im internationalen Privatrecht* (Grüsch 1985) 5; Wolf M. (*et. al.*) *AGB-Gesetz, Kommentar* 4. Aufl. (Verlag C. H. Beck 1999) Introduction, para 1. Ulmer P., in: Ulmer/Brandnen/Hensen, Intr. para 3., Piske P. I. *Die Kontrolle der Allgemeinen Geschäftsbedingungen in Spanien* (Frankfurt am Main 2002) 9 *et seq*; von Hertel B.-O. *Kontrolle von allgemeinen Geschäftsbedingungen im kaufmännischen Geschäftsverkehr gemäß § 24 AGB-Gesetz* (Heidelberg 1986) 16 *et seq*

84 *See e.g.* Trebilcock J. M. The Limits of Freedom of Contract (Cambridge, Massassuchets, and London: Harvard University Press 1993) 119; Kessler F. 'Contracts of Adhesion – Some Thoughts about Freedom of Contract' 43 *Colum. L. Rev.* (1943) 629 *et seq*

85 Yates D., Hawkins A. J. *Standard Business Contracts: Exclusion and Related Devices* (London: Sweet & Maxwell 1986) 3

France or *'dispositives Recht'* in Germany) in statutory law was inherited from Roman law. These ideas were further implemented in many civil codes of continental Europe[86]. The existence of such terms makes contracting easier as parties can agree on essential terms while other terms can be considered typical for such transactions. However, parties may also disregard typical contract terms, and these terms would remain inapplicable provided the parties explicitly deviate from typical rules included in civil codes or other special laws. Typical contracts may also provide for more legal certainty provided the contract in question does not cover all relevant situations. Hence, the standardisation of contract terms is of paramount importance not only for private business participants, but it also contributes to the efficient allocation of transaction costs as well as to the modernisation of legal orders in general[87]. In the view of a continental lawyer, standard form contracts would probably provide a better understanding of private law systems and typical contract terms as well.

Finally, many advantages of contract standardisation can be observed from the perspective of the counterparty as well. The counterparty can simply compare terms of different suppliers on the basis of quality, price, and the main object of contract. The remaining contract terms are standard in such types of contracts, and therefore there is no need to scrutinise the details any further. In cases where contract terms are fair, standard contracts contribute to legal certainty in business dealings.

To understand the academic interest in the concept of standard contract terms, it should be stressed that standard form contracts are commonly scrutinised not on their merits (*e.g.* efficiency, costs of legal transactions, *etc.*). Indeed, if standard form contracts only had a positive effect on contractual relations, there would probably be no need to provide specific legal regulation for these social practices. In industry practice, these contracts are often used by companies with strong bargaining power or a monopolistic position in the market. Such contracts deviate from default statutory rules, and the terms offered in standard forms are rarely amended even if there is a request from the counterparty.

In theory, agreements made in the free market should represent the true will of parties as well as being a fair balance of contractual relations. The parties

---

86 In relation to advantages of non-mandatory rules see *e.g.* Hesselink M. 'Non-Mandatory Rules in European Contract Law, European Review of Contract law' 1 *ERCL* (2005) 46 *et seq*

87 It should be noted that civil statutes in common law countries do not normally stipulate typical contracts. Nonetheless, the parties are bound by implied terms (*e.g.* rules on mistake, frustration), which are linked to the intention of the parties but could generally be excluded by explicit agreement of the parties (*expressum facit cessare tacitum*). For more about the comparison of contract terms in common and continental law systems see, *e.g.*: Barry N. *The French Law of Contract,* 2nd ed. (Oxford: Clarendon Press 1992) 33-34

are supposed to have absolute choice in the free market and therefore they agree that which is most beneficial for them. However, there is broad – mostly justified – criticism of the enforceability of freedom of contract, whereby completely unregulated markets do not achieve the most effective level of transactions[88].

Only under the conditions of perfect competition would individuals not exert undue influence over others, which is not the case in the real world. Some parties have weak bargaining power because of their size, specific economic circumstances or cash flow problems and it is easy for stronger parties to take advantage of them. In the absence of such prohibitions a stronger party would attempt, for example, to exclude warranties or otherwise re-allocate business risks, provided it knew that the other party did not have any other choice than to accept its standard contract terms[89]. *Lord Diplock* has notoriously described the situation where the stronger party offers to enter into contractual relations with him: 'if you want these goods or services at all, these are the only terms on which they are obtainable. Take it or leave it'[90].

In cases where unfair disadvantaging of a weaker party takes place, the obligations of the *proferens* are often reduced to the minimum allowed by law (in cases where there are minimal statutory requirements in respect of the fairness and balance of contractual obligations), while the obligations of the weaker party are substantially increased. In such situations, it must be doubted whether real consent can be expected when concluding the transaction even though, strictly speaking, the weaker counterparty was not under duress or economic hardship[91]. On the other hand, the fact that a standard form contract is offered without any negotiations does not automatically mean that the stronger

---

88 For instance, *Sunstein* convincingly argued that the market itself produces harmful or even disastrous results, measured in terms of efficiency or justice. Furthermore, he submits that the appropriate response to the paradoxes of regulations is not to return to a system of '*laissez faire*', but rather to learn of past failures. Sunstein C. R. 'Paradoxes of the Regulatory State' 57 *U. Chicago L. Rev.* (1990) 407

89 Heinrichs in: Paland before § 305 para 6; *see also:* Kessler F. 'Contracts of Adhesion – Some Thoughts about Freedom of Contract' 43 *Colum. L. Rev.* (1943) 629; Slawson W. D. 'Standard Form Contracts and Democratic Control of Lawmaking Power' 84 *Harv. L. Rev.* (1971) 529; Wilhelmsson T. 'Standard Form Conditions', in: *Towards a European Civil Code* Hartkamp A., Hesselink M. *et. al.* eds. (Ars Aequi Libri – Nijmegen Kluwer Law International 2004) 435

90 Lord Diplock in: Schroeder Music Publishing Co. Ltd v. Macaulay [1974] 3 All ER 616, 624. *See also*: Zweigert K., Kötz H. *Introduction to Comparative Law.* Trans. by Weird T. 3rd ed. (Oxford: Clarendon Press 1998) 333; Rakoff T. 'Contracts of Adhesion: An Essay in Reconstruction' 96 *Harv. L. Rev.* (1983) 1177 *et seq. Cf.* Kreienbaum B. Transparenz und AGB-Gesetz. Eine Untersuchung des Inhalts und der Schranken des Transparenzgebotes (Berlin: Duncker & Humblot 1997) 209-215

91 B&S Contracts and Design Ltd. v. Victor Green Publications Ltd. [1984] I.C.R. 419, 425

party has exerted economic pressure in the bargaining process[92]. A powerful corporation may offer to conclude a contract on the basis of its standard terms given the fact that this is its standard practice and aimed at saving legal and other costs. Such a company may well argue that many former large counterparties have accepted such terms, so they will not start negotiations with small and insignificant market participants. Should the regulator therefore interfere to protect a public interest, and if so, should it always protect the smaller enterprise?

In the conventional view, the law of contract should provide legal mechanisms for enforcing contracts that are mutually advantageous to both parties. In this regard, it is more or less unanimously agreed in legal doctrine that the free market itself cannot stop companies from offering unfair contract terms[93]. However, even if the phenomenon of proposing unfair contract terms is evident, it is not completely clear why parties are tempted to use terms that are really unfavourable to the counterparty. One may suppose that different providers should compete among themselves by offering the most favourable terms. Eventually, as a result of such competition the counterparty would end up choosing the best contract terms. However, in real life the picture is not so simple. In fact, enterprises are often tempted to increase the competitiveness of their business by transferring business risks to the other party without paying any attention to the standard contract terms of competing companies. Sometimes there are simply no competitors in the market at a given moment, sometimes negotiations with a new competitor can be even more complicated than those with the current counterparty.

The first possible explanation as to why enterprises use unfair standard terms might be that most businesses believe that they have strong bargaining power and that the other party would contract with them in any case. In fact, there are many cases where it is difficult to distinguish the actual and contractual dependency between the parties[94]. A stronger company knows that the other

---

92 *See*: Yates D. *Exclusion Clauses in Contracts* 2nd ed. (London: Sweet & Maxwell 1982) 7

93 It is worth noting that standard contract terms are ordinarily used in two types of contracts. Standard form contracts can be prepared not only by private market participants, but also by associations or other public bodies (*e.g.* standard form contracts prepared by various governmental insurance supervision commissions, International Air Transport Association, Fédération Internationale dese Ingénieurs – Conseils, standard form contracts used by *British Grain and Feed Trade Association*, the German '*Allgemeine Deutsche Spediteurbedingingen*', '*Allgemeine Bausparbedingungen*', '*Allgemeine Bedingungen für die Ausführung von Bauleistungen*', *etc*). The latter standard form contracts will not be considered in detail in this paper as they are ordinarily aimed at establishing a fair balance between both contracting parties. In fact, they have a quasi-normative character (see *e.g.* BGH, *ZIP*, 1995, 1098 *et seq*).

94 *For more discussions see:* Bayreuther F. *Wirtschaftlich-existenziell abhängige Untnehmen im Konzern-, Kartell- und Arbeitsrecht* (Berlin: Duncker & Humblot 2001) 163 *et seq*

party is subordinated to it, so it is tempted to take advantage of this; such as where the *proferens* is a single supplier of some product or service in the market, and the counterparty has no other real choice than to accept these terms[95]. For example, some huge supermarkets in Eastern and Central Europe often ask farmers and other small manufacturers to sell all products under their standard form contracts or refuse to buy at all if any amendments to their contracts are put forward. The reality is that small manufacturers have no sale outlets at which to sell their products. However, it is still more profitable for small manufacturers to sell all produce under the terms they are offered than to go to market on their own. Theoretically, such large supermarkets are not even monopolists or oligopolists, for example, they may cover less than a quarter of the market, and the regulator has little possibility of intervening in such flawed contractual relations. Even if there are other large buyers, their terms are more or less the same, as the supermarkets compete among themselves only in offering the best price to consumers.

Similar flawed practices have been noted by many academic commentators from various jurisdictions who argue that even when goods and services are not controlled by a monopoly, but by another stronger party, the terms offered by competing companies are largely, if not exactly, identical[96]. Moreover, the abuse of a dominant market position may be accompanied by intellectual or psychological superiority, which is aimed at convincing or forcing the other party to accept unfavourable contract terms[97]. Large enterprises have their own legal departments and other skilful negotiators who can invest sufficient time to persuade the counterparty that there is no other option than to accept the contract terms. Finally, lawyers who draft standard contract terms pay more attention to their professional liability, and are not really interested in making the most competitive decisions. Hence, a typical corporate lawyer would prioritise minimising the legal risks for his client, and not fair distribution of transactional risks and rewards. By contrast, account managers are mostly not able, nor authorised to amend standard contract terms drafted in sophisticated legal language even if they wished to do so.

---

95 Ratz, in: Staub § 346, note 168

96 Atiyah P. S., Smith S. *Atiyah's Introduction to the Law of Contract* (Oxford: Clarendon Press 2005) 12, 17. However, it is also true that under certain circumstances vendors in the very competitive markets can be frightened to loose even a small part of consumers if they use overtly unfair standard form contracts.

97 *See*: Zweigert K., Kötz H. *Introduction to Comparative Law*. Trans. by Weird T. 3rd ed. (Oxford: Clarendon Press 1998) 334; Alisch H. 'Zur Kontrolle von Allgemeinen Geschäftsbedingungen im rein kaufmännischen Geschäftsverkehr' *JZ* (1982) 709; Nicklisch F. 'Zum Anwendungsbereich der Inhaltskontrolle Allgemeiner Geschäftsbedingungen' *BB* (1974) 941; Hippel von, E. 'Zur Kontrolle Allgemeiner Geschäftsbedingungen' *BB* (1985) 1629 *et seq*

A weaker party may find it impossible to renegotiate more advantageous contract terms, and therefore not even attempt to do so. Furthermore, though the following argument is somewhat controversial and requires empirical examination, it is submitted that business reputation does not prevent parties from exercising unfair trade practices nor from taking advantage of insufficiently diligent clients. In fact, many newly incorporated companies in Eastern and Central Europe often seek to maximise their annual profits at any price so as to show better financial performance before they are offered for sale to large western investors. Social responsibility or reputation is difficult to measure. Moreover, even if business reputation is at stake, the company that does not possess a substantial history often just re-brands its products and services, hires public relations specialists and thereby regains public confidence. Indeed, there is little difference whether a corporation has a history of five or ten years. Sales volumes and not retaining a good business name is probably the most important goal for many corporations in that region.

Second, a so-called 'market of terms offered' is not sufficiently transparent, as information pertaining to standard form contracts is not perfectly allocated in the market. The chance of actually comparing all the contract terms of different suppliers is feasible only in theory[98]. Usually, companies submit only their price and the specification of products or services, but rarely all contract terms before entering into direct negotiations. This is often justifiable as companies disburse large amounts to lawyers to prepare standard contract terms, and therefore they do not want to make public their standard contract terms to the advantage of competing ones. Standard form contracts are often considered part of the products or services these companies offer.

On the other hand, some contract terms are often unfavourable to one party and the *proferens* does not want the counterparty to be deterred immediately by them before direct negotiations are started. After the parties have agreed the major terms, salespersons can put pressure on the counterparty by implying that insignificant paperwork remains to be signed. The counterparty may be under pressure by then, as there is no time to re-draft the contract and time is of the essence. Moreover, a company may believe that if it has been able to take advantage by including derisory contract terms, a competitor would surely also have done so. Thus, it the stronger party has little incentive to amend its contract terms. The counterparty may also consider that the issue of contractual liability rarely arises and that there would be no point contesting these contract terms and break the deal. It is worth mentioning that unfair contract terms may also be hidden in contracts and might not be immediately recognisable to an inexperienced trader. Even if such terms were noticed, the

98 Markesinis B. [*et. al.*] *The German Law of Contract* (Oxford and Portland, Oregon: Hart Publishing 2006) 165

counterparty might decide that it was not worth investing time and money in buying expensive legal advice and negotiating further, knowing that no real negotiations will take place and no substantial changes in the contract will be made. In such cases, the costs of negotiations may be even higher than reducing a hypothetical risk by amending 'auxiliary' contract terms. Finally, the counterparty normally pays more attention to the price and quality of goods, but not to so-called 'auxiliary' or 'secondary' contract terms (*e.g.* exclusion and limitation, indemnity, controls of evidence, arbitration, jurisdiction, and *force majeure* terms)[99]. This argument explains why most companies compete with other businesses by offering lower prices and better quality of goods and services, but not with respect to the 'fairness' of auxiliary contract terms. The *proferens* may be well aware of this fact and decide to take advantage of such 'laziness' of the counterparty.

Third, grossly unfair terms are still used even where the *proferens* understands that were a dispute to arise, he would not be able to enforce these contract terms. Signed contract terms have great psychological effect, especially on the weaker party, and it may reasonably be expected that the counterparty would not risk breaching the contract, so as to avoid lengthy and expensive litigation proceedings with an economically stronger *proferens*. Moreover, even where a dispute arises, the *proferens* can always counteract by offering something that was not originally included into a contract in order to finally settle the dispute. For example, a warranty could be offered, even though a signed contract included exclusion or limitation terms. However, a large number of signatories to a contract may decide not to contest unfair contracts even though it is possible to invalidate them. In short, the fact that some buyers are able to set aside unfair contract terms is not *per se* a sufficient reason for a company to be deterred from exercising unfair trade practices.

It should be also noted that Directive 93/13/EEC on Unfair Terms in Consumer Contracts as well as legislation in many European countries, deals primarily not with standard contract terms as such, but rather with *unfair* standard contract terms. For example, Recital 16 of Directive 93/13/EEC provides for the requirement of good faith that 'may be satisfied by the seller or supplier where he deals *fairly* and *equitably* with the other party whose legitimate interests he has to take into account'[100]. In this regard, the regulation of unfair standard contract terms relates to a more general and profound problem of fairness in contractual relations as well as the enforceability of freedom of

---

99 *See e.g.* Monarch Airlines Ltd. v. London Luton Airport Ltd. [1998] 1 Lloyd's Rep 403, Bacardi-Martini v. Thomas Hardy Packaging [2002] 2 Lloyd's Rep 379

100 *Cf.* Meli M. 'Unfair Terms and Unfairness Test in Contracts between Businesses and Consumers', in: *The Politics of the Draft Common Frame of Reference*, Somma A. *ed.* (Wolters Kluwer Law and Business, The Netherlands 2009) 156-59

contract. It seems that different countries have different views on this issue. Indeed, one of the most problematic issues of the theory of modern contract law relates to establishing discrimination or unfair disadvantaging in contractual relations. One can hardly describe all the ways in which unfair disadvantage may be obtained in contractual relations. For example, the liability of parties may be fixed differently for breaches following similar acts - the weaker party may be forced to indemnify against the stronger party's default, a company may be permitted to rescind an agreement only if there is misrepresentation by the other party, *etc*. For example, *Collins* distinguishes several types of unfairness when drafting contract terms: (i) cases where the price paid for goods or services appears excessive or derisory[101]; (ii) cases where unfairness involves allocation of risk; (iii) cases where unfairness concerns remedies agreed for breach of contract[102]. All these types may overlap to some extent. However, whereas there are a number of ways to discriminate against a weaker counterparty, at a general level it is difficult to conclude what contract terms genuinely disadvantage another party and to what extent standard contract terms need to be reviewed by authorised bodies.

In practice, at least at first glance, many standard form contracts include onerous and unusual contract terms. If a proposed contract were presented in standard form, one could *prima facie* suggest that such incorporated onerous terms were not desirable by the party accepting them. Moreover, one might suggest that standard contract terms could have been used not merely to speed up business dealings, but rather to disguise unfair terms so as to shift all risk in a transaction to the weaker contracting party. However, it is also possible that the other contracting party may receive some sort of 'compensation', by being offered a reduced price for accepting further onerous contracts or further parallel supply contracts, or the party proposing the contract reasonably (considering usual business practices) believes that, for example, defective goods would be repaired or replaced without relying on the signed contract because this is a standard practice. Moreover, the contract may initially seem unfair if one considers a single transaction; however, a fair proportion of contractual rights and obligations can be retained for a number of contracts. Thus such appraisal of standard contract terms should include various aspects of transactional rewards.

---

[101] Such situations are sometimes considered as *laesio enormis* under the Roman law. This expression refers to the cases where a remedy is available if the agreed price less than half (Code 4.44.2). *Cf.* Gordley J. 'Equality in Exchange' 69 *Cal. L. Rev.* (1981) 1638 *et seq.* Hatzis A., Zervogianni E. Judge-Made Contracts Reconstructing Unconscionable Contracts (downloaded from http://papers.ssrn.com/sol3/papers.cfm?abstract_id=953669 on 25 August 2009)

[102] Collins H. *Regulating Contracts* (Oxford: Oxford University Press 1999) 259. *Cf.* Eith W. 'Zum Schutzbedürfnis gegenüber Allgemeinen Geschäftsbedingungen' *NJW* (1974) 16 *et seq*; Klima P. 'Missbräuchliche Klauseln in Veträgen' *RIW* (1992) 98 *et seq*

So is it possible to measure the price of the contract and other contractual terms using the metric of fairness at all? On balance, it is submitted that the answer should be in the affirmative. It must be stressed that there are situations in which the price may be derisory and the obligations imposed upon the other party may also be derisory in comparison with similar standard transactions signed in the market at a similar point in time. In such cases, the excessive interest charged or other unfair terms imposed are agreed just because the counterparty wanted a contract at any price. It is submitted that the existence of untypical and onerous contract terms does not mean that the other party is happy, even where such terms are accepted. However, it is also possible that the counterparty may agree to pay a lower price and accept poorer quality goods (or other onerous contract terms)[103], whereas he would not enter into a similar contract otherwise. For example, auxiliary contract terms could be unsatisfactory from a buyer's perspective, but he might have no other better alternatives at that particular moment. It is mostly true that a creditor has fewer chances to recover a debt from a small business than from a large one that has a good credit rating. In this respect, it seems that the unfairness of contractual relations often depends on the perspective from which the contract terms, and indeed the business transaction as a whole, is considered. It seems reasonable for a government to maintain minimum standards for the quality of goods and services and not to tolerate a 'race to the bottom', as quality, warranty or any other similar disclaimers more adversely affect smaller and weaker companies. However, it is a matter of lengthy discussions as to what extent a weaker party needs additional protection, particularly if a weaker party is a businessman as well[104].

Finally, one may argue that regulating unfairness in contractual relations does not make sense at all. Such over-regulation may result in the *proferens* being deterred from contracting on the basis of any standard form contract at all. The regulation of standard form contracts must not undermine the stability of contractual relations. A regulator should find a proper balance between stability of contractual relations and protection of weaker parties, so that both contracting parties are able to foresee what terms are permitted. Moreover, it would seem reasonable for special regulations on standard form contracts not to differ significantly from contract law in general. Similar discrimination against a weaker party can be achieved by engaging in sham negotiations or by tailoring contracts so as to circumvent local regulations on standard form contracts.

---

[103] *Cf.* Schwartz 'A Re-examination of Nonsubstantive Unconscionability' 63 *Va. L. Rev.* (1977) 1056 *et seq*

[104] There is a broad consensus in Europe that a consumer is a weaker party in the contractual arrangements and therefore it must be offered an additional protection. These issue will be examined further in detail.

1.2 Policing the Fairness of Standard Form Contracts

The political economists of the 18th century (e.g. *Adam Smith, David Ricardo, Jeremy Bentham, John Stuart Mill*) maintained that the freedom to bargain is indispensable to further economic development[105]. Classical social theory (*Max Weber, Émile Durkheim*) – like classical political economy – presented a contract as a voluntary and self-reliant relationship between individuals, and strongly supported their discretion to shape contractual relations independently[106].

These ideas were based on the assumption that individuals know best what is good for them. Eventually, by pursuing personal interests they would contribute to the welfare of society at the same time. Following this line of argument, the influence of public authorities would be minimised, so as merely to sustain the stability and enforceability of contractual relations. For example, according to *Lord Devlin,* under the classical view free dealing was fair dealing at the same time[107].

In this regard, it must be noted that under the 'classical' law of contract[108] the doctrine of public policy has been considered to be much less meaningful. Public policy did not tackle cases where a contract created a significant disparity between contractual obligations. Judicial authorities mostly refrained from supervising contract terms, since primacy was given to the parties' intentions and protection of their expectations. It has been said that parties should be bound

---

[105] Williston S. 'Freedom of Contract' 6 *Cornell LQ* (1921) 366

[106] Collins H. *Regulating Contracts* (Oxford: Oxford University Press 1999) 14. *For some more details see:* Boucock C. *In the Grip of Freedom of Law and Modernity in Max Weber* (University of Toronto Press Toronto Buffalo London 2000) 61; Hunt A. *The Sociological Movement in London* (Maxmillan: London 1978) 85; Atiyah P. *The Rise and Fall of Freedom of Contract* (Oxford: Oxford University Press 1979) 9-11; Weber M. *Economy and Society,* Roth G., Wittich C. eds. (New York, Bedminster Press 1968) 668 *et seq*; Reiner R. *Crime, Law, Deviance: the Durkheim Legacy*, in: *Durkheim and Modern Sociology*, Fenton S. ed. (Cambridge: Cambridge University Press 1984) 176 *et seq*; Häyhä J. 'Scandinavian Techniques for Controlling Fairness in Contracts', in: *Welfarism in Contract Law*; Brownsword R., Howells G., Wilhelmsson T. eds. (Darthmouth Publishing Company Limited 1994) 130-1

[107] Grubb A., Furmston M. (eds.) *The Law of Contract* (Lexis Nexis United Kingdom 2003) 27. The similar theory of party autonomy has been endorsed in the legal doctrine of most European civil law jurisdictions. *For more see*: Grundmann S. 'Information, Party Autonomy and Economic Agents in European Contract Law' 39 *C.M.L. Rev.* (2002) 269 *et seq*

[108] The law developed during the 19th century and at the beginning of the 20th century is commonly defined as classical contract law. *Cf.* Beatson J., Friedman D. 'Introduction: From 'Classical' to Modern Contract Law', in: *Good Faith and Fault in Contract Law*, ed., Beatson J. and Friedmann D. (Oxford: Clarendon Press 1994) 7; Brownsword R. *Contract Law: Themes for the Twenty-First Century* (London: Butterworths 2001) 46 *et seq*

by a signed contract regardless of whether they understood its terms. The rule underlying this concept was the protection of the stability of commercial relations[109].

Broad acceptance of the principle of freedom of contract in the 18th and 19th centuries represented - to a certain extent – a rejection of constraints established in feudal times[110]. Freedom of contract was considered a product of the school of natural law. As a rule, agreements must be enforced (*pacta sunt servanda*), with the exception of some situations[111]. Thus the role of the state was confined to guaranteeing that private arrangements would be binding and enforceable, albeit that the legislator could enforce special mandatory rules pertaining to the public policy, such as prohibiting enforcement where a party was threatened or otherwise entered into a contract involuntarily, *etc.*

The situation changed dramatically at the beginning of the 20th century, when contract law began to be linked to distributive justice and the efficient allocation of resources. The subjugation of a weaker party was not the real outcome of freedom of contract. Judicial review of unfair standard form contracts began a new epoch of contract law that is sometimes defined as 'one of the most important and innovative developments in private law' in the 20th century[112]. At the time, it was thought that the law of contract should deal not only with ideal situations, but that one had also to take into consideration situations where the other party was economically dependent, under pressure or did not possess the necessary information before concluding a contract[113]. Regulation of contractual relations was, therefore, supposed to re-establish fair contractual relations by amending or setting aside derisory contract terms, and thereby contribute to the welfare of society in general. Judicial review evolved to stop the abuse of standard form contracts, whereby all business risks were shifted to the weaker party[114]. For example, in its early case law, the German RG

---

109 *Cf.* Hillman R. 'Debunking Some Myth about Unconscionability: a new Framework for UCC § 2-302' 67 *Cornell L. R.* (1981) 6; Yates D. *Exclusion Clauses in Contracts* 2nd ed. (London: Sweet & Maxwell 1982) 1 *et seq*

110 Zweigert K., Kötz H. *Introduction to Comparative Law.* Trans. by Weird T. 3rd ed. (Oxford: Clarendon Press 1998) 324

111 *See also:* Rutgers J. W. 'The DCFR, Public Policy, Mandatory Rules, and the Welfare State', in: *The Politics of the Draft Common Frame of Reference*, Somma A. ed. (Wolters Kluwer Law and Business, The Netherlands 2009) 123-128

112 Beale H. [*et. al.*] *Casebooks on the Common Law of Europe: Contract* (Oxford: Hart Publishing 2002) 532

113 It must be noted, however, that the duty to divulge all essential information in the pre-contractual relations is not a commonplace in Europe. There is no such general duty in England, except that section 14(3) of the Sale of Goods Act 1979 provides that the seller must ensure that goods are fit for the purpose whether or not that is a purpose for which such goods are commonly supplied.

114 Basedow in: MünchKomm, before § 305, para 2

proved that contractual obligations included in standard form contracts were often used merely as means of taking advantage of a monopolistic position[115]. Holding a leading market position in one or several industries does not mean that a company must include unfair terms in its contracts and so abuse its superior position in the market.

The notion of the Welfare State gained much support after the Second World War, and contract law was conceived as a means to achieving moral and social objectives. Currently, welfarist ideas are broadly accepted in Scandinavian countries. Case studies from these countries confirm that it is also possible to re-negotiate and adjust unfair contract terms during judicial proceedings instead of invalidating contracts[116]. The adjustment of contract terms by the judiciary may undermine the stability of contractual relations and, thus, lead to arbitrary judicial decisions. Furthermore, one may assert that judicial interference aiming to re-establish social justice creates uncertainty and augments transactional costs. In short, the redistribution of wealth is not the task of the judiciary. Criticism of the regulation of contractual arrangements is based on the assumption that the judiciary should decide merely on the enforceability or non-enforceability of contract terms and nothing more. There is merit in these arguments, as even where a contract is voided by a court, the parties are not prohibited from entering into a new agreement on substantially similar terms. However, practically speaking, it is not feasible for the parties to enter into new commercial arrangements after costly litigation.

The political determination to regulate standard form contracts should also be examined from the perspective of safeguarding fundamental rights. European contract law was heavily influenced by the German constitutional law doctrine, whereby the provisions of private law are considered subordinate not only to public order, statutory rules or good moral, but also to fundamental rights[117]. It is agreed that the respect of human rights should be somewhat higher

---

115 See RGZ, 143, 24, 28. For some notorious German case law regarding the restoration of justice in contractual relations *see*: BGH, NJW, 1976, 2345, 2346; BGHZ, 64, 238, 242; BGHZ, 70, 304, 310

116 Lehrberg B. 'Renegotiation Clauses, the Doctrine of Assumptions and Unfair Contract Terms' 3 *ERPL* (1998) 273-4. In some cases, for example, a German judge who deals with lease contracts stipulating disproportionaly expensive monthly rents may intervene and adjust the rent (*See*: BGHZ, 89, 316). However, this is not applicable for standard form contracts.

117 *See also*: Cherednychenko O. *Fundamental Rights, Contract Law and the Protection of the Weaker Party: a Comparative Analysis of the Constitutionalisation of Contract Law, with Emphasis on Risky Financial Transactions* (Sellier: European Law Publishers 2007) 57 *et seq*; Zumbansen P. 'The Law of Contract', in: *Introduction to German Law*, Reimann M., Zekoll J. eds. (Kluwer Law International 2005) 179 *et seq*; Eppig V., Lenz S., Leydecker P. *Grundrechte* (Springer 2005) 125-6; Graf von Westphalen F. 'Fallstricke bei Verträgen und Prozessen mit Auslandsberührung' *NJW* (1994) 2115 *et seq*

than the other principles of contract law. The German Federal Constitutional Court, by reviewing the constitutionality of rulings of the Federal Court of Justice (BGH), has rightly contended that the German law of contract is not completely immune to the implications arising from the doctrine of fundamental rights.

For instance, in 1990 the constitutionality of restraint of trade clauses in a contract concluded between an agent and its principal were scrutinised (generally known as the *Handelsvertreter* case in Germany)[118]. These clauses were struck out on the grounds of duress and unequal bargaining power. The excessive limitation of contractual freedom was found to be contrary to the basic freedom to exercise a profession, which is guaranteed in Article 12(1) of the German *Grundgesetz*, or Fundamental Law. Interestingly, agreeing to be barred from working with any of the principal's competitors would have been enforceable under mandatory German law provisions. However, the Federal German Constitutional Court confirmed the competence of national courts to intervene by invoking §§ 138, 242, 315 BGB in cases where the parity of contractual rights is misbalanced[119].

Another landmark ruling was adopted by the German Federal Constitutional Court in the so-called *Bürgschaft* case[120] in 1993, where the court voided a collateral contract signed by a daughter for a loan taken out by her father to finance risky professional activity. After the father defaulted, the bank sought to recover the debt under the collateral agreement. The agreement was found to breach the right to the free development of personality (Art. 2(1) German Fundamental Law) in conjunction with the principle of the social state (Art. 20(1) and 28(1) German Fundamental Law). The court concluded further that the judiciary should intervene to protect the private autonomy of the weaker party. Hence, German case law would suggest that fundamental rights can supersede the absolute freedom of contract. The courts may and probably should interfere where a contract is too onerous for one party, and therefore constitutional rights are at stake. In the last years, the Court of Justice has also faced the dilemma of whether German fundamental rights principles can justify infringing the free movement of services, particularly in the case in Bonn where games involving firing at human targets using a laser beam or other technical devices were prohibited[121]. The Court of Justice also confirmed that the protection of human dignity is compatible with Union law, which as a result permitted Germany to invoke fundamental rights that restrict the freedom of contract.

---

[118] BVerfGE 81, 242

[119] Ibid., para 48

[120] BVerfGE 89, 214

[121] Omega Spielhallen C-36/02, paras 33-41, *see also*: Schmidberger C-112/00, paras 71-94

Still, the necessity to protect a weaker party in contractual relations and interference with freedom of contract is highly controversial[122]. Even if we agree that a weaker party cannot sufficiently protect itself, and the free market cannot guarantee mutually advantageous contract terms, the problem remains as to how to maintain or restore fairness in contractual relations. The protection of a weaker party may seriously undermine the stability of contractual relations, which is not desired by any of the parties. Where parties suspect that a transaction may be invalidated at some stage of the execution of a contract, they will try to manage this risk by increasing the price of the contract or by avoiding a particular legal system or by employing other means. Conversely, a rigid rule on the enforceability of contractual relations has huge political significance. The paternalistic approach, whereby courts are entitled to re-write contract terms, reduces the value of market participants, as if they could not freely interact among themselves without governmental or judicial interference. Some other practical arguments should be outlined in detail:

First, the fact that contracting parties are in an unequal economic position can hardly in itself justify the need to regulate contractual relations. Indeed, what is the benchmark of fairness? In the author's view, only those terms which substantially deviate from contract terms normally agreed by parties of equal bargaining power and of similar economic capacity (so-called 'good commercial practice') should be seen as being *prima facie* unfair. These terms may, moreover be delegitimised by taking into consideration the particular circumstances of a case. For instance, *Beale* supports the application of the unfairness test first derived from *Ralws*. Thus, fair terms were those …

> 'that could accepted by rational agents who, without knowing on which side of the transaction they might stand, had to imagine themselves as parties to the transaction'[123].

However, this test is subject to the rather obscure criterion of 'rationality'. It may be posited that something rational should be fair at the same time. Indeed, what changes if we replace the word 'fair' with 'rational'? However one views it, this criterion is still uncertain in its meaning, and applying it may cause inconsistency when reviewing contract terms and, therefore, seriously undermine the predictability of contractual relations. Accordingly, an open-

---

[122] It may well be argued that courts are not empowered to protect or help the weaker party simply because they are not authorized to do this by law (*see e.g.* Article 20 of the German Fundamental Law, Article 109 of the Constitution of the Republic of Lithuania). From the continental lawyer's view, it could be also argued that the judiciary must just objectively apply the statutory law in respect of the factual circumstances.

[123] Beale H. 'Unfair Contracts in Britain and Europe' *C.L.P.* (1989) 206

textured statutory formula on fairness may induce businesses to opt out of the ordinary judicial system so as to avoid possible legal surprises, and submit their dispute to private adjudicators for settlement. In this respect, some additional guidelines may prove useful for safeguarding consistency when reviewing standard form contracts.

Furthermore, the question remains as to why the state should intervene in contractual relations. One can hold the view that government should set out regulations on unfairness in contractual relations by imposing general prohibitions on the activity of such companies[124]. For instance, in cases where a stronger party in a contract (*e.g.* monopolies or oligopolies) abuses its bargaining power, unfair trade practices can be regulated by antitrust legislation, but not by introducing special requirements limiting freedom of contract. In the author's view, several approaches could be employed here. One could argue that the state should be flexible and consider contract terms on a case-by-case basis. On the other hand, career judges are knowledgeable about statute and case law, but they may lack general commercial experience and awareness of common business practices. In this regard, businesses that continuously trade according to mutually agreed conventions may be afraid to be subject to the control of commercially ignorant judges. For example, a warranty might be given the basis of an established convention, even though the contract includes limitation clauses and the *proferens* is not under any obligation to provide such services.

Second, the protection of a weaker party as well as special judicial intervention may be criticised from an economic perspective (*i.e.* considering the costs of transactions)[125]. It seems that a requirement to deal fairly should reduce the costs of transactions as a contracting party can rely on minimal statutory requirements instead of hiring lawyers to check every standard contract term in detail. On the other hand, in cases where a government imposes minimal standards for products warranties, a vendor might simply increase the price of its production or services so as to absorb the costs relating to the repair of defective goods. As a result, fewer customers would be able to acquire these products and similarly fewer suppliers would be able to sell them. Such governmental intervention might have a detrimental effect on the turn-over of commodities. To sum up, even where certain contract terms are grossly unfavourable, they could

---

[124] *See:* Schwarz A., Wilde L., Louis P. 'Intervening in Markets on the Basis of Imperfect Information: A Legal and Economic Analysis' 127 *U. Pa.L.R.* (1979) 682; Collins H. *Regulating Contracts* (Oxford: Oxford University Press 1999) 258. *For more about market failures as well as the relevancy of governmental control see, e.g.,* Hatzis A. N. 'Civil Contract Law and Economic Reasoning – An Unlikely Pair', in: *The Architecture of European Codes and Contract Law*, Grundmann S., Schaue M., *eds*. (The Hague/London/ New York: Kluwer Law International 2006) 164 *et seq*

[125] *See also:* Atiyah P. S., Smith S. *Atiyah's Introduction to the Law of Contract* (Oxford: Clarendon Press 2005) 17

be agreed voluntarily by the deliberate (express or implied) consent of a contracting party. For instance, high interest rates may be agreed because of a creditor's judgement about the risk of possible default, or an obligor may consent to harsh remedial contract terms in return for low interest rates, or purchase goods with shorter warranty at a cheaper price, *etc*[126]. Furthermore, some commentators argue that there is no *prima facie* reason that the carrier in a delivery contract should always bear the responsibility for obtaining insurance[127]. It is quite clear that the possibility of insuring against risk in a transaction should be considered after deciding on the suitability of exclusion clauses[128]. However, insurance companies ordinarily refuse to cover all business risks. Insurance includes taking the risk of confiscation, theft, floods, fire, strikes, riots, malicious damage *etc*, which could generally be defined as something that is beyond the control of both parties. In many jurisdictions, insurance companies tend to refuse to insure against the default of the other party, or else high insurance premiums make the whole transaction commercially unreasonable.

Considering a government's policy on the permissibility of intervening in the allocation of business risk, it would probably be reasonable to assert that somewhat richer countries with higher gross domestic product per capita (*e.g.* the Nordic countries) would be able to afford to maintain higher standards in the quality of production and receive more expensive goods and services in return, while the poorer ones would be forced to understand that the costs of strict 'auxiliary terms' may inhibit customers to acquire certain products at a reasonable price. All in all, it is difficult to decide when strict judicial interference is desirable in reality.

Third, as noted before, some contracts may seem at first glance to be unfair; however, they are fair if one considers all the circumstances of a commercial arrangement. For example, the price of a contract may include a non-material element of value. This may happen when the purchaser deliberately decides to acquire over-valued goods, services and so on (*e.g.* because of prestige, reputation, growing expectations). The purchaser may reasonably expect that the price of real estate will increase in the foreseeable future due to,

---

[126] *See:* Posner R. 'Economic Analysis of Contract Law after three Decades: Success or Failure?' 112 *Yale L.J.* (2003) 843. *For some further criticism about regulations on standard form contracts from the economic perspective see*: Schwarz A. 'A Re-examination of non-substantive Unconscionability' 63 *Va. L. Rev.* (1977) 1054; Slawson W. D. 'Standard Form Contracts and Democratic Control of Lawmaking Power' 84 *Harv. L. Rev.* (1971) 531. *See also:* BGHZ, 77, 126, 133

[127] Atiyah P. S., Smith S. *Atiyah's Introduction to the Law of Contract* (Oxford: Clarendon Press 2005) 17

[128] For some reflections *see also*: Lutz R. *AGB-Kontrolle im Handelsverkehr unter Berücksichtigung der Klauselverbote* (München 1991) 130 *et seq*

for instance, high rates of inflation in the market or due to the increasing demand for such property. Even if the agreed price exceeds the actual market price, this price may include some other benefits in the contract or benefit via some other commercial arrangements between the same parties. Can a court in this case say that some terms in this contract are unfair? Practically speaking, judges would probably call on the experts to guide them on deciding the actual price; though such guidance is not helpful in all cases. These arguments cast much doubt on whether the regulation of standard form contracts should be based on the premise that a weaker party is discriminated against in cases where some contract terms are not similar to those used in typical business contracts.

On the other hand, it is also possible to envisage a situation in which a purchaser (say, a weaker party) was not duly informed about all the terms of a contract, and he may later find out that the price of the contract as well as some other terms were actually unfair. The purchase may be subject to unusually harsh terms that are difficult at first to understand if they drafted in a foreign language. On balance, *Collins* must be right in concluding that in some cases the purchaser may be charged more or has had to accept unfavourable contract terms. The market price of some products is relatively easy to define, and only in certain transactions does the assessment of contractual fairness require a closer inspection (*e.g.* a right to security clearly exceeds any conceivable risk of loss from default)[129]. It is, therefore, important to collect as much information as possible to find out if the contract terms are actually fair or not[130]. For these purposes, similar contracts in the market may be compared - if that is possible - before concluding whether disadvantaging actually took place or not. In the author's view, the state should, therefore, apply different approaches by assessing both material and non-material elements of a contract and thereby decide on the actual imbalance of contractual terms. By way of example, the value of aircraft can be assessed by considering sale values, but it is also always possible to consider the typical lease values on the market, and thereby decide how actual cash – flow may influence the price of the assets.

Fourth, one may argue that the possibility of assessing standard form contracts can contribute to legal uncertainty. In cases where courts are given wide discretion to decide on what is fair and what is not, parties would never be

---

[129] Collins H. *Regulating Contracts* (Oxford: Oxford University Press 1999) 265

[130] Some authors argue that many things can be measured exactly in terms of their market price, in particular by taking into account the generality of contracts of the same type concluded by parties in an equal bargaining position. In this regard, adjudication in respect of market price is not a completely subjective matter. *Cf.* Collins H. *Regulating Contracts* (Oxford: Oxford University Press 1999) 265; Lutz R. *AGB-Kontrolle im Handelsverkehr unter Berücksichtigung der Klauselverbote* (München 1991) 130 *et seq*; Atiyah P. S., Smith S. *Atiyah's Introduction to the Law of Contract* (Oxford: Clarendon Press 2005) 298; Smith A. S. 'In Defence of Substantive Fairness' 112 *L.Q.R.* (1996) 138

totally sure what contract terms would be struck out at some further stage (*e.g.* due to a changed economic environment). As a result, a counterparty may refuse to take its legal commitments seriously, expecting that the court would rectify contract terms and re-establish fairness in contractual relations. Despite this, it is submitted that tackling unfairness in contractual relations should outweigh the risk that the legal outcome of certain disputes would sometimes be inconsistent. The improvement of consistency in courts' rulings as well as legal certainty can be enhanced by issuing guidelines from the regulator and by closer supervision by higher judicial authorities of the most obvious imbalances of contractual obligations (*e.g.* establishing a 'black or grey list' of prohibitions).

To sum up, the courts should shift from a formalistic approach to the actual freedom of contract. On the other hand, the regulation of *commercial* arrangements should be regarded as a very exceptional matter, as is acknowledged in the modern law of contract[131]. A party that accepts standard form contracts should not automatically be assumed to be the weaker one. In real life, after closer examination of the case material, it seems that it is difficult to justify intervention in contractual relations merely by arguing that there is a general need to protect a weaker party. In many cases, it is difficult to distinguish cases where a weaker party was actually disadvantaged or voluntarily accepted somewhat unfavourable terms knowing that the *proferens* would not enter into the contract otherwise. Indeed, the fact that some terms deviate from the customary commercial practice does not mean that these terms are unfair. It is submitted that contract terms should not be considered *per se* unfair merely because the other party was not offered a possibility to re-negotiate the terms offered, or because the bargaining power of the parties was not exactly the same. For example, empirical research has established no connection between market concentration and the use of unfair exclusion clauses[132].

It must also be stressed that the achievement of fairness or a fair balance of contractual obligations - even though not a perfect one - should take priority over a rigid rule in respect to the enforceability of freedom of contract. Regulating standard form contracts would contribute to a fair allocation of contractual rights and obligations, which could more generally be defined as where 'a more efficient distribution of resources is achieved'[133]. From a more general perspective, the policing of fairness of contractual relations should improve the competitiveness of markets. It seems reasonable for a regulator to

131 *Cf.* Grubb A., Furmston M., ed., *The Law of Contract* (Lexis Nexis UK 2003) 32

132 Beale H. 'Unfair Contracts in Britain and Europe' 42 *C.L.P.* (1989) 199

133 Willet C. 'Introduction', in: *Aspects of Fairness in Contract*, Willet C., ed. (Blackstone Press Limited 1996) 19. *See also:* Schwarz A. 'A Re-examination of non-substantive Unconscionability' 63 *Va. L. Rev.* (1977) 1056

decide to protect the market by legislating against fraud and misleading trading practices[134]. Both parties would save more time and other resources if they knew that it was not worth scrutinising all contract terms as they must at least be in line with minimal statutory requirements or will be struck out if they do not comply with such requirements. Regulating clear imbalances of contractual relations would impede processes that are widely referred to as the 'race to the bottom', where all traders compete only in shifting all possible risks to the other party in order to reduce the price of the contract.

On the basis of these considerations, it is submitted that the judiciary should not be discouraged from engaging in an evaluation of substantive unfairness in contractual relations. Unfair results may derive not only from unfair negotiations, but also from asymmetry of information. In many cases, it is possible to compare clauses incorporated in a contract with similar clauses used in customary commercial transactions[135]. In this respect, fairness in contractual relations can be deduced from typical contractual relations on the basis of the best available information in the market.

1.3 Difficulties in Finding an Appropriate Formula for Appraising Fairness in Contractual Relations

A more controversial issue in the contemporary theory of contract law is not whether to regulate unfairness in contractual arrangements, but *how* to regulate it. Businesses of different sizes have different needs, and therefore it is difficult to find a common denominator as to the most effective model of market regulation. Where politicians do decide to intervene in the contractual relations, the question remains as to what contract terms should be covered by this regulation and what terms should be left to the complete discretion of the parties? Moreover, the regulator should make a decision on whether a special rule should cover merely non-individually negotiated contract terms or all contract terms.

Many European countries have enacted special laws that authorise the state to set aside unfair contracts or at least some terms thereof. Nowadays one finds special laws dealing with unfair standard contract terms in the Baltic countries, Germany, Scandinavia, Austria, Portugal, Spain, the Benelux countries, *etc.* These special laws mostly cover consumer contracts, while reviews of business-to-business contracts are ordinarily set out in the general

---

134 Collins H. *Regulating Contracts* (Oxford: Oxford University Press, 1999) 279

135 It must also be noted that it is not always possible to ascertain the precise price where the price fluctuates or there are no similar products on the market. However, such cases are the exception rather than the rule. For more views on this issue *see*: Gordley J. 'Equality in Exchange' 69 *Cal. L. Rev.* (1981) 1589 *et seq*

provisions of contract law. As set out above, Directive 13/93/EEC on Unfair Terms in Consumer Contracts leaves aside purely commercial arrangements. In this respect, there is no unanimous agreement on the question of whether SMEs should also be protected by enacting special regulations tackling unfair contract terms in commercial contracts.

Thus further analysis of European private law systems will be based on a comparison of the following points: (a) how far should the judiciary intervene in assessing contractual relations?; (b) how specifically should the national regulator deal with unfair terms in business-to-business contracts?; (c) what is the most appropriate formula for defining standard contract terms?; (d) should regulations on unfair contract terms cover terms pertaining to the price and quality of the main object of a transaction?

First, at a very basic level both civil and common law systems - though they do not share the same legal terminology and legal reasoning - acknowledge that a contract must be held to be unenforceable only if it was concluded under undue influence, misrepresentation, duress, mistake, *etc*. Different governments tend to enact special minimal requirements on contract terms from which parties may not deviate. However, there are many important discrepancies in the approach to assessing unfair contract terms in civil law systems. The first and most important issue is how far the judiciary should interfere with freedom of contract. English case law draws a clear line between procedural fairness and substantive fairness. Generally, English law is more concerned with the preservation of procedural fairness that refers to the formation of a contract, but not to the results agreed by the parties or substantive fairness[136]. Procedural fairness requires that the terms offered by a party should be disclosed in order to avoid unfair surprises. In other words, contracts should not be offered on a '*take-it-or-leave-it*' basis. The counterparty should always be given a choice[137]. Lord Reid in the Suisse Atlantique Societe d'Armament SA v NV Rotterdamsche Kolen Centrale case said that 'the freedom to contract must surely imply some choice or room to bargain'[138]. Summarising its different positions, the English judiciary seems to tackle unfair contracts by applying such principles as

---

[136] However, the House of Lords in *Director General of Fair Trading v. First National Bank plc* [2002] 1 AC 481 suggested that it would consider both procedural and substantive fairness. This development is considered a significant civil law influence on the common law.

[137] *See more*: Brownsword R., Howells G., Wilhelmsson T. 'Between Market and Welfare: Some Reflections on Art. 3 of the EC Directive on Unfair Terms in Consumer Contracts, in: *Aspects of Fairness in Contract*, Willet C., ed. (Blackstone Press Limited 1996) 40

[138] [1967] A.C. 361, 406

inequality of bargaining power[139], a duty to bargain in good faith[140], and testing the adequacy of consideration[141], *etc*. Conversely, most continental European countries put a stronger emphasis on the assessment of substantive provisions of contracts. Procedural fairness is important in reaching a decision on the effective incorporation of standard terms in a contract.

Generally, continental European countries have implemented an interventionist approach widely, and consequently contemporary private law serves as a device of cooperation and fairness[142]. For example, an entrepreneur must actively cooperate by informing the other party about all circumstances that may later inhibit the enforcement of the agreement[143]. Moreover, some commentators have argued that European law of contract can be labelled as 'welfarist' in its aims[144]. Indeed, most continental European countries reject the classical *laisser-faire* concept of contract law, in contrast with the dominant legal doctrines in England. In short, common law countries are more concerned with the assessment of the bargaining power of parties, while continental law countries focus more on the actual contents of standard form contracts and their conformity to the notion of good faith.

---

139 Strictly speaking, the doctrine of inequality of bargaining strength is not broadly recognised in England as such. However, it often comes into consideration when the exclusion clauses in standard form contracts are reviewed. *Cf.* Grubb A., Furmston M. (ed.) *The Law of Contract* (Lexis Nexis UK 2003) 42 *et seq*; Dalhuisen HJ 'Domestic Contract Laws, Uniform International Contract Law and International Contract Law Principles. International Sales and Contractual Agency' 11(7-8) *EBLR* (2000) 221 *et seq*

140 It must be noted that the concept of good faith is not an established fact of English law. As Lord Ackner in Walford v. Miles [1992] 2 AC 128, HL noted: *'Each party to negotiations is entitled to pursue his (or her) own interest, so long as he avoids making misrepresentations. To advance that interest he must be entitled, if he thinks it appropriate, to ... withdraw'*. *See also*: Bingham, LJ in: Interfoto Library v. Stilleto Ltd [1988] 1 All E.R. 348

141 Collins H. 'Fairness in agreed Remedies', in: *Aspects of Fairness in Contract.* Willet C., eds. (Blackstone Press Limited 1996) 100

142 *Cf.* BGH, NJW, 1976, 2346. *See also* Zweigert K., Kötz H. *Introduction to Comparative Law.* Trans. by Weird T. (Oxford: Clarendon Press 1988) 332; Wolf M. 'Harmonisation of Protection against unfair Contract Terms in Private European Law', in: *European Legal Traditions and Israel*, Rabello A. M., ed. (Jerusalem: The Harry and Michael Sacher Institute for Legislative Research and Comparative Law 1994) 382; Hesselink M. 'The Politics of European Contract Law: Who has an Interest in what kind of Contract Law for Europe?' 2(1) *Global Jurist Frontiers* (2002); Adams J. N 'Unconscionability and the Standard Form Contract', in: *Welfarism in Contract Law*, Brownsword R., Howells G. and Wilhelmsson T. *eds*. (Darthmouth Publishing Company Limited, 1994) 233

143 *Cf.* the decision of Lithuanian Supreme Court No. 3K-3-558/2008.

144 *See*: Wilhemsson T. *Social Contract Law and European Integration* (Dartmouth: Publishing Company 1995); Brownsword R. 'The Philosophy of Welfarism', in: *Welfarism in Contract Law*, Brownsword R., Howells G. and Wilhelmsson T., eds. (Darthmouth Publishing Company Limited 1994) 23 *et seq*

Second, one notices some further discrepancies by analysing special statutory provisions dealing with unfairness in standard form contracts. Most modern Civil Codes enacted in continental Europe deal explicitly with unfair contract terms. Some others still rely on the general provisions of civil law. A good example is the Italian *Codice Civile*, which provides for some basic rules. Thus, general contract terms ('*condizioni generali di contratto*') prepared by one of the parties shall be effective only if at the formation of the contract the latter knew of them or should have known of them by using basic due diligence. Pursuant to Article 1341(2) *Codice Civile*, standard contract terms that limit liability bind the other contracting party only if they were approved in writing[145]. This means, the Italian *Codice Civile* provides merely some hints to the judiciary on how to deal with such unfair contract terms. The Code does not contain any exhaustive rules about how unfair disadvantaging should be evaluated.

The LCC provides for some general rules. It establishes a prohibition regarding the incorporation of surprising terms into commercial contracts. Still, the LCC lacks detailed rules on standard form contracts. In this regard, the Lithuanian judiciary may employ general principles (*e.g.* the principles of integrity, reasonability, and justice) to evaluate the enforceability of contract terms. Detailed rules on assessing the effectiveness of standard form contracts – probably some of the most exhaustive in Europe - are set out in the German BGB. § 307 BGB stipulates a general rule that unfair disadvantaging *inter alia* takes places if essential rights and duties that arise from the contract are so limited that the attainment of contract aims is jeopardized. Some particular rules, *i.e.* 'black' and 'grey' lists of prohibited terms are enumerated in §§ 308-309 BGB. The exhaustive statutory rules have given a big momentum to the further development of judicial practice in Germany. The so-called 'standard contract terms law' (German *'AGB-Recht'*) gives numerous examples of how to deal with various situations relating to the striking out of standard contract terms[146].

The common law pursues a slightly different policy in the assessment of fairness of contract terms from that of continental Europe. As noted above, English judges tend to adhere to the market individualism approach and maintain a more neutral stance towards the evaluation of contents of contract terms. However, English statutes do also contain some rules on the regulation of unfair terms. After UCTA 1977 came into force in England, almost all unfair contract terms – whether or not they are pre-formulated – can be found to be void if they are unreasonable for the counterparty (*see:* Section 3 UCTA). In

145 *For more comments see e.g.* Lena S. J., Mattei U. *Introduction to Italian Law* (The Hague, London, New York: Kluwer Law International 2002), Wolf M., in: Wolf/Horn/Lindacher, Introduction, para 55

146 Some of these aspects will be examined in the subsequent chapters of this book.

general, it seems that the English courts still retain vast discretion – which is, however, rarely used in practice - to decide on the effectiveness of standard contract terms on a case-by-case basis.

Several other European countries (*e.g.* France, Belgium, and Luxembourg) have no special statutory provisions for the review of standard contract terms in business-to-business transactions[147]. In those countries, the concept of standard form contracts has a more doctrinal meaning. For example, the French concept of *contrat d'adhésion* implies that contract terms are not intended to be amended by the other contracting party. The enforceability of standard form contracts in commercial arrangements is ordinarily assessed taking into consideration the compatibility of the terms with *ordre public* or proper conduct (*see*: Article 6 of the French CC)[148]. Moreover, the enforceability of standard form contracts is also evaluated by employing general principles of contract law acknowledged by the Civil Code. Finally, standard contract terms may sometimes be tested by the court when it interprets contract terms that are detrimental to the other party.

The third major problem concerns the definition of standard form contracts. The experience of different countries confirms the difficulty of adopting more or less acceptable unified rules for different jurisdictions in defining standard form contracts. In legal doctrine, standard form contracts are sometimes called 'mass' or 'form' contracts. Such different definitions stress either the form of the contract, its economic purposes or the fact that it is intended for multiple uses[149]. Two aspects are usually stressed when defining these contracts: (i) multiple application of the terms, and (ii) the fact that the other party merely adheres to the contract, and therefore is not able to influence the content of the terms.

Some laws in continental European countries entail special prescriptive definitions or provide some specific elements to enable a contract to qualify as standard. For example, pursuant to German law protection against unfair standard contract terms in business-to-business contracts is provided in accordance with §§ 305 *et seq*. BGB. The controlled standard contract terms fall within these provisions only if they are not individually negotiated. It may be assumed here that individually tailored contracts should hold no surprises for a counterparty. Thus special statutory rules need not be drafted for the

---

147 Wolf M. 'Harmonisation of Protection against unfair Contract Terms in Private European Law', in: *European Legal Traditions and Israel*, Rabello A.M., ed. (Jerusalem: The Harry and Michael Sacher Institute for Legislative Research and Comparative Law 1994) 379. *See also*: Basedow in: MünchKomm, before § 305, para 34

148 *See*: Articles 6 and 1131 the Belgian Civil Code. Moreover, the terms may be struck out in some cases where they constitute an abuse of rights contrary to good faith.

149 Brunner A. *Allgemeine Geschäftsbedingungen im internationalen Privatrecht* (Grüsch 1985) 20-21

enforceability of such contracts. In practice, a distinctive characteristic of the multiple application of a contract means that the terms are intended to be used at least three to five times[150]. Generally, before including such terms in a contract the *proferens* should intend to use the same contract terms several times[151]. Thus the contract would be considered standard even if its terms were used for the first time, as they were intended to be used continuously in future. In other words, special protection under §§ 305-310 BGB would not be provided in Germany if contract terms were tailored for individual transactions.

The shortcoming in this approach is that some contracts where substantive disparities are found can be used on very few occasions, perhaps just twice (*e.g.* the sale of aircraft engine or other aircraft spares to, for example, two customers only) and therefore they would fall out of the scope of regulatory oversight. Moreover, a powerful company with a large legal department could propose individually tailored contracts to all of its clients; which all included substantially similar disadvantageous terms and where it was unlikely that successful negotiations would take place. In this regard, the courts should consider whether the contract was drafted individually for one party and whether there are no companies in the market to sign contracts of similar contents.

It must also be stressed that German law does not require contract terms to be in writing in order to qualify as standard form terms. Likewise, a party may be informed about these contract terms – for example - over telephone. For example, Article 6:231 Dutch BW treats standard contract terms similarly[152]. Furthermore, it is not relevant whether these terms were printed in small letters or in some other form. Special provisions relating to the regulation of standard form contracts are defined in other European Civil Codes as well (*see e.g.* Article 1341 of Italian *Codice Civile*, Articles 6.1285 - 6.187 of LCC, §§ 864a, 879(3) of Austrian ABGB).

It is worth noting that Article 3(2) of Directive 13/93/EEC on Unfair Terms in Consumer Contracts defines the terms that are to be reviewed as those 'which were prepared by one contract party and … '*consumer has therefore not been able to influence the substance of the term*'. This means that the Directive

---

[150] BGH, NJW, 1997, 135; BGH, NJW, 1998, 2287. It is not, however, required the terms to be offered to several different companies. *See also:* Wolf M. 'Harmonisation of Protection against unfair Contract Terms in Private European Law', in: European Legal Traditions and Israel, Rabello A. M., *ed.* (Jerusalem: The Harry and Michael Sacher Institute for Legislative Research and Comparative Law 1994) 381; Bayreuther F. *Wirtschaftlich-existenziell abhängige Unternehmen im Konzern-, Kartell- und Arbeitsrecht* (Berlin: Duncker & Humblot 2001) 163

[151] BGH, NJW-RR, 2002, 13

[152] *Cf.* Hondius E. 'Protection of the Weaker Party in Dutch Contract Law', in: *Welfarism in Contract Law*, Brownsword R., Howells G. and Wilhelmsson T. eds. (Darthmouth Publishing Company Limited 1994) 266

is applicable in relation to contracts that were tailored for single use as well. Pursuant to the wording of the Directive, the most important feature of the regulated terms is not their multiple application, but the fact that the counterparty was not in a position to influence the content of contractual terms. Thus some European countries take account of this provision by changing their national law in order to ensure the uniform protection of consumer contracts. For instance, by implementing the Directive into German law there a special § 310 (3) No. 2 (*ex* Art. 24a No. 2 AGBG) BGB was introduced. This provision extended the scope of the regulation of standard form contracts and covered such cases as where the contract was prepared for single use, but a consumer was not able to influence the substance of it[153].

Another indispensable characteristic of standard form contracts is that the terms are not negotiated with the counterparty. In most cases, it is not difficult to identify non-negotiated contract terms. However, the situation is not very clear if one tries to draw a clear line between:

(a) contract terms that were individually negotiated, but those negotiations did not lead to any substantial changes (provided the counterparty could potentially influence the substance of the term) or
(b) contract terms that were offered in standard form, but which establish a fair balance of both contracting parties[154].

In other words, the fact that a party offers to conclude a contract on standard terms does not irrefutably suggest the unfairness of the contract, and *vice versa*. Furthermore, some terms of a contract may be individually negotiated and some not. A formal invitation to negotiate on contract terms also does not mean that the contract will be actually negotiated.

By virtue of § 305(1) BGB terms may be qualified as standard only if they were not individually negotiated between parties under German law. The burden of proof lies with the party proposing them to prove the terms were actually individually negotiated. German legal doctrine rightly supports the position that formal negotiations do not mean that the terms in question were negotiated[155].

---

153 BGBl. 1996, 1013. *For more comments see*: Hommelhoff P., Wiedermann K. U. Allgemeine Geschäftsbedingungen gegenüber Kaufleuten und unausgehandelte Klauseln in Verbraucherverträgen: Grundsätzliches zur Transformation der EG - Klauselrichtlinie ins deutsche Recht, *ZIP* (1993) 562

154 *See:* Joint Report 'Unfair Terms in Contract' English and Scottish Law Commissions (Law Com No 292, Scot Law Com No. 199, 2005) para 5.72-5.74. For this distinction compare: Lord Diplock in: Schroeder Music Publishing Co Ltd. v. Macaulay [1974] 1 WLR 1308 (1316)

155 Wolf, in: Wolf / Horn / Lindacher, § 1, para 34 *et seq*; Ulmer, in: Ulmer/Brandner/Hensen § 1, para 48; Basedow in: MünchKomm, § 305, para 35

The proposing party needs to show its seriousness and readiness to amend contract terms as well as offer the opportunity to the other party to amend the proposed terms and so protect its interests[156]. As a result, the contract terms offered to the other party need not necessarily be amended; though this would be an indication that a party was ready to tailor its terms to individual needs. The fact that several options are offered to the counterparty in a standard form contract does not suggest that the terms were individually negotiated[157]. In short, the other party must have a real; and not just hypothetical opportunity to influence the contents of a contract for the contract to qualify as being individually negotiated. This notwithstanding, the German judiciary faces similar problems to other countries in interpreting such loose concepts as the 'seriousness of the offer to enter into negotiations' or 'actual chances to amend the terms'. It is sometimes argued that it is more or less impossible to verify these criteria objectively, and that the courts should rely on objective factors, such as checking whether discussions between the parties took place[158].

In practice, a weaker party may be offered the opportunity to start negotiations, but in view of its lesser bargaining power it often understands the futility and costs of such negotiations and accepts the standard form contract offered instead. Thus the abstract notion of 'non-negotiated contract terms' is of little use in those situations where the stronger parties contracts on the principle *'take it or leave it'*[159]. Furthermore, this approach is open to criticism, as a weaker party may voluntarily refuse to begin negotiations even though it presumably actually has the chance to do so, as it loses the special protection under civil laws whereby the terms no longer qualify as standard contract terms[160].

It must also be borne in mind that some contracts are not actually negotiated even though a *proferens* is ready to lead negotiations and to amend its terms where a request to do so is put forward. In some cases, transactions have to be concluded within a fixed timescale (for example, aircraft maintenance agreements, where lenghy negotiations may lead to higher costs), or else there are no lawyers or other staff to make any proposals to amend the contract. In this regard, it is arguable whether all non-negotiated contracts should be judged on their enforceability using a different metric from that applied to other contracts.

---

[156] See *e. g.* BGH, NJW, 1998, 2600, 2601; BGH, NJW, 2002, 2388, 2389

[157] Coester in: von Staudingers Kommentar (Walter de Gruyter, 2005) 161

[158] *See*: Reinelt E. 'AGB-Klausel oder Individualvereinbarung? Zum Begriff Aushandeln' (downloaded from www. reinelt-bghanwalt.de/veroeffentlichungen/vo_r45_c.htm)

[159] We will return to the concept of standard form contracts when assessing the legislation of different European legal systems in subsequent chapters.

[160] Bayreuther F. *Wirtschaftlich-existenziell abhängige Unternehmen im Konzern-, Kartell- und Arbeitsrecht* (Berlin: Duncker & Humblot 2001) 165

Interestingly, the English UCTA 1977 covers all unfair contract terms, no matter if they were individually negotiated or not[161]. Special provisions were established (*e.g.* regarding breach of contract) for cases where the terms were included in a party's written standard terms of business (*e.g.* section 3 UCTA 1977). It seems that English judges take a more flexible approach than their colleagues in continental Europe when defining these terms as standard. The willingness of a *proferens* to discuss contract terms does not make them automatically negotiable. It is obvious that the other party could alter insignificant terms. Minor changes to a contract do not mean that it no longer qualifies as a standard contract[162]. Furthermore, English courts, among other things, pay attention to the degree to which the 'standard terms' are understood by the other party when agreeing to the terms, as well as the extent and nature of any agreed alterations to the 'standard terms'[163]. This means that the particular circumstances of a case must be analysed in order to discern whether the contract terms used in the particular transaction were the 'written standard terms of business'. The English position seems to be reasonable because it tackles effectively those cases where contract terms are amended just enough to circumvent strict statutory regulations on standard form contracts.

Many German lawyers argue that the well-structured regulation of standard form contracts provided by German law is more suitable for consumer protection. On the other hand, it is easy to circumvent regulation, particularly so in the case of complex and important transactions[164], and therefore it is relatively ineffective in tackling all cases of inequality in contractual relations. Interestingly, in contrast to the German approach, the French *Code de la Consommation* applies to all contract terms, regardless of whether they are standard form or were negotiated individually (*see*: Art. L132-1). This Code is, however, applicable only to the '*non-professionel ou consommateur*'.

The fourth problem relates to the scope of terms covered by regulation. It is moot whether an assessment of the fairness of standard form contracts should include the adequacy of price and the contract's chief objectives. Parties entering into a contract normally have a good idea of the market price, and this is usually the basic issue the parties negotiate and agree upon. As outlined earlier,

---

161 Other European countries established special regulations for unfair terms even though they were individually negotiated. See *e.g.* § 36 of Law on Contracts that is applicable in Sweden, Norway and Finland, similarly, § 12 of Danish Law on Contracts. *For more compare:* Lehrberg B. 'Renegotiation Clauses, the Doctrine of Assumptions and Unfair Contract Terms' 3 *ERPL* (1998) 272

162 See *e.g.* St. Albans City and District Council v. International Computers Ltd. [1996] 4 All ER 481, 491; Chester Grosvenor Hotel v. McAlpine [1991] 56 Build LR 115

163 *Cf.* Salvage Association Ltd. v. CAP Financial Services Ltd. [1995] FSR 654

164 Bayreuther F. *Wirtschaftlich-existenziell abhängige Unternehmen im Konzern-, Kartell- und Arbeitsrecht* (Berlin: Duncker & Humblot 2001) 166

unfavourable contract clauses can be compensated for by a low contract price. So regulating price or quality may prevent the party proposing the contract from concluding any contracts at all. For instance, a market participant might be hindered from receiving credit[165] because the probability of default was high and creditors refused to form a contract otherwise. It would be right to assume that policing the fairness of contractual relations ought to cover only those non-core (or 'auxiliary') contract clauses that were not negotiated. These clauses include, for instance, remedies for breach of contract, penalty clauses, dispute resolution clauses, *etc*.

The theoretical debate over policing terms relating to price and quality is reflected in the current legislation of the European Union as well. Article 4(2) of Directive 13/93/EEC on Unfair Contract Term in Consumer Contracts explicitly excludes price terms from judicial scrutiny as long as these terms are in plain intelligible language. However, the Directive introduces a system of minimum and partial harmonisation and does not preclude Member States affording consumers a higher level of protection. This provision was taken from the German and Dutch legal systems[166], where special judicial consideration is not given to the adequacy of price in relation to the services or goods received[167]. From a more general perspective, this attitude derives from the classic Roman principle that a price did not need to be fair[168]; the court cannot change it, because it is what the parties really intended to agree[169]. This rule is, however, subject to a number of exceptions under the German BGB and civil codes of other countries, because – as a matter of principle – it is applicable only in relation to the core issue of performance[170]. Contract terms that substantially alter the scope of performance are subject to such control.

---

[165] Collins H. *Regulating Contracts* (Oxford: Oxford University Press 1999) 258

[166] *See e.g.* Hondius E. 'European Approaches to Fairness in Contract Law', in: *Aspects of Fairness in Contract* Willet C., ed. (Blackstone Press Limited 1996) 62

[167] BGHZ, 93, 358, 360 *et seq*, BGHZ, 100, 157, 174 *et seq*. *See also*: Dylla-Krebs C. *Schranken der Inhaltskontrolle Allgemeiner Geschäftsbedingungen* (Baden-Baden 1990). Wolf, in: Wolf/Horn/Lindacher, § 8, para 4, *et seq*. Interestingly, a similar provision was established in Article 4:110(2) PECL.

[168] Zimmermann R. *The Law of Obligations Roman Foundations of the Civilian Tradition* (Oxford: Oxford University Press 1990) 255-6. *See also*: Gordley J. 'Equality in Exchange' 69 *Cal. L. Rev.* (1981) 1589; Kötz H., Flessner A. *Europäisches Vertragsrecht Band I.* (Tübingen: Mohr Siebeck 1996) 193

[169] Conversely, *Lando*, by following the practice of the Nordic countries, submits that the fairness of the price should be reviewed as well. Lando O. 'Liberal, Social and 'Ethical' Justice in European Contract Law' 43 *C.M.L. Rev.* (2006) 828

[170] *Compare*: BGH, NJW, 1993, 2369

Thus, the so-called '*Preisnebenabreden*', *i.e.* terms that influence the price and can be replaced by the default statutory norms, can be reviewed and struck out by the court if they are not in line with statutory requirements[171]. Having said that, it is possible to envisage a situation where the price demanded was actually grossly unfair. Again, in England there is no absolute requirement to review primary obligations or the main subject matter in such a case[172]. The English courts are generally reluctant to police the fairness of the main contractual obligations. Thus it is also unlikely that judges would scrutinise the fairness of price either.

On balance, common law judges appear to adhere more to freedom of contract and tend to remain more neutral than judges from continental Europe when assessing what the parties agreed. That said, there are no strict boundaries as to what terms can be reviewed and what the formal features of standard form contracts are. Continental European legal systems have developed a high degree of abstraction *vis-a-vis* the definition of standard form contracts as well as the limits of this control. A proper statutory definition of unfair contract terms would not *per se* prohibit unfair trade practices. Unfortunately, this strict definition of standard form contracts may give the *proferens* a better chance of circumventing regulation by conducting sham negotiations, for example by including derisory amendments, or in some other way. This is why in practice many businesses include clauses on so-called 'negotiated agreements', which clarify some terms such as 'excusable delay', 'exclusion of liability', 'indemnification and insurances' were fully understood by the parties when entering into the contract, and the prices established in the agreement were arrived at after consideration of such provisions. Upon signing a standard form contract including such terms, it becomes much more difficult to prove that the counterparty had no chance to amend the contract terms.

In general, it is not easy to draw general conclusion as to the effectiveness of different models in tackling unfair standard form contracts. Sometimes, statutes do not explicitly deal with standard form contracts; however, the

---

[171] BGH, NJW, 2001, 2635; BGH, NJW, 1999, 2276. *Cf.* Joost D. 'Der Ausschluss der Inhaltskontrolle bei Entgeltregelungen in allgemeinen Geschäftsbedingungen' *ZIP* (1996) 1685 *et seq.*; Wolf M. *Preisanpassungsklauseln im Allgemeinen Geschäftsbedingungen unter Kaufleuten*, ZIP, 1987, 341 *et seq;* Basedow in: MünchKomm, § 307, paras 14-16.

[172] *Cf.* Beale H. 'Legislative Control of Fairness: the Directive on Unfair Terms in Consumer Contracts', in: *Good Faith and Fault in Contract Law*, Beatson J. and Friedmann D. *eds.* (Oxford: Clarendon Press 1994) 241. However, under Article 4(2) of the Directive, whereby the definition of main subject of contract and the adequacy of price and remuneration as against the goods and services supplied are not subject to the assessment of fairness in plain intelligible language, was implemented in England in Regulation 6(2) UTCCR 1999. Regarding application of the Regulation in England and Wales see *e.g.* Director General of Fair Trading v. First National Bank [2002] 1 AC 481

disadvantaged party can seek remedies under the general principles of civil law. The experience of different countries bears witness to the fact that the regulator should be cautious about introducing strict criteria that are decisive in order to designate the contract as a standard form contract. The author advocates a flexible approach, as where strict regulation of standard contracts was introduced, businesses would be able to find gaps to circumvent these. On the other hand, a regulator should encourage businesses to protect their rights through their own due diligence instead of blindly expecting judicial intervention to rectify a contract that was agreed of their own accord.

One implication is, however, noticeable: countries that have enacted special statutes to regulate standard form contracts ordinarily have greater case law on this matter than countries lacking such statutes. Indeed, clear and explicit statutory regulation should encourage parties to protect their rights in a more effective way. In the author's view, more case law would also enhance legal certainty. Both contracting parties would then know exactly what contract terms would not be enforced. Taking this into consideration, exhaustive statutory regulation balancing contractual rights and obligations in standard form contracts is advisable. The Dutch BW illustrates a proper model to follow. Section on standard contract terms (section 6.5.3) is one of the most important developments since the Dutch BW was substantially amended on 1 January 1992. Furthermore, as was the case in Germany, the code includes so-called 'grey' and 'black' lists (Art. 6:237 and 6:236 BW) of prohibited terms, while under the old version of the Dutch Code unfair standard contract terms were measured solely using the general benchmark of good faith (*see*: Art. 1374(4)).

2. REGULATING FAIRNESS IN BUSINESS-TO-BUSINESS CONTRACTS

2.1 Similarities and Differences between Consumer Contracts and Business-to-Business Contracts

It is a commonplace in European contract law that unfairness in contractual obligations is more evident in consumer contracts than in commercial contracts. Consumers are ordinarily treated as the weaker party[173]. Indeed, one can hardly expect that common consumers would be informed about the peculiarities of the transactions they enter into. Even if individuals can understand the contents of the agreements they enter into, they are often ignorant of the legal importance of

[173] For differences between consumer and business-to-business contracts in assessing undue advantage in standard form contracts see *e.g.*: Hollier v. Rambler Motors (AMC) Ltd. [1972] 2 QB 71 and British Crane Hire Corporation v. Ispwich Plant Hire Ltd. [1974] 1 All ER 1059

certain terms, particularly the legal implications in cases where the contract is breached and the kinds of remedies are available, or what kinds of remedies are waived. Conversely, enterprises are ordinarily better informed than consumers about possible business risks[174]. Except where companies are small, they usually have an organisational structure and separate legal departments and can often recover the value added tax paid on purchases (provided they are registered as a value added tax payer), they have better access to wholesalers, *etc.* Furthermore, commercial contracts are concluded with the goal of making profit; whereas these objectives are not so apparent in consumer contracts[175]. Commercial purchases are ordinarily larger; so contracts are drafted more diligently. These assumptions are largely supported by economic analyses of the law, whereby the necessity for consumer protection is often considered from the perspective of market failures in business-to-consumer transactions and the irrational behaviour of consumers. It should be noted that commercial arrangements are often based on trust and not purely on short-term economic gain. Often companies seek to create long-term business relations and trust with their partners rather than to take advantage through a single contract. Moreover, unfavourable terms in commercial contracts can be offset by favourable terms in the present or other contracts. Consumers – irrespective of whether they are powerful or not - concluding a single transaction cannot expect to be treated in a similar way. In this respect, unfair standard contract terms in commercial contracts should be appraised taking into account all business relations between the contracting parties. The fact that, owing to their commercial experience, companies are less vulnerable than consumers, is recognised both in German and Lithuanian case law[176]. Similarly, the English experience confirms that the common law has

---

[174] *See*: Hertel B. O. *Kontrolle von allgemeinen Geschäftsbedingungen im kaufmännischen Geschäftsverkehr gemäß § 24 AGB-Gesetz* (Heidelberg 1986) 92; Basedow in: MünchKomm, § 307, para 71

[175] Hesselink M. The New European Private Law. Essays on the Future of Private Law in Europe (The Hague, London New York: Kluwer Law International 2002) 103-4. *See also:* Lutz R. AGB-Kontrolle im Handelsverkehr unter Berücksichtigung der Klauselverbote (München 1991) 4 *et seq*

[176] See: BGH, NJW, 1976, 2346, compare with decision No. 3K-3-24/2009 of the Lithuanian Supreme Court. *For more discussions see*: Alisch H. 'Zur Kontrolle von Allgemeinen Geschäftsbedingungen im rein kaufmännischen Geschäftsverkehr' *JZ* (1982) 709; Bastian G., Böhm K. 'Schutz der Kaufleute vor Allgemeinen Geschäftsbedingungen' *BB* (1974) 100 *et seq*; Eberstein H. H. 'Allgemeine Geschäftsbedingungen und Kaufleute' *BB* (1974) 1185 *et seq*; Pauly H.-J. 'Anwendung des AGB - Gesetzes auch auf Kaufleute' *BB* (1976) 534 *et seq*; Hermann H. 'Allgemeine Geschäftsbedingungen und Kaufleute' *BB* (1974) 1185 *et seq*; Brandner E. H. 'Kaufmännische Vertragsgestaltung under den Zwängen des Rechts der Allgemeinen Geschäftsbedingungen' *DZWiR* (1992) 177 *et seq*; Pfeiffer T. 'Vom kaufmännischen Verkehr zum Unternehmensverkehr' *NJW* (1999) 169 *et seq*; Pauly H.-J. 'Anwendung des AGB - Gesetzes auch auf Kaufleute' *BB* (1976) 534 *et seq*

found it very difficult to develop common doctrines that can be applied equally to both consumer and commercial transactions[177].

The distinction between consumer and business transactions has also been a constant in Union law as well. A resurgence in consumer protection law began in the 1980s, after the Union issued a number of directives on issues of consumer protection. For example, Directive 2005/29/EC on Unfair Commercial Trade Practices was promulgated to achieve maximum harmonisation in business-to-consumer fair trading law, which should reduce diffirences in consumer protection laws, but sustain a good level of consumer protection. Conversely, businesses are mostly not covered by the special protectionist consumer regime created by the Union law.

The Court of Justice has also drawn a distinction between consumers and businesses. For example, by considering the question of protection entrenched in Directive 85/577/EEC in the so-called 'di Pinto' case, the Court of Justice noted that the directive would not protect businesses even where the transaction was not its usual business[178]. A trader would be regarded as a consumer only if a transaction was made for family or personal needs[179]. This means that the Court of Justice was reluctant to give a commercial party consumer status, except where the link between the party's ordinary business activities and the activities in question were really weak[180]. On balance, it seems that Union law is of little help in extending to other businesses the protection afforded to consumers. As noted above, the term 'consumer' applied in Article 2(b) of 93/13/EEC Directive on Unfair Terms in Consumer Contracts does not include legal persons[181].

---

177 Furmston M. *Cheshire, Fifoot & Furmston's Law of Contract* (Butterworths Lexis Nexis 2001) 172

178 Criminal Proceedings v. Di Pinto C-361/89, para 18. *Cf.* Shearson C-89/91, whereby the Court of Justice has acknowledged that a plaintiff acting in pursuance of his trade or professional activity cannot enjoy the benefits of the rules laid down for consumer protection.

179 *See also*: Beale H. [*et. al.*] *Casebooks on the Common Law of Europe: Contract* (Oxford: Hart Publishing 2002) 537; Nebbia P. *Unfair Contract Terms in European Law. A Study in Comparative and EC Law* (Oxford and Portland, Oregon: Hart Publishing 2007) 71 *et seq*

180 According to Lithuanian case law, a natural person would not be granted the status of the consumer where some goods or services were purchased in accordance with his profession or business. *See:* the decisions of the Lithuanian Supreme Court No. 3K-3-458/2005; 3K-3-211/ 2008; 3K-3-579/2008

181 According to the directive, a consumer was defined 'a natural person who is acting for purposes which are outside his trade, business and profession'. For comment on the interpretation of this provision *see e.g.:* Reid K. 'Unfair Terms in Consumer Contract Regulations' 16(9) *Comp. Law* (1995) 280-2; Brothers S., Herington M. 'Unfair Terms and Consumer Contracts Regulation' 3(8) *International Insurance Law Review* (1995) 262 *et seq*

Advocate General *Mischo* has noted:

> 'Legal persons and companies did not generally find themselves in that weaker position and there is therefore no reason to grant them protection which, as an exception to contractual freedom, must, moreover, by strictly interpreted'[182].

It would probably be reasonable to contend that the scope of protection of Directive 93/13/EC on Unfair Terms in Consumer Contracts should not be extended with respect to businesses, because this was not what the Union's regulator originally intended. However, the AG's position cannot generally be regarded as correct; practically speaking, there are very few good arguments for leaving business transactions completely outside judicial review of standard form contracts[183].

It has already been noted that those large companies that dominate in some industries offer their standard contract terms to all customers (suppliers, consumers and others). Sometimes these terms are accepted just because the other contracting party completely depends on the large company's orders and wishes to conduct further business in that particular area. This so-called 'supply side market failure' does not significantly differ whether in consumer or commercial contracts, as many businesses – especially small ones – are also discriminated against through inherently unequal bargaining power. In fact, small businesses cannot expect large conglomerates to negotiate all contract clauses with them, especially where the volumes of trade are not significant. In this regard, some commentators argue convincingly that the market does not prevent an automobile manufacturer from drafting a contract to serve his interests whether the other party is a supplier, dealer or a new car buyer[184]. This means that giants of manufacturing treat all other market participants in the same manner. Even if a small party notices an imbalance in contractual rights and obligations, the company can do nothing but accept these clauses. Furthermore, many small businesses do not have in-house lawyers, and they are less likely to seek legal advice. They may, therefore, be just ignorant as an ordinary consumer of the possible legal ramifications of contracts they conclude.

It should, moreover, be noted that the protection of companies from unfair standard form contracts is not covered by secondary Union legislation and does not fall within the exclusive competences of the Union. A national regulator is

---

182 AG Mischo in: Idealservice C-541 and 542/99, para 14

183 *Cf.* Zweigert K., Kötz H. *Introduction to Comparative Law.* Trans. by Weird T. 3rd ed. (Oxford: Clarendon Press 1998) 344

184 *For more see*: Brownsword R. *Contract law: Themes for the Twenty-First Century* (London: Butterworths 2001) 89

not prevented by Union law from applying whatever regulation is desired. National regulators may decide not to distinguish consumer and business transactions, in order to provide necessary protection for the weaker party in a contract. Contrary to current developments in Union law, the English Court of Appeal in the case of *R&B Customs Brokers Co Ltd. v. United Dominions Trust Ltd.*[185] has conceded that a company may act as a consumer 'where a transaction was only incidental to the business activity' of the company, as 'a degree of regularity was required before the transaction'. Thus, the English judiciary interprets the notion of 'consumer' more broadly than the Court of Justice. In the author's view, this position is reasonable. British consultancy businesses report many examples in which terms have been used that prevent a small retailer - which must incur liability when it resells defective goods to the consumer - from passing that liability 'back up to the chain' to its supplier. It is rightly submitted that the small retailer is 'squeezed between consumer and manufacturer' as he would be forced to accept exclusion clauses, but these same exclusion clauses cannot normally be shifted to the consumer[186].

German courts have reached a similar conclusion that the actual level of protection of companies and consumers against unfair disadvantaging is more or less the same[187]. In France the French Consumer Commercial Code is not applicable to contracts between businesses[188]. A somewhat stricter protection of businesses can be derived from the general provisions of the French Civil Code. For example, Article 1646 of the French Civil Code sets out that a seller in good faith is 'only liable for restitution of the price and to reimburse the buyer for the expenses incurred in the sale'. However, the concept of expenses was interpreted broadly by the *Chambre des Requêtes* of *the Cour de Cassation* in 1847 (and confirmed in 1925)[189]. Following the argument that a professional seller must be treated as knowing the quality of his goods, it was decided that a professional seller is not allowed to exclude liability for defective goods. There is an irrefutable presumption that a vendor knows the hidden defects of the goods he is selling (*vices cachés*)[190]. This conclusion is based on the assumption that a professional seller should bear greater responsibility because of his experience and special knowledge.

185 [1988] 1 All ER 847, 847, compare, however, Stevenson v. Rogers [1999] 1 All ER 613

186 Joint Report 'Unfair Terms in Contract'. English and Scottish Law Commissions (Law Com No 292, Scot Law Com No 199, 2005) paras 4.8, 5.7

187 For more details about the German experience see the following chapters.

188 The application of the *Loi Scrivener* in France is extended to the legal persons who act outside their business competence.

189 *For more about this case law see:* Bell J. *French Legal Cultures* (Butterworths: London Edinburgh, Dublin 2001) 81-2

190 *See*: Müller H., Otto H.-H. *Allgemeine Geschäftsbedingungen im internationalen Wirtschaftsverkehr* (Neuwied, Kriftel, Berlin 1994) 147

On the other hand, this case law is relevant only in some areas, *e.g.* in cases where a professional seller is liable only for injury or the exclusion clauses were included in the contract[191].

On balance, the examples from the selected jurisdictions discussed above lead to the conclusion that, on the one hand, it is justifiable to treat a commercial vendor more strictly. A professional vendor should not take advantage just because of his stronger market position. Stronger bargaining power may be exerted both against consumers and other customers. However, it must be borne in mind that a commercial buyer has better chances than the consumer does generally to identify business risks and not enter into risky transactions.

Finally, these are merely general statements and an adequate level of protection should be guaranteed on a case-by-case basis considering the bargaining power of both commercial parties to a transaction. In light of this, one may infer that rigid rules on the enforceability of contract terms would not be a practicable solution for regulating business-to-business transactions in all cases.

2.2 PROTECTION OF SMALL AND MEDIUM SIZED ENTERPRISES

Some European countries have a long historical tradition of treating purely commercial arrangements differently from all other transactions. Austrian and German experience offers an interesting example of regulating commercial and other contracts[192]. These countries developed a dualist civil law system, whereby civil codes co-existed along with special trade codes.

The Austrian Trade Code was first promulgated by the Kaiser in 1862. It entitled traders to invoke principles of business by seeking remedies at the courts. Since January 1st 2007 instead of the old Austrian Trade Code, a special Companies' Code (*Unternehmensgesetzbuch* – 'UGB') has been in force in Austria. Again, the code sets out rules for commercial transactions among traders. However, unfair non-negotiated contract terms in business-to-business contracts may be reviewed under the general provisions of contract law and in accordance with § 879 of the Austrian BGB. A contract can be voided if, *inter alia*, it violates explicit statutory prohibitions or good practices. Similarly, the German HGB co-exists together with the German BGB and provides somewhat

[191] *See more:* Bell J. *French Legal Cultures* (Butterworths: London Edinburgh, Dublin 2001) 83; Muir W. H., Sefton-Green R. Fitting the Frame: an Optional Instrument, Party Choice and Mandatory / Default Rules, in: *European Private Law after the Common Frame of Reference*, Micklitz H. - W., Cafaggi F. eds. (Edward Elgar 2010) 211-212

[192] Some elements of codified commercial law as it is understood in continental Europe may be found in Section 14 of the Sale of Goods Act 1979 in England.

stricter rules for commercial transactions that originally derive from recognised business practices[193]. Some companies incorporated in Germany must be subject (German *Einzelkaufmann*) and some enterprises have the choice to decide (German *Kannkaufmann)* to be registered in the trade register and be subject to the special provisions of the German HGB. On the other hand, there are many other jurisdictions that did not enact special commercial codes (the Netherlands, Italy, *etc.*). Many Central and Eastern European countries decided to follow the monist civil law tradition as well. For example, Lithuania enacted its new LCC in 2001 and thereby finally repealed the Soviet Civil Code. The new LCC is applicable to all commercial and non-commercial private arrangements[194]. As to the regulation of standard form contracts, the LCC provides only for some very general rules applicable to commercial contracts. The general provisions of the LCC may be used to tackle all kinds of unfair trade practices. Nevertheless, practically speaking, the regulations on unfair standard form contracts were not very different, whether or not special trade codes were enacted. For example, the Netherlands has no special trade code; however, Dutch law stipulates that unfair terms may be struck out in cases where they are not in line with the concept of good faith. Furthermore, Article 6:248(2) of the Dutch BW makes it possible to assess these terms in the light of reasonableness and equity. A similar notion is established in § 36 of the Nordic Law on Contracts.

In many countries special prohibitions applicable to consumer contracts may be used as a base when conducting further assessment of business-to-business contracts. Indeed, there is a broad consensus in Europe that a consumer has less experience and is therefore *per se* more vulnerable than a business. On the other hand, it is possible to envisage that an experienced lawyer acting as a private consumer may be even better acquainted with the legal risks of concluding a transaction than small businesses. Such cases do not mean that consumer protection is unreasonable, as a company would rarely bargain with a consumer on small deals irrespective of its power in the market. On balance, most European laws make a distinction between consumer-to-consumer, business-to-business and business-to-consumer transactions. However, the

---

[193] *See*: §§ 347, 348, 349, 352 of the German HGB. For more comments on these statutory provisions see: Handelsgesetzbuch Großkommentar. Dritter Band, 1. Halbband §§ 343-351 (Berlin New York: de Gruyter 1978); Lutz R. *AGB-Kontrolle im Handelsverkehr unter Berücksichtigung der Klauselverbote* (München 1991) 6-7; Basedow J. 'Handelsbräuche und AGB-Gesetz' 150 *ZHR* (1986) 469 *et seq*

[194] When drafting their national civil laws many Eastern and Central European countries recently considered new developments in Dutch law. The Burgerlik Wetboek (BW) of 1992 has abolished the distinction between civil and commercial law. *For a general comment about Lithuanian experience see e.g.*: Mikelėnas V. 'Unification and Harmonisation of Law at the Turn of the Millennium: the Lithuanian Experience' *Uniform Law Review* (2000) 243 *et seq*

fourth category of transactions, namely transactions between weak and strong businesses, has consistently been neglected by national regulators. This is typical not only of local laws, but also for international agreements. For example, the CISG does not make any special reference to the special needs of SMEs, except inasmuch as the convention would not be applicable if goods were bought for 'personal, family or household use' (Art. 2(a) CISG).

It is obvious that while there are one-person businesses (for example, artisans and family businesses), there are also large multinational corporations whose budget may exceed the budget of smaller sovereign states. Large companies are more able to protect themselves. Many large companies force the other contracting party to accept cross-default clauses, which means that a contract counterpart is treated as being in default where a breach occurs under another term, for example a term relating to lease, hire purchase, conditional sale, or credit sale agreement between a subsidiary of the contract counterparty and the stronger company. Should a regulator interfere and offer all businesses equal protection? In the author's view, it would not be appropriate to equalise relations between a one-person-company and a large corporation just to protect the weaker party. The English and Scottish Law Commissions expressed similar concerns when elaborating proposals on the regulation of standard form contracts for the British government, where they advised that:

> 'the court should have regard to whether the contract is a consumer contract, a small business contract or general business-to-business contract[195]'.

On the other hand, is it possible to find a unanimous approach that is suitable for all businesses? Most European legal systems do not provide for comprehensive regulation of contract law in respect of SMEs exploited by standard from contracts, except insofar as, for example, Article 6:235(1) of Dutch BW prescribes that a grey and black list of unfair terms that are presumed unfair are applicable not only to consumer, but also to small enterprises. It is difficult to draw general conclusions as to the courts' readiness to protect specifically small and medium sized enterprises. These enterprises' vulnerability, as well as the protection to be afforded them, should probably be considered on a case-by-case basis, as businesses are different in their staff, annual income, the book value of assets, links with their subsidiaries, *etc.* For example, according to § 267 of the German HGB, limited companies (German *Kapitalgesellschaft*) are divided into small, medium-sized and large companies. A small company meets at least two of the three following characteristics: (i) 4.84 million euro total assets minus an

[195] Joint Report 'Unfair Terms in Contract'. English and Scottish law Commissions (Law Com No 292, Scot Law Com No 199, 2005) para 4.70

identified shortfall in the assets; (ii) 9.68 million euro revenues in the 12 months preceding the completion date, (iii) the annual average not exceeding fifty workers. Many other countries have special legislative definitions of small and medium sized enterprises. According to the Law on Small and Medium-sized Business Development of the Republic of Lithuania, a medium sized enterprise would have fewer than 250 staff and the annual income in Litas cannot exceed 24 million (roughly 6.95 million euro) and the book value in assets cannot exceed 17 million Litas (roughly 4.9 million euro). Since the beginning of the 1990s the institutions of the Union have paid attention to the unification of the concept of SMEs. The definition of SMEs was first developed in a 'Recommendation of the Commission' in 1996. In 2003, the Commission adopted new Recommendation 2003/361/EC that amended the concept of SMEs and replaced Recommendation 96/280/EC[196] with effect from 1 January 2005. The new recommendation has raised the financial ceiling and introduced new financial thresholds for the staff headcount to categorise enterprises into medium-sized, small and micro enterprises. According to 'a legally secure and user-friendly definition', a medium sized enterprise should consist of fewer than 250 of people with annual turnover not exceeding 50 million euro turnover and/or an annual balance sheet not exceeding 43 million euro[197]. In short, a company with fewer than 10 employees would be considered a 'micro' company, while a company with fewer than 50 employees as 'small', and those with fewer than 250 employees as 'medium'[198]. In determining whether or not a company is micro, small or medium sized, subsidiaries are also considered. In addition, one should also consider whether one company holds a majority of members' voting rights, whether the company is entitled to appoint or remove the majority of administrative or management personnel, to exercise control of the company, whether the company is a subsidiary, *etc*. From this analysis it becomes clear whether enterprises are genuinely small or medium sized.

SMEs play an important role in promoting innovation, partnership, competitiveness, development and the growth of jobs. In June 2008 the Commission issued a Communication to the Council, the European Parliament, the European Economic and Social Committee and the Committee of the Regions "Think Small First" – A "Small Business Act" for Europe, where it was

---

[196] Commission Recommendation 96/280/EC of 3 April 1996 concerning the definition of small and medium-sized enterprises (Text with EEA relevance) O.J. L107 p. 4-9 of 30 April 1996. *For comparative review see also*: United Nations Economic Commission for Europe. Small and Medium–Sized Enterprises in Countries in Transition. (United Nations New York and Geneva 2003)

[197] *See*: Commission Recommendation 2003/361/EC of 6 May 2003 concerning the definition of micro, small and medium-sized enterprises (Text with EEA relevance), O.J. L 124, p. 36-41, of 20 May 2003

[198] Ibid., p. 39

acknowledged that the Member States and the Union have made progress in creating an SME-friendlier business environment[199]. Among other things, the Commission acknowledged that the European Union and Member States should create an environment within which entrepreneurs and family businesses can thrive and entrepreneuership is rewarded[200]. Unfortunately, there were no special explicit provisions addressing the approximation of contract laws, except some references to developing a legal and business environment supporting timely payments in commercial transactions[201]. In light of this, it seems that strengthening protection of SMEs and facilitating cross–border transactions for SMEs is consistent with current developments in Union law. Furthermore, a decade ago, there already were voices in favour of the scope of Directive 93/13/EEC on Unfair Terms in Consumer Contracts being expanded with regard to SMEs[202]. On the other hand, the concept of an SME is a very broad one. According to the Commission, such enterprises represent about 99% of all enterprises[203]. Roughly speaking, almost all enterprises should be considered small or medium sized.

Hesellink convincingly argued that whether or not SMEs are in a similar position to consumers is an empirical question and cannot be answered in categorically either way[204]. In fact, different scenarios are possible – a company may be large, but it has to deal with an even more powerful one, and it is completely dependent upon the orders from this larger company. At the same time, a medium-sized company may sign contracts that are outside its professional knowledge and lack experience in some areas. Finally, there are also micro companies that have neither strong bargaining power nor sufficient human resources to engage in negotiations with more powerful companies. Thus, one may question whether small businesses should be protected from all larger companies or whether all small and mid-sized companies should be

---

199 Communication from the Commission to the Council, the European Parliament, the European Economic and Social Committee and the Committee of the Regions 'Think Small First'. A 'Small Business Act' for Europe, COM (2008) 394 Final, p. 2

200 Ibid., p. 2

201 *See*: Directive 2000/35/EC on combating late payment in commerical transactions. Some other directives, e.g., Directive 86/653/EEC on self-employed commercial agents and Directive 2000/31/EC on E-Commerce are also relevant for commercial transactions

202 ECOSOC Opinion OJ 1991, C159; Lando O. 'Liberal, social and "ethical" justice in European Contract Law' 43 *C.M.L. Rev.* (2006) 829

203 Enterprise and Industry Publications, the New SMEs definition. User Guide and Model Declarations. European Commission

204 Hesselink M. SMEs in European Contract Law. Background note for the European Parliament on the position of small and medium-sized enterprises (SMEs) in a future Common Frame of Reference (CFR) and in the review of the consumer law acquis. Final version – 5 July 2007 (Centre for the Study of European Contract Law. Working Paper Series No 2007/03) 15

protected from large ones. Finally, should a legislator protect a micro company against another micro company assuming that they have more or less similar bargaining power, or whether they are both inexperienced in specific areas of goods or services?

It should be noted further that it is difficult to define SMEs in practice. A contract counterparty concluding a contract may not know that a company is an SME; on the other hand, a small company may not genuinely be an SME, but rather a special purpose vehicle incorporated to transact risky deals or to manage risky assets. It is often difficult to prove ownership links between a special purpose vehicle and a large parent or subsidiary, so that the special protection owed to it as a small company is not required. Bearing this in mind it is suggested that only genuinely small enterprises (*e.g.* individual entrepreneurs, artisan companies) should be afforded a higher level of protection against unfair disadvantaging. In the author's view, if similar protection were afforded to all SMEs, this would amount to over-protecting, which would eventually inhibit enterprises agreeing business terms as they wished.

All in all, an analysis of unfairness in commercial arrangements requires a careful consideration of a particular transaction, the size of the participating companies, their bargaining powers and other relevant issues. The regulator should establish a special protective regime similar to that afforded by the consumers only for genuinely small companies. However, this special regime should only cover commercial relations, as consumer protection should not be diminished by introducing new protective regimes for small enterprises. Finally, there should be clear disclosure rules whereby a contracting party should be made aware that it is dealing with a small business that is covered by a special protective regime.

2.3 Administrative Supervision of Standard Form Commercial Contracts

In order to ensure impartiality in disputes, contested contract terms should be reviewed by a third party. Traditionally, standard contract terms have been reviewed *ex post facto* by applying direct statutory prohibitions and general principles derived from case law. Even in continental law systems, many statutory prohibitions were often first developed in case law, and somewhat later incorporated into civil laws. The German RG originally considered the content of a contract under § 138 BGB (*bonos moros*) to establish whether a company was abusing a dominant position[205]. The illegality of a contract in the sense of

205 *See*: RGZ, 62, 264, 266. *See also:* Pohlhausen R. *Zum Recht der allgemeinen Geschäftsbedingungen im 19. Jahrhundert* (Ebelsbach 1978). *Cf.* Art. 1448 of Italian Civil Code, Art. 1072 of the French CC

bonos mores is established where one company is controlled by another. Statutory prohibitions ordinarily deal with the most evident abuse of standard form contracts, while case law proves to be more selective and flexible by evaluating the circumstances of individual cases. For example, in England, common law can be applied separately or together with statutory prohibitions[206].

Nevertheless, litigation is a costly and lengthy matter. Businesses may still be tempted to use abusive terms assuming that not all weak contract counterparties would initiate litigation. In light of this, it is worthy considering whether administrative supervision of standard terms may replace the judicial control. Administrative bodies would interfere upon their own initiative and instruct businesses what terms should not be tolerated in practice. Thus, in addition to judicial review, some European countries have established administrative bodies to review unfair contracts. This practice found wide support in the Scandinavian countries. For example, there is a special official in Sweden who is tasked with guaranteeing good commercial practices. Likewise, the Financial Ombudsman Service was created in England under the Financial Services and Markets Act 2000. The Financial Ombudsman Service deals with complaints from consumers and small businesses in respect of financial products, and is entitled to strike out unfair contract terms and impose an order for damages[207]. A person can, however, further complain about a decision of the Ombudsman Service. In France the *Conseil d'Etat* can also prohibits some terms, though this happens rarely[208]. The Netherlands has a special commission that elaborates standard contracts for certain economic areas that can be used for individual contracts[209]. The Lithuanian Consumer Protection Agency (*Vartotojų teisių gynimo tarnyba*) is authorised to deal with consumers' complaints only. To

---

206 For more about the common law doctrines to strike out the expressed contract terms see: Atiyah P., Smith S. *Atiyah's Introduction to the Law of Contract* (Oxford: Clarendon Press 2005) 306 *et seq*

207 It should also be borne in mind that under the Fair Trading Act 1973 the office of General Director of Fair Trading was created to review contracts that are detrimental to consumers. The General Director issues recommendations on the regulation of unfair trade practices.

208 The French *Counseil E'tat* has reserved a right 'to prohibit, limit or regulate clauses dealing with the way the price is determined or to be determined as well as with its payment, the integrity or delivery of the object party for, the placement of risk, the extent of liabilities and warranties, the conditions of performance, rescission, dissolution or renewal of agreements, as well as those clauses which seem to be imposed on non-professionals or consumers by an abuse of the other party's economic power and confer on him an excessive damage'. *See*: Gordley J. [*et. al.*] *An Introduction to the Comparative Study of Private Law* (Cambridge: Cambridge University Press 2006) 492-3. *See also*: Zweigert K., Kötz H. *Introduction to Comparative Law*. Trans. by Weird T. 3rd ed. (Oxford: Clarendon Press 1998) 339

209 Remien O. *Zwingendes Vertragsrecht und Grundfreiheiten des EG-Vertrages* (Tübingen: Mohr Siebeck 2003) 466

sum up, in some countries administrative authorities simply solve disputes that arise in cases where parties use unfair standard form contracts. However, similar institutions in other countries are authorised not only to prohibit unfair terms, but also to approve model or sectorial contract terms.

In the author's view, administrative control of unfair standard contracts should be viewed positively. In particular, administrative officers add value by not only striking out unfair terms, but also by consulting with businesses, for instance advising them on how to eliminate unfavourable terms from their standard form contracts without incurring sanctions, preparing general guidelines for the businesses, *etc*. In practice, some SMEs may be discouraged from contesting unfair standard contract terms in the courts as they run that no other contract will be concluded with them in future. So it is probably still better for SMEs to have an unfair contract rather than no contract at all. It is submitted that it would be useful if a government agency were entitled to intervene and strike out obviously unfair commercial arrangements (*e.g.* terms whereby small manufacturers are charged an additional fee for concluding a contract with large supermarkets or an additional fee for placing their goods; having to indemnify the supermarket against losses if their products were not sold; special fees for refurbishing trading facilities, *etc*.).

It may also be questioned whether administrative authorities are the most appropriate bodies to revolve purely business-to-business disputes. Indeed, commercial transactions are often sophisticated and sometimes make reference to trade customs and business practices (e.g. *Incoterms* or the *Uniform Customs and Practices for Documentary Credits, Hague-Visby rules* that regulate the carriage of goods by sea). As mentioned above, in cases where companies conclude a batch of contracts, it would probably be right to evaluate unfavourable terms not only in the light of a single transaction, but also considering all business arrangements between the companies. Administrative bodies may lack experience in dealing with such complicated and time consuming issues. Hence the activity of such administrative bodies should be closely supervised, and they should not become an additional burden to businesses that act fairly. Finally, the establishment of a new special review body is a costly matter. However, in cases where no special administrative institutions are established, it is not completely clear which body ought to review business-to-business transactions. For instance, the British Office of Fair Trading has said that it is unwilling to take on the role of policing small business contracts[210]. Thus the role of judicial bodies should not be underestimated when regulating unfair trade practices in business-to-business contracts.

---

[210] Joint Report 'Unfair Terms in Contract'. English and Scottish Law Commissions (Law Com No 292, Scot Law Com No 199, 2005) paras 5.93-5.95

3. PROVISIONAL ASSESSMENT

The regulation of standard form contracts is closely linked to the issue of how to find a proper balance between freedom of contract and fairness in contractual arrangements. In essence, the regulation of standard form contracts means not just public interference in the stability of contractual relations, but also support for the legitimate expectations of a weaker party not to be unfairly discriminated against or otherwise disadvantaged on the basis of standard form contracts. Nowadays, it is a commonplace across various jurisdictions in Europe that modern contract law should address situations where one party is exploited and so the terms incorporated in a contract deviated from those considered as reasonable in a free market. The analysis carried out in Chapter I of this book supports the assumption first posed in the introductory part of the book that judicial intervention is sometimes necessary to protect a weaker contracting party and thereby facilitate the implementation of good commercial practice. In the author's opinion, the free market itself will not deter businesses from implementing unfair trade practices and fairly allocate contractual risks (so-called 'market failure'). There is little transparency in what auxiliary contract terms are offered in the market, and therefore there is almost no competition in offering the most favourable contract terms. From an economic point of view, the fair allocation of contract obligations should positively contribute to the business environment and the quality of goods and services.

In general, terms incorporated in standard form contracts often represent not a free agreement made by parties, but rather a misuse of bargaining power. However, unfairness in contractual relations is subordinate to the perspective from which a contract or a bundle of contractual arrangements is considered. In difficult cases, it is not really clear if the terms incorporated into the contract were the result of what both parties initially wanted or that one party - usually a weaker one - was reckless, or the party had no other choice than to accept unfair contract terms. Given the difficulties in uncovering true unfairness in private arrangements, some jurisdictions put more emphasis on supporting fair bargaining, rather than on appraising the final result the parties actually agree on.

It must be conceded that judicial intervention in evaluating unfairness in contractual obligations can be criticised for a number of reasons. Judicial assessment of the fairness of a contract may undermine or at least weaken the stability of commercial relations. In that case companies may opt for those jurisdictions that give more certainty and security that the terms agreed between them will be enforced. Laws should create an incentive to parties to take their contractual obligations seriously and not just allow parties to rely on a court to rectify a contract if the contract appears to be less commercially attractive or a better offer is received. In this respect, the law should establish very clear criteria as to the circumstances in which contract terms can be considered unenforceable.

In practice, an examination of fairness in contractual obligations requires very close scrutiny. Firm and concrete rules are usually unhelpful. It is submitted that the judiciary should not be afraid to be involved in undertaking detailed economic analysis to decide about the costs of a transaction or the economic reasonableness of other terms. Intervention in freedom of contract is justified where there is an obvious abuse of bargaining power, or where a stronger party refuses to disclose important information in order to gain a substantive advantage in contractual obligations. The efficient allocation of contractual obligations by way of review of unfair standard form contracts seems to be a more important goal than a rigid rule enforcing contractual terms.

It seems that judicial oversight of unfair contract terms would be appropriate for both consumer and purely commercial contracts. In the author's view, companies are usually better positioned than consumers to assess business risks, as well as being able to afford qualified legal advice. Because of that, regulation of standard form contracts in business-to-business transactions should be more flexible than that for consumer contracts. The scope of review should encompass not only the substance of contract terms, but also the size and market strength of both contracting parties. In view of this, it can be stated that national statutory provisions that protect genuinely small businesses against unfair standard form contracts are consistent with developments in Union law and should be welcomed from a social and economic perspective.

It is now time to examine in detail the approaches of selected Member States to the question of unfair standard terms in commercial contracts.

II. Regulating Standard Form Contracts in Selected Jurisdictions: Germany, France, England and Lithuania

1. GEOPOLITICAL DIMENSIONS TO THE REGULATION OF STANDARD FORM CONTRACTS

The nations of Eastern and Western Europe experienced different political developments following the end of the Second World War, and again after the fall of the 'iron curtain' in the 1990's. Compared with the new European Union Member States from Central and Eastern Europe, Germany, France, England and other Western European jurisdictions did not undergo radical changes to their private law systems after 1945. Their current regulations on the assessment of fairness in contractual relations were first developed through case law. Later, case law was systematised and transposed into civil codes or other statutes. Currently, therefore, in these national legal systems even seemingly insignificant provisions contain core legal elements. To some extent, this fact explains why it is so difficult to harmonise national private laws in Europe. Even slight changes can represent substantial interference in internally balanced national private law systems.

Conversely, Central and Eastern European countries had to almost completely rearrange their legal systems following the collapse of the Soviet regime at the end of the 20th century[211]. These countries wanted to get do away with the Soviet regime as quickly as possible, as most of its legal rules were suitable for a command economy, not for the liberal market economy that was adopted thereafter.

Generally speaking, Central and Eastern European countries tend to follow the legal traditions of Western European countries[212]. To a large extent, new laws enacted in Central and Eastern Europe are based on international conventions and other instruments developed to unify private law (*e.g.* the UNIDROIT Principles, PECL, *etc.*). Thanks to this, there are less the revised or newly adopted civil codes of Central and Eastern Europe are more streamlined than equivalent laws in Germany, England and France. Hence, Lithuania, which adopted a new civil code in 2000, is a good example of developments experienced by Central and Eastern European countries over the last decade.

---

211 For more see *e.g.* Vékás L. 'Models in Central-Eastern European Codes', in: *The Architecture of European Codes and Contract Law*, Grundmann S. and Schaue M. eds. (The Hague/London/ New York: Kluwer Law International 2006) 120 *et seq*

212 It is important to note that the new Dutch BW was a source of inspiration for many Eastern European countries in re-arranging their legal systems. *For more comments see:* Smits J. *The Making of European Private Law. Towards ius Commune Europeum as a mixed legal system* (Intersentia 2002) 60

1.1. The Role of the Doctrine of Good Faith in early German Case Law

The German BGB became effective on January 1, 1990. It was the major codification of German civil laws ever since. Historically, German private law was based on the principle of freedom of contract. However, the issue of unfair standard form contracts was raised in Germany at the beginning of the 20th century after typical supply terms began to be used widely in different sectors (*e.g.* insurance, carriage contracts). The old case law of the German RG[213] stated that businesses should not be excluded from protection against unfair standard terms. In the absence of special statutory rules, the fairness of standard contract terms was assessed under § 138 BGB (*bonos mores*). Moreover, § 315(3) BGB provided the German courts with power to act in the interests of fairness in cases where only one party was in a position to determine the core contents of a contract at its discretion[214]. These occasional rulings gradually developed into a consistent case law aimed at preventing monopolies from abusing their dominant positions and including favourable terms in contracts at the expense of counterparty[215]. In addition, in the absence of special rules, the courts reviewed unfair standard contract terms by construing narrowly contract terms that exclude or limit contractual liabilities[216]. The German BGB norms prescribed for typical transactions (so–called *dispositives Recht*) were taken as a benchmark for evaluating the fairness of contractual obligations. Moreover, contract terms were to be drafted in plain and unambiguous language so as to bind the other party. It is important to note that German courts did not act arbitrarily: they did not strike out contracts merely because they deviated slightly from those default statutory rules of the BGB that were typical for certain contracts[217]. In this respect, the German approach did not differ much from the approaches employed in other European countries, as general provisions of the BGB were only invoked to set aside unfair contract terms.

---

[213] *cf.* Raiser L. *Das Recht der Allgemeinen Geschäftsbedingungen* (Gentner, Nachdruck Bad Homburg 1961) 26; Ulmer P. 'Zehn Jahre AGB–Gesetz–Rückblick und Ausblick', in: *Zehn Jahre AGB-Gesetz* Heinrichs H., Löwe W., Ulmer P., Hrgs. (Köln 1987) 12

[214] In particular, § 315(3) BGB provides that 'where the specification is to be made at the reasonably exercised discretion of a party, the specification made is binding on the other party only if it is equitable. If it is not equitable, the specification is made by judicial decision; the same applies if the specification is delayed' – Bundesministerium für Justiz. Übersetzung der Bücher 1 und 2 des Bürgerlichen Gesetzbuches durch ein Übersetzer-Team des Langenscheidt Übersetzungsservice.

[215] Basedow, in: MünchKomm, before § 305, para 9

[216] *See:* BGHZ, 54, 299

[217] Markesinis B. [*et. al.*] *The German Law of Contract* (Oxford and Portland, Oregon: Hart Publishing 2006) 164

Substantial changes the law came in the late 1950's. Starting in 1956, the German BGH began applied judicial oversight of standard contract terms under § 242 BGB (good faith)[218]. It is thus sometimes argued that the 'abandonment of neutrality towards contractual bargains should be seen as a heroic deed of German courts'[219]. In other words, the German courts refused to enforce contracts in cases where the content of those contracts seemed unfair. Since then, fairness in contractual relations has been assessed taking into consideration the need to protect the weaker party[220]. Judicial review is exercised according to the abstract notion of the inequality of parties, which obviates the need for special assessments in respect of individual transactions[221]. The concept of good faith is the starting point for striking out those terms presumed unjust.

As noted above, German private law has drawn a clear line between consumer contracts and pure business contracts. As a result of this dualistic system, business transactions must also be entered into in line with special provisions, *e.g.* §§ 350, 373(2), 377, 391 of the German HGB[222]. At a general level, German case law has consistently supported the position that businesses are supposed to be more experienced market participants than ordinary consumers. Nevertheless, before the enactment of special statutes in Germany, the review of standard form contracts was general and largely unsophisticated.

1.2 From the Classical to Modern Law of Contract in England

It would be artificial to draw too many similarities between German and English contract law, as those jurisdictions are traditionally attributed to different legal families. Historically, the English courts have showed more respect for freedom of contract than the judiciary in continental European countries. Generally, common law developed the principle that in the absence of fraud, duress, *non est factum*[223], mistake or misrepresentation, everything agreed should bind the

---

[218] BGHZ, 22, 90, 97 *et seq.* Lutz R. *AGB-Kontrolle im Handelsverkehr unter Berücksichtigung der Klauselverbote* (München 1991) 3. *For some further case law see:* BGHZ, 20 164, 167, BGHZ, 60, 243

[219] Markesinis B., *et. al., The German Law of Contract* (Oxford and Portland, Oregon: Hart Publishing 2006) 164

[220] von Hertel B. *Kontrolle von allgemeinen Geschäftsbedingungen im kaufmännischen Geschäftsverkehr gemäß § 24 AGB-Gesetz* (Heidelberg 1986) 128. *Cf.* Heinrichts H. 'Die Entwicklung des Rechts der Allgemeinen Geschäftsbedingungen im Jahre 1988' *NJW* (1998) 1604 *et seq*

[221] Munz M. *Allgemeine Geschäftsbedingungen in den USA und Deutschland im Handelsverkehr* (Heidelberg 1992) 175

[222] For these reasons the old German AGBG included special provision § 24 I No. 1 (now § 310(1) BGB)

[223] *See*: Lord Wilberforce in *Gallie v. Lee* (Saunders v. Anglia Building Society) [1971] A.C. 1004 [1970] 33 All ER 961

contracting parties, regardless of the content of contracts[224]. This attitude was based on the idea that a person should be aware of a contract into which he enters. Traditional English doctrines deal only with cases where a party did not actually and voluntarily agree the contract terms. In other words, the contract could not be struck out merely because some of the contract terms were unreasonable or possibly unfair to the other contracting party. However, it should be also noted that the contract could not be enforced according to the rules of offer and acceptance in cases where a contract was ambiguous or some terms were disguised and a party's assent was not ascertained. The doctrine of public policy did not protect the weaker contracting party either, such that even disproportionate contractual obligations were not considered to be contrary to public policy. Furthermore, the doctrine of consideration did not specifically tackle unfair contracts either. On balance, classical English law clearly fostered the freedom of individuals and corresponded to the philosophy of *laissez-faire*[225]. Freedom of contract was sacrosanct provided the contract was a result of free bargaining.

Furthermore, it should be noted that the classical English law of contract gives the highest priority to achieving stability in contractual relations. This is supposed to prevent an agreement being struck out at the discretion of a judge. Nonetheless, this non-interventionist approach was not the product of any plan or conscious design. Rather it can be explained by the fact that the judges who decided cases had a traditional commercial background[226]. Historically, English judges paid relatively little attention to the protection of the weaker party. Parties to a commercial arrangement were expected to take care of themselves and act in strict conformity with their obligations. Judicial intervention was considered to adversely influence contractual relations. For example, in the case of *Smith v. Hughes*[227] it was attempted to implement the 'objective theory' in English contract law. In that case, the passive acquiescence of the seller in the self-deception of the buyer did not entitle the buyer to avoid contractual obligations arising from the contract. Thus it was acknowledged that the vendor was not under any obligation to inform the buyer that he was acting under a mistake induced by the vendor.

---

224 Leake S. M. *The Elements of the Law of Contracts* (London: Stevens and Sons, 26, Bell Yard 1867) 125-210. *See also:* Adams J. N 'Unconscionability and the Standard Form Contract', in: *Welfarism in Contract Law* Brownsword R., Howells G. and Wilhelmsson eds. (Darthmouth Publishing Company Limited, 1994) 242-3; Lütkenhaus A. M. *Unfair Contract Terms Act 1977 und AGB-Gesetz 1976: Rechtsregeln zu Allgemeinen Geschäftsbedingungen im Vergleich* (Frankfurt am Main [u. a.] 1987) 134

225 *Cf.* Williston S. 'Freedom of Contract' 6 *Cornell LQ* (1921) 365-67

226 Atiyah P., Smith S. *Atiyah's Introduction to the Law of Contract* (Oxford: Clarendon Press 2005) 21

227 (1871) LR 6 QB 597, 607

All in all, classical common law did not provide legal instruments whereby an exclusion clause could be declared unenforceable[228], though the existence of unfair terms was recognised to a certain extent. In particular, contract terms were sometimes struck out if one contracting party exerted undue influence or undue pressure over the other party or the transaction was unconscionable. Cases abound where a weaker party is in desperate need of the benefit of the transaction or unfair terms are included into, e.g., a salvage agreement[229]. Furthermore, it is often contended that the judiciary actually paid more interest to the enforceability of contract terms, even though this could not easily be established from the language of judgements:

> '... in England, standard terms have been subject to closer scrutiny by the courts that is noticeable from the (sometimes superficially) tough (freedom of contract-respecting) language of their judgements'[230].

Because of the ambiguity of actual and formal approaches classically pursued by the English judiciary, it is difficult to draw general conclusions as to what extent the courts have actually considered the needs of a weaker party. In cases where a weaker party acted under economic duress, unfair bargaining could be tackled. Furthermore, the rules of contractual interpretation can be applied to make contract terms unenforceable where they have contradictory provisions. Finally, the general duty to disclose contract terms can also be applied to strike out hidden terms in standard contracts.

1.3 General Safeguards in the Code Napoleon

The most significant statute to regulate contract law is the famous Code Civil (or French Napoleonic Code) enacted in France in 1804. The most important achievement is that the Code represents a departure from old feudal and royal laws and created a new uniform law for all parts of France. Indeed, the creators of Code succeeded in achieving a high degree of legal standardisation. The French courts were expected to interpret these abstract norms and to fill the gaps in laws and regulations where was necessary.

The Code does not have special rules with regard to standard form contracts. Like most other European civil laws, the French Code Civil

---

[228] Poole J. *Textbook on Contract Law* (Oxford: Oxford University Press 2003) 262

[229] *See:* Lord Denning in: *Lloyds Bank v. Bundy* 3 All ER 757, 763-765

[230] Markesinis B. *et. al. The German Law of Contract* (Oxford and Portland, Oregon: Hart Publishing 2006) 166

recognizes the freedom of contract (see: Art. 1134(1))[231]. Since an agreement of contracting parties 'takes the place of *loi*', it was in principle open to the parties to agree damages in case of breach of contract[232]. Furthermore, terms that limit remedies for breach of contract (French *clause limitative de responsabilité)* are basically permitted in France. Likewise, the French courts tend to adhere to the limits of recoverable damages agreed by the parties. The Code, together with dominant legal doctrine, has paid relatively little attention to the protection of a weaker tries, interest in the regulation of standard form contracts arose first at the beginning of the 20th century. Some French scholars (*e.g. Saleilles*) submitted proposals on how to deal with contract terms that were prepared unilaterally by one party (French *clauses abusives).* However, French legal doctrine did not settle a clear position for some time. In particular, discussion centred on whether another party adhering to terms put forward by the *preferens* was sufficient to conclude a contract. A position of the so-called *contractualistes* ultimately received broader approval in French case law[233]. It was acknowledged that economic inequality between the parties did not impede the proper conclusion of contracts as such as a weaker party still has a choice either to accept or decline the offer[234]. Nonetheless, it was commonly believed in France that case law was not authorised to rectify the substance of a contract. The government, but not the judiciary, was supposed to be responsible for reviewing the contents of pre-formulated contract terms (French '*pas de nullité sans texte*'). Freedom of contract was affected by *lois imperatives* that aimed to rectify the inequality of contractual obligations[235]. Furthermore, the French National Assembly was supposed to protect *d'ordre public* as well as *bonnes mœurs* (*cf.* Art. 6 of the French CC). The practical significance of the *d'ordre public* clause was quite similar to English law in that it was not aimed at protecting a weaker party from unfair standard contract terms[236].

---

[231] *See more*: Tunc A. 'The Grand Outlines of the Code', in: *The Code Napoleon and the Common-Law World*, Schwartz B. ed. (New York: New York University Press) 1956

[232] Barry N. *The French Law of Contract* 2nd *ed.* (Oxford: Clarendon Press 1992) 232. *See also:* Routhette G. 'The Obligatory Force of Contract in French Law', in: *Contract Law Today. Anglo-French Comparisons*, Harris D., Tallon D., eds. (Oxford: Clarendon Press 1991) 40

[233] *See:* Müller H., Otto H.-H. *Allgemeine Geschäftsbedingungen im internationalen Wirtschaftsverkehr* (Neuwied, Kriftel, Berlin 1994) 131

[234] Sonnenberger J. 'Das französische Recht der allgemeiner Geschäftsbedingungen (*conditions générales*)' *RIW* (1990) 166

[235] This position has a historical explanation in France. The discretion of judges was negatively assessed during the French revolution whereas the judges applied the law in the way to protect their own privileges.

[236] *See more:* Wolf M. *et. al. AGB-Gesetz, Kommentar*, 4. Aufl. (1999) Intr., para 50

On balance, the French courts still pursue a non-protectionist approach[237]. They have remained strangely reluctant to strike out unfair terms. The French parliament's endeavours to systematise and introduce regulation of standard form contracts in the Code Civil were neither systematic nor numerous[238]. Historically, clauses excluding liability for non-performance or mis-performance were more often struck out in England or Germany, rather than before French courts[239]. French legislators have left commercial contracts free of intervention, except for some statutory safeguards in respect of consumer transactions[240]. Thus French case law confirms the hypothesis that in the absence of exhaustive legislative provisions the courts are not eager to exercise discretion conferred on them to strike out unfair terms. It is, therefore, submitted that detailed provisions should contribute more to legal certainty as well as to the fair allocation of contractual obligations.

1.4 Historical Foundations of the Lithuanian Law of Contract

Lithuania, along with a further nine Central European countries, joined the European Union on 1st May 2004. It should not be forgotten that all these Central European countries have different legal systems. So the fundamentals of Lithuanian contract law are not exactly the same as in other Northern and Central European countries. The Lithuanian legal system – contrary to, for example, the Latvian and Estonian legal system – was much less influenced by German legal doctrine[241].

After the Declaration of the Independence in 1918, four civil legal systems *de facto* co-existed in the Republic of Lithuania: (i) the German BGB was applicable in Klaipėda district, (ii) the Restatements of Civil Law of the Baltic provinces of 1864 were applicable in the districts of Palanga and Zarasai, (iii) in the rest of the territory the Russian Collection of Laws (Russian *Zvod Zakonov*) of 1832 was applicable, except (iv) in the South-Eastern part of

237 Niglia L. *The Transformation of Contract in Europe* (The Hague London New York: Kluwer Law International 2003) 14

238 Sonnenberger J. 'Das französische Recht der allgemeiner Geschäftsbedingungen' (*conditions générales*) *RIW* (1990) 166

239 Niglia L. *The Transformation of Contract in Europe* (The Hague London New York: Kluwer Law International 2003) 14-5

240 *See*: Law on Information and Protection of Consumer in Credit Businesses as of 10 January 1978

241 Historically, the first written source of Lithuanian law of contract is the Code of King Casimir (1468). Some provisions of contract law were included in the Lithuanian Statutes of 1529, 1566 and 1588. All these statutes were autonomous legal acts of the Grand Duchy of Lithuania.

Lithuania, where the Code Napoleon of 1804 was in force[242]. After the occupation of Lithuania by Soviet troops in 1940 and again in 1944, uniform Soviet civil laws gradually replaced all former civil legislation. Soviet civil laws were aimed at developing a planned economy[243]. In the author's opinion, it would not be relevant to pay much attention to the old post-war Soviet case law because a planned economy differs so completely from the capitalist system of a free market economy. Moreover, the judiciary was highly influenced by politicians and any generalisations as to case law would be inaccurate.

The old Soviet Civil Code of 1964 – with some subsequent amendments - was applied in Lithuania from 1990 until 2001, as it was impossible to prepare a new civil code directly after re-gaining independence in 1990. According to the Soviet Civil Code, freedom of contract existed only insofar as it was permitted by the mandatory rules of private law. The problems of regulation of standard form contracts were almost never extensively handled in Lithuanian jurisprudence and case law. Moreover, the old Soviet Civil Code provided no special rules with regard to standard contract terms. On the other hand, the application of standard form contracts was not prohibited either. In fact, during Soviet rule such standard contract terms were often used by large government companies.

Theoretically, standard form contracts could have been challenged in the same manner as other contract terms. Contract terms could have been struck out in cases where they were not in line with other statutory provisions (Art. 47 of Civil Code 1964). The absolute basis (*ab initio*) for striking out a contract lay in whether a contract was falsified and there was clearly no intention of creating legal relations (Art. 51); whether the contract contradicted to the interests of society (Art. 48); and whether the requirements for approval of the notary were disregarded (Art. 58). The other legal bases were mistake (Art. 56), fraud, intimidation, hardship (Art. 57), cases where the capacity was restricted due to the abuse of alcohol or drugs (Art. 55). Contractual terms could be struck out by the court where only some contract terms were invalidated, and where the other contractual rights and duties could have been filled by statutory default provisions of contract law (*inter alia* by taking into consideration the criteria of justice and reasonableness). Interestingly, the Soviet Civil Code did not have explicit statutory provisions that could be invoked to invalidate a contract that was contrary to public order or good morality. It is thus quite evident that the general provisions of the Soviet Civil Code could not be applied effectively to tackle unfairness in standard form contracts.

---

242 Interestingly, Lithuania had two criminal jurisdictions at that time. Unlike the rest of the country, the Klaipėda district applied the German Criminal Code (StGB) of 1871

243 'Speculation' (or ordinary commercial activity) was considered a crime under the Soviet Criminal Code.

In general, the Soviet Civil Code resembled the situation in Germany and England until those countries enacted special statutes regulating unfairness in contractual relations. The Code entailed neither special rules on incorporation, nor rules pertaining to the interpretation or control of contents of standard form contracts. Generally, case law inclined towards the view that the effectiveness of unfair standard form contracts might be assessed having regard of the interests of society (Art. 48 of the Code). Finally, it must be borne in mind that Lithuania enacted special laws in parallel with the old Civil Code (*e.g.* the Law on Consumer Protection of 1994[244]), though these laws did not deal explicitly with commercial arrangements. Thus the lack of special provisions contributed to making the case law on the validity of standard form terms less substantial than under the old Soviet Civil Code.

2. CONTEMPORARY REFORMS OF ENGLISH AND GERMAN LAW IN THE CONTEXT OF EUROPEAN INTEGRATION

2.1 GERMAN PERSPECTIVE

Efforts to better safeguard consumers' interests became noticeable in Germany in the 1970s. To a certain extent these tendencies were reflected in other European countries after the European Council adopted a preliminary programme for a policy on consumer protection and information in 1975. These trends resulted in the adoption of the Law on Standard Contract Terms (hereafter - AGBG) in Germany. In essence, the German AGBG codified the pre-existing case law into extensive statutory prohibitions rather than creating completely new regulations[245]. The act came into force on 1 April 1977 and was not repealed until 2002. In addition, allegedly unfair trade practices could also be assessed using the general notion of good faith under § 242 of German BGB.

[244] *See*: Valstybės žinios (Official Gazette), 1994, No. 94-1833

[245] BGBl. I, 1976, 3317. *For more comments on the German AGBG and historical developments see: e.g.*, Stein A. *Gesetz zur Regelung des Rechts der Allgemeinen Geschäftsbedingungen* (Stuttgart 1977); Schmidt–Rimpler W. 'Das Gesetz zur Regelung des Rechts der Allgemeinen Geschäftsbedingungen' *NJW* (1977) 135 *et seq*; Wolf D. 'Vorschläge für eine gesetzliche Regelung der Allgemeinen Geschäftsbedingungen' *JZ* (1974) 41 *et seq*; Tillmann W. 'Das AGB – Gesetz und die Einheit des Privatrechts' 142 *ZHR* (1978) 52 *et seq*; Lang T. *Die Anwendung des AGB-Gesetzes auf Formularmietverträge und deren Inhaltskontrolle eine Bestandaufnahme und kritische Würdigung der Rechtsprechung* (Stuttgard 1999); Löwe W. Graf von Westphalen F., Trinkner R. *Kommentar zum Gesetz zur Regelung des Rechts der Allgemeinen Geschäftsbedingungen* (Heidelberg 1977); Schlosser P., Coester–Waltjen D., Grabe H.-U. *Kommentar zum Gesetz zur Regelung des Rechts der allgemeinen Geschäftsbedingungen* (Bielefeld 1977); Hippel von E. 'Zur Kontrolle Allgemeiner Geschäftsbedingungen' *BB* (1985) 1629

Indeed, in recent years the regulation of standard form contracts has mostly been associated with the Law for the Modernisation of the Law of Obligations (hereafter – 'SMG')[246]. Though the initial purpose of the reform was to transpose directives[247] into German law, as a consequence unaltered provisions of *ex* AGBG were transposed into §§ 305 - 310 of the German BGB[248]. The new rules are now applicable to contracts that were concluded under German law post 1 January 2002 or continuous contracts as of 1 January 2003.

The incorporation of the AGBG norms into the German BGB was, nonetheless, only a small part of the modernisation of the German law of obligations[249]. Furthermore, it would be wrong to assert that the AGBG made substantial changes in respect of the regulation of the effectiveness of standard form contracts in Germany, though physically the number of norms relating to the regulation of standard form contracts was significantly reduced. For instance, the revised § 310 of the BGB took the place of the former Article 24 AGBG. Essentially, by virtue of § 310 BGB regulation of business-to-business contracts remained similar to that under the old provision. Moreover, similar prohibitions applicable to consumer transactions were transposed into §§ 308 and 309 of the BGB[250].

Finally, as stated above, detailed prohibitions stipulated in the German BGB in respect of consumer contracts were still not directly applicable to business-to-business contracts. Other substantive amendments first implemented by the SMG (*e.g.* the amendment of limitation clauses, introduction of the single

---

246 See BGBl. I, 3138

247 *e.g.* Directives 1999/44/EC on Certain Aspects of the Sale of Consumer Goods and Associated Guarantees, 2000/35/EC on Combating Late Payments in Commercial Transactions, 2000/31/EC on Certain Legal Aspects of Information Society Services, in particular Electronic Commerce, in the Internal Market ('Directive on Electronic Commerce'). *For more on the German law reforms see*: Möllers T. 'European Directives on Civil Law. The German Approach: Towards the Re-codification and New Foundation of Civil Law Principles' 6 *ERPL* (2002) 779 *et seq*

248 *For criticism and advocacy of this reform see, e.g.,* Grundmann S. 'Structural Elements in the Contract Law Parts of the German Civil Code' in: *The Architecture of European Codes and Contract Law,* Grundmann S. and Schaue M., eds. (The Hague/London/ New York: Kluwer Law International 2006) 78

249 For some interesting contributions in English about the new German Law of Obligations see *e.g.* Zimmermann R. 'Contract Law Reform: The German Experience', in: *The Harmonisation of European Contract Law. Implications for European Private Laws, Business and Legal* Publishing 2006) 71 *et seq;* Krajewski M. 'The New German Law of Obligations' 14 *EBLR* (2003) 201 *et seq*

250 Articles 10 and 11 AGBG (old version)

concept of the impairment of the performance of an obligation, *etc.*) were not directly aimed at the review of standard form contracts[251].

2.2 English approaches

A consensus on adopting special statutes to deal with unfair contracts was only achieved in England in the 1960s in those areas which had not previously been protected by legislation. A number of statutes were enacted in England - the Misrepresentation Act 1967, the Unfair Contract Terms Act ('UCTA') 1977, the Civil Liability (Contribution) Act 1978, the Minors Contract Act 1987. Some acts, *e.g.*, the Supply of Goods and Services Act 1982, the Law of Property (Miscellaneous Provisions) Act 1989, and the Carriage of Goods by Sea Act 1992 regulate only certain types of contracts.

In comparison with German law, the English UCTA 1977 was very different, as it introduced many new rules that had not yet been applied in English case law. On the other hand, UCTA did not deal with all standard contract terms, but rather with one type of unfairness, particularly where contractual obligations were not onerous enough on the *proferens*. Cases where the burden was too onerous on the counterparty (*e.g.* excessive penalties), were not included in its scope. Furthermore, before UCTA 1977 can be invoked, the terms in question must satisfy common law requirements as to incorporation and construction.

In short, UCTA dealt mostly with exclusion and limitation terms and limits the applicability of disclaimers of liability. Bearing this in mind, the name of the act is somewhat misleading, as all contract terms and notices cannot be scrutinised under this act. Moreover, the act applies to all contracts concluded after 1 February 1978[252]. It should be noted that UCTA was not the only act prohibiting exclusion clauses in England[253]. However, the other acts only included sporadic prohibitions, and therefore UCTA 1977 remains the most comprehensive major statute to deal with the enforceability of commercial contracts[254].

---

251 For example, the new provisions on standard form contracts re-enacted in the BGB explicitly consider the principle of transparency (Germ. *Transparenzgebot*) (§ 307(3) BGB); and make reference to the striking out of a contract for minor negligent physical damage (§ 309(1)(7) BGB); permissibility of shortening limitation clauses in respect of claims for loss except in consumer purchase contracts ((§ 309(1)(8b) BGB); and some other minor amendments in comparison with the former AGBG.

252 *For more comment see*: Macdonald E. *Exemption Clauses and Unfair Terms* (London Edinburgh Dublin: Butterworths 1999) 77-96

253 *See also*: the Road Traffic Act 1960, section 151, the Transport Act 1962, section 43(7)

254 The consumer contracts are controlled both by the Act and the Regulations in Unfair Terms in Consumer Contracts.

In recent years, the UK has launched a reform of UCTA; though it is not yet complete. Under instruction from Parliament, the English and Scottish Law Commissions prepared a new Unfair Contract Terms Bill and in March 2005 both Law Commissions published their joint report on Unfair Contract Terms in Contracts[255], together with a draft Unfair Contract Term Bill. In general the British government viewed these recommendations favourably. If the assessment proves favourable, the Department of Trade and Industry will seek an opportunity to introduce appropriate legislation to implement most recommendations as soon as practicable. However, the proposed Bill broadly replicates the existing regulations imposed by UCTA[256]. The main stimulus for reforming UCTA was that, as noted above, UCTA and the UTCCR overlap somewhat. UTCCR covers some contracts that are excluded from UCTA (*e.g.* insurance, sale of land). However, the protection provided by UTCCR is less certain than that in UCTA, as UTCCR contains only indicative list of terms which may regarded as unfair. Therefore, the Law Commissions have set out to prepare a unified statute on unfair contract terms that would contribute to the simplification and clarification of existing regulations.

On balance, the anticipated reforms in England are of a much smaller scope than recent German amendments to the law of obligations. On the other hand, the Law Commissions also submitted some proposals regarding the regulation of business-to-business contracts. The most important anticipated change in this area concerns small businesses. The proposals envisage similar protection to that afforded to consumers by UTCCR (which affects a wide range of potentially 'non-core' unfair contract terms) also being applied to small businesses. As discussed in Part I, SMEs are not necessarily less vulnerable than consumers. For this reason, special statutory rules would enhance legal certainty and encourage small businesses to protect their rights more effectively. However, under the proposal, only those small businesses with nine or fewer employees would be granted the extended protection.

Indeed, in general the English judiciary is prominent in its adherence to freedom of contract. In this respect, the extension of protection to all parties was rejected, as it might imply a certain degree of uncertainty[257]. Furthermore, it was proposed that contracts with a value of more than £500,000 (including a series of similar transactions entered into over a period of two years, which have a value exceeding £500,000) should not be regulated in the similar manner as those of small businesses[258] except small businesses would still bear the burden

---

[255] Law Com No. 292

[256] Joint Report 'Unfair Terms in Contract' English and Scottish Law Commissions (Law Com No. 292, Scot Law Com No. 199, 2005) para 4.4

[257] Ibid., paras 4.10-4.12

[258] Section 29(6) Draft Bill

of proving that the terms in question were unfair[259]. These amendments are supposed to provide better protection to small businesses, and therefore similar provisions would be highly beneficial for other European jurisdictions as well. In general, the English draft bill seems to be a valuable solution in defining the size of small companies, albeit that the trade volumes applicable to small businesses may be applied differently in other countries.

3. SPECIAL STATUTORY INTERVENTIONS: ENGLISH UCTA 1978 AND GERMAN BGB IN BRIEF

3.1 THE GERMAN BGB: THE PROBLEM OF SEPARATING CONSUMER AND BUSINESS-TO-BUSINESS CONTRACTS

The German BGB (before 2002 the provisions of *ex* AGBG) sets out the basic rule first developed in case law, whereby standard contract terms may be struck out if they unfairly disadvantage the other contracting party. With regard to standard form contracts, the principle rule permitting the policing of unfairness in contractual relations was established in § 307(2)(2) BGB (*ex* Art. 9(2)(2) AGBG). According to this paragraph, unfair disadvantaging would be *inter alia* established in cases where parties do not infringe mandatory rules of contract law, but where the essential rights or duties inherent in the nature of the contract are so restricted that the attainment of the objective of a contract is jeopardised. Thus unfairness in contractual relations can also take place in those cases where, formally speaking, no prohibitions of the code have been breached, but essential contractual rights or duties are unreasonably limited.

Viewed in its historical context, Germany's acknowledgement of the need for additional consumer protection can be traced to 1971, when a special 'Report on the Consumer Matters', following trends in the EEC was published[260]. In the first draft of the AGBG of March 1974 the working group proposed confining special review to consumer contracts. Corporate bodies were completely excluded, while small businesses were partly excluded from the scope of protection under the first draft law. Furthermore, small businesses would not able to attract protection if they concluded contracts in the course of regular business activity[261]. The proposed scope of application of the draft law was controversial[262].

---

[259] Joint Report 'Unfair Terms in Contract' English and Scottish Law Commissions (Law Com No 292, Scot Law Com No 199, 2005) para 5.31

[260] BT-Drucks: VI/2724

[261] *See:* Paulusch B.-A. 'Haftung und Haftungsbegrenzung im kaufmännischen Geschäftsverkehr' *DZWiR* (1992) 182

[262] See: Wolf M. 'Gesetz und Richterrecht bei AGB' *JZ* (1974) 469

Opponents argued that artificial separation of ordinary enterprises, be it consumers or small businesses, made no sense; the courts were themselves to assess the vulnerability of enterprises that needed such special protection on a case-by-case basis. Accordingly, the CDU and CSU (Christian-Democrats) prepared a second draft of the AGBG, whereby both consumers and businesses were offered special statutory protection[263]. The law finally enacted by the German Parliament was mostly based on the second draft law[264], so that all businesses were included in the scope of protection of the new law.

Thus judicial review of business contracts was sanctioned by virtue of § 307 BGB (historically *ex* Art. 9 AGBG) in conjunction with § 310(1) BGB (*ex* Art. 24 AGBG)[265]. Though both companies and consumers enjoyed special protection thanks to this law, the German regulator decided that the same level of protection for business-to-business contracts and consumer contracts might inhibit the protection of consumers[266]. Companies were protected under general provisions of the BGB (former AGBG), while the exhaustive 'grey' and 'black' lists of prohibitions were approved only in respect of transactions with consumers. The provisions of § 305(2), (3) BGB (*ex* Art. 2 AGBG), § 308 BGB (*ex*. 10 AGBG), § 309 BGB (*ex*. 11 AGBG) were not to be directly applicable in assessing the validity of business-to-business contracts.

Many German lawyers contended that the decision not to exclude companies from special statutory protection was correct, following the principle that the law should not make distinctions as to the origin of a disadvantaged party[267]. However, other commentators regarded the possibility of judicial review of standard contract terms in business-to-business contracts as 'sand in business transactions'[268] mainly because such control would encumber rapid, flexible and safe business transactions. Indeed, generally speaking, the

---

263 *See:* Graf von Westphalen F., in: Löwe / Graf von Westphalen / Trinkner, 2 Aufl. § 24, para 3; Wolf M. *et. al. AGB-Gesetz, Kommentar*, 4. Auflage 1999) § 24, para 2; Horn, in: Wolf /Horn/ Lindacher § 24, para 2; Basedow in: MünchKomm, before § 305, para 13-4; Teske W. *Schriftformklauseln in allgemeinen Geschäftsbedingungen* (Köln Berlin Bonn München 1990) 91-103; Hensen H.-D. 'Die Auswirkung des AGB-Gesetzes auf den kaufmännischen Verkehr' *NJW* (1987) 1986 *et seq*

264 *For more about historical developments see:* Baudenbacher C. 'Zur Bedeutung der Klauselkataloge des AGB-Gesetzes für den kaufmännischen Verkehr' *JA* (1987) 218 *et seq*

265 DT–Drucks: 7/3919

266 *For more see*: BT-Drucks 7/3912, 43

267 Hensen H.-D. 'Die Auswirkung des AGB-Gesetzes auf den kaufmännischen Verkehr' *NJW* (1987) 1986-8

268 Strumpf H. 'Sand in Getriebe unternehmerischen Handeln' *BB* (1985) 963; Ulmer P. 'Zehn Jahre AGB–Gesetz–Rückblick und Ausblick', in: *Zehn Jahre AGB-Gesetz* Heinrichs H., Löwe W., Ulmer P., Hrgs. (Köln 1987) 19

protection of business meant that large companies started paying more attention to the reasonable expectations of less powerful business partners. That said, businesses in Germany are able to circumvent a review of their standard contract terms where they offer their standard contracts for individual negotiation but permit no substantial amendments[269]. Moreover, the new law has made it more difficult for the businesses to structure deals as they wish, by shifting more liability in return for a lower price[270]. In any case, the positive thing about including businesses under the scope of statutory protection against unfair standard terms was that these amendments brought about intense discussion in Germany as to the kind of terms that are enforceable and those that are not in business to business transactions.

In essence, the former AGBG did not create detailed rules on how businesses should be protected from unfair standard form contracts in practice. For example, the *Landgericht* (*i.e.* the regional Court) of Cologne in its prominent decision of 28 April 1986 formulated a functional approach to the application of the AGBG. In particular, it was submitted that this law was not aimed at protecting any party that accepted a contract on standard contract terms. A counterparty may have sufficient economic and commercial resources to be in a position to safeguard his own interests[271]. Rather, the *ex* AGBG (now §§ 305-310 BGB) was created to protect only those persons who cannot influence the contents of the contract, which is determined on a case-by-case basis. The structure of this law was praised for the flexibility in addressing different life situations[272].

Following the adoption of a special law to tackle unfair standard contract terms, a further significant issue was how to draw a line between a benchmark used for consumer transactions and that for business-to-business transactions. The most important prohibitions of the AGBG were established in Articles 10 AGBG (now § 308 BGB) and 11 AGBG (now § 309 BGB), commonly known as 'grey' and 'black' lists of prohibitions. However, according to *ex* Article 24 AGBG (now § 310(1) BGB), these prohibitions among other things are not directly applicable in respect of standard contract terms used in business-to-business transactions. In March 1984 the 7th Civil Senate of BGH (*Foam Insulation case*) formulated an important rule that considerably blurred the distinction between consumer and business-to-business contracts:

---

269 *For some more analysis see:* Bayreuther F. Wirtschaftlich-existenziell abhängige Unternehmen im Konzern-, Kartell- und Arbeitsrecht (Berlin: Duncker & Humblot 2001) 161

270 In some cases, the German courts permitted exclusion clauses with lower price as consideration. See: BGH, NJW, 1980, 1953, 1955

271 *See*: NJW, 1987, 10 *et seq*

272 Horn in: Wolf M. (*et. al.*) *AGB-Gesetz, Kommentar*, 4. Aufl. (Verlag C. H. Beck 1999) § 24, para 4

'If the applicable term in the non-business transactions is qualified as a prohibited term pursuant to Article 11 AGBG, this is an indication (German *Indiz)* that this term also leads to the unfair disadvantaging in business transactions, except where it may be vindicated with respect to special interests or needs of business transactions[273]'.

This *obiter dictum* was confirmed in many further similar cases and gave impetus to the development of further case law relating to judicial control of standard form contracts. Accordingly, *ex* Article 11(1)(2) AGBG (now § 309(1)(2) BGB) (refusal to execute agreed performance) was found to be relevant[274] to business-to-business transactions[275]. In other words, the German courts conceded that prohibitions in relation to consumer transactions can also lead to the business-to-business contracts being struck out, though the legal basis for the striking out of business-to-business contracts and consumer contracts is different[276]. In particular, one should examine whether the contract counterparty was a related organisation of the *proferens*; whether the particular transaction was incidental to its activity; and many other factual circumstances showing the bargaining power and experience of a business accepting such standard terms. For example, in the case of a single transaction for a small business, it is probably true to say that the weaker party has no time and experience to discover all business risks, which puts it in a similar position to that of consumers.

Interpretations of the provisions of the BGB (*ex*. AGBG) regarding the indicative significance of prohibitions on consumer contracts have been assessed differently at times in German law[277]. It was argued that the German regulator used different provisions to strike out contract terms for consumer transactions as opposed to business-to-business transactions (*cf.* Art. 24 AGBG (now § 310(1) BGB)). Accordingly, the same contract terms were to be treated differently in business-to-business and consumer contracts. However, there is no

---

273 BGHZ, 90, 273, 278, NJW 1984, 1750, ZIP, 1984, 493. *See also*: Rabe D. 'Die Auswirkung des AGB-Gesetzes auf den kaufmännischen Verkehr' *NJW* (1987) 1982 *et seq*; Paulusch B.-A. 'Haftung und Haftungsbegrenzung im kaufmännischen Geschäftsverkehr' *DZWiR* (1992) 184 *et seq*; Lutz R. *AGB-Kontrolle im Handelsverkehr unter Berücksichtigung der Klauselverbote* (München 1991) 28 *et seq*

274 So-called '*Indizwirkung*' or derive inspiration (sometimes named also as '*Ausstrahungswirkung*') from particular provisions prescribed for consumer transactions.

275 BGHZ, 92, 313, 316, *also*: BGHZ, 91, 375, 383

276 BGHZ, 103, 316, 328; BGH, NJW, 1996, 389; BGHZ, 122, 241

277 *Cf.* Paulusch B.-A. 'Haftung und Haftungsbegrenzung im kaufmännischen Geschäftsverkehr' *DZWiR* (1992) 182 *et seq*; Munz M. *Allgemeine Geschäftsbedingungen in den USA und Deutschland im Handelsverkehr* (Heidelberg 1992) 15; Lutz R. *AGB-Kontrolle im Handelsverkehr unter Berücksichtigung der Klauselverbote* (München 1991) 202-3

concrete prohibition in the BGB in respect of consumer contracts that is provides sufficient legal justification to strike out entire business-to-business contracts. The effect of particular contract terms is assessed individually on a case-by-case basis, taking into account the particular nature of the business dealings in question.

According to German case law, fairness of standard contract terms is assessed first stage using formal statutory provisions. For instance, if a term proves to be important in respect of its hypothetical fairness, it is likely that the same prohibition would be applicable both in consumer and business-to-business transactions. In this respect, it is clear that essential contractual rights and obligations, as well as the exclusion of contractual liability, are to be given most consideration in both consumer and business transactions[278]. Further, the German courts would take into account the necessity of protecting businesses from unfair disadvantaging. In this respect, the court can apply different benchmarks in respect of small, medium sized and large businesses while assessing the effectiveness of the same terms. Indeed, large businesses are less exposed to information deficit, as they have better ways of insuring their liabilities and stronger bargaining power, and therefore need less judicial protection. The effectiveness of the term in question is assessed commercially, applying typical business interests.

Finally, when evaluating the effectiveness of business-to-business transactions the courts also take into consideration both business practices and the special needs of business transactions[279]. As already noted, the German HGB has drafted certain rules in such a way that traders may speed up business dealings. Thus the prohibitions set out for consumer transactions would not automatically apply to pure business-to-business transactions. Established business practices would take priority when deciding the effectiveness of these contracts and in striking out clearly unreasonable terms. In general, the special needs of business-to-business transactions are assessed separately from the validity or otherwise of business practices[280].

In summary, the German BGB establishes a clear distinction between consumer and business-to-business transactions. Standard form business contracts in Germany are assessed by virtue of § 307 BGB (*ex* Art. 9 AGBG) in conjunction with § 310(1) BGB, but not in accordance with §§ 308 und 309 BGB (*ex* Art. 10, 11 AGBG). The former AGBG and similar provisions now provided for by the BGB have consistently been interpreted functionally,

---

278 These issues will be closely examined in subsequent chapters.

279 *See*: BGH, NJW 1985, 426, 427, BGH, NJW 1985, 853, 854

280 Paulusch B.-A. 'Haftung und Haftungsbegrenzung im kaufmännischen Geschäftsverkehr' *DZWiR* (1992) 1983. *See also*: Horn in: Wolf M. (*et. al.*) *AGB-Gesetz, Kommentar* 4. Aufl. (Verlag C. H. Beck 1999) § 24, para 18

maintaining that the law is aimed at protecting the legitimate interests of any *weaker* party, regardless of whether they are a consumer or a company. Furthermore, it is important to note that clauses §§ 242, 134, 138 BGB, of more general application, may also be invoked where some terms - *e.g.* non-normative trade practices - do not fall within the scope of the special provisions set out in §§ 305-310 BGB.

Thus in German case law there is no significant difference in assessment of standard form contract terms in consumer and business-to-business contracts. Business-to-business contracts are ordinarily measured in a more flexible way though the particular prohibitions relating to consumer contracts in the BGB may also be relevant in voiding business-to-business contracts. In practice, German courts tend to refrain from intervening in purely business-to-business transactions.

3.2 Striking out Unfair Terms in Commercial Contracts at Common Law and UCTA

Similar efforts to establish a statutory framework dealing with unfair trade practices have been made in England. UCTA does not, however, provide unified legislation for the whole of the United Kingdom; the act contains separate provisions in Part 2 for Scotland. Moreover, UCTA entails references to other statutes (*e.g.* the Misrepresentation Act 1967). Generally speaking, the rules of the Misrepresentation Act are complex indeed. For instance, the English and Scottish Law Commissions acknowledged that 'it is difficult to understand [UCTA] without very careful reading'[281]. Though the Act substantially widened the scope of the terms that could be considered unfair, UCTA did not completely replace common law rules. For instance, in *AEG (UK) v. Logic Resource Ltd.*[282], it was concluded that common law rules may be also invoked to strike out certain contract terms (*e.g.* terms like 'purchaser shall return the defective parts at his own expense'). Furthermore, the English courts can also employ the doctrines of public policy, inequality of bargaining power or overriding express contractual terms that stipulate loss or damages[283]. Thus, some contract terms can be still struck out even though UCTA does not explicitly provide for this.

[281] Joint Report 'Unfair Terms in Contract'. English and Scottish Law Commissions (Law Com No 292, Scot Law Com No 199, 2005) para 1.14. This position has been endorsed by many commentators. *See e.g.* Zweigert K., Kötz H. *Introduction to Comparative Law.* Trans. by Weird T. (Oxford: Clarendon Press 1998), Markesinis B., [*et. al.*] *The German Law of Contract* (Oxford and Portland, Oregon: Hart Publishing 2006) 166, Beale H., Goriely T. 'An Unfairly Complex Law' 155 *N. J. L.* (2005)

[282] [1996] CLC 265

[283] Atiyah P., Smith S. *Atiyah's Introduction to the Law of Contract* (Oxford: Clarendon Press 2005) 307 *et seq*

As in Germany, preventive regulation of unfair business-to-business contracts was rejected England[284]. It was argued that such review would impose unreasonably high compliance costs on businesses. In such an event, businesses would be exposed to expensive procedures when registering their standard form contracts[285]. However, preventive regulation has been introduced with respect to consumer transactions under UTCCR in England[286]. UTCCR is generally considered successful because major groups of businesses have decided to draw up voluntary codes of practice based upon it, to be followed when supplying certain goods and services to consumers[287].

UCTA deals with exclusion or restriction of liability for negligence. Negligence means a breach of any common law duty to take or exercise reasonable care and skill, but not any stricter duty[288]. In this respect, some commentators rightly submit that the title of the act is grossly misleading[289]. The actual scope of application of the act is far less wide than may be expected from the name of the law. In particular, under the act, negligence can arise from infringements of: (a) express and implied contract terms, (b) from every other infringement of due diligence obligations at common law, (c) from the infringement of contractual duties that arise from the Occupier's Liability Act 1957 as well as the Occupier's Liability Act (Northern Ireland) 1957 (section 1(1) UCTA). The act deals with liability for negligence in contracts and torts[290]. It is also noteworthy that the Act applies not only to contractual terms, but also to non-contractual notices that exclude or limit liability (*vide* section 2 UCTA). Furthermore, UCTA has not implemented all-encompassing regulation of pre-formulated contract terms; it is basically concerned with exclusion and limitation clauses. Moreover, some types of contracts are explicitly excluded

---

284 On the merits of such preventive control see, *e.g.:* Kötz H., Flessner A. *Europäisches Vertragsrecht* Band I. (Tübingen: Mohr Siebeck 1996) 230

285 Sobich C. *Die verfahrensrechtliche Kontrolle 'unfairer' Allgemeiner Geschäftsbedingungen in England. Zur praktischen Wirksamkeit von AGB – Kontrollverfahren im Vergleich zum deutschen Recht* (Frankfurt am Main [u. a.] 1997) 39

286 *See*: Beale H., Goriely T. 'An Unfairly Complex Law' 155 *N.J.L.* (2005)

287 *For more comments see:* Zweigert K., Kötz H. *Introduction to Comparative Law.* Trans. by Weird T. 3rd ed. (Oxford: Clarendon Press 1998) 346-7

288 Lawson R. *Exclusion Clauses and Unfair Contract Terms*, 8th *ed.* (Thomson Sweet & Maxwell 2005) 138. *Cf.* Occupier's Liability Act 1957

289 Furmston M. *Cheshire, Fifoot & Furmston's Law of Contract* (Butterworths Lexis Nexis 2001) 197

290 It should be noted that contractual liability at common law – unlike in the civil legal system - is assumed to be absolute. This means that a party is liable for failure to perform a duty regardless of whether he was liable for the failure. The common law does not apply the principle of *impossibilium nulla obligation. See*: Barry N. 'Fault and Breach of Contract', in: *Good Faith and Fault in Contract Law,* Beatson J. and Friedmann D. eds. (Oxford: Clarendon Press 1994) 337-355

from the ambit of the act, *e.g.* contracts of insurance, and any contract as far as it relates to the forming or dissolution of any body of corporate or incorporated association or partnership (section 15(3) UCTA). The act does not affect some of those contract terms that impose additional obligations; it is not of assistance in cases where a party is required to pay damages for the loss caused by a third party, accept variations of price after contracts have been agreed, *etc.*[291] In fact, there are many ways beyond using exclusion or limitation clauses whereby business risks and unfair disadvantage can be shifted.

The regulations set out in UCTA are applicable mostly to 'business liability' (*see:* section 2 to 7 UCTA). Despite some overlapping provisions, consumer contracts are principally controlled under the UTCCR 1999. For example, *Weick*[292] expressed concerns that it was difficult to understand why UCTA was confined mostly to business liabilities. The concept of 'business' is not comprehensively explained in the act either, which has invited criticism in academic circles[293]. Many commentators hold that business liability should not be confined to commercial activities, but rather cover professions, government departments, local authorities, and other public authorities[294]. 'Business liability' covers obligations or duties arising in the course of businesses[295] or from the occupation of premises used for the occupier's business purposes (section 1(3) UCTA). Thus, a buyer that does not act in the course of business acquires the status of a consumer and can thus be given broader protection. The academic commentaries advocate a broad interpretation of 'business': it must be more than simply the selling of goods[296].

In the view of the author, the adoption of UCTA is a positive development. Following the adoption of explicit statutory rules, unfair standard form contracts could now be invalidated without making reference to the doctrines of common law. Thanks to the new act, there was no need to construe artificially excluded terms so as to prevent the enforceability of overtly unfair standard form contracts. It is also important to note that common law doctrines cannot be changed rapidly and do not respond promptly to evolving economic realities. For example, common law did not deal specifically with cases where a weaker party was not able to make a rational decision when concluding a contract. That said, UCTA does not cover many areas in which a stronger party

---

291 Joint Report 'Unfair Terms in Contract'. English and Scottish Law Commissions' (Law Com No 292, Scot Law Com No 199, 2005) para 5.8. *See also:* Beale H., Goriely T. 'An Unfairly Complex Law' 155 *N.J.L.* (2005)

292 Weick G. 'Unfair Contract Terms Act und AGB-Gesetz' 145 *ZHR* (1981) 74

293 Furmston M. *Cheshire, Fifoot & Furmston's Law of Contract* (Butterworths Lexis Nexis 2001) 198

294 Yates D. *Exclusion Clauses in Contracts* 2nd ed. (London: Sweet & Maxwell 1982) 104

295 Whether his own business or another's business.

296 *See more:* Brown I. 'Business and Consumer Contracts' *J.B.L.* (1988)

may still exert unfair influence over the weaker one. All in all, the English courts received additional and - probably more importantly - less ambiguous legal rules with which to strike out the clearest unfair trade practices. Furthermore, though it is difficult to measure the actual effect of the act, the enactment of special statutory rules probably discourages enterprises from including prohibited terms in the contracts at the very preliminary stage, instead of seeing them struck out in numerous and costly court proceedings.

3.3 Comparison of Regulations on Standard Form Contracts under English UCTA and the German BGB

UCTA, and the provisions on standard form contracts set out in the German BGB, are quite similar in many respects - they both deal with unfair contract terms. On the other hand, there are many significant differences between the two statutes. Probably the most important difference is their different scope of application. The BGB is aimed at regulating all types of contracts, whereas UCTA reviews mostly exclusion as well as limitation of liability clauses in contract and tort law in England, Wales and Northern Ireland (*see:* section 1(3) UCTA). As noted above, the name UCTA is somewhat misleading: it does not fully correspond to the content of the statute[297]. In this regard, the initial proposed title 'Avoidance of Liability Bill' would have been more relevant[298].

Regulation of standard form contracts is not exercised exclusively via UCTA in England, common law rules (*e.g.* restrictive interpretation of exclusion clauses) remain applicable alongside it. Traditionally common law was only concerned with matters of procedural fairness in relation to contractual validity, whereas UCTA was expected to regulate the substantive fairness of contracts as well[299].

In contrast to the German BGB, UCTA does not stipulate a statutory definition of unfair contract terms. This omission is easy to understand, as statutes must be interpreted in a very strict manner under English law, without giving discretion to judicial interpretation, which is permitted only with respect to unwritten common law. Thus in cases where situations are not covered by UCTA, English judges have little chance to intervene. This is not the case in

---

297 *For more see:* Butterworths Law of Contract (1999) 515

298 Weick G. 'Unfair Contract Terms Act und AGB-Gesetz' 145 *ZHR* (1981)

299 Bradgate R. 'Unreasonable Standard Terms' 60(4) *M.L.R.* (1997) 591; *see also:* McKendrick *E. Contract Law: Text, Cases and Materials* 2nd ed., (Oxford: Oxford University Press 2005) 792-4. Recently, the House of Lords explained that the test of good faith should embrace both substantive and procedural fairness. Their Lordships attempted, thus, to reconcile the test of reasonableness as established in UCTA 1977 and matters indicated in the UTCCR 1999. *Cf.* Director General of Fair Trading v. First National Bank [2002] 1 AC 481

Germany, where German judges fill the gaps left by the BGB or other civil statutes. § 305 of the German BGB permits the review of terms prepared for multiple contracts that were individually negotiated. However, even if contract terms were individually negotiated, certain protection may still be provided. Protection regarding unfair standard form contracts is provided not only by special provisions set out in §§ 305-310 BGB, but also in general norms, in particular § 242 (*infringements against good faith*) as well as § 138 BGB (*bonos mores*).

Conversely, the basic idea underlying UCTA was not to deal with standard form contracts exceptionally, but rather to regulate unacceptable business practices relating to the application of exclusion clauses. For these reasons, UCTA contains prohibitions on individual agreements between parties even if these terms were not standard or were individually negotiated. Some sections of UCTA also deal explicitly with 'written standard terms of business'[300]. The English Parliament has not defined the exact meaning of this term either. Generally speaking, the content of this term seems to correspond to the German concept of 'form contract', which is not mentioned in the BGB (as well as provisions of the *ex* AGBG)[301]. Not establishing a statutory definition of 'written standard terms of business' in UCTA was a deliberate decision. It was expected that the courts would decide on a case-by-case basis if the terms in question should be treated as standard terms or not[302]. There is some evidence that 'written standard terms of business' are interpreted restrictively in England. The mere fact that the terms are standard does not automatically mean that they qualify as 'written standard terms of business'. For instance, in *Brigden v. American Express Bank Ltd*[303] the court said that, by mentioning 'written standard term of business', UCTA 1977 does not refer to 'standard form of contract or standard terms in a contract', and held that the standard terms included in a bank's employment contract were not the other party's written standard terms of business.

It seems that the prohibitions established in UCTA went somewhat further than those of the BGB. For example, pursuant to section 2(1) UCTA, exclusions or limitations of liability for death or personal injury resulting from negligence

---

[300] *Cf.* section 3(1) UCTA. It should be noted that the business liability under UCTA 1977 can arise in cases where the occupation of premises was used for business purposes of the occupier.

[301] *See*: Lütkenhaus A. M. *Unfair Contract Terms Act 1977 und AGB-Gesetz 1976: Rechtsregeln zu Allgemeinen Geschäftsbedingungen im Vergleich* (Frankfurt am Main [u. a.] 1987) 5

[302] Joint Report 'Unfair Terms in Contract'. English and Scottish Law Commissions (Law Com No 292, Scot Law Com No 199, 2005) para 4.55. *See also*: Beale H. 'Unfair Contract Terms Act 1977' 5(1) *British Journal of Law and Society (*1978) 118-9

[303] [2000] I.R. L.R 94

are banned[304]. Furthermore, absolute prohibitions apply in respect of sale and hire-purchase contracts governed by the Sale of Goods Act 1979 (*e.g.* seller's implied undertakings as to title, *etc.*). § 307 of the German BGB provides no absolute prohibitions on business-to-business contracts. However, similar legal results can often be derived from general stipulations of the BGB. By virtue of § 309(1) (7) *lit a* BGB, excluding liability for bodily injuries and damage to health is absolutely and explicitly prohibited in consumer transactions, though this - according the German case law[305] - is also an indication that these terms may not be used in business-to-business contracts either. Most German business contracts include terms to the effect that death, bodily injury or damage to health where caused negligently cannot be excluded.

As outlined above, German law has constantly made a clear distinction between consumer and business-to-business contracts. The strictest prohibitions of the BGB are not directly transferable to business-to-business contracts nor for cases where the counterparty was a legal person whose activity is regulated by public law. This is different from the scope of UCTA.

In essence, UCTA makes only a few exceptions with regard to the 'persons dealing as consumer' (*see*: section 6(2) UCTA). UCTA was not aimed primarily at protecting the specific interests and needs of a consumer. Nonetheless, it should also be noted that Directive 93/13/EEC on Unfair Terms in Consumer Contracts was implemented in the UK by enacting the UTCCR rather than amending UCTA. Therefore, the UTCCR provides special protection for consumer transactions only, which reiterates the position in UCTA to some extent. Clearly, UCTA and the UTCCR have overlapping provisions[306] as they both deal with unacceptable trade practices in respect of a consumer. In practice, the English FTO apply both acts when dealing with consumer complaints[307].

It is worth noting that not all rules regarding the regulation of standard contract terms emanate exclusively from the German BGB. It is common in Germany that contract terms may be struck out where they collide with statutory prohibitions and no permissible construction of these terms is possible (the so-

---

[304] For some relevant case law *see*: *Johnstone v. Bloomsbury HA* [2001] 2 All ER 239

[305] BGH, *NJW*, 2007, 3774. The German court concluded that a distinction should not be made between consumer and business transactions when protecting the most important personal legal values.

[306] *See:* Aquaro G. 'Enhancing the Legal Protection of the European Consumer. Beyond the wording of the E.U. Directive 93/13/EEC' 14(4) *E.B.L. Rev.* (2003) 411; Beale H., Goriely T. 'An Unfairly Complex Law' 155 *N.J.L.* (2005); Chen-Wishart M. *Contract Law* (Oxford: Oxford University Press 2005) 442 *et seq*; Padfield A. 'The Impact on English Contract Law of the EC Directive on Unfair Terms in Consumer Contracts' 10(5) *Journal of International Banking Law* (1995) 175 *et seq*

[307] *See:* Hartwell N. 'The Application of the Reasonableness Test under UCTA 1977: a Schism between Certainty and Fairness' 3(2) *Hertfordshire Law Journal* (2005) 55

called '*geltungserhaltende Reduktion*'). The German BGB does not explicitly refer to this prohibition. The case law of the German BGH confirms that the circumvention of statutory prohibitions must lead to the entire contracts being struck out[308]. This position has both theoretical and practical justification. In theory, it may be argued that it is not the task of the court to re-write a contract so that terms will be acceptable to both contracting parties and remain consistent with mandatory statutory provisions. Some other countries, however, permit courts greater discretion[309].

The strict German position underlies practical considerations. In particular, it was assumed that in cases where a judge would be permitted to adjust contract terms to the minimal level permitted by the law, business would be encouraged to include such terms to the minimal level permitted by the law unilaterally, without fear of severe legal consequences. UCTA makes no express reference to the consequences of using unfair contract terms. However in the commentaries, it is sometimes contended that the existence of unreasonable terms prevents a party from relying on a clause for the purpose of excluding liability but not for any other purposes[310]. Thus, apart from these unreasonable terms the remaining contract terms would bind the parties. The legal implications of a breach usually depend on the nature of the term that was breached. However, it must be also borne in mind that it is highly unlikely that new contract terms would be read into a contract by the English judiciary in order to fill in the gaps in a contract between private parties. Furthermore, a party may rely on common law, where the remedy for abuse of bargaining power is rescission of the contract, though partial rescission of contract was

---

308 BGHZ 84, 109, 91, 375, 92, 312, BGH, NJW 2000, 1110. *For more on the German case law see:* Heinrichs H. *Maßstäbe und Anwendungsbereich der Inhaltskontrolle, in: Zehn Jahre AGB-Gesetz* Heinrichs H., Löwe W., Ulmer P. (Hrgs.) (Köln 1987) 35; Wilke P.J. *Inhaltskontrolle und deren Rechtsfolgen im System der Überprüfung Allgemeiner Geschäftsbedingungen* (München 1983); Neumann J. *Geltungserhaltende Reduktion und ergänzende Auslegung von Allgemeinen Geschäftsbedingungen* (Nomos Verlagsgesellschaft Baden Baden 1988); Boemke-Albrecht B. 'Rechtsfolgen unangemessener Bestimmungen in Allgemeinen Geschäftsbedingungen' *DZWiR* (1992) 77 *et seq;* Rabe D. 'Die Auswirkung des AGB-Gesetzes auf den kaufmännischen Verkehr' *NJW* (1987)1984

309 For the Lithuanian experience see the following chapters.

310 *See, e.g.*, Joint Report 'Unfair Terms in Contract'. English and Scottish Law Commissions (Law Com No 292, Scot Law Com No 199, 2005) para 4.75; Lawson R. *Exclusion Clauses and Unfair Contract Terms* 8th ed. (Thomson Sweet & Maxwell 2005) 210. Interestingly, a similar approach is supported in Scandinavian countries. However, contrary to the English practice, a judge in Sweden may intervene even more into contractual relations; in particular a judge may even adjust contract terms if they are unreasonable with reference to the contents of a contract. *See*: Lehrberg B. 'Renegotiation clauses, the doctrine of assumptions and unfair contract terms' 3 *ERPL* (1998) 272

resisted by the English judiciary for a long time. All in all, it would seem that stringent German case law provides a somewhat better means of deterring companies from consciously disadvantaging a weaker party. However, in any case, there is nothing to stop the seller or supplier from using the same unfair terms in similar transactions[311].

Another important feature in the comparison of English and German laws on the regulation of standard contract terms is that neither German nor English statutes regulate the issue of construction of standard contract terms comprehensively. English common law (which corresponds to case law in Germany) deals with these issues in a broadly similar way. The judiciary in all the selected jurisdictions - including France and Lithuania - apply a *contra proferentem*[312] rule with respect to the terms put forward by the *proferens*. It means that doubtful and ambiguous terms should be interpreted against the party that put these terms into contracts[313]. However, this principle is only applied in respect of those terms that are genuinely ambiguous[314]. Where they are precise and unambiguous the judiciary may not interpret the terms in favour of any party. Thus a party wishing to apply exclusion clauses or limit its liability should use very clear and unambiguous wording. In general, the effect of interpretation rules is relatively limited in both jurisdictions, as the rule of *contra proferentem* in itself would not inhibit parties from exerting superior bargaining power and drafting a contract with unbalanced terms.

Finally, comparing both sets of laws solely on the basis of their wording might be inaccurate. The actual outcome of some cases is highly dependent on other rules, as well as the judicial discretion.

For example, English common law is widely applied to limit the validity of unfair trade practices in England. It would seem that the rules on the incorporation of pre-formulated terms are somewhat stricter in common law[315]

---

311 Willet C. 'The Directive on Unfair Terms in Consumer Contracts and its Implementation in the United Kingdom' 2 *ERPL* (1997) 227

312 See *e.g.* § 305c (2) BGB, BGHZ, 24, 39, BGHZ, 62, 63. *For the English case law see*: Wallis v. Pratt and Haynes [1911] AC 394 HL, Webster v. Higgin [1948] 2 All ER 127; Association of British Travel Agents v. British Airways plc. [2002] Lloyds LR 209. *For the case law of the Lithuanian Supreme Court see*: No. 3K-3-535/2005, 3K-3-600/2006, 3K-3-320/2008

313 *See:* Thomas Witter Ltd v. TBP Industries Ltd. [1996] 2 All ER 573, 575, Lee & Son Ltd v. Railway Executive [1949] 2 All ER 581, 584. *Cf.:* Macdonald E. 'Y2K and Contractual Exemption Clauses' 2 *The Journal of Information, Law and Technology* (1999)

314 *See*: Aqua Design and Play International Ltd v. Kier Regional Ltd. [2003] BLR 111

315 *See:* Treitel G. *The Law of Contract,* 11th ed. (London: Sweet & Maxwell 2003) 216-21 Parker v. South Eastern Railway (1877) 2 C.P.D. 416; Frank Mass (UK) Ltd. v. Samsung Electronics (UK) Ltd. [2004] EWHC 1502 (Comm); OK Petroleum v. Vitol Energy [1995] 2 Lloyd's Rep. 160; Extrudakerb v. Whitemountain Queries Ltd. [1996] C.L.C. 1747

than in German law[316] though this is a general conclusion subject to many exceptions. Furthermore, it is also important that special statutory provisions on the incorporation of standard terms are not applicable to business transaction (cf. § 310 (1) BGB). The incorporation of standard terms in business transactions is assessed in the light of general provisions regulating the conclusion of transactions. This means that standard terms may be included through tacit agreement in Germany provided, however, that the *preference* uses its standard terms and the counterparty does not oppose their incorporation[317]. Moreover, German case law confirms that the effective incorporation of standard terms in business transactions does not require that the counterparty was actually aware of the standard terms[318], it suffices that a clear reference to such standard term was made, or that the counterparty was given a chance to get acquainted with such terms. On the contrary, the issue of the valid incorporation of contract terms is not explicitly regulated by UCTA. In English law the distinction is made between signed documents and all other types of agreement. It is assumed that the signature incorporates the terms of a contract, and a party is bound by the terms that he signs[319]. Thus, in practice, exclusion clauses are sometimes inserted using capital letters to show that additional steps were taken to draw the attention of the counterparty. In other cases, for example, where a document was handed by one party to another party, English common law has developed a requirement to give the other party 'a reasonably sufficient notice of the condition'[320], which is also applicable in business transactions. This rule was explained persuasively by *Lord Denning M. R.* in *White v. Blackmore*:

---

[316] Special provisions of German law requires to make an explicit reference to the standard contract terms as well as to offer an opportunity to take notice of their contents in an acceptable manner in accordance with § 305(2) BGB so as to incorporate these terms into a contract effectively in consumer contracts. However, this provision by virtue of § 310(1) BGB is not applicable for purely business-to-business transactions. For more discussions on the incorporation of standard terms see, *e.g.* Fischer F. O. 'Praktische Probleme der Einbeziehung von AGB under Kaufleuten insbesondere bei laufenden Geschäftsbedingungen' *BB* (1995) 2491 *et seq*; Wolf M. *et. al.*, *AGB-Gesetz, Kommentar* (Verlag C.H. Beck 1999) § 2 AGBG, para 6 *et seq.*

[317] Brandner E. H. 'Kaufmännische Vertragsgestaltung under den Zwängen des Rechts der Allgemeinen Geschäftsbedingungen' *DZWiR* (1992) 180; Basedow in: MünchKomm, before 305, para 91

[318] See, e.g. BGHZ, NJW, 1964, 1788

[319] *See*: L'Estrange v. F Graucob Ltd. [1934] 2 K.B. 394, [1934] All ER Rep 16

[320] Interfoto Library v. Stilleto Ltd [1988] 1 All E.R. 348, developed from Parker v. South Eastern Railway (1877) 2 C.P.D. 416; Frank Maas (UK) v. Samsung Electronic (UK) [2004] EWHC 1502 (Comm). *See also:* Bradgate R. 'Unreasonable Standard Terms' 60(4) *M.L.R.* (1997) 586-90; Macdonald E. *Exemption Clauses and Unfair Terms* (London Edinburgh Dublin: Butterworths 1999); Stone R. *The Modern Law of Contract* (London Sydney Portland Oregon: Cavendish Publishing Limited 2005) 225

'The court must be satisfied that the particular document relied on as containing notice of the excluding or limiting term is in truth as *integral part* of the contract'[321].

The effectiveness of incorporation of such exclusion clauses depends on various factors, *e.g.* the nature of the agreement, the degree and time of notice. Interestingly, the means of incorporating contract terms can sometimes be linked to the substance of a particular term: 'the more unreasonable a clause is, the greater notice must be given of it'[322]. The classic example regarding notice of incorporation is from *Interfoto Picture Library Ltd. v Stiletto Visual Programmes Ltd*[323]. In that case the defendants were absolved from the obligation to pay a fee for the late returned of negatives because the defendant was not given adequate notice, and therefore these terms were considered not to have been effectively incorporated in the contract. This means that unfair terms may be struck out not because they unfair or largely disadvantage the other party, but because a weaker party was not properly informed about the meaning of such terms[324]. In essence, this rule is a bit more relaxed with regard to business transactions. The fact that parties conduct business several times on the same terms and conditions leads the other party to reasonably expect that the other party has accepted its terms[325]. Evidence that a contract is signed may be insufficient to conclude that the terms were effectively incorporated[326]. As noted above, the inclusion of exclusion or limitation clauses will be valid only if a term has been included in clear and unambiguous wording[327]. In cases where a contract term is unusual the other party must bring the term to the other party's attention during negotiations.

In consideration of this, it may be concluded that English judges have fewer means at their disposal than their German colleagues to assess the fairness of the substance of business transactions, which is sometimes negatively referred to as the policing of contractual relations. Neither jurisdiction has extensive rules on the incorporation of contract terms in commercial contracts. The English judiciary has some discretion to strike out unfair rules by invoking common law rules on incorporation of contract terms in documents that were not

---

321 [1972] 3 All ER 158, 167

322 Lord Denning in: Spurling Ltd. v. Bradshaw [1956] 2 All E.R. 121, 125

323 [1988] 1 All ER 348

324 *For some relevant examples see*: Frank Maas (UK) v. Samsung Electronic (UK) [2004] EWHC 1502 (Comm). It should be noted that English courts might deem that reasonable notice can be given by the way of usual business dealings.

325 Motours Ltd. v. Euroball (West Kent) Ltd. [2003] EWHC 614 (QB)

326 *See the arguments of the Court of Appeal in*: Grogan v. Robin Meredith Plant Hire Triact Civil Engineering Ltd. [1996] C.L.C. 87

327 *See*: Sugar v. London, Midland & Scottish Railway [1941] 1 All ER 172

signed, whereas the issue of incorporation of standard contract terms in commercial contracts in Germany is scrutinised according to the general provisions of the BGB.

4. HIDDEN REGULATION OF UNFAIR CONTRACT TERMS UNDER THE FRENCH CODE CIVIL

As noted above, there is no special statutory system of regulation of standard form contracts for business-to-business contracts in France. Nonetheless, a hidden attempt at regulation is discernable from the restrictive construction of some provisions of the Code Civil[328]. The French regulator stipulated certain requirements for the incorporation of terms into a contract; contract terms should be clear and unambiguous to be effectively included into a contract. Pursuant to Article 1156 CC, the common intention of the contracting parties must be sought in agreements rather than ascertaining merely the literal meaning of terms. For instance, in cases where a limitation of liability clause is incorporated into a contract, this will bind the party if it is proven that the party knows of its existence[329]. On the other hand, the effectiveness of incorporated contract terms is generally assessed on a case-by-case basis.

There are cases where limitation clauses were considered enforceable under French law, even though the defendant relied on standard terms (*e.g.* conditions for the carriage of passengers in public places), as the plaintiff 'could not have been ignorant of the existence of the clause concerned'[330]. Under some circumstances, it can reasonably be expected that the counterparty must know the exclusion and limitation clauses and therefore should be considered to be binding on both contracting parties. In the case where standard form contracts put forward by both parties contradict each other, default statutory provisions should be applicable (*annulation réciproque des clauses contradictoires*). By virtue of Article 1162 CC, the burden of proving that contract terms are fair is shifted to the party that insisted on them. Terms excluding contractual liability may be incorporated into a contract silently or impliedly. In any way, these terms

---

328 Wolf M. 'Auslegung und Inhaltskontrolle von AGB im internationalen kaufmännischen Verkehr' 153 *ZHR* (1989) 300-1

329 *See*: 'Tragic Flying Lesson case' (Cass. Civ. 1 re, 4 July 1967), cited in: Beale H., Hartkamp A., Kötz H., Tallon D. *Cases, Materials and Text on Contract Law* (Oxford and Portland, Oregon: Hart Publishing 2002) 499. *Compare also:* Sonnenberger J. 'Das französische Recht der allgemeiner Geschäftsbedingungen (*conditions générales*)' *RIW* (1990) 168

330 Case '*Air Passenger in a Hole*' (Bull. Civl. I 190, D. 1971, 373), cited in: Beale H., Hartkamp A., Kötz H., Tallon D. *Cases, Materials and Text on Contract Law* (Oxford and Portland, Oregon: Hart Publishing 2002) 500

need to be known to both parties and be mutually accepted[331]. French law gives importance to the fact that contract terms must be signed by both parties. This is to confirm that the parties are actually aware of the terms which they agree.

Finally, it should be noted that countries outside the German legal tradition do not enforce contracts concluded through so-called 'tacit acceptance' (so-called '*das kaufmannische Bestätigungsschreiben*'), even if a contract includes standard terms[332]. Simple non-response to a proposal cannot be regarded as an expression of assent to the proposed contracts terms. Nonetheless, the acceptance of contract terms can be also done tacitly in France *('silence circonstancié')*[333].

5. THE MAIN AMENDMENTS TO THE NEW LITHUANIAN CIVIL CODE

5.1 GENERAL FRAMEWORK

After the re-establishment of independence in 1990 it was impossible to enact a new civil code immediately, In fact, the transition from Soviet law to a completely new autonomous Lithuanian legal system took roughly a decade. At the beginning of the 1990's, Lithuanian authorities introduced minor amendments to the old Soviet laws, giving due consideration to new conditions in a market economy. In the first five years after independence, most Soviet laws were changed. In 1998, Lithuania enacted a special law whereby all Soviet laws adopted before 1990 were officially repealed. However, some exceptions were made, and the effectiveness of some Soviet laws was expressly extended for a short period of time[334]. The old civil code was among these laws.

In fact, laws generally corresponding to European Union benchmarks were introduced gradually after 8th December 1995, as Lithuania submitted an official application to join the Union. Lithuanian progress in promulgating new laws was evaluated positively by the Commission before it officially invited Lithuania to join the Union. Indeed, contemporary Lithuanian private law - along with other branches of law - is similar to continental European laws in many respects. As a matter of principle, Lithuanian law does not acknowledge the binding character of precedent though some published rulings of the

[331] Ibid., p. 33

[332] The so-called '*das kaufmännische Bestätigungsschreiben*' in German law countries, *see e.g.* § 346 HGB, compare also with § 362 HGB. *For more comments see:* Basedow J. 'Handelsbräuche und AGB-Gesetz' 150 *ZHR* (1986) 469 *et seq;* Basedow in: MünchKomm, § 305, para 100

[333] Sonnenberger J. 'Das französische Recht der allgemeiner Geschäftsbedingungen (*conditions générales*)' *RIW* (1990) 168

[334] Valstybės žinios (Official Gazette), 1997, No. 118-3045

Supreme Court as well as resolutions of the Senate of the Supreme Court must be considered[335]. In judicial hearings, however, case law is often cited to support arguments put forward by the parties. Lithuanian contract law is based on the rules of the relatively new civil code (hereafter – LCC), which came into force on 1st July 2001[336]. The new LCC replaced the Soviet Civil Code of 1964[337].

Interestingly, the Lithuanian parliament declined the opportunity to implement a dualistic private law system. The new LCC contains the most important rules applicable for civil, consumer and business transactions. The default rules of contract law are set out in the 6th book 'The Law of Obligations' ('*Prievolių teisė*'). In general, the new LCC was heavily influenced by developments to private law in the Netherlands, Italy, and the Canadian Province of Quebec. Some valuable experiences from Germany, France, and Sweden were also adopted. Finally, it must be also noted that this new Lithuanian law of contract widely replicated the major rules established in the UNIDROIT Principles as well as the PECL[338].

5.2 THE CONCEPT OF GOOD FAITH IN THE LCC

In common with many other civil codes in continental European countries, the LCC is based on the principle of good faith. Pursuant to Article 6.158 LCC every contracting party must act honestly (in other words, according to the principle of good faith). In essence, this provision is mandatory in nature as contracting parties cannot modify or contract out of it. Any term that is contradictory to public order or norms of good morals shall be null and void (Art. 1.81 LCC)[339]. The LCC is not sufficiently comprehensive in defining the norm requiring parties to act honestly. The author submits that this means that parties should disclose all necessary information, retain a due balance of interests as well as perform contractual obligations in accordance with the principles of fairness and reasonableness. The duty to act honestly is applicable to pre-contractual arrangements (Art. 6.163 LCC[340]), so a party may legitimately

335 Valstybės žinios (Official Gazette), 1998, No. 38-101. *See also*: The Resolutions of the Constitional Court of the Republic of Lithuania dated 28 March 2006, 5 July 2007, 24 October 2007, the decisions of the Lithuanian Supreme Court in the cases No. 3K-3-52/2008, No. 3K-3-120/2008

336 Valstybės žinios (Official Gazette), 2000, No. 74-2262

337 For the old Soviet Civil Code see: Valstybės žinios (Official Gazette), 10 July 1964, No. 19-138

338 *For more see e.g.* Mikelėnas V. Lietuvos Respublikos Civilinio kodekso komentaras. Šeštoji knyga prievolių teisė (1) (Vilnius 2003) 191

339 *See also:* the decision of the Lithuanian Supreme Court in the case No. 3K-3-641/2006

340 *As for the relevant case law see*: the decision of Lithuanian Supreme Court No. 3K-3-38/2005

engage in pre-contractual negotiations only if it has a real intention to conclude a contract.

Lithuanian case law has confirmed that each contract must be interpreted in accordance with the principles of rightness, reasonableness, and fairness as set forth in Article 1.5 LCC. In particular, this means that contract terms must be construed in such a way that such interpretation would not result in unfairness in respect of one party[341]. On the one hand, this provision may be interpreted as obliging a party to abide by the obligations it has voluntary agreed upon, which is required by Article 6.189 LCC. Thus the court should retain a proper balance between parties by discouraging discriminatory trade practices. In general, the principle of freedom of contract is not absolute under Lithuanian law. The Lithuanian Supreme Court has concluded that freedom of contract is properly exercised only if contracting parties are in an equal position. Where one contracting party dominates the other, one may doubt if freedom of contract is actually in evidence, except where agreement between the parties is based on mandatory provisions of law[342].

It is important to note that the notion of 'gross disparity' stipulated in Article 6.228 LCC largely reiterates Article 3.10 of the UNIDROIT principles. Furthermore, Article 6.228 LCC takes into consideration Article 4.109 PECL (*ex* Article 6.109 PECL), which deals with 'excessive benefit or unfair advantage'. A party may rescind a contract or an individual term, if, at the time of conclusion of the contract, the whole contract or some terms in it unjustifiably gave the other party an excessive advantage[343]. Among other factors, regard is to be had to the fact that one party has taken unfair advantage of the other party's dependence, economic distress or urgent needs, or of its ignorance, inexperience or lack of bargaining power and the nature and purpose of the contract[344]. Upon a request by the party entitled to rescind, a court may adapt the contract or some terms thereof in order to make it accord with reasonable commercial standards of fair dealing. A court would adapt contract terms upon the request of the party receiving notice of rescission, provided that party informed the other of its request promptly after receiving such notice, and before the other party reasonably acted in reliance on it.

---

[341] *See*: the decisions of the Lithuanian Supreme Court in the cases No. 3K-3-406/2005, 3K-3-203/2007, 3K-3-18/2006, 3K-3-15/2008

[342] The decision of the Lithuanian Supreme Court in the case No. 3K-3-579/2008

[343] Following the authorative interpretation of Article 3.10 UNIDROIT principles, the term 'excessive' does not refer to arithmetical measures. *See*: Bonell M. J. *An International Restatement of Contract Law. The Unidroit Principles of International Commercial Contracts.* 3rd *ed.* (Transnational Publishers Inc. Ardsley, New York USA 2005)169

[344] It must also be noted that pursuant to Article 1.91 LCC a transaction may be struck out according to general provisions, provided it has been concluded due to fraud, economic duress, exceptional circumstances, *etc*.

Similarly, as with the UNIDROIT Principles, Article 6.228 LCC provides a twofold test[345]. First, any disparity between the obligations of parties that gives an excessive advantage to one party must be identified. Second, the excessive advantage must be unjustifiable, for example economic distress or urgent need, or lack of bargaining power. In this respect, the LCC combines the test of substantive and procedural unfairness. The test covers both the content of the contractual terms as well as the behaviour of the parties[346].

The successful implementation of this provision shows that it is practical and possible to transpose the UNIDROIT principles, which combine elements of both common and civil legal systems. One possible point of criticism may be that the test is cumbersome to apply in practice, as it is difficult to ascertain both substantive and procedural disparity in business-to-business contracts.

5.3 Special Regulations on Tackling Unfairness in Standard Form Contracts

There is some evidence that Lithuanian case law recognises that a corporation may be considered a weaker party in business-to-business contracts in cases where one contracting party is a dominant market force[347]. The case law is, however, not abundant on this point. Thus special provisions regarding the striking out of standard contract terms by virtue of Articles 6.185-6.186 LCC may be employed here. The LCC stipulates the concept of standard contract terms similar to that in other European countries. Standard contract terms are defined as those provisions which are prepared in advance for general and repeated use by one party, and which are actually used without negotiation with the other party (Art. 6.185(1) LCC, *cf.* Art. 2.1.19 UNIDROIT Principles). Standard contract terms can be prepared as a separate document, and they can also be executed as an appendix to the major agreement[348].

In essence, the regulation of standard form contracts was transposed to a large extent from Articles 2.19, 2.20, 2.21, 2.22 of the UNIDROIT Principles. Bearing this in mind, the means by which the UNIDROIT Principles and the

---

345 At the stage of preparation of the UNIDROIT Principles there were two separate articles drafted: ‘Unequal Bargaining Power’ and ‘Gross Unfairness’. Basically, they both reconcile two different approaches used in the continental and civil law systems aimed at tackling unfairness in contractual relations.

346 In exceptional cases, unfair advantage can be established without abuse of superior bargaining power provided due consideration is given to the nature and purpose of the contract.

347 The arguments of the Vilnius District Court (Vilniaus apygardos teismas) in: UAB ‘Tele2’ v. UAB ‘Vortumas’ case No. 2A-653-340/08.

348 Cf. the decisions of the Lithuanian Supreme Court in cases: No. 3K-3-141/2006; 3K-3-545/2007, 3K-3-80/2008

PECL are applied is highly relevant to the interpretation of provisions of the LCC. Contract terms drafted by government institutions are not considered standard contract terms within the meaning of the LCC.

The LCC contains rules regarding both the incorporation of standard contract terms and the regulation of their content (Art. 6.179, 6.185, 6.186 LCC). For example, a contract containing standard terms may be concluded only if the counterparty had a reasonable opportunity to become acquainted with the contract terms (Art. 6.185(2) LCC). The very basic rule established in the LCC is that a stipulator should behave honestly or in good faith. According to the law, the duty to acquaint oneself with contract terms in business-to-business transactions would be satisfied in cases where: (a) a stipulator submits contract terms in writing before signing a contract or at the time of signing a contract, or (b) before signing a contract, a stipulator notifies the counterparty that a contract shall be concluded on standard contract terms and the counterparty may become acquainted with them at the place indicated by the stipulator, or (c) a stipulator offers to send a copy of standard terms to the counterparty (Art. 6.185(3) LCC). Indeed, there are no strict requirements as to how standard contract terms should be submitted to the counterparty. In practice, Lithuanian courts find it sufficient if the counterparty confirms by signature that it has received a contract or a copy[349]. Nevertheless, according to the wording of the LCC, standard contract terms may be effectively incorporated in business-to-business contracts if the counterparty was duly offered the chance to familiarise itself with the standard contract terms, which does not necessarily imply that the counterparty need sign the contract. In theory, the effective incorporation of standard contract terms does not require the *proferens* to attach its standard contract terms to the offer. As far as business-to-business contracts are concerned, a stipulator is merely bound to offer the counterparty the chance to familiarise itself with them. According to Lithuanian case law, the *proferens* must prove he has undertaken all actions in relation to the incorporation of standard contract terms required by law. A challenging party must prove that the standard contract terms in question were not property presented and incorporated at the time[350].

The new LCC introduced certain special limitations with regard to regulating the content of standard contract terms in business-to-business contracts as well. In particular, Article 6.186 LCC stipulates that unusual standard terms would not bind a counterparty in cases where it does not reasonably expect these terms as part of the contract. As for substance, this provision largely reiterates Article 2.20 of the UNIDROIT Principles. The enforceability of standard contract terms is assessed by virtue of their content,

---

[349] *See*: the decision of the Lithuanian Supreme Court in case No. 3K-3-545/2007

[350] *See* the decisions of the Lithuanian Supreme Court in cases No. 3K-3-486/2000; No. 3K-3-911/2000; 3K-3-689/2006

language and presentation (Art. 6.186(2) LCC). In some cases, the Lithuanian Supreme Court has said that allegedly unusual terms must be evaluated in the context of whether they were sufficiently clear with regard to content, formulation or form, and whether they were duly disclosed to the counterparty[351]. For example, a contract term may cause alarm in cases where it has been prepared in a foreign language or in small letters, or it has been put in the wrong place[352]. On the other hand, the Lithuanian courts are not ordinarily concerned with whether the particular standard terms were fair. Case law seems to follow the statutory provisions without giving sufficient explanation. Unusual contract terms may also entail the exclusion of liability. Provisions regarding the effectiveness of unusual contract terms are not applicable in cases where pre-formulated contract terms were expressly accepted by the counterparty. According to the UNIDROIT Principles, some additional safeguards regarding the effectiveness of unusual contract terms were added to the LCC because Lithuanian rules on the incorporation of standard contract terms are not sufficiently rigid. The existence of such provisions would mitigate a situation where a counterparty was not properly informed of the peculiarities of a set of standard contract terms, but did not challenge them[353]. Finally, it is worth noting that these provisions are applicable solely in business-to-business transactions, while a separate Article 6.188 LCC safeguards the interests of a consumer.

By way of comparison with the provisions set out in the UNIDROIT Principles, the LCC provides for some additional safeguards to protect a weaker party. In particular, a counterparty may also be required to rescind a contract or to change standard terms (Art. 6.186(3) LCC). This possibility can be exhausted in cases where standard contract terms do not necessarily contradict the mandatory provisions of Lithuanian law. In such cases, a contracting party is either deprived of the rights typical to such contracts or the liability is excluded or limited, the balance of interests of the contracting parties is not sustained, or the contract terms are not in line with the principles of rightness, reasonableness, and fairness. This provision largely replicates Article 4.110 PECL (*ex* Art. 6.110) that regulates the effectiveness of individually non-negotiated terms.

On balance, the Lithuanian regulator sets out somewhat stricter requirements for the enforcement of standard form contracts rather than that for individual contracts. Undoubtedly, standard contract terms should be suggested by the party stipulating in a reasonable, honest and fair way.

---

351 The decision of the Lithuanian Supreme Court No. 3K-3-689/2006

352 Mikelėnas V. Lietuvos Respublikos Civilinio kodekso komentaras. Šeštoji knyga prievolių teisė (1) (Vilnius 2003) 235-236

353 *See also:* Bonell M. J. *An International Restatement of Contract Law. The Unidroit Principles of International Commercial Contracts.* 3rd ed. (Transnational Publishers Inc. Ardsley, New York USA 2005) 155-6

In Lithuanian case law disputes as to the enforceability of standard contract terms have mostly arisen between insurers and the insured. However, case law confirms that it is difficult for a counterparty to have standard contract terms struck out. Sometimes, the courts conclude that there is no evidence that the counterparty either had the opportunity to acquaint itself with the standard contract terms (Art. 6.185 (2), (3) LCC), nor that the contract terms in question were surprising. The court would also consider whether the counterparty required an amendment to the terms it was challenging or whether it wanted to rescind a contract[354]. On the one hand, insured parties were often treated as a weaker party if they entered into a contract on standard terms[355]. In Lithuanian judicial practice, standard terms in insurance contracts were not ordinarily considered to be unusual if the insured risks were explicitly mentioned in the contract[356]. Furthermore, it was acknowledged that the benchmark of diligence is somewhat higher for companies than it is for consumers. Companies are considered as being more experienced in contractual arrangements - they know their rights and obligations better[357]. This assumption makes the striking out of standard contract terms in business-to-business contracts even more difficult.

6. ASSESSMENT

It is a commonplace in Europe that judges do not tolerate unfair trade practices. However, all the jurisdictions observed here have somewhat different approaches to the regulation of standard form contracts. For example, Germany and England, where unfair contract terms were historically contested more often than in France, have introduced extensive statutory frameworks aimed at protecting a weaker party from unfair trade practices.

The English UCTA principally tackles the fairness of exclusion clauses, whereas §§ 305-310 of the German BGB (transposed from the AGBG) *inter alia* provide for some common rules on the incorporation and interpretation of standard contract terms. UCTA established special rules for business-to-business contracts; however, it seems that English courts remain morally neutral in practice when evaluating the content of agreed terms. In general, the English courts are very reluctant to strike out terms that are incorporated into a commercial contract, and an English court would probably not consider the effect of negotiations held prior to contract in deciding on the effectiveness of these standard terms. In other words, English courts are more interested not in

354 *See:* the decision of the Lithuanian Supreme Court in case No. 3K-3-24/2009

355 *See e.g.* the decisions of the Lithuanian Supreme Court in cases No. 3K-3-581/2000; 3K-3-911/2002, *etc.*

356 Decision of the Lithuanian Supreme Court in case No. 3K-3-213/2006

357 *See:* the decisions of the Lithuanian Supreme Court in case No. 3K-3-689/2006

assessing the content of a contract, but rather in the way a contract was agreed. The theoretical background underlying this approach is that the contract was assumed to be the result of mutual bargaining by the parties. However, this is more relevant for contractual arrangements that are not executed. It is assumed that signature incorporates terms into the contract and the judiciary has little discretion to intervene under English common law. Therefore, traditionally neutral common law judges would be reluctant to interfere in agreements parties agreed among themselves.

This is, however, not the case in Germany and Lithuania and many other continental European countries; the courts there endeavour to establish a fair balance of contractual duties and obligations, which from a common law perspective is sometimes negatively regarded as market regulation. Moreover, judges in Lithuania - similar to those in Nordic countries - are entitled only not to examine the contents of a contract for the purposes of setting aside unfair contract terms, but also to rectify it, taking into consideration the commercially reasonable interests of both parties. In light of this, it would seem that continental European countries adhere less to the idea of market individualism, and therefore their judges possess more discretion to reinforce fairness in contractual relations, even where a contract initially passes the so-called 'fair bargaining test'.

On the other hand, judges from civil law countries are more bound by the mandatory provisions of civil codes (for example, the notions of good faith, fair trading), while common law rules link the reasonableness of contract terms to the particular situation. As a consequence, a standard contract term in continental Europe may correspond to the particular expectations of a party - for example, a party agrees to take all possible risks for a lower price – but, by using abstract prohibitions set out, for example, in the German BGB or Lithuanian Civil Code as a benchmark, these terms may be found to be unfair. On the other hand, a contract term may be in line with the minimal requirements of statutory law, but greatly disadvantage the particular interests of a party and so be held to be unreasonable and void in England, but not in most jurisdictions in continental Europe. For these reasons, although statutory law provides similar means for striking out contract terms, the legal outcome after assessing the fairness of contract terms will be different in the different countries observed here. This analysis confirms that Lithuanian and German law are lenient with regard to assessing the effectiveness of incorporation of standard terms in business-to-business contracts. It may suffice for the *proferens* to prove that he offered the counterparty the chance to familiarise itself with standard contract terms under Lithuanian law so as to prove the effectiveness of standard contract terms. In Germany the incorporation of standard terms in business-to-business transactions is assessed under general rules of formation of contract.

Minor discrepancies are noticeable with regard to evaluating the effectiveness of the content of standard contract terms in jurisdictions selected here. German laws only allow for the fairness of auxiliary ('non-core') contract terms to be assessed, but not the adequacy of price and main subject of a contract. There is no such general limitation in England and France. The assessment of fairness of the main object of a contract as against price is only explicitly excluded in consumer contracts in Lithuania where they are clear and transparent (Art. 6.188(5) LCC). However, there is no such general requirement in relation to business-to-business contracts. This means that the Lithuanian judiciary – at least in theory - has significant discretion to restore substantive fairness in contractual relations, while English law controls mostly procedural fairness. German law lies somewhere in between these two approaches, though these are simply theoretical assumptions based on an analysis of statutory law.

In practice, unfair contracting is linked closely to the unfair terms offered. It is likely that the same contract terms would be unenforceable in all the selected jurisdictions, but possibly for different reasons. These findings support the comparative analysis's initial hypothesis that in practice there are far-reaching parallels between the four jurisdictions and that the legal outcome with regard to the enforceability of similar standard form contracts is not as divergent as one might suppose. It is thus submitted that, despite different statutory provisions as well as differing theoretical approaches to market regulation, following an appraisal of unfair standard terms in domestic transactions the jurisdictions selected here are more likely to guarantee similar legal outcomes than not.

III. Regulation of Exclusion Clauses in Standard Form Contracts

1. PRELIMINARY OBSERVATION

> 'Exemption clauses differ greatly in many respects. Probably the most objectionable are found in the complex standard conditions which are now so common. In the ordinary way the customer has no time to read them, and if he did read them he would probably not understand them. And if he did understand or object to any of them, he would generally be told he could take it or leave it. And if he then went to another supplier the result would be the same'.
>
> Lord Reid in: Suisse Atlantique Societe d'Armament SA v NV Rotterdamsche Kolen Centrale [1967] 1 AC 361, 363

In general both common law and continental legal systems accept the principle that the plaintiff has to be compensated for loss he has suffered as a consequence of non-performance or misperformance of a contract. For instance, § 249(1) of the German BGB expressly stipulates that 'a person who is liable in damages must restore the position that would have existed if the circumstance obliging him to pay damages had not occurred'. At the same time, parties enjoy freedom of contract and may consequently exclude one or both parties from liabilities arising from a breach of contract to which they are ordinarily subject[358]. However, the existence of the exclusion clause does not necessarily mean that actual liability would always be shifted to the other party. Terms could merely be included to have a deterrent effect on the other party.

It is sometimes contended that exclusion clauses may secure better compliance with an agreement; since they leave a counterparty with the impression that it has few enforceable contractual rights[359]. From a more general perspective, the actual exclusion of liability means that one contracting party must accept reduced remedies. However, most European legal orders consider exclusion clauses enforceable provided that parties were not under undue influence or ignorant when they included the terms in the contract. The level of permissibility of exclusion and limitation clauses depends on whether they were individually negotiated or included in standard terms and conditions.

---

[358] *See*: Yates D. *Exclusion Clauses in Contracts* 2nd ed. (London: Sweet & Maxwell 1982) 1; Lewison K. *The Interpretation of Contracts* (London: Sweet & Maxwell 2004) 359

[359] Yates D. *Exclusion Clauses in Contracts,* 2nd ed. (London: Sweet & Maxwell 1982) 26

A comparison of the permissibility of exclusion of contractual liabilities across jurisdictions is complex, because contractual liabilities and damages are understood differently. For example, in many contracts governed by continental civil law – contrary to the common law system – it is not necessary to list various types of damages (direct, indirect, consequential, *etc.*[360]), and there is no requirement to include third parties (*e.g.* officers, directors, agents, trustees, beneficiaries) in exclusion clauses terms, or to distinguish between various forms of fault, *e.g.* 'deliberate', 'wilful' and so on. Furthermore, statutes differentiate between a breach of primarily and secondary obligations. The infringement of primary obligations makes the enforcement of a contract impossible, while a breach of secondary obligations should not ordinarily prevent the exercise of primary obligations.

It goes without saying that the exclusion of liability is not always expressly formulated in clear languages such as *e.g.* 'all claims in respect of the exclusion clauses will be excluded'. The actual exclusion of liability may *de facto* take place where contractual obligations are significantly reduced (*e.g.* in respect of supply, limitation clauses) or the liability or its enforcement is subject to restrictive or onerous conditions. Thus, there are no ordinary exclusion clauses, but terms that have been drafted to achieve the same result. For instance, a representative of a counterparty after inspecting goods could be asked to sign an acknowledgement that they complied in both nature and performance, with the contract specification[361]. LJ Donaldson J. in *Kenyon, Son & Craven Ltd. v. Baxter Hoare & Co. Ltd* gives an authorative explanation in respect of the factual effect of exclusion clauses:

> 'Protective conditions are of three different types: first those which limit or reduce what would otherwise be the defendant's liability for the breach of specified aspects of that duty, second those which exclude the defendant's liability for breach of specified aspects of that duty and third, those which limit the extent to which the defendant is bound to indemnify the plaintiff in respect of the consequences of breaches of that duty'[362].

All three aspects can overlap in certain circumstances. However, as a consequence the plaintiff would have limited rights or remedies less than those that he would ordinarily have in law. Indeed, exclusion or limitation of

---

360 Many exclusion clauses drafted in contracts to be governed by one of the common law systems ordinarily list: indirect, special, incidental or consequential loss or damage; damage to or loss of property or equipment; loss of profits or revenue; loss of use of customer's material or equipment; loss of data; increased costs of any kind, *etc.*

361 Yates D. Exclusion clauses in contracts 2nd ed. (London: Sweet & Maxwell 1982) 26

362 *Kenyon, Son & Craven Ltd. v. Baxter Hoare & Co. Ltd* [1971] 1 W.L. R. 519

contractual liability is probably one of the most frequently used methods for exploiting a counterparty when offering a standard form contract[363].

In practice, limitation clauses – as opposed to exclusion clauses – are not abused as often. Limitation clauses still leave some rights or remedies to the other party, though they may also go beyond what is reasonably expected by the other party. Thus limitation clauses are ordinarily assessed in a much looser manner than are exclusion clauses. For example, limitation clauses are frequently used in construction and carriage agreements where the other party fails to complete delivery on the agreed date. Ordinarily, such contracts fix the maximum remedies available. It is much easier to justify governmental intervention in contractual relations with rules on exclusion or limitation clauses than with for other terms (for example, penalties in a contract securing due performance of agreed obligations). Indeed, it is quite clear that the unreasonable limitation of remedies cannot be tolerated as it corrupts the fair distribution of business risks and increases general transactional costs. In light of this, rules on the enforceability of exclusion or limitation clauses in the selected jurisdictions will be discussed in detail. By examining these statutory provisions, one may also draw a more general conclusion about the optimal level of protection for weaker parties across jurisdictions.

2. The German Approach to the Exclusion of Contractual Liabilities

The most important rule in setting out whether standard form contract terms in business–to–business contracts are ineffective is whether, contrary to the requirement of good faith, they unreasonably disadvantage the other party to the contract (§ 307(1) BGB). The German BGB does not give any clearer judicial direction on how to deal with those standard contract terms that exclude or limit contractual liabilities in business-to-business contracts. In fact, these rules were first developed in legal doctrine and afterwards adopted in German case law. It was generally acknowledged in Germany that the freedom to limit or exclude contractual liabilities should be based on the idea that contracting parties may themselves establish the optimal and proportional distribution of risks[364]. Generally speaking, the permissibility of the exclusion of liabilities depends on several factors: (i) whether the party relying on the standard contract terms

---

[363] *Cf.* Macdonald E. *Exemption Clauses and Unfair Terms* (London Edinburgh Dublin: Butterworths 1999)

[364] *For more comment see:* Haas M. *Haftungsfreizeichnungsklauseln in Allgemeinen Geschäftsbedingungen. Eine rechtsdogmatische und ökonomische Analyse* (Frankfurt am Main 1991) 17. *See also:* Markesinis B. (*et. al*) *The German Law of Contract* (Oxford and Portland, Oregon: Hart Publishing 2006) 164

infringes the essential duties or essential rights inherent in the nature of the contract (so-called '*Kardinalpflichten*'[365]), and (ii) the responsibility of the party for breach of contract.

Contrary to the common law approach and in common with other continental law systems, German law makes an essential distinction between intentional and negligent infringements of a contract. Pursuant to § 276(3) of the BGB, an obligor's liability cannot be excluded in advance where the obligor has behaved with the intention of harming the other party. Furthermore, the validity of an exclusion of liability depends on whether the *essential* contractual rights of the counterparty and duties owed to the counterparty by the party relying on the standard contract terms were infringed. Liability for infringements of essential rights of, and duties toward, the counterparty cannot be excluded or otherwise reduced in cases where parties contract on standard contract terms. Similarly, § 307(2)(2) BGB allows an obligor to exclude its liabilities only if no essential contractual rights and duties inherent in the nature of the contract are infringed and if there are no other general vitiating elements under the general provisions of BGB to render the contract ineffective[366]. Thus, the German theory of contract law states that the responsibility of a party must be ascertained only if examining them in the light of the essential duties and rights so jeopardised does not void the standard contract terms.

2.1 Breaches of Essential Contractual Rights and Duties

The concept of essential contractual rights and duties is a core principle of the German BGB that is established in § 307(2)(2) BGB. This principle had been developed in case law long before the AGBG was enacted[367]. In general terms, the 'essential contractual rights and duties' cover the most important contractual expectations of both parties. For instance, performance of the main object of a contract should *prima facie* be considered an essential contractual right from the point of view of the party entitled to that performance, and a duty from the point of view of the party that must perform that obligation. The German BGH makes clear that ordinarily every contract brings with it essential contractual rights and

---

365 Generally, the concept of '*Kardinalpflichten*' could be generally compared with the notion of '*Breach of Fundamental Term*' in England.

366 *See:* BGH, NJW, 1988, 561; BGH, NJW, 1993, 1063; BGH, NJW, 1991, 2630

367 *Cf.* Schlosser P. 'Freizeichnungsklauseln im kaufmännischen Verkehr', in: *Zehn Jahre AGB-Gesetz* Heinrichs H., Löwe W., Ulmer P. (Hrgs.) (Köln 1987) 124; Heybrock H. *Zur Dogmatik der Kardinalpflichte* (Frankfurt am Main 1990) 4; Paulusch B.-A. 'Haftung und Haftungsbegrenzung im kaufmännischen Geschäftsverkehr' *DZWiR* (1992) 185-7; Graf von Westphalen F. 'Vetragsrecht und AGB- Klauselwerke', in: *Vertragsrecht und AGB-Klauselwerke*, Graf von Westphalen F. Hrsg. (Verlag C. H. Beck München 2007) 115-24

duties[368]. However, recent German case law shows much interest in the transparency of this concept[369]. For instance, the German OLG explained that such terms as the party shall be 'liable for the breaches of essential contractual rights and duties as well as intentional and grossly negligent infringements' shall be ineffective as they are not in line with the requirements of the doctrine of transparency[370].

The German BGB prevents the parties from derogating from those provisions that are supposed to be essential. Essential contractual rights and duties may derive both from the nature and the purpose of a contract. The decisive factor here is that deciding which contractual rights and duties are considered essential depends whether an infringement jeopardises the attainment of the purpose of the contract[371]. Other contract terms are not directly subordinated to the purpose of the contract, but rather serve its implementation. In this regard, one should treat delay in performing contractual duties differently from absolute non-compliance with contractual duties under German law. Nevertheless, under certain circumstances even a delay may also be essential in assessing the performance of contractual obligations. For instance, some services are time-critical, and in the performance of these obligations time is of the essence. Moreover, some duties that are auxiliary by nature - *e.g.* duties to consult and to obtain and provide information - can be considered essential duties in particular circumstances[372]. In fact, it is sometimes still difficult to draw a clear line between essential and auxiliary contractual rights and duties. Essential rights and duties are not necessarily those listed in § 308 BGB (*i.e.* prohibitions which *may lead* to the invalidity of contract, or the so-called 'grey list' of prohibitions) and § 309 BGB (*i.e.* prohibitions that *must lead* to the invalidity of contract, or the so-called 'black list' of prohibitions). The list

---

368 *See:* BGH, NJW, 1991, 2631; BGH, NJW, 1993, 335

369 *For more see*: Schäfer J. *Das Transparenzgebot im Recht der Allgemeinen Geschäftsbedingungen* (Verlag Peter Lang GmbH Frankfurt am Main 1992); Kreienbaum B. *Transparenz und AGB- Gesetz. Eine Untersuchung des Inhalts und der Schranken des Transparenzgebotes* (Berlin: Duncker & Humblot 1997)

370 OLG Celle, Urteil vom 30.10.2008, 11 U 78/08 § 12 Abs. 1 S. 1, S. 2 UWG, § 307 Abs. 1 Satz 2 BGB

371 For some relevant case law *see:* BGH, NJW, 1998, 1785; BGH, NJW, 1990, 764. In this respect, the German approach has many similarities with the English doctrine of repugnancy, whereby a court can disregard an exclusion clause that is repugnant to the main purpose of the contract. *For more see*: Lord Denning in: Sze Hai Tong Bank Ltd. v. Rambler Cycle Co. Ltd. [1959] 3 All ER 182

372 It is sometimes argued that German case law is not very consistent in defining essential rights and obligations. *See e.g.* Westermann H. P. 'Abgrenzung von Neben- und Hauptleistungspflichten im Hinblick auf die Inhaltskontrolle', in: *Zehn Jahre AGB-Gesetz*, Heinrichs H. Löwe W., Ulmer P. Hrsg. (Köln 1987); Lutz R. *AGB-Kontrolle im Handelsverkehr unter Berücksichtigung der Klauselverbote* (München 1991) 138-40

established in § 308 BGB provides for indicative factors that are for interpretation by the courts.

In some cases, however, even non-essential breaches may lead to the striking out of contracts under German law. For example, in cases where a vendor negligently breaches duties that are insignificant in themselves but the consequences of the breach are sufficiently serious, the proportionality of standard contract terms would be assessed under § 307(1) of the BGB, but not § 307(2)(2). Accordingly, § 307(1) BGB prohibits acts by one contracting party that unfairly disadvantage the other contracting party where the relevant acts are contrary to the essential principles of the statutory provisions from which they deviate. In other words, even if serious breaches do not qualify as breaches of 'essential contractual rights and duties', the contract would still be measured according to the notion of good faith under § 307(1) BGB.

2.2 Intentional and Negligent Infringements of Contractual Obligations

Under German law, a person is liable for breach of contract only where the breach results from *culpable* behaviour (§ 276(1) BGB). § 276 BGB makes a distinction between intentional and negligent breaches. Intentional infringements occur where an obligor knew that he could/would be breaching his obligations under the contract, and in addition he must be shown to have intended to breach those duties. Thus intentional infringements cannot be made by mistake. Intentional infringements may sometimes also lead to stricter liability under § 826 BGB[373]. As already noted, § 276(3) BGB expressly prohibits the exclusion of liability for intentional breaches, whether or not this exclusion was stipulated by a standard form or individually negotiated contract. The same prohibition is applicable both to consumer and business-to-business contracts.

Conversely, under § 276(1) BGB, negligence is defined as 'a failure to take reasonable care'. Negligence is ordinarily established by evaluating objectively the circumstances in question, *i.e.* a person's ability to foresee damage, circumstances that could have prevented possible damage occurring, or possible alternative courses of behaviour that were available to the person in breach.

Gross negligence (*culpa lata*) is established where the reasonable man would consider that a higher than normal standard of care existed. Where the other party had no intention to breach contractual duties, the exclusion of liability for low levels of negligence is generally permitted, though there is little

[373] By virtue of § 826 BGB, a person who, in a manner contrary to public policy, intentionally inflicts damage on another person is liable to the other person to make compensation for the damage.

German case law on this point (provided, however, no essential contractual rights and duties are breached)[374]. Whether gross levels of negligence (German *grobe Fahrlässigkeit*) can also be excluded depends on the interpretation of § 276(1) BGB - 'the obligor shall be liable for intentional as well as negligent behaviour' - in all commercial contracts[375]. Pursuant to § 309(1)(7) *lit b* BGB, excluding liability for grossly negligent breaches of duty is prohibited absolutely in consumer contracts. In many instances, German case law opts to treat the validity of consumer and business-to-business contracts in a similar way – in other words, liability for grossly negligent infringements by businesses as well as grossly negligent behaviour by persons acting on behalf of the company[376] may not be excluded from standard form contracts, under § 307 BGB[377].

The same principles would apply in cases where it is established that several businesses acted recklessly in concert. Practically speaking, it is difficult to prove that a party intentionally breached its obligations, therefore it is often submitted that intentional and grossly negligent infringements should be treated similarly[378]. On the other hand, customary rules on transportation can also be relevant to those German businesses that permit more flexibility for business-to business contracts as to the exclusion or limitation of liability (see, *e.g.*, German Freight Forwarders' Conditions - ADSp[379]). The exclusion of liability shall not be permitted for the freight forwarder if the damage was caused by intent or gross negligence or by violation of essential contractual rights or duties, however, in which case damage claims may be limited to foreseeable, typical damage.

On balance, whether excluding the liability of an obligor is permitted is assessed similarly in both consumer and business-to-business transactions. To the extent the liability of a *proferens* is limited in accordance with the aforementioned sections of the BGB, such liability may also be also limited in respect of the corresponding personal liability of its employees, auxiliary persons (German *Erfüllungsgehilfen*), and legal representatives.

---

374 BGH, ZIP, 1985, 687, 689; BGH NJW, 1985, 623, 627; BGHZ, 71, 226, 228 *et seq*

375 *For more debates on this issue see e.g.:* Kötz H. Zur Wirksamkeit der Freizeichnungsklauseln, *NJW* (1984) 2447; Bunte H.-J., Hinrichs H. *Aktuelle Rechtsfragen zur Freizeichnung nach dem AGB-Gesetz* (Köln 1985); Henseler P. 'Beispiele zur Haftung und Haftungsbegrenzung im kaufmännischen Geschäftsverkehr - § 24 AGB-Gesetz' *DZWiR* (1992) 193 *et seq*

376 *See:* BGH, NJW, 1968, 1718, 1720; BGH, NJW, 1978, 1918

377 *Cf.* BGH NJW, 1983, 1681. *See also*: BGHZ, 89, 363, 368

378 Lutz R. *AGB-Kontrolle im Handelsverkehr unter Berücksichtigung der Klauselverbote* (München 1991) 125

379 Eickmeier F. *Rechtsweite und Grenzen der Hafungsfreizeichnung gemäß § 41a ADSp unter dem Einfluss der neugefaßten Speditionsversicherungsbedingungen* (Hamburg Verlag Versicherungswirtsch) 1993; Horn in: Wolf / Horn / Lindacher § 24, para 39

2.3 LIMITATION OF REMEDIES IN STANDARD FORM CONTRACTS

Both in Germany and elsewhere[380] contractual liabilities are often limited to the maximum quantum of damages recoverable[381]. In many international business contracts parties agree that total aggregate liability in contract or otherwise will not exceed the total price paid under the contract, except for gross negligence or wilful misconduct. In other words, the parties seek to limit contractual liability to a certain reasonable percentage of the contract price, and attach maximum liability to down payments, via a security deposit or in similar ways. The main reason for a company to use limitation terms in the broadest sense is to protect itself against unforeseen liability. In practice, it is easy to convince the contract counterparty to limit its liability at a time when both parties need the contract and the default of the other contracting party is improbable. However, owing to market fluctuations, the market price of the object of the contract may change, and the aggrieved party may seek full compensation for reduced income or lost opportunities.

In cases where the amount of compensation is limited absolutely, such terms may *de facto* operate as an exclusion clause. German case law has developed a principle that essential contractual rights and duties may be affected where remedies are limited[382]. This means that the scope of remedies may be reduced only if no essential rights and duties were breached. Read together, § 276(3) BGB (*i.e.* 'liability cannot be excluded for intentional infringements') and § 309(1) (7) *lit b* BGB - *i.e.* 'exclusion of liability for *grossly negligent* breach of duty is absolutely prohibited in consumer contracts' - leads one to the conclusion that limitation of liability for intentional infringements is absolutely ineffective. The legal basis for such invalidation is § 307 BGB[383]. Thus, all limitations of liability must expressly preserve liability for gross negligence. On the other hand, German case law acknowledges that businesses are more professionally experienced than consumers, and that therefore they are more able than consumers to assess risk.

Nevertheless, German case law permits the exclusion of liability for atypical or unforeseeable damage[384]. Contracting parties may agree on the

---

380 Strictly speaking, at common law clauses on liquidated damages are not regarded as exclusion clauses.

381 Basedow in: MünchKomm, § 309(1)(8), para 36

382 Horn in: Wolf / Horn / Lindacher § 24, para 36, BGHZ, 164, 11, 36

383 Schlosser P. 'Freizeichnungsklauseln im kaufmännischen Verkehr', in: *Zehn Jahre AGB-Gesetz* Heinrichs H., Löwe W., Ulmer P. (Hrgs.) (Köln 1987) 121. As for the exemption of liability for the other negligent infringements *see*: Graf von Westphalen F. 'Die Wirksamkeitsgrenze von Haftungsfreizeichnungs- und Haftungsbegrenzungsklauseln bei leichter Fahrlässigkeit gem. § 9 AGBG' *WM* (1983) 974

384 BGH, NJW, 1985, 3016, 3018

maximum amount of contractual damages that approximates to the average typical damages in claims under such contracts[385]. Hence, a reasonable pre-estimation of damages is permissible provided that it is not just a clause that fixes a maximum amount of damages to be recovered. Given the fact that case law tolerates agreements on foreseeable damages, German businesses ordinarily include such terms as "liability shall be limited to foreseeable damages which must be typically expected to arise, provided the party is not liable for intent, gross negligence, loss of life, bodily injury or damage to health". This helps businesses to limit the effect of negative implications arising out of unforeseeable business risks.

Finally, many businesses seek to limit their total aggregate liability in respect of all or any losses they attract to the maximum amount to which they are insured under professional insurance. It is not clear whether such terms would always be enforceable under German law[386]. One should probably consider them on a case-by-case basis, particularly whether such maximum insurance covers typical losses incidental to the transaction and whether the incorporation of such terms may affect the other party in unexpected ways.

3. THE ENFORCEABILITY OF EXCLUSION AND LIMITATION CLAUSES UNDER ENGLISH LAW

3.1 EXCLUSION AND LIMITATION CLAUSES IN BUSINESS-TO-BUSINESS CONTRACTS

To a certain extent, UCTA adopts common law rules whereby exclusion or limitation clauses should not be effective in cases where the parties had unequal bargaining power. According *to Lord Denning M. R.*[387] common law does not allow a party to exclude liability when it would be unconscionable for him to do so[388]. However, this view is not common in England. It is sometimes submitted that open review of unfair contract terms at common law was merely a 'single-handed attempt by *Lord Denning M.R.*'[389]. Contractual liability in England

385 *See:* Basedow in: MünchKomm, § 309(1)(8), para 36; Wolf M. (*et. al.) AGB-Gesetz, Kommentar*, 4. Auflage (1999) § 11, No. 7, para 55; *see also:* BGH, NJW 1993, 335

386 *See*, e.g., Paulusch B.-A. 'Haftung und Haftungsbegrenzung im kaufmännischen Geschäftsverkehr' *DZWiR* (1992) 189

387 Gillespie Bros. v. Roy Bowles Transport Ltd. [1973] 1 QB 400, 416

388 *See also: Levison v. Patent Carpet Cleaning Co. Ltd.* [1977] 3 All ER 498, 499. In the following case the plaintiffs were given a carpet for cleaning. The contract had a term that limited the defendant's liability to £40. The Court of Appeal has decided that the liability may be limited only if terms do not constitute a fundamental breach.

389 Beale H., Hartkamp A., Kötz H., Tallon D. *Cases, Materials and Text on Contract Law,* (Oxford and Portland, Oregon: Hart Publishing 2002) 512

usually means strict liability. It means that common law has traditionally treated contractual obligations as in principle absolute, though subject to modification in modern times via the doctrine of supervening impossibility or frustration[390]. UCTA did not invent anew rules prohibiting exclusion of liability in 1977[391]. A clear and express formulation was required to exclude liability for negligence under common law. In cases where no clear and unambiguous expression is used, the ordinary meaning of the word should be used. If a clause covers any other sort of liability, it should not be interpreted so as to exclude liability for negligence[392]. On the other hand, the effect of rules of incorporation and interpretation created by common law should not be over-estimated[393]: UCTA sets out both general principles and concrete prohibitions as to what kind of liabilities should not be excluded in a contract.

Probably the most important innovation of UCTA is the introduction of 'the test of reasonableness' along with major rules pertaining to the effectiveness of the exclusion of liability. Generally speaking, rights, duties or liabilities arising out of contracts can be amended by mutually binding agreement. Only certain limitations are absolute in UCTA, and several of these depend on whether the term that seeks to limit or exclude liability 'satisfies the requirements of reasonableness'.

The most important prohibitions are outlined below:

(a) Exclusion or restriction of liability for breach of sellers' implied undertakings as to title, *etc.* is not permitted[394]. Sellers' implied undertakings as to conformity of goods with description or sample, or as to their quality or fitness for a particular purpose can be excluded in business dealings only insofar as the term satisfies the requirements of reasonableness (section 6(2), 6(3) UCTA).

(b) Exclusion or restriction of liability for death or personal injury resulting from negligence is not permitted[395]. In cases concerning other kinds of loss or damage, this will be allowed insofar as the term or notice satisfied the requirements of reasonableness (section 2(1), 2(2) UCTA). This prohibition is of

---

[390] Barry N. *The French Law of Contract* 2nd ed. (Oxford: Clarendon Press 1992) 31-2

[391] *See e.g.* Canada Steamship Lines Ltd. v. the King [1952] AC 192; HIH Casualty and General Insurance Ltd. v. Chase Manhattan Bank [2003] 2 Lloyds Rep 61

[392] Shell Chemical UK Ltd. v. P&Q Roadtanks Ltd 1 Lloyds Rep 297

[393] In common law, companies are often treated as initially having equal bargaining power, and therefore terms that are in common use are often considered as being effectively incorporated in contracts. *See e.g.* British Crane Hire Corporation Ltd. v. Ipswich Plant Hire Ltd [1975] Q. B. 303

[394] Section 12 Sale of Goods Act 1979, 6(1) UCTA

[395] *See also:* Johnstone v. Bloomsbury, HA. [1991] 2 All ER 293; Ashdown v. Samuel William & Sons Ltd. [1957] 1 QB 409

huge practical importance, because parties rarely take out personal accident insurance. For instance, *Beale* submits that terms requiring one contract party to indemnify the other contract party against liability incurred as a result of a former party's negligence are still permitted under English law[396].

(c) If one party deals on another party's written standard terms of business, then the other party cannot (i) when himself in breach of contract, exclude or restrict any liability of his in respect of breach, or (ii) claim to be entitled to render contractual performance substantially different from that which was reasonably expected of him. A party is also not permitted to render no performance at all in respect of the whole or any part of his contractual obligation, except insofar as the contract term satisfies the requirements of reasonableness (section 3(2) UCTA)[397]. It is basically not permitted to terminate a contract with another party because of minor breaches of contract[398].

(d) Liability in respect of (i) the right to transfer ownership of the goods, or give possession, or (ii) the assurance of quiet possession to a person taking goods in pursuance of the contract cannot be excluded or restricted insofar as the term satisfies the requirements of reasonableness (section 7(4) UCTA).

The somewhat clumsy drafting of the act means that the same contract clause may be assessed under different sections. For instance, standard contract terms may exclude or restrict liability for negligence; however, certain terms that exclude or limit liability may at the same time constitute a breach of certain terms implied by UCTA or common law in contracts for sale of goods, hire-purchase and in other contracts for the supply of goods[399]. Generally speaking, exclusion or limitation of liability for damage to property is only permitted if the contract terms were proportional under the test of reasonableness.

By enacting UCTA, English legislator has for the first time explicitly acknowledged the need to review written standard terms of business. However, as in Germany, a distinction was made between consumer and business-to-business transactions. The exclusion of liability is not totally prohibited in business-to-business transactions. In this respect, UCTA shows some similarity

---

396 Beale H. 'Unfair Contract Terms Act 1977' 5(1) *British Journal of Law and Society* (1978) 117. A term where one party agrees to indemnify against the liability which that other party may have towards him is sometimes called 'the obverse of an exemption clause'. *See*: Lewison K. *The Interpretation of Contracts* (London: Sweet & Maxwell 2004) 392

397 *For some leading English case law on these issues see:* Philips Products Ltd. v Hyland [1987] 2 All ER 620, Thompson v. Lohan Plant Hire [1987] 1 WLR 649; Timeload v. BT [1995] 3 EMLR 459, 468; Paragon Finance v Nash [2002] 1 WLR 686

398 *For more see*: Beale H. 'Unfair Contract Terms Act 1977' 5(1) *British Journal of Law and Society* (1978)

399 *See more*: Beale H., Hartkamp A., Kötz H., Tallon D., *Cases, Materials and Text on Contract Law* (Oxford and Portland, Oregon: Hart Publishing 2002) 518

to §§ 308 and 309 of the German BGB, which also contains some absolute and relative prohibitions, albeit that UCTA does not make any references to the 'guilt' of the obligor. It should also be noted that the term 'standard' is interpreted slightly differently in Germany and England. The notion of 'standard contract terms' in Germany implies that terms should be used on a regular basis, whereas English case law is much looser on this issue; it must be shown that contracts were altered so frequently that the terms in question cannot be regarded as standard[400].

UCTA contains some provisions addressing cases where parties agree to limit the scope of remedies available (section 11(4) UCTA). Generally, the act contains a 'grey-letter rule', whereby the court must assess such terms on a case-by-case basis. In cases where contract terms or notices restrict liability to a specified sum of money, the following factors must be considered by the court: (a) the resources which a person could expect to be available to him for the purpose of meeting liability for damages should these arise, as well as the remuneration the party receives under the contract and (b) how far it was open to him to insure against his losses. Thus, although German law also permits the limitation of remedies, the approaches used in the two countries are slightly different. Generally, the rules of UCTA are aimed at addressing situations where the limitation of remedies was actually agreed by the parties, whereas German law would assess the limitation of liability in having regard to industry-typical contracts. Finally, English case law also provides that the rules of construction on interpreting limitation of liability clauses are not applied as rigorously as in the case of exclusion of liability clauses[401].

It is further submitted that the prohibitions established in UCTA are much more specific than those in the German BGB for business-to-business contracts. Indeed, continental lawyers may have difficulties comprehending the English approach. Similar (*e.g.* relating to sellers' implied undertakings as to title) legal outcomes can be derived from the general provisions of the German law of obligations (as in other continental European laws). Judges in continental Europe may ordinarily apply a purposive interpretation of a contract and subjectively establish the intent of the parties. Parties in continental Europe may rely more on default statutory rules instead of negotiating every single aspect of a transaction. In light of this, it may be difficult to measure the effectiveness of both laws in practice merely by considering German and English statutes.

It would not be correct to assert unambiguously that English statutory law in respect of the regulation of exclusion of liability is stricter than the German BGB, as most of the prohibitions in UCTA are subject to the test of

[400] Chester Grosvenor Hotel v. McAlpine [1991] 56 Build LR 115

[401] *See*: Ailsa Craig Fishing Co Ltd v. Malvern Fishing Co Ltd [1983] 1 All ER 101; Suisse Atlantique v. Rotterdamische Kolen Centrale [1966] 2 All ER 61

reasonableness. Furthermore, UCTA remains inapplicable for a wide number of contracts, *e.g.* contracts of insurance, contracts related to the creation, transfer or termination of interests in land, contracts related to the creation or formation or dissolution of a company and other forms of contract (*see:* Schedule 1, sections 2, 3, 4 and 7 of UCTA).

3.2 The Test of Reasonableness: Practical Implementation of the Act

The most famous provision of UCTA establishes that most terms and conditions that exclude or restrict any liability are permitted insofar as they were fair and reasonable, having regard to the circumstances which were, or ought reasonably to have been known or in the contemplation of the parties when the contract was made (section 11(1) UCTA). The burden of proving that a clause is reasonable is borne by the party that claims that the term satisfies the requirements of reasonableness (section 11(5) UCTA).

Practically speaking, the test of reasonableness means that a party relying on the term must prove that both contracting parties had actual knowledge of the agreed terms or had the inclusion of these terms into the contract in contemplation. The English courts would ordinarily assess contract terms from the time the contract terms were incorporated and not simply from the point at which circumstances changed after the contract was signed.

Similar tests can be found in other jurisdictions as well. For example, the test of reasonableness fixed in UCTA bears some similarity to the United States Uniform Commercial Code, which also allows courts to refuse to enforce a contract, or to refuse to enforce a contract with an unconscionable clause, or to limit the application of an unconscionable clause so as to avoid an unconscionable result[402]. At a very general level, one can also link the test of reasonableness with the concept of good faith (*e.g.* the duty of loyalty ensures that a party will use the contract in a way that as can reasonably be expected), which is a core principle of the German BGB[403]. However, it is difficult to

---

402 *See:* §§ 2-302 UCC. The doctrine of unconscionability is often considered as being looser than the English test of the 'reasonableness'. *For more see*: Dugan R. 'Good Faith and the Enforceability of Standardized Terms' 22 *William and Mary Law Review* (1980); Hillman R. 'Debunking Some Myth about Unconscionability: a new Framework for UCC § 2-302' 67 *Cornell L.R.* (1981) 1; Leff A. 'Unconscionability in the Code, the Emperor's New Clause' 115 *U. Pa. L.R.* (1967) 485; Ellinghaus M. P. 'In Defence of Unconscionability' 78 *Yale L. J.* (1969) 757

403 *See:* Hesselink M. *The New European Private Law. Essays on the Future of Private Law in Europe* (The Hague, London New York: Kluwer Law International 2002) 205; Beale H. [*et. al.*] *Casebooks on the Common Law of Europe: Contract* (Oxford: Hart Publishing 2002) 495

measure the effectiveness of these provisions as a test of reasonableness will always be applied in respect of a particular situation, and any generalisations would not be based in hard fact. Section 11(4) UCTA therefore mentions some other specific factors to be considered when evaluating reasonableness where by reference to a contract term or notice a person seeks to restrict liability to a specified sum of money, *i.e.* the resources available for the purposes of meeting liability, or whether it was open to a party to take out insurance. Thus the test of reasonableness is a flexible and open-ended test.

Strictly speaking, the test of reasonableness is not a direct development from case law[404]. Earlier English courts had few means of altering unfair contract terms or declaring the terms void, where necessary. Before UCTA, common law did not allow substantial amendment, though under certain circumstance, public policy could be invoked to strike out unfair contracts[405]. Common law also often held void those damages provided for in a contract in place of financial loss or loss of property.

It is worth noting that the applying the principle of inequality of bargaining power was even more controversial. The English courts have rarely been willing to apply this doctrine; however they have also been unwilling to renounce it entirely[406]. Historically, the Courts of Equity would use the doctrine of unconscionability to put aside contract terms. It meant that one party took advantage of or exploited the other party because of its weakness or vulnerability, though no fraud was committed. However, it is not clear how often the Courts of Equity employed the doctrine of unconscionability to tackle unfair contracts[407]. In modern English law the doctrine of unconscionability is linked with the efforts of *Lord Denning M.R.* to revive the doctrine[408].

However, it does not seem that his views have much support in contemporary English contract law unless treated as a matter of exception. The House of Lords in *National Westminster Bank v. Morgan* was reluctant to accept the doctrine of unconscionability[409]. As some commentators note, the real difficulty remains in establishing what kind of behaviour is improper[410]:

---

404 Section 3 of the Misrepresentation Act 1967 imposes a similar test of reasonableness on clauses excluding liability for misrepresentation.

405 Basically, an agreement to commit a crime, intending to injure government by bribing official, intending to pervert the course of justice or any similar overtly illegal agreements would be considered as being contrary to public policy under the English law.

406 Atiyah P. S., Smith S. *Atiyah's Introduction to the Law of Contract* (Oxford: Clarendon Press 2005) 308

407 Ibid., p. 310

408 *See*: Lloyds Bank v. Bundy 3 All ER 757

409 *For more see:* Atiyah P. S., Smith S. *Atiyah's Introduction to the Law of Contract* (Oxford: Clarendon Press 2005) 310-1

410 Ibid., p. 311

'It seems impossible to explain unconscionability as either a purely consent-based or purely wrongdoing based excuse, or, more generally, to reduce unconscionability to some other, more familiar idea. In this respect, unconscionability appears similar to the broader idea of good faith'[411].

Another attempt to strike out unfair contract terms uses the doctrine of fundamental breach of contract. The doctrine was developed by common law in the 1950's, and allowed a party to repudiate a contract[412]. A fundamental breach refers to the situation where a person breaches a contract and the consequences for the injured party are so grave that the breach can be considered fundamental[413].

Lord Denning M.R. made several efforts to gain wider support for the doctrine of fundamental breach (as a rule of construction) in English law. However, it was later rejected by the House of Lords in the case *Photo Production v. Securicor Transport*. In this case the defendants relied on exclusion clauses which provided that under no circumstance were the

---

411 Ibid., p. 312. On the other hand, strictly speaking, English law (despite underlying conceptions of duress, misrepresentation, mistake) did not acknowledge a general duty to negotiate or perform contracts in good faith. This attitude may be explained by a general scepticism as to why contracts should be subject to the moral criteria. Moreover, it is not completely clear which benchmark should be used to appraise the morality of contracting. The English courts have a wide discretion; therefore in theory the notion of good faith can be avoided by invoking other doctrines. *For more debates on this issue see*: Walford v. Miles [1992] 2 AC 128; Hesselink M. 'Special issue on Critical Legal Theory and European Private Law' 3-5 *ERPL* (2002) 217; Whittaker S., Zimmermann R. 'Good Faith in European Contract Law', in *Good Faith in European Contract Law* Zimmermann R., Whittaker S. *eds*. (Cambridge: Cambridge University Press 2000) 39 *et seq.*

412 Beale H. 'Unfair Contract Terms Act 1977' 5(1) *British Journal of Law and Society* (1978) 116; Lewison K. *The Interpretation of Contracts* (London: Sweet & Maxwell 2004) 384. *See also*: Harbutts Plasticine v. Wayne Tank [1970] 1 QB 447

413 English legal doctrine distinguishes fundamental breach and the breach of a fundamental term. The latter refers to the non-performance of primary obligations. For example, exclusion clauses could have been struck out if contractual behaviour differed substantially from what was initially agreed by the parties, *e.g.* something 'different in kind' was delivered. This matter was famously clarified by Lord Wilberforce in *Photo Production Ltd. v. Securicor Transport Ltd*: *'I have no second thoughts as to the main proposition that the question whether, and to what extent, and exclusion clause is to be applied to a fundamental breach or a breach of a fundamental term, or indeed to any breach of contract, is a matter of construction of the contract'*. *Cf.* Karsales (Harrow) Ltd v. Wallis [1956] 2 All ER 866, 869. *See also:* Yates D., Hawkins A. J. *Standard Business Contracts: Exclusion and Related Devices* (London: Sweet & Maxwell 1986) 98

defendants 'to be responsible for any injuries act or default by any employee … unless such act or default could have been foreseen and avoided by the exercise of due diligence'. According to the House of Lords the term was fair and reasonable in this case[414]. The decision implies that the courts must allow parties to decide for themselves the allocation of business risks in commercial arrangements. For example, a company can minimise risks through insurance. The decision seems to mean that it would even be legitimate to exclude liability for a fundamental breach in England, provided that the wording of the exclusion was sufficiently clear. In some cases, however, the courts have been reluctant to accept exclusion clauses unless they are clearly drafted[415].

After Parliament adopted UCTA in 1977, the situation was not completely reversed, but it became much clearer how to measure what contracts should be enforced. It is submitted that the implementation of the test of reasonableness is a positive development because of its clarity and flexibility. However, judges are still not completely free to alter contracts where terms are thought to be unfair. Schedule 2 of UCTA contains an indicative list of relevant circumstances to be considered when deciding on reasonableness:

> (a) The strength of the bargaining position of the parties taking into account (among other things) alternative means by which the customers' requirements could have been met,
>
> (b) Whether the customer received an inducement to agree to the term, or in accepting it had an opportunity of entering into a similar contract with other persons, but without having to accept a similar term,
>
> (c) Whether the consumer knew or ought to know reasonably to have known of the existence and extent of the term (having regard, among other things, to any custom of the trade any previous course of dealing between the parties),
>
> (d) Where the term excludes or restricts relevant liability if some condition is not complied with, whether it was reasonable at the time of the contract to expect that compliance with that condition would be practicable, and

---

[414] *See:* The House of Lords' arguments in Suisse Atlantique Societe d'Armament SA v. NV Rotterdamsche Kolen Centrale [1967] 1 AC 361; Photo Production v. Securicor Transport [1980] 1 All ER 556

[415] *Cf.* Ailsa Craig Fishing Ltd. v. Malvern Fishing [1983] 1 All ER 101; Tor Line v. Alltrans Group of Canada Ltd. (The TFL Prosperity) [1984] 1 All ER 103

(e) Whether the goods were manufactured, processed or adopted to the special order of the consumer.

The circumstances detailed in the Schedule apply to all provisions of UCTA[416]. Strictly speaking, the guidelines are applicable only in respect of the exclusion or restriction of implied obligations as to description and quality in supply and hire–purchase contracts as well as contracts of sale of goods. However, the guidelines are often considered to be of general application by deciding on what is a reasonable term[417].

Some criticism is made of the test of reasonableness because of its possible uncertainty, which is intrinsically connected to the flexibility of its rules. Even in the parliamentary debates on the Bill that became UCTA there was discussion about the objectivity (or not) of the test[418]. For instance, *Treitel* argued convincingly that the guidelines helped to reduce the uncertainty to which the requirement of reasonableness gives rise, but that they have uncertain scope[419]. Another point of criticism is that the test is relevant only for assessing liability under exclusion or limitation clauses and is unsuitable for testing other contract terms[420].

Nevertheless, application of this test did not cause significant problems in practice. English case law tends to take a restrictive (non interventionalist) approach when applying this test[421]. *Chadwick L.J.* noted that:

> 'in circumstances in which parties of equal bargaining power negotiated a price for the supply of product under agreement … the courts should be very cautious before reaching the conclusion that the agreement which they have reached is not a fair and reasonable one'[422].

---

416 *See e.g.* Philips Products Ltd. v. Hyland [1987] 2 All ER 620, 628

417 *Cf.* Stewart Gill v. Horatio Myers [1992] QB 600; Smith v. Eric Bush [1990] AC 831, 848

418 Lütkenhaus A. M. *Unfair Contract Terms Act 1977 und AGB-Gesetz 1976: Rechtsregeln zu Allgemeinen Geschäftsbedingungen im Vergleich* (Frankfurt am Main [u. a.] 1987) 135; Poole J. *Textbook on Contract Law* (Oxford: Oxford University Press 2003) 287-8

419 Treitel G. *The Law of Contract,* 11th *ed.* (London: Sweet & Maxwell 2003) 259. *See also:* Beale H. 'Legislative Control of Fairness: the Directive on Unfair Terms in Consumer Contracts', in: *Good Faith and Fault in Contract Law,* Beatson J. and Friedmann D. *eds.* (Oxford: Clarendon Press 1994) 246

420 *See:* Hartwell N. 'The Application of the Reasonableness Test under UCTA 1977: a Schism between Certainty and Fairness' 3(2) *Hertfordshire Law* Journal (2005) 55

421 *Cf.* Brownsword R. *Contract Law: Themes for the Twenty-First Century* (London: Butterworths 2001) 60. *Cf.* Watford Electronics Ltd. v. Sanderson CFL Ltd. [2001] EWCA Civ 317; Granville Oil v. Chemicals Ltd v. Davis Turner & Co Ltd. [2003] 2 Lloyd's Rep. 356

422 *For further discussions see:* Carey S. 'Exclusion Clauses – What is Reasonable?' 12(6) *Cons. Law* (2001); Peel E. 'Reasonable Exemption Clauses' *L.Q.R.* (2001)

In essence, in commercial agreements where the parties are initially not of equal bargaining power, it may be assumed that they are not free to establish contractual relations. This assumption can, however, be rebutted. Judges should consider on a case-by-case basis factors such as what kind of opportunity the parties had to prevent damage without making the contract significantly more onerous; the actual insurance position of the parties; whether the parties were able to enter into a contract without the exclusion term; whether there was an alternative source of supply in the market; whether there are any unusual elements and other relevant factors[423]. In some cases it may be reasonable to exclude liability if parties can insure themselves. Indeed, it is true that one cannot expect that the party offering a contract would be always under obligation to take care of insurance. This is especially true when one party has special knowledge and is able to get cheaper insurance[424]. There is no reason to deny the commercial parties a possibility to allocate business risks among themselves as they wish.

However, courts consider each case on its merits, and all generalisations may be inaccurate. For instance, in the case *George Mitchell (Chesterhall) Ltd v. Finney Lock Seeds Ltd*[425] the defendants supplied an inferior variety of seed, the claimant suffered considerable losses planting and clearing the field, and the crop completely failed. However, the contract contained a term limiting the liability of the defendants to a trivial sum, but it was held that this clause was void as unreasonable. The main factor relied upon by the House of Lords in reaching this decision was that in practice the seed merchants often negotiated settlements and paid proper compensation in cases of this kind even where their

---

423 *See:* Hartwell N. *The Application of the Reasonableness Test under UCTA 1977: a Schism between Certainty and Fairness*, 3(2) *Hertfordshire Law* Journal (2005) 56. *Also*: Lord Wilberforce and Lord Diplock in *Photo Production v. Securicor Transport Ltd.* [1980] 1 All ER 556, 568; Markesinis B. (*et. al.*) *The German Law of Contract* (Oxford and Portland, Oregon: Hart Publishing 2006) 170; Adams J. N. 'Unconscionability and the Standard Form Contract' in: *Welfarism in Contract Law* Brownsword R., Howells G. and Wilhelmsson T. eds. (Darthmouth Publishing Company Limited, 1994) 246; Thalmair P. *Von Postulat der Überraschungsfreiheit von AGB-Klauseln zu ihrer Transparenskontrolle* (München 1999); Peel E. 'Making More Use of the Unfair Contract Terms Act 1977: Steward Gill Ltd. v. Horation Myer & Co Ltd.' 56 *M.L.R.* (1993) 98, 102; Lawson R. *Exclusion Clauses and Unfair Contract Terms*, 8th *ed.* (Thomson Sweet & Maxwell 2005) 177-86; Yates D. *Exclusion Clauses in Contracts* 2nd *ed.* (London: Sweet & Maxwell 1982) 97

424 Atiyah P. S., Smith S. *Atiyah's Introduction to the Law of Contract* (Oxford: Clarendon Press 2005) 314

425 [1983] 2 AC 807

contracts contained the relevant clause[426]. In practice, courts apply various criteria flexibly in evaluating the reasonableness of contract terms, particularly with regard to business-to-business contracts. In *R. W. Green Ltd v. Cade Bros. Farms*[427] the plaintiff sellers claimed a particular sum as well as interest for potato seed they had sold to the defendant buyers. The defendants asked to set it off against a counterclaim because the potato seeds sold were infected with a virus, which resulted in a loss of profit. The plaintiff argued that any claim was to be limited to the price the defendants agreed to pay. The court decided that the defendants' counterclaim was limited to the price of the seed because: (a) the parties had equal bargaining power, (b) the buyer received no inducement to accept the terms, and neither of the parties knew that potatoes were infected, (c) the farmers could avoid the damage that occurred by buying certified potato seed, and (d) the contract had been in force for several years.

Such reasoning suggests that the reasonableness of contract terms is based on many practical criteria. Indeed, the benchmark for assessing business-to-business contracts is looser than that applied in the case of consumer contracts. In cases where both commercial parties are not of unequal bargaining power they are free to allocate risk as they see fit[428]. In this respect, UCTA did not bring radical changes to the assessment of exclusion clauses in commercial arrangements. According to *Lord Wilberforce* in *Photo Production Ltd v. Securicor Transport Ltd*:

> 'After this Act, in commercial matter generally, when the parties are not of unequal bargaining power, and when risks are normally borne by insurance, not only in the case for judicial intervention undemonstrated, but there is everything to be said, and this seems to have been Parliament's intention, for leaving the parties free to apportion the risks as they think and for respecting their decisions'[429].

As one sees in the other cases discussed above, even after UCTA came into force, English case law did not depart significantly from the inductive legal reasoning normally applied in the common law. Common law reasoning

---

[426] Atiyah P. S., Smith S. *Atiyah's Introduction to the Law of Contract* (Oxford: Clarendon Press 2005) 316. This ruling has been sometimes criticized as undermining the stability of commercial arrangements. *For more see:* Adams N. J., Brownsword R. 'The Unfair Contract Terms Act: a Decade of Discretion' 104 *LQR* (1988) 94 *et seq*

[427] R. W. Green Ltd v. Cade Bros. Farms Queen's Bench Division [1978] 1 Lloyd's Rep 602

[428] *Cf.* White Cross Equipment Ltd. v. Farrel [1982] 2 T.L.R. 21. However, as already noted, this does not necessarily mean that the exclusion clauses in commercial arrangements would always be upheld. *See also*: Rasbora Ltd. v. J. C. L. Marine [1977] 1 Lloyd's Rep. 645

[429] [1980] 2 AC 827, 843

employs open-textured rules in order to examine the facts of each case[430]. The reasonableness of contractual terms is assessed in the light of a particular situation, considering the concrete interests of the contractual parties. This approach is different from the legal reasoning applied in Germany and most other civil law countries, where the fairness of contract terms is judged in the light of more general statutory provisions and typical transactions. Practically speaking, English judges enjoy broader legal discretion to decide on the reasonableness of contractual relations without directly referring to the normative text of UCTA.

It is generally agreed that appellate courts are likely to uphold the decisions of lower courts with respect to the interpretation of reasonableness. For example, Lord *Bridge of Harwich* in *George Mitchell (Chesterhall) Ltd v. Finney Lock Seeds Ltd* contended that there should be room for a legitimate difference of judicial opinions:

> 'When asked to review such a decision on appeal, the appellate court should treat the original decisions with the utmost respect and refrain from interference with it unless satisfied that it proceeded on some erroneous principle or was plainly and obviously wrong'[431].

On balance, it seems that by enacting UCTA Parliament provided the courts with additional means of revising contractual obligations. However, English courts still adhere to freedom of contract as well as an economic analysis of business relations. In future, the concept of the test of reasonableness may be amended slightly, as the Commissions have suggested switching to a 'fair and reasonable' test for contract terms in the new Draft Bill. This draft proposes leaving no gaps in social regulation in respect of some types of contracts, and the test would be applicable to them all. Moreover, in line with developments in some other European countries, the proposed new tests put special emphasis on the transparency of contract terms[432]. Thus, English law is making a slight movement towards convergence with other continental European laws.

---

[430] For legal reasoning in common law see *e.g.*: Collins H. 'Formalism and Efficiency: Designing European Commercial Contract Law' 1 *ERPL* (2000) 228-32

[431] [1983] 2 AC 803, 816. The other judges' opinions were concurring in this case. *See also:* Lord Wilberforce in: Photo Production v. Securicor Transport [1980] 1 All ER 556

[432] Joint Report 'Unfair Terms in Contract'. English and Scottish Law Commissions (Law Com No 292, Scot Law Com No 199, 2005), para 4.70

4. THE FRENCH APPROACH

4.1 GENERAL PROHIBITIONS ON LIMITING THE AVAILABILITY OF REMEDIES

French civil laws have not established special statutory rules for the review of standard contract terms. Indeed, the French 'Code Civil' (CC) is much more general in character than the German BGB, which was strongly influenced by the school of Pandectism. It was believed in Germany that the civil code should be the sole source of law and, therefore, should not be complemented by case law or legal doctrine. The area of unfair disadvantage long remained unregulated, as the prevailing attitude in France was that of the regulation of contract law should not reverse inequality in the bargaining power of contracting parties[433].

It should also be noted that the French CC was first enacted in 1804, whereas judicial concern for the regulation of unfair disadvantage in unfair standardised terms only arose much later. Nonetheless, French legislators also ultimately intervened to tackle unfair contracts[434]. Probably the most prominent example is the Decree of 24 March 1978 (*Loi Scrivener*) that listed a number of clauses said to be '*abusives*'. However, the *Loi Scrivener* dealt mainly with contracts of sale between professionals and consumers and therefore the act was irrelevant for purely commercial arrangements. The French CC itself provides only very general rules in respect of the exclusion of liability in business-to-business contracts. Article 1382 CC sets out a basic rule that a party should compensate a counterparty for loss: 'any act whatever of man which causes damages to another obliges him by whose fault it occurred to make reparation'. Freely negotiated agreements were traditionally held valid unless public policy (*see*: Art. 6 CC) was successfully invoked to void the contract. The French courts have taken a view that it would be incompatible with the requirements of public policy for a party to fully exclude liability for all infringements.

As in the German BGB and many other European Civil Codes, so the French CC links liability to the fault of an obligor. Pursuant to Article 1150 CC, a party whose fault does not amount to *dol* (intentional infringement) is liable for damages which were foreseen or which could have been foreseen at the time of the contracting. The statutory limitation with respect to foreseeable damage was based on the idea that parties should be able to enter into a contract and

---

433 Sonennberger H.-J., Schweinberger E. *Einführung in das französische Recht* (Darmstadt 1986) 56

434 For instance, in 1905 there was a special act enacted establishing that contracts for the transport of goods by land might not exclude liability for loss or damage to the goods as opposed to the delay of their arrival. Barry N. *The French Law of Contract* 2nd ed. (Oxford: Clarendon Press 1992) 234

reasonably estimate what risks may be expected. In essence, the French courts tolerate agreements regarding the exclusion of liability in the case of minor negligence (*'faute légère')*, whereas it does not permit the exclusion or limitation of liability for *dol* or *faute lourde* infringements[435]. For example, *Barry* explains that the prohibition on exclusion of liability for *faute lourde* is based on 'the fear that the removal of the risk of liability would encourage negligence or recklessness'[436].

Article 1151 CC provides that in the event of intentional infringements a party shall be liable for direct and immediate damages, with regard to the loss incurred by the obligee and the gain of which he has been deprived, whether or not the damage incurred was foreseeable. In a similar to UCTA, this means that persons cannot agree to limit liability for personal injury. Though there is no such explicit prohibition, liability for personal injury cannot be excluded, as a human body cannot be the subject matter of a contract in France[437]. In this respect, French civil laws show a high degree of similarity to laws in other continental European jurisdictions.

4.2 LIMITATION OF LIABILITY UNDER '*VENDEUR PROFESSIONEL*' CASE LAW

Apart from general statutory provisions, French case law has developed special rules relating to the exclusion of liability for defects in goods sold by commercial vendors (the so-called '*vendeur professionel*' case law). These special rules also apply in cases where a vendor sells goods on the basis of standard form contracts. The French *Cour de Cassation* in its famous ruling of 28 April 1987 established that where a business contract was concluded outside the ambit of the contract counterparty's professional competence it should be treated as a consumer contract[438]. Among other things, the court explained that the contracting party 'was unfamiliar with the highly specialised technology of alarm systems and was therefore as ignorant about the contents of the contract in issue as any other consumer would have been'[439]. For this reason, the party was

---

435 In practice, the concept of *dol* has also embraced *faute lourde* or gross negligence – '*Dol ou faute loured équivalente au do'*. *See:* Zweigert K., Kötz H. *Introduction to Comparative Law.* Trans. by Weird T. 3rd ed. (Oxford: Clarendon Press 1998) 338-9; Sonennberger H.-J., Schweinberger E. *Einführung in das französische Recht* (Darmstadt 1986) 65; Kleinwächer K. 'Möglichkeiten einer Haftungsbeschränkung im französischen Recht' *RIW* (1984) 692

436 Barry N. *The French Law of Contract* 2nd ed. (Oxford: Clarendon Press 1992) 233

437 Ibid., p. 233

438 *See*: Cass. civ. 1re, 28 April 1987, in: Beale H. [*et. al.*] *Casebooks on the Common Law of Europe: Contract* (Oxford: Hart Publishing 2002) 529

439 Beale H. [*et. al.*] *Casebooks on the Common Law of Europe: Contract* (Oxford: Hart Publishing 2002) 529

given protection similar to that established by Law No. 78-23 of 10 January 1978 (*Loi Scrivener*). Indeed, pursuant to Article 35 of the *Loi Scrivener*, any term having as its object the exclusion or limitation of the right of a non-professional or consumer to compensation for breach of any of his obligation is forbidden. Moreover, by virtue of Article 35 of *Loi Scrivener* the French government is empowered to issue a decree that prohibits specified terms in contracts between consumers and professionals. Accordingly, the '*Commission des clauses abusives*' was established to deal with these issues[440]. The *Loi Scrivener* was incorporated into the French Consumer Code in 1993[441]. It is sometimes contended that the principles that apply to the exclusion and limitation of liability should not be confined solely to contracts for sale, but should be interpreted extensively and therefore also be applicable in respect of other types of contracts[442].

However, to interpret a party as being 'a person acting as consumer' merely on the basis that he was not familiar with certain types of transactions seems to be going too far. The other contracting party could have been *de facto* perfectly informed about all risks of business transaction as well as other peculiarities of the deal both parties are involved in. Thus the courts started to consider not the actual acquaintance of the business concerned with the area in question, but rather whether the transaction can be considered intrinsic to the business in which it is involved. The *Cour de Cassation* took a much narrower approach in a case of 24 January 1995. Here, the court decided that the purchaser *Société Héliogravure Jean Didier,* which concluded a contract with dominant French electricity company EDF, was a business user of electric energy. The contract came within the usual sphere of its commercial activity. For this reason, the company would *not* be covered by the protection offered by *Loi Scrivener*[443]. By deciding on the enforceability of exclusion clauses French courts paid attention to whether the vendor and purchaser were professionals in the same sector *(professionels de la mēme spécialité).* It is decided on a case-by-case basis whether such a direct relationship between contracting parties exists. Professionals in the same business are expected to recognise transactional risks for themselves.

Finally, it should be borne in mind that the concept of professionals working in the same sector is construed narrowly in French case law. For instance, a construction company and a producer of construction materials are

440 Ibid., 520

441 Similar Consumer Codes are also enacted in Austria, Belgium, Greece and other countries.

442 *See*: Barry N. *The French Law of Contract,* 2 ed. (Oxford: Clarendon Press 1992) 234

443 Cass. Civ. 1re 24 January 1995 (*Contract for electricity*), cited in: Beale H. [*et. al.*] *Casebooks on the Common Law of Europe: Contract* (Oxford: Hart Publishing 2002) 529

not considered to be working in the same sector[444]. It will be presumed that owing to their different professional activities the enterprises possess different kinds of knowledge, though they are in fact knowledgeable about products or services they acquire. For example, some enterprises may be treated as acting in the same sector if they both manufacture the same product, but work on different stages of the production cycle.

Finally, it should be noted that developments in French law exhibit similarity to the English case *R&B Customs Brokers Co Ltd. v. United Dominions Trust Ltd.* [445], where it was concluded that a company may act as a consumer if a transaction was only incidental to a business activity. However, the implications of this case were not as dramatic as in the French experience, as most of the prohibitions established in UCTA are subject to the requirement of reasonableness.

5. THE LITHUANIAN APPROACH TO THE EXCLUSION OF LIABILITY IN CONTRACTUAL RELATIONS

The LCC stipulates both general prohibitions pertaining to the exclusion of liability and special provisions with regard to unfair standard contract terms. Moreover, as outlined in previous chapters, the LCC contains special rules regarding the striking out of unusual standard contract terms that were not reasonably foreseen by the counterparty (Art. 6.186 LCC).

In common with civil laws in other continental European countries, the possibility of excluding liability is subordinated to mens rea in Lithuania. Pursuant to Article 6.252 LCC, it is absolutely prohibited to exclude or limit liability for intentional or grossly negligent behaviour. Moreover, it is absolutely prohibited to exclude liability for death of personal injury or non-material damage (6.252(1) LCC). Conversely, the exclusion of liability for minor negligence is permitted under the LCC. In this respect, the LCC shows similarity to German and French laws that set out prohibitions applicable to intentional and grossly negligent infringements. Moreover, the LCC functionally replicates section 2(1) of UCTA 1977, which prohibits the exclusion of liability for death or personal injury.

In addition, the LCC provides general legal grounds that entitle a party to exclude liability in cases where a contracting party cannot influence the course of fulfilment of contractual obligations. For example, a contracting party is not liable for damages provided it is caused, among other things, by *force majeure*,

---

444 Hennemann M. *AGB-Kontrolle im UN–Kaufrecht aus deutscher und französischer Sicht.* (Tübingen 2001) 60

445 [1988] 1 All ER 847, 847. *Cf.* Rasbora Ltd. v. J. C. L. Marine [1977] 1 Lloyd's Rep. 645; Bridgen v American Express [2000] IRLR 94

governmental actions, the acts of a third person, an aggrieved party's acts, or damage caused as a result of absolute necessity or in self-defence (Art. 6.253 LCC). However, the obligor is not permitted to exclude liability for the acts of a third party engaged by him, except where statutes provide for rules whereby the third party is to be directly liable to the aggrieved party (6.257 LCC).

Beyond this, the LCC contains special provisions for the exclusion of liability, in particular Article 6.211 LCC (reiterating Article 7.1.6 UNIDROIT Principles), which states that contract terms - that limit or exclude one party's liability for non-performance or that permit one party to render performance substantially different from what the other party reasonably expected - may not be invoked if they are unfair.

It is worth noting that this provision is also included in the UNIDROIT Principles, as the commission working on the drafting of the UNIDROIT Principles considered the notions of intentional and grossly negligent non-performance too vague. It was therefore decided to include a provision that deals directly with unilateral alteration of a performance agreed by the parties[446], but state of mind is completely irrelevant in assessing the unfairness of substantially different contractual performance. As reported, the fact that a party acted intentionally or with gross negligence may be sufficient to conclude that it would be grossly unfair for it to rely on an exclusion clause[447]. On the other hand, the term 'unfair' may suggest that a party taking advantage acted deliberately. The intention of the drafters of Article 7.1.6 of the UNIDROIT Principles should be taken into account when interpreting Article 6.211 LCC.

All in all, the LCC, like German law, makes a distinction between breaches based on intention as well as other factors involving non-performance of core contractual liabilities. In this respect, Articles 6.252 and 6.211 LCC overlap somewhat. As noted above, under § 307(2)(2) BGB, in standard form contracts German law prohibits exclusion of contractual rights and duties inherent and essential to the nature of the contract. Strictly speaking, Lithuanian law is more lenient on this issue. It merely deals with those situations where performance may substantially differ from what was reasonably expected by an aggrieved party. In theory, an agreement should be enforced under Lithuanian law in cases where parties agree on the non-performance of contractual liabilities, provided that the other party would reasonably foresee this.

---

[446] Bonell M. J. *An International Restatement of Contract Law. The Unidroit Principles of International Commercial Contracts.* 3rd ed. (Transnational Publishers Inc. Ardsley, New York USA 2005) 161

[447] Ibid., p. 161-2

6. ASSESSMENT

Despite the different legal terminology and legal reasoning employed, there is a high degree of functional similarity in the regulation of exclusion and limitation clauses in all four jurisdictions observed. The author's analysis of this chapter confirms that there is a broad consensus in Europe that contract terms excluding liability should be construed restrictively. Disputed standard form contracts in business-to-business contracts are ordinarily assessed on a case-by-case basis in the context of good faith or reasonableness. Special emphasis is often given to the enforceability of standard terms that are unusual or not within reasonable contemplation.

From a practical point of view, probably the most important issue for international businesses is to decide which law is more favourable towards the seller and which the purchaser. However, given the complexity of English, German, Lithuanian and French laws, this question cannot be answered unambiguously. UCTA, together with English common law, provides more explicit prohibitions than the German BGB or the LCC for business-to-business transactions. However, in practice English law permits the incorporation of terms limiting or excluding liability where both contracting parties had similar bargaining power. As for assessing the content of exclusion clauses, English law takes a pragmatic approach. Exclusion clauses are not classified according to the way they are formulated, and they may be set aside where the other party considers them unreasonable. The basic principle underlying German and Lithuanian approaches in this respect is the concept of good faith. Generally, German and Lithuanian law require that parties should act in good faith, but should also exercise their bargaining powers fairly. Both countries distinguish between infringements based on the state of mind and other cases where exclusion of liability is not possible due to non-performance. A contracting party cannot avoid liability by deliberately (intentionally or with gross negligence) disregarding contractual obligations. Moreover, in Germany including unfair standard contract terms cannot breach essential contractual rights and obligations. Lithuanian law does not permit parties to exclude liability where performance is substantially different from what the other party reasonably expected.

Another important practical difference between Lithuanian law on the one side, and English and German law on the other, is that German and English courts may decide what exclusion clauses are fair and what not; however, they are not permitted to adjust or otherwise amend contract terms. In Germany, the whole contract will be set aside where unfair contract terms were included. This is quite different from Lithuanian law which, by implementing the international (UNIDROIT) principles in its domestic legislation, took over welfarist ideas from Scandinavian countries. The Lithuanian courts are able to 're-write' contract terms in cases where the clauses render an excessive advantage to one party. Furthermore, the LCC employs many other criteria - reasonableness, honesty, justice, balance of contractual rights and obligations - to assess the validity of contract terms without giving extensive guidance as to the content of these definitions. In this respect, a Lithuanian judge is less constrained when assessing contested standard contract terms than German or even English colleagues. Interestingly, French case law provides for some special rules. A French vendor is generally subject to somewhat stricter liability than his counterparts in Germany or England acting in domestic transactions, unless both French contracting parties are professionals acting in the same sector. Therefore, it is possible that a French wholesaler may exclude particular liabilities, whereas the retailer would not be able to enforce similar exclusions in respect of his consumers.

On balance, all jurisdictions observed in this book have established certain safeguards for the protection of a weaker contracting party from unfair exclusion or limitation clauses. However, once a judge has struck out largely unfair terms, the issue remains as to how the judiciary should deal with the remaining contract terms. Should a judge merely set aside unfair contract terms or should he strike out the entire contract?; or should he simply adjust the contract terms to what is typically considered fair and reasonable? The analysis confirms that before any proposals to harmonise regulations on standard contract terms in business-to-business transactions are drafted, on the question of how far a judge should be permitted to intervene in restoring contractual justice must be answered. It seems that here we encounter once again certain fundamental differences between legal systems.

1. REGULATION OF STANDARD FORM INTERNATIONAL CONTRACTS

1.1 THE QUESTION OF REGULATION OF NATIONAL AND INTERNATIONAL BUSINESS CONTRACTS

In both domestic and international business transactions the same goals are sought after as those that prompted the use of standard form contracts - *e.g.* reduction of business costs, speeding up negotiations between parties - as well as similar implications in the failure of the market to stipulate free contractual relations. A strong company will ordinarily seek to offer the same standard forms to both domestic and foreign partners. Thus, one may surmise that international companies are exposed to the same risks as domestic ones. However, there are some significant differences between domestic and international transactions. Generally, international transactions are less likely to be concluded using standard form contracts. From an economic point of view, it is more expensive to contract at international level. The parties face language, cultural, legal and other barriers when they cross national boundaries. It would probably be reasonable to concede that parties conclude international business contracts only if they can gain substantial advantages compared with similar domestic transactions (*e.g.* as for the price, assortment of goods, quality, *etc.*). It is also possible that some companies only have partners abroad as there is no demand for their goods or services in the domestic market. For example, aviation training centres based in a small country seek clients from larger foreign jurisdictions as there are few pilot trainees in the home jurisdiction. Furthermore, international contracts are ordinarily more sophisticated; they include agreements on jurisdictions, choice of law, arbitration clauses, *etc*[448]. Internationally contracting parties tend to include as many terms in their contracts as possible because unknown default national civil laws may come into play and fill gaps in relations that were not expressly stipulated in an agreement.

[448] For general comments as to standard contract terms in international contracts *see:* Meyer-Sparenberg W. 'Rechtswahlvereinbarungen in Allgemeinen Geschäftsbedingungen' *RIW* (1989) 347; Rühl Ch. *Rechtswahlfreiheit und Rechtswahlklauseln in Allgemeinen Geschäftsbedingungen* (Baden-Baden 1999); Schiller K.V. 'Gerichtsstandsklauseln in AGB zwischen Vollkaufleuten und das AGB-Gesetz' *NJW* (1979) 636 *et seq;* Hübner U. 'Allgemeine Geschäftsbedingungen und Internationales Privatrecht' *NJW* (1980) 2601 *et seq;* Jayme E. 'Allgemeine Geschäftsbedingungen und internationales Privatrecht' 142 *ZHR* (1978) 103 *et seq*

The issue as to what law is to govern an international contract often depends on which party is more vulnerable and would seek to enforce contract provisions. For example, where a supplier is paid after providing services, he would ordinarily seek to enforce a contract within his home jurisdiction so as not to be subject to unknown foreign laws. However, where a customer agrees to make a deposit for the services he will receive, the supplier would probably be less reluctant to agree on a neutral jurisdiction. In practice, much depends on the nature of the arrangement and bargaining power of both parties. Some types of contracts (*e.g.* aircraft lease agreement, aircraft maintenance agreement, other aviation agreements) are generally governed by the laws of England, as there is held to be more case law and more certainty about the customary rights and obligations of parties.

Though this is not the case for all transactions, parties involved in international business are normally more experienced and tend to be more informed about possible business risks pertaining to the transaction. Given this fact, it is often argued that rules aimed at regulating the effectiveness of standard contract terms in international business dealings should be looser in than in similar domestic transactions, so as not to over-burden international trade[449]. Thus intervention is different if one compares domestic and international transactions.

Some calculations would suggest that large companies doing business internationally rely more on long-term business relationships than formal legal norms[450]. Confidence in each other and a good reputation are very important for long-term business partners. They would probably be more interested in retaining good business relations rather than taking advantage of the negligence or trust of a contracting party. Small misunderstandings would more often be settled between partners who traded for longer. On the other hand, it is also true that many large companies enter into contracts only on their standard forms, regardless of whether the other party is a foreign or domestic company. Such standard forms are typically included in contracts of carriage, sale of goods, and international loan contracts. In light of this, it is more difficult to reach a firm conclusion as to whether or not weak parties dealing with international partners should be offered equivalent protection to that available in their domestic markets.

As noted in the first chapters of the book, the idea of regulation of standard form contracts in modern contract law is based not only on the

[449] *Cf.* Wolf M. 'Auslegung und Inhaltskontrolle von AGB im internationalen kaufmännischen Verkehr' 153 *ZHR* (1989) 300 *et seq*; *also*: Horn, in: Wolf / Horn / Lindacher § 24, para 22 *et seq*; Hoffmann von B. 'Über den Schutz des schwächeren bei internationalen Schuldverträgen' 38 *RabelsZ* (1974) 396 *et seq*

[450] These issues will be further discussed in the subsequent chapters.

mitigation of existing substantive and procedural inequality among parties, but also on the general assumption that regulated markets - in particular, markets protected from unfair terms - generate a better outcome for both parties and for society. Though this assumption is probably true at least at the theoretical level, it is not so easy to identify the frontiers of an international market to be protected. The regulation of fairness or fair bargaining in contractual relations has traditionally been a matter of domestic policy. It is difficult to envisage mandatory international rules that may not be opted out of by free agreement. For example, contracting parties may not choose national law, but rather decide to be subject to *lex mercatoria* rules (*e.g. Incoterms*, *ICC Uniform Customs and Practice for Documentary Credits*) provided their dispute is referred for scrutiny to a private adjudicator. In this case, neither party has the advantage of relying on its own national law. However, these international rules cover only specific areas and they are not applicable for all types of contract.

It is possible that extensive regulation can make a jurisdiction less attractive, and that therefore parties may seek to circumvent such rules after taking advice from local counsel where their standard terms could be struck out. Moreover, the *proferens* would also probably seek to include an arbitration clause where material provisions of the contract led to an uncertain legal outcome owing to mandatory rules in the relevant jurisdiction. Hence, it is submitted that over-regulation of international transactions may induce parties to choose the most liberal legal order or even *lex mercatoria* rules. Nevertheless, if we assume that international contracting in the Union internal market should not be considered a purely international transaction, the development of unified regulations across the Union on unfair standard form contracts is not completely out of the question. Ideally, the internal market of the Union should achieve the same level of integration as the domestic markets of Member States. In that event, the same advantages of a regulated market would be enjoyed by all enterprises incorporated in the Union.

In this context, different national approaches to the regulation of standard form contracts are considered next.

1.2 Comparison of National Mandatory Rules on International Contracts

Differences in national regulations on unfair standard form contracts seem to be even more important in international business transactions than domestically, as unless the contracting parties choose the law of a third country or internationally recognised *lex mercatoria* rules, at least one party has to abide by foreign law. As outlined above, the legal systems of our selected Member States do not have exactly the same approach with regard to the regulation of standard form contracts. As a consequence, stringent national mandatory rules on contract law will ordinarily put a vendor at competitive disadvantage in international contracts[451].

It is worth noting that most jurisdictions do not regulate contract law differently for international transactions. In most European jurisdictions, both international and domestic transactions are regulated in a similar way (Germany, France, Lithuania, *etc.*). For example, the general prohibitions established in §§ 305-310 of the German BGB should be applicable to international contracts agreed on standard terms in cases where German law is the governing law of the contract[452]. Lithuanian law of contract does not make any distinction as to whether a contract is concluded between domestic or foreign parties. Taking this into consideration, it seems that French law - provided it governs the international contract in question - seems to be more risky for professional vendors, unless both parties are professionals trading in the same sector. Thus reasonable suppliers would seek to avoid the mandatory effect of French laws where this is possible in a particular situation.

Interestingly, the regulation of international contracts concluded on standard forms is slightly different in England when compared to the selected European counterparts. This contributes to the popularity of English law among foreign enterprises. UCTA 1977 provides a number of prohibitions where a party on the 'receiving end' concludes a contract on the basis of 'written standard terms of business'[453]. However, the act was basically drafted for the purpose of regulating domestic transactions. As a rule, international supply contracts remain outside the scope of application of the act as they have nothing to do with the protection of domestic customers. UCTA is not applicable for transactions involving the passing of possession or ownership, nor for a contract made between parties whose place of business is in the territories of different states. For example, the Channel Islands and the Isle of Man are expressly termed different states (section 26(3) (b)). Section 26(4) of UCTA specifies the terms whereby international supply contracts are excluded from the scope of UCTA. In particular, the act says that 'at the time of conclusion of the contract, the goods should be in the course of carriage or be carried, from one state to another, the contract provides for the goods to be delivered to the territory of a state other than in whose territory the acts offer and acceptance were effected'. English case

[451] Under the Rome I Regulation, in the absence of governing law being chosen, a contract of sale or purchase of movable property will be governed by the law where the seller and not the buyer has its habitual residence or its central administration. For further details see the following chapter.

[452] The original version of § 12 AGBG prescribed that AGBG could be applied if a contract shows close links with the Federal Republic of Germany. § 12 AGBG was amended after the implementation of the Directive 93/13/EEC on Unfair Terms in Consumer Contracts.

[453] *See: e.g.* 3(1) UCTA

law is not extensive on the application of the act with respect to international contracts. For example, in the case *Amiri Authority v. BAE Systems Plc.*[454] a dispute arose about the interpretation of the statutory formula 'from one state to another', as the contract had been concluded in one state. The English judiciary extensively interpreted section 26 of UCTA, by explaining that the act was aimed at excluding all exporters from the protective regime. This approach was also confirmed in *Ocean Chemical Transport and Ocean Ships Inc. v. Exnor Craggs Ltd* case[455]. According to this ruling, transactions cannot be regulated by UCTA, even where the contract is concluded on behalf of the buyers' agents based in the UK[456]. A principal residing in the Delaware state was considered a party in the contract, so qualifying it as an international supply contract excluded from the scope of UCTA. Given the effectiveness of UCTA, the English courts found the actual place of incorporation of the buyer to be decisive. Nonetheless, UCTA contains safeguards where the act could otherwise be circumvented by the parties. English law may govern contractual relations only if it is in some way closely linked to the contractual relations (for example, the seller has his habitual residence in England[457]). Thus, in exceptional cases, the act can be applicable where the parties choose a foreign law for the purposes of evading UCTA (section 27(2) UCTA). On the other hand, a continental judge would be able to recognise the mandatory effect of its national law *ex officio*.

On balance, traditionally liberal and conservative English law has implemented the idea that participants in international business transactions have enough experience to fix their relations as they wish. The English legislator probably assumed that regulation under UCTA might deter foreign enterprises from choosing London as a forum and weaking the role of the English law in comparison with other popular jurisdictions (such as the law of the State New York). Moreover, many international business disputes are referred for arbitration under the London Court of International Arbitration rules. Parties often choose London for arbitration to evade local rules. By way of example, if two Irish and Lithuanian companies enter into an aircraft lease agreement and choose a London commercial court as the forum, this does not prohibit the Lithuanian court from hearing a dispute regarding rights *in rem* in Lithuania. This is because an aircraft is considered immovable property in Lithuania, contrary, for example, to the categorisation of aircraft as a movable asset in England, Estonia and other jurisdictions. In this case, the Lithuanian court would have exclusive jurisdiction to hear the case under Lithuanian civil procedure

---

454 [2003] All ER(D) 306

455 [1999] All ER (D) 1516

456 Alfred R. *Exclusion Clauses and Unfair Contract Terms* 8th ed. (Thomson Sweet & Maxwell 2005) 129

457 *See*: Article 4 of the Rome I Regulation.

laws (Art. 31 of the Lithuanian Civil Procedure Code). If the dispute is heard in London, an English judgement might be found to be unenforceable in Lithuania.

The liberal approach of English law with respect to commercial arrangements also makes the City of London an attractive place for many businesses trying to avoid strict compliance costs and rely more on customary trade practices. Many international contracts are drafted in English and therefore they include many terms that are typical only for common law (*e.g.* tax and general indemnity clauses, conditions precedent). Moreover, parties have wide discretion to agree that some rights are absolute even if the party invoking such rights is in breach of its obligations; finally, it is possible for only one party to be given an alternative to choose between arbitration or ordinarily judicial proceedings, *etc.* It seems that the evident disparity of contractual rights and obligations would be called into question in jurisdictions in continental Europe. Probably for this reason, many large businesses exercising strong bargaining power choose English law as governing law though the transaction has no connection with England[458].

The attitude to excluding international business transactions from the scope of national regulations remains atypical if one compares it with the dominating attitude in other European countries. All enterprises incorporated in the European Union should enjoy the same opportunities to compete both in domestic and other markets of the Member States. One Member State should not take advantage of other countries of the Union by loosening requirements for the control of standard form contracts and thereby rendering a competitive advantage to its domestic exporters. Ideally, contract law throughout the Union should be based on good faith and fair performance of contractual obligations. Ultimately, the legal outcome should be more or less the same whether parties choose English, German or other laws. For example, in German or Lithuanian law there are only slight differences with respect to the regulation of domestic and international contracting, while some trade customs are theoretically applicable only in Germany and Austria[459].

---

458 *Cf.* McKendrick E. 'Harmonisation of European Contract Law: the State we are' in: *The Harmonisation of European Contract Law. Implications for European Private Laws, Business and Legal* Publishing 2006) 20; Furmston M. *Cheshire, Fifoot & Furmston's Law of Contract* (Butterworths Lexis Nexis 2001) 198-9; Beale H. 'The European Civil Code Movement and the European Union's Common Frame of Reference', *Legal Information Management* (2006) 9-10; Yates D., Hawkins A. J. *Standard Business Contracts: Exclusion and Related Devices* (London: Sweet & Maxwell 1986) 15

459 The so-called commercial letter of confirmation (German *das kaufmännische Beschtätigungsschreiben*). As to the relevant legal basis, see*:* § 346 of German HGB. Legal stipulations regarding the commercial letter of confirmation were not included in the Vienna Convention (CISG), and therefore they are not recognised internationally.

2. CHOICE OF LAW IN INTERNATIONAL BUSINESS DEALINGS

2.1 THE FREEDOM OF CHOICE OF LAW IN STANDARD FORM CONTRACTS

Before a judge decides on the enforceability of contracts having foreign elements, he must deal with the issue of whether the forum has jurisdiction to hear a case at all. Only after the question regarding a court's competence is examined, would a judge ordinarily consider the issue of the law that is to govern contractual relations.

Several decades ago, the Members States recognised the necessity of promoting uniformity in solving international disputes. The major stimulus to unifying laws in this area was to prevent parties bringing claims of a civil and commercial nature in the most favourable jurisdiction (so-called *forum shopping*), which distorted the justice system in Europe. In the end, these efforts resulted in the enactment of the Brussels Convention[460].

At the same time, the success of the Brussels Convention inspired contracting parties to take a step further by harmonizing national laws regarding choice of law in contracts. After long negotiations the so-called Rome Convention was signed on 19 June 1980 and entered into force on 1 April 1991[461]. This convention came into force after the United Kingdom joined the European Economic Community, and most Member States managed to reconcile the approaches of common law and continental law. According to the authoritative *Gulliano-Lagarde* Report, the main purposes of preparing the convention were to enhance legal certainty, confidence in the stability of contractual relations, and the protection of rights acquired in the whole field of private law[462]. For example, pursuant to Article 18, the Rome Convention should be interpreted uniformly in order to achieve a unanimous application by all contracting parties. At the same time, the harmonisation of applicable laws has considerably reduced the discretion of the forum, as under certain circumstances

---

460 *See*: EC Convention on Jurisdiction and the Enforcement of Judgments in Civil and Commercial Matters, Brussels 1968. The Brussels I Regulation (officially: Council Regulation (EC) No. 44/2001 on jurisdiction and the recognition and enforcement of judgement in civil and commercial matters) superseded the EC Convention that was applicable before the Brussels I Regulation came into force.

461 The Convention was initially signed by the six original EEC Member States and Ireland. Germany and Denmark implemented the Convention before it came into force. The Accession Conventions were concluded with countries that joined the EEC (EU) later. *See*: OJ 1980 L 266, *for the consolidated version see*: OJ 2005 C334. For example, the Rome Convention was implemented in the UK by Contracts (Applicable Law) Act 1990.

462 *Guliano-Lagarde* Report on the Convention on the Law Applicable to the Contractual Obligation, OJ 1980 C282/32

the court may be obliged to apply foreign material law[463]. However, the Rome Convention created much controversy regarding its effect on Union law, international law and domestic law.

It is important to note that the Commission was successful some time later in addressing the shortcomings of the Rome Convention and implementing its plan to convert the Rome Convention into a Regulation of the European Parliament and Council[464]. On 17 June 2008 Regulation (EC) No. 593/2008 on the Law Applicable to Contractual Obligations (hereinafter – the Rome I Regulation) was adopted[465]. The new draft Regulation was much discussed in the United Kingdom in particular, [466] however, in June 2008 the United Kingdom decided to opt into the Regulation[467]. Now the new rules of conflict of law would apply to contracts concluded after 17 December 2009 throughout the European Union, with the exception of Denmark. It must also be noted that the Rome I Regulation did not harmonise the substantive law of Member States.

The conversion of the Rome Convention and adoption of the Regulation was necessary in order to approximate the wording of the Rome Convention with the Brussels I Regulation and the Rome II Regulation. Apart from this, the new Rome I Regulation has *inter alia* revised the provisions regarding the applicable law in the absence of choice (Art. 4 Rome I Regulation), included new provisions on contracts of carriage and insurance (Art. 5 and 7 Rome I Regulation), revised the rules regarding consumer contracts (Art. 6 Rome I Regulation) as well as newly drafted the concept of overriding mandatory provisions (Art. 9 Rome I Regulation) *etc*. As of 1 December 2009 the Regulation replaced the Rome Convention in Member States except as regards the territories of Member States that fall within the territorial scope of the Rome Convention and to which this Regulation does not apply (Art. 24 Rome I Regulation).

---

463 For some discussion about the effects of the Rome Convention that is sometimes defined as 'the most unnecessary, useless attempts at unification and harmonisation of law' *see, e.g.*, Collins L. (ed.) Dicey, Morris & Collins *The Conflicts of Law* (London: Sweet & Maxwell 2006), Vol. 2. 1543; Hill J. *International Commercial Disputes* 2nd ed. (LLP: London Hong Kong 1998) 425-6; North P. *Essays in Private International Law* (Clarendon Press Oxford 1993) 5-22; North P., Fawcett J.J. *Cheshire and North's Private International Law,* 13th ed. (Butterworths: London, Edinburgh, Dublin 1999) 536-7

464 *See the proposal in:* Commission to the European Communities '*Proposal for a Regulation of the European Parliament and the Council on the law applicable to contractual obligations (Rome I)*' COM (2005) 650 final.

465 [2008] O.J. L177/6

466 Ministry of Justice. Rome I – should the UK opt in? Consultation Paper CP 05/08 published on 2 April 2008

467 In England and Wales and Northern Ireland the Regulation was implemented by the Law Applicable to Contractual Obligations (England and Wales and Nothern Ireland) Regulations 2009

Probably the most important principle entrenched in the Rome Convention, which is – in essence - later reiterated in the Rome I Regulation is freedom of contract (*ex* Art. 3 of the Rome Convention, Art. 3 Rome I Regulation). Private parties are permitted to decide at their own discretion what laws are to govern their contractual relations[468]. Agreements, by which a foreign legal system is chosen, could also be concluded on the basis of standard form contracts[469]. Interestingly, under English law this choice must not necessarily be made in good faith. It is, therefore, sometimes argued that agreements with to the objective of evading laws should not be declared void[470].

The Rome I Regulation does not connect parties' choice of law to a particular country. The choice of law, barring some exceptions, *e.g.* carriage of passenger – Article 5(2), may be made freely even where all relevant elements are related to one jurisdiction[471]. It is, thus, not completely clear if a party may invoke national mandatory regulations that would ordinarily be applicable, but they were circumvented by free choice of the parties. For example, a Lithuanian or French vendor may choose English law to govern contractual relations, because it is more liberal in enforcing international transactions, in particular exclusion or limitation clauses. However, this interpretation would mean that a stronger party may have a chance of exerting its bargaining power in international business dealings by offering a foreign law that has few safeguards with respect to the regulation of unfair terms or that enforces disproportional contractual rights and obligations.

Parties are generally allowed to choose a whole legal system or only a part thereof (Art. 3(1) Rome I Regulation). One could suggest that this provision permits contracting parties to avoid unfavourable national provisions in cases where they have a negative impact on the enforceability of contractual relations.

---

[468] It should be noted that the Rome Convention was not aimed at harmonising non-contractual obligations in the EC. The unification of conflict of law rules regarding obligations arising out of, among other things, unjust enrichment, *culpa in contrahendo*, *negatorum gestio*, etc. was done by adopting Regulation (EC) No 864/2007 of the European Parliament and the Council of 11 July 2007 on the law applicable to non-contractual obligations (Rome II). This Regulation shall, except for some provisions, apply from 11 January 2009 (Art. 32). *As to the implementation in Germany see*: BGBl. I S. 2401

[469] *For relevant English case law see e.g.:* Aim Rasheed Shipping Corporation v. Kuwait Insurance Co [1984] AC 50; James Miller & Partners Ltd. v. Whitworth Street Estates (Manchester) Ltd. [1970] AC 583. *As for the German experience see:* Rühl Ch. *Rechtswahlfreiheit und Rechtswahlklauseln in Allgemeinen Geschäftsbedingungen* (Baden-Baden 1999)

[470] *See also*: Hill J. *International Commercial Disputes* 2nd ed. (LLP: London Hong Kong 1998) 437

[471] Collins L. (ed.) Dicey, Morris & Collins *The Conflicts of Law*, Vol. 2 (London: Sweet & Maxwell 2006) 1563

For example, parties may agree that national mandatory rules with respect to the exclusion of liability would be excluded. There is no unambiguous answer as to whether such practices should be tolerated. Experts who prepared the Rome Convention believed that the severability of a contract should be limited to cases where the contract consisted of several contracts[472]. Other commentators argued that severability should be limited to freedom of contract, which is difficult to foresee. It seems that a reasonable solution is offered by the *Guliano-Lagarde* Report. It was suggested that parties should not be able to avoid mandatory provisions of national law by virtue of the Rome Convention[473]. Indeed, no legal system is completely liberal. Thus, parties are always forced to abide by mandatory regulations of at least one jurisdiction, which is not always desirable to both parties.

In practice, it can sometimes be difficult to decide if a choice of law has been made at all. The parties should at least show their intention to be subject to one particular legal order. Some difficulties may arise in distinguishing cases where an implied choice was made and where there was no choice at all. In cases where an implied choice was made, it must be ascertained whether a particular law was to govern contractual relations or whether parties subjectively wanted it. Sometimes the choice of law may be only inferred from the circumstances[474]. Thus, in such unambiguous cases the law of the country with which the contract is most closely connected should probably govern the contract. Accordingly, the Rome I Regulation emphasises that an implicit choice of law must be demonstrated clearly by the terms of the contract or the circumstances of the case. In such cases, a party would be able to rely on business negotiations the parties conducted before entering into formal contractual arrangements. In general, the Rome I Regulation contributes to the simplification of determining the law applicable to specific contracts where parties have not selected a particular governing law, or if the contract was not listed in the Article 4(1), in the absence of choice of law the governing law would be that of the habitual residence or, in the case of a body corporate or unincorporate, its central administration, of the party required to effect the characteristic performance of the contract (*see*: Art. 4(2)). Finally, the Rome I Regulation provides that despite these two rules, if it is clear from all the circumstances of the case that the contract is manifestly more closely connected with the other country, the law of that other country shall apply (Art. 4 (3) Rome I Regulation).

---

[472] Guliano-Lagarde Report on the Convention on the Law Applicable to the Contractual Obligation, OJ 1980 C282/32, para 4

[473] Ibid., para 4

[474] *See also:* Collins L. (ed.) Dicey, Morris & Collins *The Conflicts of Law*, Vol. 2 (London: Sweet & Maxwell 2006) 1567, 1573

Article 3(1) of the Rome I Regulation permits parties to choose the *law* applicable to the whole or part only of the contract. In light of this, it may be argued whether the choice of law should be confined to the choice of one domestic legal system or the parties may choose internationally developed principles to govern their contractual relations (*e.g.* UNIDROIT Principles or *lex mercatoria*)[475]. Since the Regulation, like the Rome Convention before it, refers to the 'law', it would seem more reasonable to argue that parties should be able to choose only a recognised legal order. Initially, the Commission proposed that the new Rome I Regulation would allow a choice of principles and rules from the substantive law of contract recognized internationally or in the Community[476]. However, these ideas were not implemented in the Rome I Regulation, except for Recital 13 of the Rome I Regulation setting forth that this Regulation does not preclude parties from incorporating by reference into their contract a non-State body of law or an international convention; then these terms would be considered as a part of contract. On the other hand, many countries in Central and Eastern Europe functionally implemented UNIDROIT Principles into their domestic legal systems. At least theoretically, this offers a possibility for parties to choose a legal order that actually restates these internationally acknowledged principles.

It is submitted that even if in theory parties are free to choose a legal order to govern their international contracts; in fact both parties are inherently affected by an information deficit in international trade. In practice, choice of law is often made sporadically as a matter of compromise, considering the general political climate in the jurisdiction in question or the bargaining power of parties, not after comprehensive assessment of the mandatory rules of a foreign jurisdiction. It seems obvious that every unknown legal system has negative side effects. An enterprise that accepts a foreign legal system usually takes more risk, as it will not ordinarily be able to exhaust all remedies guaranteed by foreign law unless a sophisticated local law firm is assigned to assist it[477]. In addition,

---

475 *Negatively*: North P., Fawcett J. J. *Cheshire and North's Private International Law*, 13th ed. (Butterworths: London, Edinburgh, Dublin 1999) 559-60. *See also*: van Bar Ch. *Internationales Privatrecht. Zweiter Band. Besonderer Teil* (München: C.H. Beck'sche Verlagsbuchhandlung 1991) 315

476 *For more see:* COM (2005) 650 final

477 It could, however, be conceded that this is not a sufficient argument for the harmonisation of European law. Improving access to information might possibly solve these problems. Sometimes it is argued that divergent legislation induces not only information costs, but also litigation, instability, drafting costs as well as decreasing the efficiency of the whole market. *See*: Smits J. 'Diversity of Contract Law and the European Internal Market' in: *The Need of a European Contract Law. Empirical and Legal Perspectives* Smits J. *ed.* (Groningen: Europa Law Publishing 2005) 168. Joint response of the Commission on European Contract Law and the Study Group on A European Civil Code Osnabrück 25 October 2001, 6 *et seq*

foreign enterprises incur comparatively more expenses for legal advice and to discover the peculiarities of foreign legal systems. For example, many law firms have different fees for domestic and foreign clients, which makes it more expensive for a foreign company to receive legal advice. Moreover, it is clear that the same company would probably be able to get better legal service in its home jurisdiction, where it deals with similar legal issues on a daily basis. In the author's view, a domestic competitor would, therefore, gain competitive advantage over foreign enterprises that are less familiar with domestic regulations.

2.2 MANDATORY AND OVERRIDING PROVISIONS

The Rome I Regulation accepts that there are certain restrictions[478] on the choice of law. Mandatory rules may derive from different sources – the *lex causae* country, the country of the forum, or even a third country. The Rome I Regulation does not extensively explain what rules the parties cannot contracted out of. For example, Article 3(3) of the Rome I Regulation, states that:

> 'the fact that the parties have chosen a foreign law … shall not, where all the other elements relevant to the situation at the time of the choice are connected with one country only, prejudice the application of rules of the law of that country'.

This restriction on freedom of contract may be justified only in very exceptional cases. Recital 15 of the Regulation sets out that these rules should be applied whether or not the choice of law was accompanied by a choice of court or tribunal. The purpose of Article 3(3) of the Rome I Regulation was to address the evasive choice of law in domestic contracts[479]. The court may decide flexibly under which circumstances the mandatory requirements of the *lex causae* country law should come into application.

Some further exceptions are set out in Article 9 of the Rome I Regulation. The first paragraph deals with the concept of overriding mandatory provisions, while the second one explains the application of mandatory provisions of the forum, and the third permits the application of overriding mandatory provisions of foreign law.

Generally, the scope of application of Article 9(1) is somewhat narrower than that established in Article 3 of the Rome I Regulation. The overriding mandatory provisions in laid down in Article 9(1) are not those that parties cannot derogate from, but those that must be applied whatever the law

478 Consumer and employment contracts will not be observed in detail.

479 Hill J. *International Commercial Disputes* 2nd ed. (LLP: London Hong Kong 1998) 463

applicable to the contract (or overriding rules). The major difference here is that these overriding provisions would be applicable regardless of whether the governing law has been determined by taking into consideration the closest related legal order or where parties explicitly choose the governing law. The issue of whether a national statute may be interpreted as containing a mandatory provision is decided on a case-by-case basis. Recital 37 of the Regulation makes clear that the concept of 'overriding mandatory provisions' should be distinguished from the expression 'provisions which cannot be derogated from by agreement' (*see*: Art. 3(3) Rome I Regulation). Hence, according to Article 9(1) of the Rome I Regulation, overriding mandatory provisions are provisions the respect for which is regarded as crucial by a country for safeguarding its public interests, such that they are applicable to any situation falling within its scope, whether or not the law is otherwise applicable to the contract under this Regulation. In general, the definition introduced should contribute to the uniform interpretation of overriding mandatory provisions in the Union. In some unambiguous cases, the Court of Justice would be able to provide further guidelines.

Article 9 of the Rome I Regulation contains several provisions: Article 9(3) Rome I Regulation establishes the overriding rules of third countries, while Article 9(2) Rome I Regulation sets out the overriding rules of the court. Historically, the notion of overriding rules was first developed in Germany and afterwards accepted by the Dutch Supreme Court in the *Alnati* case, whereby foreign public law, in particular regulations on the import and export, should be observed even outside of its territory[480]. Thus, foreign rules under Article 9(3) Rome I Regulation are applied if the facts of the case suggest a close connection with that third country. Article 9(3) Rome I Regulation sets out that 'effect may be given' to such mandatory overriding provisions, which means that the application of the mandatory provisions of foreign law may be, but need not be, applied.

Initially, some countries, *e.g.* Germany, Luxembourg, Ireland, and the UK, had reservations with respect to the application of 7(1) of the Rome Convention, which prescribed that 'the mandatory rules of the law of another country [may be given effect] with which the situation has a close connection, if and in so far as, under the law of the latter country, those rules must be applied whatever the law applicable to the contract'. This provision was criticised for the uncertain legal outcomes that may arise in different jurisdictions. In this respect, it seems that Article 9(3) of Rome I Regulation should bring more flexibility by stating

---

480 Collins L (ed.) Dicey, Morris & Collins *The Conflicts of Law* Vol. 2 (London: Sweet & Maxwell 2006) 1592-3; Plender R., Wilderspin M. *The European Contracts Convention. The Rome Convention on the Choice of Law for Contracts* (London: Sweet & Maxwell 2001) 184

that the overriding mandatory provisions of the law of the country in question must be given consideration where the obligations arising out of the contract have to be or have been performed, in so far as those overriding mandatory provisions render the performance of the contract unlawful. Originally, the scope of *ex* Article 7 of the Rome Convention (now Article 9 of the Rome I Regulation) should have been extended to protective rules only where there is a public non-discriminatory interest. For example, the Court of Justice considered that Articles 17 and 18 of Directive 86/653/EEC that guarantee certain rights to commercial agents after the termination of agency contracts – *e.g.* indemnity or compensation for the damage they suffer as a result of the termination of relations with the principal - are mandatory in nature and must be applied where the situation is closely connected with the Community, in particular where the commercial agent carries on his activity in the territory of a Member State. Thus, according to the Court of Justice, these rules cannot be evaded by the simple expedient of a choice-of-law clause[481].

Some contractual terms may also be considered unenforceable because of mandatory provisions of the law of the forum chosen, such as where they are not in line with Competition Law in the European Union and they lead to the abuse of monopolistic position, or terms in agreements detrimental to consumer protection or similar abuses[482]. Practically speaking, Article 9(2) Rome I Regulation is probably even more important than Article 9(3) as it establishes the overriding rules of the forum. The effect of such provisions is unrestricted; these provisions would be applicable regardless of the governing law of the contract[483]. Indeed, overriding rules ought to be construed restrictively as they are of a very exceptional nature. It should be noted that Article 9(2) of the Rome I Regulation largely replicates *ex* Article 7(2) of the Rome Convention, except that the Regulation does not require that the provisions of the law of the forum must be crucial to the country for safeguarding its public interests[484].

It is also worthy of note that general requirements to act in accordance with good faith, as established in many civil codes of continental European countries, are considered instruments of private control, and they are not overriding rules in the spirit transposed by the former Rome Convention into domestic law. National regulations pertaining to the exclusion or limitation of contractual liabilities are also not considered mandatory requirements by virtue of Article 9(2) of the Rome I Regulation. For example, Articles 27 to 34 of the

---

481 Ingmar GB Ltd. C-381/98, para 25

482 *Cf.* Guliano-Lagarde Report on the Convention on the Law Applicable to the Contractual Obligation, OJ 1980 C282/32

483 Collins L. (ed.) *Dicey, Morris & Collins The Conflicts of Law* (London: Sweet & Maxwell 2006) 1590

484 Hartley T. *International Commercial Litigation. Text, Cases and Materials on Private International Law* (Cambridge: Cambridge University Press 2009) 608

German EGBGB incorporated the Rome Convention 1980. *Ex* Article 34 EGBGB stipulated that an agreement on the applicable law shall not be affected by application of German laws that cover social-political matters and are necessary to govern the relevant situation at an international level. The Article did not contain any explicit list of laws that should be mandatory. Generally, this issue had to be decided by considering the purpose of the law[485]. However, special regulations on standard form contracts were not considered mandatory rules for business-to-business transactions in the sense of Article 34 of German EGBGB[486]. Articles 27 to 37 of the German EGBGB were repealed as of 17 December 2009 by giving direct effect to the Rome I Regulation in Germany[487].

The concept of mandatory rules is not completely harmonised in Europe, though Article 9(1) of the new Rome I Regulation includes the definition of overriding mandatory provisions. Under English law, in cases where the contract was governed by foreign law, implied terms contained in the Sale of Goods Act 1979 do not apply[488]. However, it is not completely clear if UCTA (together with, for instance, the Employment Rights Act 1996, the Carriage of Goods by Sea Act 1971) should be considered mandatory rules[489]. Some commentators considered UCTA as having a limited overriding effect[490]. If the statute does not expressly identify the circumstance in which it applies, the court has to decide whether or not its provisions are mandatory[491]. UCTA explicitly established rules regarding its application; however, the act basically excludes international supply contracts from its scope of review. In principle, English courts enjoy vast discretion to decide whether laws have an overriding effect, taking into consideration the policy pursued. It must be stressed that according to Recital 37 overriding mandatory provisions should be construed restrictively. Thus, one may surmise that English judges became less tempted to give effect to mandatory overriding rules via UCTA after the Regulation became fully applicable. Finally, in accordance with the Rome I Regulation the choice of

---

485 Kropholler J. *Internationales Privatrecht* (Tübingen: Mohr Siebeck 2004) 490

486 *Cf.* Remien O. *Zwingendes Vertragsrecht und Grundfreiheiten des EG-Vertrages* (Tübingen: Mohr Siebeck 2003) 493; Stoffels M. *AGB-Recht* (Heidelberg 2003), para 232

487 BGBl. I. S. 1574.

488 Clarkson C.M.V., Hill J. *The Conflicts of Law* 3rd *ed.* (Oxford: Oxford University Press 2006) 199

489 Hill J. *International Commercial Disputes* 2nd ed. (LLP: London Hong Kong 1998) 465; North P., Fawcett J. J. *Cheshire and North's Private International Law*, 13th *ed.* (Butterworths: London, Edinburgh, Dublin 1999) 576

490 *See*: North P., Fawcett J. J. *Cheshire and North's Private International Law*, 13th ed. (Butterworths: London, Edinburgh, Dublin 1999) 579-580; Kayer P. *The New Private International Law of Contract of the European Community* (Dartmouth: Aldershot, Brookfied USA, Hong Kong Singapure Sydney 1993) 167

491 Clarkson C.M.V., Hill J. *The Conflicts of Law* 3rd ed. (Oxford: Oxford University Press 2006) 201

parties may be limited not only by mandatory provisions of the forum, but also by public policy. Article 21 of the Rome I Regulation sets out:

> 'The application of a provision of the law of any country specified by this Regulation may be refused only if such application is manifestly incompatible with the public policy (*ordre public*) of the forum'.

From the wording of Article 21, as with Article 16 of the Rome I Convention, it seems that the requirements of public policy are negative. The forum is authorised to eliminate rules that are not in line with the public law of the forum. However, Article 21 of the Regulation includes the word 'manifestly', which means that a concept of public policy as laid down in the Regulation should be construed in a very restrictive way.

The benchmark of public policy is much higher for international transactions. For example, it is sometimes contended that the fundamental English ideas of justice and morality should be breached[492] (*e.g.* an agreement to commit a crime or civil wrong or to perpetrate a fraud[493], agreement tending to inure good government[494], anti-competitive agreements[495], restrictive covenants that are contrary to the English doctrine of restraint of trade[496]) to invoke former similar provisions of the Rome Convention. In many jurisdictions there is a general reluctance to invoke public policy to strike out foreign rulings in order to override the explicit choice of law. By virtue of Article 6 of the German EGBGB, domestic rules should *inter alia* be given priority over foreign laws that govern contractual relations. However, as in English law, Article 6 of the German EGBGB refers only to the most important principles of German law. Thus, the provision of public order may be invoked if applying foreign laws, as entrenched in the German Fundamental Law, pertaining to the general public order, human rights, Union law or the rules of public international law breaches fundamental rights. German laws are sometimes criticized for the reason that they do not offer an exhaustive statutory list of the provisions that may be considered mandatory[497]. The importance of public order can be measured by the following formula: the more closely the contract is connected to the *lex fori* legal system, the less important should the implications for a foreign law system

---

492 *See*: Collier J. G. *Conflict of Laws* 3rd ed. (Cambridge: Cambridge University Press 2001) 216

493 Alexander v. Rayson [1936] 1 K.B. 169, Tinsley v. Millingan [1994] 1 A.C. 340

494 Parkinson v. College of Ambulance Ltd. [1925] 2 K.B. 1

495 Petrofina (Great Britain) Ltd. v. Martin [1966] Ch. 146, 180; Schroeder Music Publishing Co. Ltd. v. Macaulay [1974] 1 W.L.R. 1308

496 Duarte v. Black and Decker Corp [2008] 1 All E.R. (Comm) 41

497 Kropholler J. *Internationales Privatrecht* (Tübingen: Mohr Siebeck 2004) 492

be[498]. Finally, it is possible to foresee that foreign mandatory rules may contradict each other. In such cases, the public policy rules of the forum would overrule the mandatory rules of the other country.

3. ASSESSMENT

Under the Rome I Regulation, which is applicable in most Member States, parties are permitted to decide what national rules of contract law are to govern their contractual relations. However, the Rome I Regulation merely sets out the rules as to which contract law would be applicable, but it does not deal with cases where a weaker party had to accept the legal order offered by a stronger contracting party. Thus, when the Rome I Regulation superseded the Rome Convention at the end of 2009 not many substantial changes were made. A weaker party would still be exposed to unknown legal regulations and incur additional costs relating to the discovery and adaptation of contracts to foreign regulations. In this regard, it seems that the Rome I Regulation, like its predecessor the Rome Convention, does not contribute sufficiently to the simplification and maintenance of fairness in international business transactions. However, this issue relates to the general principles of contract law (*e.g.* the notion of good faith, fair bargaining, *etc.*) that - as explained in previous chapters – are slightly different in the jurisdictions analysed in this book.

Overriding mandatory provisions and the scope of their application to limit the choice of law vary from jurisdiction to jurisdiction. Historically, in most jurisdictions prohibitions on the exclusion or limitation of liability were not ordinarily treated as 'mandatory or overriding rules' in the sense laid down in Article 7 of the Rome Convention and should probably not be treated as 'overriding mandatory provisions' as stipulated in the Rome I Regulation. In general, contracting parties are completely free to decide on all terms they hope to govern their international contractual relations. As a rule, parties based in different jurisdictions choose only one country's law to govern the whole of the contract. For example, in cases where German and Lithuanian traders negotiate with each other, a party can avoid mandatory prohibitions pertaining to the exclusion of liability under German law, but then Lithuanian law will be applicable, or *vice versa*. Consequently, parties would be subject either to mandatory German or Lithuanian laws. It is also true that none of the legal orders of the Union are completely liberal, except insofar as some laws (*e.g.* English laws) provide for a somewhat looser legal regime for international transactions. Thus it is submitted that *Collins* is right when he argues that 'choice of law rules does not offer a solution to the potential deterrent to trade threatened by diversity in the laws applicable to contracts in the Member States

[498] Ibid., p. 244

of the European Community'[499]. It seems unavoidable that even if parties are well informed about the law in a foreign jurisdiction, they may be wrong in not choosing the most appropriate legal system, or else some mandatory provisions of foreign law remain undiscovered. Simply because many businesses mistrust unknown foreign legal systems a favourable legal regime may not be chosen.

As seen in the previous chapters, the mandatory rules of one country (*i.e.* of the forum) are sometimes regarded as being able to override the mandatory rules of a foreign country. In many cases, the forum retains a wide degree of discretion to decide whether there is a connection to their jurisdiction and what national rules are mandatory and therefore should come into play. In light of this, it is submitted that certain efforts aimed at unifying or harmonising rules relating to the regulation of standard form contracts would be desirable.

Can the Union interfere by setting aside discrepancies arising from intra-Union trade? Unfortunately, the answer seems not to be simple. Though many European law systems show a high degree of similarity in how they deal with standard form contracts, at the same time some discrepancies in substantive law regulations can cause considerable uncertainty for foreign enterprises. This seems unacceptable, as the internal market comprises an area without internal frontiers in which the free movement of goods, persons, services and capital is guaranteed. Thus one may hypothesise that different conditions of competition exist in the internal market. Moreover, it is possible to envisage divergent national contract law regulations inducing higher transactional costs and, therefore, these can be considered prohibited measures in Union law.

In the view of the author, in order to identify unjustifiable trade obstacles the effect of this legal uncertainty should be scrutinised first by examining market freedoms and the development of the internal market. After analysing this development, we shall turn to the question of the legitimacy of national regulations on standard form contracts.

---

499 Collins H. 'Good Faith in European Contract Law', 14(2) *O.J.L.S.* (1994) 231

PART 2:

THE INTERACTION OF UNION LAW AND NATIONAL REGULATIONS ON STANDARD CONTRACT TERMS

European Community law 'is like an incoming tide.
It flows into the estuaries and up the rivers. It cannot be held back'
Lord Denning M. R. in:
HP Bulmer v J Bullinger SA [1974] 2 All ER 1226, 1231

1. IMPACT OF THE MARKET FREEDOMS ON INTRA-UNION TRADE

1.1 THE POSITIVE AND NEGATIVE INTEGRATION OF NATIONAL LEGAL SYSTEMS

Article 26(2) TFEU provides that the "internal market shall comprise an area without internal frontiers in which the free movement of goods, persons, services, capital is ensured in accordance with the provisions of the Treaties". Thus the internal market refers to the area where the freedom of goods, services, persons and capital are protected so as to enable free market activity for the European Union's market participants. These market freedoms[500] together with the customs union, were created to underpin the internal market[501].

The TFEU - as recently amended by the Treaty of Lisbon - sets out the major principles of free movement of goods (Art. 28-38 TFEU), free movement of persons (Art. 45-55 TFEU), freedom of services (Art. 56-62 TFEU) and free movement of capital (Art. 63-66 TFEU). It is sometimes asserted that these four market freedoms are supplemented by the free movement of payment which is considered the fifth market freedom (Art. 63(2) TFEU). Generally speaking, the market freedoms define the free flow of economic factors across the Union, and at the same time they form the substantive Union law. They are intended to increase competition and strenghten economies of scale in the internal market. There is some force in the argument that the concept of market freedoms has more historical relevance nowadays[502]. In 1985 the European Council instructed

[500] German law has developed a term *'Grundfreiheiten'* that has no exact equivalent in English and refers to the free movement of economic factors (the so-called 'fundamental freedoms' or 'four freedoms'). The Court of Justice suggested other terms for defining the fundamental freedoms, *e.g.* 'a fundamental Community provision', 'one of the fundamental principles of the Treaty'. *For more see*: CIA Security C-194/94. Pfeil W. *Historische Vorbilder und Entwicklung des Rechtsbegriffs der 'Vier Grundfreiheiten' im Europäischen Gemeinschaftsrecht* (Frankfurt am Main 1998)

[501] *For more about the concepts of the common market and the internal market see*: Mortelmans K. 'The Common Market, the Internal Market and the Single Market, What's in the Market' 35 *C.M.L. Rev.* (1998) 102 *et seq*

[502] For example, quantitative restrictions on exports were abolished as of 31 December of 1969 (*see*: Regulation (EEC) No. 2603/69), and the EEC entered into the 'definitive' stage.

the Commission to adopt measures with the aim of progressively establishing the internal market by 31st December 1992[503]. However, some areas, in particular the field of services, had not yet been fully integrated.

Rapidly growing volumes of case law of the Court of Justice on this issue still cause uncertainty, as the market freedoms are constantly covering new areas. From time to time, the Court of Justice reconsidered the legitimacy of certain national regulations in the internal market. In essence, the market freedoms should be designed in order to guarantee that unjustified barriers do not distort access to foreign markets and that free competition is not distorted[504]. In other words, the market freedoms make it possible for national market participants to act according to the rules of the most liberal jurisdictions in the internal market unless there are justifiable reasons for not enforcing the rules. Thus the market freedoms impose an obligation on the Member States not just to refrain from adopting certain regulations infringing them, but rather to actively implement all necessary measures aimed at ensuring that the market freedoms are respected in their territories[505]. In particular, this means that any rules inhibiting free trade in intra-Union trade may not be enacted and, if already enacted, are to be repealed so as not to infringe the market freedoms by omission. As a consequence of the existence of the market freedoms, in theory goods, services, labour and capital would move to those jurisdictions of the Member States where the costs are the lowest. This should increase the competitiveness of the Union as well as optimally allocate production costs throughout the Union[506]. If some Member States are put at a disadvantage because of the free flow of economic factors, supporting the poorest regions and integrating infrastructure at the European level should ensure the coherent development of all Member States.

---

503 Most of the Commission's proposals set out in the Single White Paper were implemented by the end of 1992 (*see*: Seventh Report from the Commission to the Council and the European Parliament on the Implementation of the Commission's White Paper on completing the internal market COM (92) 383 final, 2 September 1992). However, the Commission has permanently expressed much skepticism regarding full accomplishment of the internal market.

504 *Cf.* AG Fennelly in: Volker Graf C-190/98

505 Commission v. France C-265/95, para 32, Schmidberger v. Austria C-112/00, para 59. This is sometimes defined as anti-protectionist approach. *For more see*: Snell J. *Goods and Services in EC Law. A Study of the Relationship Between the Freedoms* (Oxford: Oxford University Press 2002) 2; Koenig Ch., Haratsch A. *Europarecht* (Tübingen: Mohr Siebeck 2004) para 487. With reference to the *Angonese* case (C-281/98) it may be asserted that the market freedoms may sometimes have a direct horizontal effect on private individuals. However, it is still far from clear if the case law will be consistent on this issue further.

506 Craig P. 'The Evolution of the Single Market', in: *The Law of the Single European Market,* Barnard C. Scott J. *eds*. (Oxford and Portland, Oregon: Hart Publishing 2002) 2

The market freedoms are often linked (though not exclusively) with negative integration[507]. This means that Member States ought to refrain from enacting rules that entail discriminatory provisions or restrictive practices with respect to other Member States[508]. Negative integration suggests that the Union should not actively seek to implement harmonised secondary legislation, but rather implement reasonable means by which Member States do not create unnecessary obstacles to intra-Union trade. It is sometimes contended that is the Court of Justice encourages negative integration by inducing Member States to act pro-actively and agree on 'consensual political measures' or else a so-called 'race to the bottom' may occur by national regulations being repealed[509]. However, since the Court of Justice does not deal with reverse discrimination towards national producers, negative integration may actually work to the competitive advantage of foreign producers from less regulated markets[510].

It must also be noted that the TFEU entitles the Union to act *inter alia* positively in order to achieve the objectives set out in Article 26 TFEU. For example, pursuant to Article 114 TFEU [*ex* 95(1) EC] the Union was authorized to enact 'the measures from the approximation of the provisions laid down by law, regulation, or administrative action in Member States which have as their object the establishment and functioning of the internal market'[511]. In short, harmonisation means that national rules will be replaced by rules that are common in all Member States. This, however, does not suggest that common rules must be identical. Where a directive is enacted, according to Article 288(3) TFEU national authorities are permitted to choose the form and method by

---

[507] The terms 'negative' and 'positive' integration have been originally used by Jan Tinberger. *See*: Tinberger J. *International Economic Integration* (Elsevier Amsterdam 1965) 77-9

[508] *See e.g.* Van de Haar C-177 & 178/82, paras 11-2. However, the prohibition on state aid does not relate directly to the market freedoms, cf. Article 107 TFEU.

[509] Davies G. *EU Internal Market Law* (Cavendish Publishing Limited London Sydney Portland Oregon 2003) 154. The 'race to the bottom' induces businesses to migrate to the least regulated legal systems. However, there is a general lack of empirical evidence as to whether a fall in quality of production or services really occurs due to a lack of public regulation. These debates are very popular in the US, where is largely discussed about the efficiency of the American federalism. This is relevant for Europe as well, as, for example, owing to the competing systems, there was a flight of capital to Luxembourg because of weaker reporting duties in that jurisdiction. For more discussion on these issues: Smits J. *The Making of European Private Law. Towards ius Commune Europeum as a a mixed legal system* (Intersentia 2002) 63

[510] In Lithuanian practice, it was sometimes argued that foreign suppliers of low-budget air itinerary services received more gratuitous benefits from the municipalities several years ago, whereby an incentive to establish and render their low fare services has been secured. The national air itinerary companies were not entitled to these benefits.

[511] *See also:* Article 18 Single European Act of 1 July 1987

which the result is to be achieved. As early as 1985, the Commission announced a new approach regarding harmonisation, whereby it called for retrenchment away from detailed rules. The European legislator was encouraged thereby to indicate merely the essential principles in regulations aimed at approximating laws in the Community[512]. Accordingly, Member States would implement these abstract rules in national legislation of their own accord - the regulations of other Member States would be mutually recognized. Secondary legislation aimed at harmonisation of the laws of Member States and the market freedoms, as a means of negative integration, would be applied concurrently.

In short, the effect of the market freedoms means that Member States now lack authority to enact certain rules that would not be compatible with the market freedoms, while positive integration requires Member States to take some steps towards completing the internal market. Both negative and positive integration in the Union should be reconciled in order to ensure the proper functioning of the single market. However, there is a broad consensus in academic circles that the concept of an 'area without internal borders' does not imply the over-whelming elimination of all differences, but rather the creation in the Union of an economic area without internal borders. The creation of the single market did not result in the creation of a single legal system or complete unification of all legal orders. Rather, the harmonisation of national legal systems should merely moderate, but not completely eliminate legal difference between Member States.

1.2 Structural Convergence of the Market Freedoms

Generally speaking, the market freedoms are concerned essentially only with those regulations that have an effect on cross-border intra-Union transactions[513]. They are not applicable when measuring activities that are exercised within one country of the Union only[514]. Economic factors protected by Union law may not be purely domestic, but should be in some way related to Union commerce. Hence, Union law would not apply if non-exported goods were treated less

[512] *For more see:* Completing the Internal Market. White Paper from the Commission to the European Council, COM (85) 310, 14 June 1985

[513] It is noteworthy that the market freedoms also protect the cross-border movement of workers, providing services in the other Member States, as well as cross-border movement of capital.

[514] See *e.g.* Waterkeyn C-314-316/81 & 83/82, para 12; Oosthoek C-286/81, para 13; Driancourt C-355/85, para 10, *etc.* However, the Court of Justice had sometimes difficulties to distinguish domestic and foreign wares - *e.g.* in cases where foreign integrients were used to produce domestic products. *See*: Angonese C-281/98, *cf.* Ritter C. 'Purely Internal Situations, Reverse Discrimination, Guiomnt, Dzodzi and Article 234' 31 *E.L.R.* (2006) 1617 *et seq*

favourably than imported goods from other Member States. The market freedoms do not attempt to equalise legal regulation for all goods, but rather to guarantee unrestricted access to goods in the markets of other Member States.

It must also be noted that the prohibition on restricting the import and export of goods legally circulating throughout the Union encompasses not only overt, but also disguised discrimination. For example, market participants can be overtly discriminated against on the basis of their nationality or country of incorporation, but Member States tend to avoid such discrimination unless there is sound justification. Disguised forms of discrimination can be employed deliberately or recklessly by a Member State, though only some criteria are tackled that are typical for companies from other Member States. In practice, addressing disguised discrimination is of greatest importance, as governments seldom decide blatantly to breach their commitments as set out in TFEU and discriminate against goods and services from other Member States. There is an argument that discrimination can be also established in those cases where rules are applied indistinctly; however, these rules do not take effect indiscriminately (*so-called* other restrictions), or rules that ban trade in respect of goods that would not otherwise be produced in the market of the country of destination. In fact, disguised discrimination leads to the same results as overt discrimination, except that this discrimination cannot be derived directly from the wording of legal acts but rather from tangible effects.

Historically, the most significant freedom was the pioneer freedom of free movement of goods. TFEU - like the EC Treaty - stipulates that the free movement of goods should be developed through the following processes:

(a) Customs union (Art. 30-32 TFEU);
(b) Prohibiting all quantitative restrictions on exports, and all measures having equivalent effect between Member States (Art. 34-37 TFEU);
(c) Elimination of the discrimination by any state monopolies of a commercial character so as to ensure that no discrimination regarding the conditions under which goods are procured and marketed exists between nationals of Member States (Art. 37(1) TFEU).

Over recent decades, the customs union and free movement of goods have had a major effect on the liberalisation of intra-Union trade. It must be noted that only Union goods are eligible for protection pursuant to Article 28(2) TFEU. Such goods should either originate in one of the Member States or come from third countries, but be admitted for free circulation in Member States. In fact, such goods should be either produced in one Member State or a significant part of processing should take place there[515].

[515] For more see, *e.g.*, Brother International C-26/88, paras 19-24

For a long time all four market freedoms were considered in isolation[516]. This attitude was based on the assumption that different market freedoms can be breached by different means, and TFEU provides different lists of justifications for these breaches (cf. Art. 36 and Art. 45(3) TFEU). A major change came after the *Säger* ruling in 1991, whereby the Court of Justice arrived at the conclusion that the commercial activities of a foreign supplier of services may restricted under Article 56 TFEU [*ex* 49 EC] provided the restrictions indistinctly affect domestic and foreign suppliers lawfully providing similar services[517]. Moreover, as the Court of Justice concluded in the *Kraus* ruling, the same principles were relevant with regard to the free movement of workers as well as with regard to the right of establishment:

> 'Article 45 and 49 TFEU [*ex* 39 and 43 EC] preclude any national measure governing the conditions under which an academic title obtained in another Member State may be used, where that measure, even though it is applicable without discrimination on grounds of nationality, is liable to hamper or to render less attractive the exercise by Community nationals, including those of the Member State which enacted the measure, of fundamental freedoms guaranteed by the Treaty. The situation would be different only if such a measure pursued a legitimate objective compatible with the Treaty and was justified by pressing reasons of public interest. It would however also be necessary in such a case for application of the national rules in question to be appropriate for ensuring attainment of the objective they pursue and not to go beyond what is necessary for that purpose'[518].

Thus, in many cases the effect of the market freedoms is inter-related and the restriction of several market freedoms may be observed concurrently. The Court of Justice has confirmed that in relation to different market freedoms there should not only be a prohibition against discrimination, but also as a much broader prohibition on imposing other measures to restrict the cross-border movement of economic factors (the approach of restriction prohibition)[519].

---

[516] Riesenhuber K. *System und Prinzipien des Europäischen Vertragsrechts* (Berlin: de Gruyter 2003) 29. *Cf.* Behrens P. 'Die Konvergenz der wirtschaftlichen Freiheiten im Europäischen Gemeinschaftsrecht' *EuR* (1992) 145 *et seq*

[517] Säger C-76/90, para 12

[518] Kraus C-19/92, para 32

[519] See: Gebhard C-55/94, para 37, *see also*: Alpine Investments C-384/93 paras 35-38; Bosman C-415/93, para 103; Säger C-76/90, paras 12, 15. *For more about the restrictions of the free movement of workers see*: Steindorff E. 'Anmerkung zur EuGH Rechtsprechung' *JZ* (1994) 96; Mülbert O. P. 'Privatrecht, die EG-Grundfreiheiten und der Binnenmarkt' 159 *ZHR* (1986) 28

Though the basic elements of the doctrine of market freedoms was first formulated by assessing the effects of Article 34 TFEU (the free movement of goods), they were later functionally transferred to the other market freedoms, *i.e.* the free movement of persons (Art. 45-55 TFEU) and services (Art. 56-62 TFEU) as well as the free movement of capital (Art. 63(1), 64 TFEU). Thus, all market freedoms can be assessed structurally using the uniform test, in particular by:

(a) assessing whether the contested measure falls into the scope of protection of the market freedoms,

(b) whether the measure could constitute a prohibited restriction (*e.g.* whether Member States set out different rules that impose additional burden and differs from those enacted in the country of origin, whether the measure in fact or in law restricts the access to the market, *etc.*), and

(c) if a prohibited measure can be justified.

In essence, this is an abstract imperfect framework for dealing with the prohibited restrictions. Nevertheless, these developments suggest that the Court of Justice is steadily moving towards a uniform approach, which is to produce more legal clarity with respect to the interpretation of infringements of the TFEU. On the other hand, the uniform approach should also consider fundamental differences among different economic factors. It would probably be right to contend that the case law of the Court of Justice on the interpretation of the market freedoms is not fully consistent. As a matter of fact, the Court of Justice has employed different reasoning in ascertaining the prohibited measures; at the same time, however, the list of possible justifications for interventions in cross-border transactions has also been expanded. It seems that *Oliver* and *Roth* rightly conclude that the convergence of market freedoms cannot be considered absolute, whereas unwarranted divergences should be avoided between purely economic transactions and the movement of human beings[520].

After considering the case law of the Court of Justice, it appears that the freedoms of free movement of persons and services are slightly overtaking the freedom of free movement of goods, which is assessed very loosely – this is basically because of the concept of mandatory requirements was developed by the *Cassis* case - and therefore a higher degree of discretion is still left to national governments[521]. For these reasons, in respect of violations of Article 56

[520] Oliver P., Roth W.-H. 'The Internal Market and the Four Freedoms' 41 *C.M.L. Rev.* (2004) 440-1; Hatzopoulos V. 'Recent Developments of the Case Law of the Court in the Field of Services' 37 *C.M.L. Rev* (2000) 47; however, *contra*: Snell J. *Goods and Services in EC Law. A Study of the Relationship Between the Freedoms* (Oxford: Oxford University Press 2002) 16 *et seq*

[521] *Cf.* Säger C-76/90; Schindler C-275/92 *versus* Keck C-267/91 and C-268/91

TFEU (it ordinarily suffices to show that the measure makes it more difficult to render some services) traders are urged to bring claims under the free movement of services rules, even where these actions concern goods[522]. Finally, it should be noted that breaches of several market freedoms concurrently can be in issue. In the *Schindler* case the Court of Justice explained that it would examine only one market freedom, even though on the facts of the case one of them was entirely secondary in relation to the other and could be considered together with it[523]. However, much depends on the particular circumstances of the case, as in the *Gourmet* ruling where the provisions of TFEU regarding the market freedoms of goods and services were examined simultaneously[524].

2. DIFFICULTIES IN ASSESSING THE NATURE OF A RESTRICTION: 'BEFORE AND AFTER KECK'

2.1 GENERAL

The enactment of the customs union is closely linked with the prohibition on establishing restrictions on imports and exports. As noted above, Article 34 TFEU establishes that quantitative restrictions on imports and all measures having equivalent effect (hereafter – 'MEEs') shall be prohibited between Member States. Explicit discriminatory restrictions constitute the basic type of restriction and are thereby an infringement of TFEU. As already mentioned, direct quantitative restrictions - quotas and bans - are rarely applied in intra-Union trade, as it is easy to identify their existence and they are justified only in the very exceptional cases listed in Article 36 TFEU.

In practice, the prohibition of all MEEs is much more important than the quantitative restrictions on imports and exports. Generally speaking, these measures are applicable both to domestic and foreign products, but they in fact impose a larger burden on imported goods. An importer could be subject to the so-called 'dual burden', which ordinarily puts him at competitive disadvantage. Beginning in the 1970s there was a directive issued that listed a number of examples of MEEs. The prohibited 'measures' under Article 34 TFEU [*ex* 28 EC] can be laws, regulations and administrative practices as well as similar instruments issued by public authorities, including restrictive practices which do

---

[522] *See e.g.* Schindler C-275/92, para 24. *See also*: Hatzopoulos V., Do T. U. 'The Case Law of the Court concerning the Free Provision of Services: 2000-2005' 43 *C.M.L. Rev.* (2006) 956 *et seq*

[523] *Cf.* Schindler C-275/92, para 22

[524] *See*: Gourmet C-405/98, paras 13-43

not have a binding effect, recommendations, and individual decisions[525]. The content of MEEs has since been detailed in the extensive case law of the Court of Justice. In essence, case law makes it clear that the interaction of national and Union interests shall not be static, but rather subject to dynamic development. Article 34 TFEU should not be considered as a pure prohibition on discrimination. Rather, the extensive case law of the Court of Justice on this matter considered it an overwhelming prohibition on imposing any kind of limitation on goods from foreign Member States[526].

The case law of the Court of Justice is not entirely consistent in many respects. The new developments are not unwelcome; it is clear that the judiciary should address the new disguised forms of unpermitted restrictions. However, not every kind of discrimination inhibits free intra-Union trade. The Court of Justice has rarely given rulings deemed to be overruled by subsequent case law, and which rulings must be still referred to. Despite some controversial cases, it now is settled law that three milestone rulings - *Dassonville*, *Cassis de Dijon* und *Keck* – together with the subsequent case law brought more clarity to the issue of what kind of measures should not be tolerated in Union law. These developments are considered further below.

2.2 The early Case Law of the Court of Justice: 'Dassonville'

An extensive outline of restrictions on imports was defined in the so-called *Dasonville* ruling in 1973. It was established that the Belgian traders Gustave and Benoit Dassonville imported 'Scotch Whiskey' to Belgium without possessing a certificate of origin from British customs authorities, thereby infringing Belgian rules, which was punishable in Belgium. However, the *Tribunal de premiere* applied to the Court of Justice for a preliminary ruling. The question asked was whether national provisions prohibiting the import of goods bearing a designation of origin, where such goods are not accompanied by an official document issued by the government of the exporting country certifying their right to such designation, constitutes a measure having an effect equivalent to a quantitative restriction. In this case, the Court of Justice adopted a very wide interpretation of Article 34 TFEU by questioning the legitimacy of the Belgian legislation that required attaching a label of origin for importers from other Member States:

525 *See:* Directive 70/50/EEC [1970] OJ L13/29. *See also*: Ciola C-224/97, para 32; Commission v. Ireland C-249/81, para 28. *For some general comments see*: Burrows F. *Free Movement in European Community Law* (Clarendon Press Oxford 1987) 39-40

526 Some restrictions (*e.g.* selling arrangments) should, however, be considered. *See*: Jarass D. H. 'A Unified Approach to the Fundamental Freedoms' in: *The Law of the Single European Market*, Barnard C. Scott J. *eds*. (Oxford and Portland, Oregon: Hart Publishing 2002) 147

> 'All trading rules enacted by Member States which are capable of hindering, directly or indirectly, actually or potentially, intra-Community trade are to be considered as measures having an effect equivalent to quantitative restrictions'[527].

Thus, as early as 1973 the Court of Justice in the *Dassonville* case recognised that not all indistinctly applicable measures have indistinct effect. Article 34 TFEU may also be invoked to tackle those rules that do not explicitly discriminate against foreign suppliers. It suffices that measures having indirect or potential effect restrict intra-Union trade. On the basis of this interpretation, even those measures that potentially influence intra-Union trade can be assessed as being measures having equivalent effect and prohibited in the sense of Article 34 TFEU[528]. The actual effect of the restriction must not necessarily be proved. Finally, the restriction should not be of a legal nature[529]. The *Prantl* ruling, whereby the issue was raised whether the contested measure should lead to perceptible restrictions of inter-Union trade, later extended the *Dassonville* rule. The Court of Justice held to be irrelevant the issue of whether quantitative restrictions as well as measures of equivalent effect should lead to perceptible limitations on intra-Union trade[530].

A relatively wide '*Dassonvile formula'* led to the conclusion that in essence every regulation may be subject to scrutiny under the market freedoms, provided they are capable of adversely affecting import volumes or otherwise adversely affecting intra-Union trade. With reference to the *Dassonville* ruling, it could even be argued that any differences in national legislation can at least have a potential effect on imports. Similar arguments were used in the *Rau* case, where the Court of Justice was dealing with the requirement that margarine should be packed in cube-shaped containers. Though the Court of Justice consistently avoided being involved in detailed economic analysis[531], arguments as to costs were used to qualify the equivalent measures that are prohibited under TFEU [*ex* the EC Treaty]. The Court of Justice in this case outlined that:

---

527 Dassonville C-8/74, para 5. *For some early case law see e.g.:* Consten and Grundig C-56&58/64; Geddo C-2/73; van Haaster C-190/73. *For the newer case law*: Commission *v.* Italy C-420/01, para 24, etc. *See also:* Connor T. 'Accentuating the Positive: the "Selling Arrangement" the First Decade and Beyond' 54 *I.C.L.Q* (2005)

528 In some cases the potential effect is recognised as sufficient to find an infringement of TFEU. *See e.g.* Commission v. France C-184/96, paras 17-18

529 *Cf.* Brigola A. *Das System der EG–Grundfreiheiten: vom Diskriminierungsverbot zum spezifischen Beschränkungsverbot* (Verlag V. H. Beck: München 2004) 8

530 Prantl C-16/83, para 20. *Compare also*: Conforama C-312/89; Criminal Proceedings v. Marchandise C-332/89

531 For example, the Court of Justice referred to the potential obstacles to trade in the '*Buy Irish*' case. *See:* Commission v. Ireland C-249/81

'nevertheless it is such nature as to render the marketing of those products more difficult or *more expensive* either by barring them from certain channels of distribution or owing to the additional costs brought about the necessity to package the products in question....'[532]

Though no explicit references were given, the Court of Justice later deviated from its position in the *Dassonville* case. In some decisions, the Court of Justice declined to consider these restrictions as prohibited measures in the sense laid down in Article 34 TFEU, in essence because the measures in question were too unclear and therefore led only to indirect restrictions[533]. For example, in the *Council of the City of Stoke-on-Trent and Norwich City Council v. B & Q* case the Court of Justice explained that the application of Article 34 TFEU [*ex* 28 EC] depended on whether a measure can indirectly, directly or plainly hypothetically restrict intra-Union trade[534]. Moreover, in the *Yves-Rocher* ruling, the Court of Justice agreed that rules leading solely to uncertain possibilities of indirect restrictions in cross-border transactions do not fall within the meaning of the restrictive measures prohibited under TFEU. Thus, a hypothetical restricting effect on intra-Union trade remains relatively irrelevant[535].

Somewhat similar reasoning was restated in *Krantz, Graf* and the *CMC Motor Vehicles* rulings, whereby rules that lead only to the indirect possibility of restrictions to intra-Union trade are not restrictions under Article 34 TFEU [*ex* 28 EC][536]. For example, in the *CMC Motor Vehicles* case, the Court of Justice analysed whether obligations deriving from so-called '*culpa-in-contrahendo'* relations[537] under German law were compatible with the prohibitions of Article 34 TFEU. It was held that a pre-contractual duty to inform customers that authorised dealers would refuse to provide services for goods delivered to the country by way of parallel import, though under guarantee, would definitely influence trade volumes. It seems likely that many customers would not choose a product if they knew they had limited rights under guarantee to get their vehicles repaired. Surprisingly, the Court of Justice explained that the restricting effect deriving from obligations to notify the other contracting party were, equally, not aimed at regulating trade and, furthermore, that they were too uncertain and indirect to restrict trade between Member States[538]. It seems that in this case the Court of Justice weighed the importance of fairness of contractual relations against the importance of unfettered intra-Union trade. One

---

532 Rau C-261/81, para 13
533 Krantz C-69/88, para 11; CMC Motor Vehicles C-93/92, para 12
534 B&Q C-169/91, para 15
535 *Cf.* Yves Rocher C-126/91, para 21
536 Krantz C-69/88, para 11; Volker Graf C-190/98, para 25
537 In common law countries such cases may be considered within the tort of fraud.
538 CMC Motor Vehicles C-93/92, para 12; BASF C-44/98, para 16

may argue that a pre-contractual duty to disclose all facts relevant to a transaction is reasonable as it prevents inattentive customers from being confused. On the other hand, this ruling creates uncertainty as to what further national regulations might be considered too remote to hinder inter-state trade.

It would seem that every legal difference between the country of origin and country of destination brings with it additional costs, *e.g.* additional costs for legal advice - at least for one party. This is especially relevant for enterprises that do not trade with foreign partners on a regular basis. Thus, *prima facie*, every legal difference acts as a deterrent, and may therefore constitute a restriction on intra-Union trade. Somewhat stricter national provisions would always require a certain degree of adaptation for exporters in foreign markets. However, it is doubtful whether the fact that a foreign supplier of goods must adapt itself to the rules of the country of delivery is sufficient argument in concluding that such strict national regulations constitute a restriction of intra-Union trade in the sense of the TFEU.

It is submitted that intra-Union trade - like any other international trade - is inherently affected not only by different legal regulations but also by cultural differences, ordinarily by language barriers linked to misunderstandings and resulting in cross-border delivery delays, disputes, *etc*. Looking at the case law of the Court of Justice, it is not completely clear how to distinguish such pure non-discriminatory differences in laws from cases where different rules can still potentially interfere with the market freedoms. Indeed, what are the criteria for making this distinction? It seems reasonable that prohibitions set out in Article 34 TFEU should be measured *inter alia* in the light of a cost-benefit analysis. The increased costs for international transactions can be compared with the operational costs in the domestic jurisdiction in order to assess the restrictive actual effect of the national measure in question. Unfortunately, the Court of Justice has almost never gone into detailed economic calculations when deciding on the legitimacy of national measures in the sense of Article 34 TFEU.

Finally, it is worth noting that the Court of Justice has never fully required the integration of the internal market by abolishing all divergent national regulations. The principle of country of origin has already been mentioned in relation to the *Dassonville* case[539], and its meaning was further developed in the later *REWE Zentral v. Bundesmonopolverwaltung für Branntwein* (also known as '*Cassis de Dijon*') case. The implications of this case will be observed further.

539 '...the requirement by a member state of a certificate of authenticity which is less easily obtainable by importers of an authentic product which has been obtainable by importers of an authentic product which *has been put into free circulation in a regular manner in another member state* than by importers of the same products coming directly from the country of origin constitutes a measure of having an effect equivalent to a quantitative restriction as prohibited by the Treaty', *see:* Dassonville C-8/74, para 9

2.3 CHANGE OF DIRECTION: THE RATIO OF THE *CASSIS DE DIJON* CASE

Another milestone decision was the '*Cassis de Dijon'* case, handed down in 1979. In the case of '*Cassis de Dijon'*, the Hessian Finance Court applied to the Court of Justice for a preliminary ruling, as the plaintiff applied for an authorisation to import liquor. The administration was informed that the liquor had insufficient alcohol strength and therefore did not have the characteristics required in order to be marketed within the Federal Republic of Germany. Liquor not exceeding 20% proof was permitted to be traded in other jurisdictions of the Union without any restrictions, while German law required that fruit liquors have a minimum alcohol content of 25%. The importer Rewe Zentral AG argued at against the refused import permit. The German court handling the case enquired with the Court of Justice whether or not indistinctly applicable German rules could be considered an MEE in the sense laid down in Article 34 TFEU. The Court of Justice arrived at the conclusion that:

> 'There is therefore not valid reason why, provided that they have been lawfully produced and marketed in one of the member states, alcoholic beverages should not be introduced into any other member State; the sale of such products may not be subject to a legal prohibition on the marketing of beverages with an alcohol content lower than the limit set by the national rules'[540].

Probably the most important innovation in this ruling was the introduction of the principle of country of origin. Indeed, in some cases, the principle of equal treatment of national and foreign goods may be insufficient and put foreign suppliers at a disadvantage. The major idea was to encourage the country of destination to abolish all trade barriers so that a foreign supplier would get access to the market, provided that the supplier abided by the regulations of his country of origin. Ultimately, a foreign supplier should not be forced to change any physical qualities of production in order to comply with the requirements of the country of destination and enter the markets of other jurisdictions of the Union. Goods that were produced or legally introduced into one Member State were to be guaranteed free circulation in the whole internal market unless a government was able to invoke an acceptable justification. The origin of production is established under different criteria, essentially taking into consideration whether production took place, fully or in part, in a Member State[541]. It is irrelevant for the implementation of the principle of origin whether

[540] Rewe-Zentral 'Cassis de Dijon' C-120/78, para 14. *See also:* Criminal Proceedings v. Fietje C-27/80, paras 10, 15

[541] *See more*: Brother International C-26/88, paras 20-25

a domestic supplier would be put at a disadvantage in cases where the regulations of the country of origin are more lenient. Given the different treatment of domestic and foreign suppliers, it may be concluded that the principle of country of origin is aimed at protecting intra-Union trade rather than interests of private parties.

The implementation of the principle of country of origin may also have negative consequences. Theoretically, the country of origin may establish 'zero regulation' on certain goods, which would lead to a decline in the quality of the goods circulating in the internal market – generally known as the 'race to the bottom'. It seems that the country of destination should have the authority to tackle such cases and at least regulate the marketing of the imported goods. Finally, it should be borne in mind that the *Cassis de Dijon* case was basically dealing with the restrictive effect of import regulations. The Court of Justice constantly refused to transfer the *Cassis de Dijon* test on export restrictions Article 35 TFEU [*ex* 29 EC][542]. In fact, domestic suppliers may also be disadvantaged *vis-a-vis* foreign enterprises by strict national rules. On the other hand, most countries tend not to impede, but rather to stimulate exports, which is completely different from establishing barriers for imported goods. These arguments underlie the different construction of Articles 34 and 35 TFEU.

The *Cassis de Dijon* ruling should not be read as establishing the total equalisation of all Member State regulations. Another important achievement of the *Cassis de Dijon* ruling was the development of the concept of mandatory requirements of general interest. These requirements are sometimes also called imperative requirements, the rule of reason[543] or overriding requirements justifying a restriction on free movement of goods[544]. In the *Cassis de Dijon* case, the German authorities sought to justify the application of a prohibition regarding minimum alcohol content on the ground of public health, the protection of consumers against fraud as well as the suppression of unfair competition, which seems to be reasonable and fair. In fact, the Court of Justice did not follow its earlier *Dassonville* case law this time, explaining that:

> '... in absence of common rules[545], obstacles to movement within the community resulting from disparities between the national laws relating to the marketing of a product must be accepted in so far as those provisions

---

[542] *See, e.g.*, Groenveld C-15/79; Alpine Investments C-384/93; Komikalieinspektion C-473/98; Kingdom of Spain v. Council of the European Communities C-9/89; Criminal Proceedings v. Grilli C-12/02, *etc*

[543] Commission v. Germany C-178/84, para 30; Boscher C-239/90, para 17

[544] Familiapress C- 368/95, para 18

[545] It must be noted that the rule of mutual recognition should be applied not only in the absence of common rules, but also in cases where these common rules establish minimum standards.

may be recognized as being necessary in order to satisfy mandatory requirements...'[546].

Article 36 TFEU [*ex* 30 EC] set out a number of justifications with respect to prohibitions or restrictions that are not in line with Article 34 and 35 TFEU (*e.g.* public morality, public policy or public security, the protection of health and life of humans, animals and plants, *etc.*). Pursuant to Article 36 TFEU, the contested measures can be saved provided they do not have the same effect on foreign and domestic goods. Thus, the mandatory requirements from '*Cassis de Dijon*' are *quasi* in the second group of justifications, along with those listed in Article 36 TFEU[547]. National regulations should be first scrutinised using Article 36 TFEU and only afterwards, if still needed, using the *Cassis de Dijon* case law. It is clear that the derogations stipulated in Article 36 TFEU should be construed restrictively, as they permit different treatment as between domestic and foreign trade[548]. Conversely, the mandatory requirements of general interest justify indistinctly applicable rules that impede both domestic and foreign goods. The list of mandatory requirements of general interest as enumerated in the *Cassis* ruling was merely exemplary[549] and included:

(a) the effectiveness of fiscal supervision;
(b) the protection of public health;
(c) the fairness of commercial transaction;
(d) and defence of the consumer[550].

---

546 Rewe-Zentral 'Cassis de Dijon' C-120/78, para 8. *For the later case law see e.g.* Commission v. Spain C-358/01. It should be noted that the necessity of such rules should be checked for whether they are proportional in respect of the aim pursued. *See:* Rau C-261/81, para 12

547 Interestingly, *Oliver* advocated the view that 'mandatory requirements' constitute additions to the list of justifications set out in Article 36 TFEU [*ex* 30 EC]. Following this line of reasoning, mandatory requirements are subject to the same test as the grounds of Article 36 TFEU [*ex* 30 EC]. *See*: Oliver P. *Free Movement of Goods in the European Community under Articles 28 to 30 of the EC Treaty* (London: Sweet and Maxwell 2003) 217; Oliver P., Enchelmaier S. 'Free Movement of Goods: Recent Developments in the Case Law' 44 *C.M.L. Rev.* (2007) 690-1. It should be noted that fundamental rights could also be employed as an exception to the market freedoms, along with the mandatory requirements. This can be inferred from the case law of the Court of Justice as the market freedoms cannot be invoked to justify infringements of the human rights (for the relevant case law see *e.g.* Schmidberger v. Austria C-112/00, para 68). However, these issues will not be examined in this book in detail.

548 van Duyn C-41/74, para 19

549 De Kikvorsch C-94/82; 3 Glocken C-407/85

550 Rewe-Zentral 'Cassis de Dijon' C-120/78, para 8

The Court of Justice also later named *inter alia* protection of working conditions and maintenance of press diversity as supplementary mandatory requirements[551]. The protection of public health and consumer protection remained the most common grounds invoked to justify the restrictions[552]. For example, national measures that are aimed at protecting the fairness of commercial transactions would be justified only as mandatory requirements (provided they are applied without distinction to both domestic and imported products), but not as a derogation established under Article 36 TFEU. From a functional point of view, this innovation means that the Court of Justice has extended a list of the permitted justifications[553].

On balance, *Cassis de Dijon* has re-defined the scope of Article 34 TFEU. The introduction of the principle of country of origin does not aim to set international trade free from every foreign rule that may constitute an obstacle to intra-Union trade. The *Cassis de Dijon* rule makes it clear that not only the direct channelling of imports, but also all other indistinctly applicable measures that directly or indirectly, actually or potentially, restrict intra-Union trade are prohibited provided they *inter alia* cannot be saved by mandatory requirements of general interest.

2.4 The Case of *Keck and Mithouard*: did the Court of Justice get it right?

Though the *Cassis de Dijon* case offered additional justifications in the form of the mandatory requirements of general interest, the '*Dassonvile formula*' still seemed to define the legal boundaries of Article 36 TFEU too widely. They were, therefore, teleologically confined by the prominent *Keck* ruling[554].

The efforts of the Court of Justice to limit the scope of Article 36 TFEU could have been discerned in other cases before the famous *Keck* ruling was handed down[555]. For example, in the *Torfän Borough Council* case the Court of Justice explained that the prohibition whereby single traders were banned from opening their businesses on Sundays was not aimed at restricting intra-Union trade between Member States[556]. The Court of Justice was *inter alia* dealing with domestic legislation on the working hours of bakeries (German *Gesetz über*

---

551 *See*: Oebel C-155/80, para 12, Familiapress C-368/95, para 18

552 Commission v. Germany C-178/84, *but compare with*: De Kikvorsch C-94/82; Clinique C-315/92

553 *See also*: Becker U. 'Voraussetzungen und Grenzen der Dienstleistungsfreiheit' *NJW* (1996) 180; Jarass H. D. 'Elemente einer Dogmatik der Grundfreiheiten' *EuR* (1995) 224

554 Koenig Ch., Haratsch A. *Europarecht* (Tübingen: Mohr Siebeck 2004), para 557. *See also:* Keck C-267/91 and C-268/9, para 16

555 *See*: *e.g.* Oebel C-155/80; Blesgen C-75/81; Quietlynn and Richards C-23/89

556 Torfän Borough Council C-145/88, para 13; B&Q C-169/91, para 14

die Arbeitszeit in Bäckereien und Konditoreien) in the *Öbel* case. These provisions, in respect of night work in bakeries as well as the export and import of fresh baker's wares, were analysed as to whether they could be considered to be measures having equivalent effect to quantitative restrictions on imports and exports[557]. The rules that prohibited night work in bakeries were deemed to be a part of economic and social policy and apply by virtue of objective criteria to all undertakings in a particular industry[558]. According to the Court of Justice, regulations prohibiting a delivery of bakery products to consumers and retailers did not have the effect of restricting exports among Member States, subject to the exception that delivery to consumers and retailers is restricted to the same extent to all producers[559].

In the *Blesgen* case, the Court of Justice concluded that national regulations prohibiting the sale of drinks of over 22 % proof were in line with Article 34 TFEU, as it was unconnected to importing products and would not affect trade between Member States[560]. In this case the Court of Justice did not refer to specific agreements, except to mention that the rules in question were not capable of restricting intra-Union trade[561]. The Court of Justice believed that these measures did not influence in any way the importing of the products and did not, as such, impede intra-Union trade.

The fundamental point from the *Keck* ruling was to differentiate between product requirements and selling arrangements by deciding on the competence of the country of destination. Interestingly, the Court of Justice did not explicitly refer to earlier rulings that were actually overruled by the *Keck* decision. The facts of the case were straightforward: traders Keck and Mithouard breached French laws on selling alcoholic beverages and coffee. In particular, goods were resold at a loss (*vente à perte*), which was prohibited under French law. Even though the situation did not involve any other Member States, *Keck* and *Mithouard* argued in their defence that indistinctly applicable prohibitions with respect to the sale of goods at a loss can deter foreign enterprises, and therefore this prohibition was not in line with the free movement of goods and distorted competition within the Community. The Court of Justice scrutinised their arguments and concluded:

> 'in the absence of harmonisation of legislation, national rules cannot be regarded as the breach of Article 34 TFEU [*ex* 28 EC] as long as those provisions apply to all relevant trade operating within national territory

---

557 *See*: Oebel C-155/80, para 11
558 Oebel C-155/80, para 16
559 Ibid., para 20
560 Blesgen C-75/81, para 9
561 Ibid., para 11. *Cf*: Quietlynn and Richards C-23/89, para 11-12

and affect in the same manner, in law and in fact, the *marketing* of domestic products and of those from the other Member States'[562].

National competences defining minimum prices of goods were considered compatible with TFEU even though they reduced the volumes of intra-Union trade. The French rules whereby goods were not permitted to be sold at a lower price than that paid, were defined as selling arrangements. According to the Court of Justice, so-called non-discriminatory selling arrangements should not impede free inter-Union trade, and therefore national authorities were permitted to regulate them[563]. On the other hand, the true purpose of 'selling arrangements' should not be a disguised regulation of trade in goods between the Member States[564].

Despite the clear theoretical background to this ruling, the 'selling arrangements' – sometimes defined as 'a living organism' in the case law of the Court of Justice - were not defined clearly enough by the Court of Justice, which caused uproar in academic circles and in subsequent case law on this issue[565]. For example, *Barnard* and *Deakin* argued that 'certain non-discriminatory selling arrangements, such as a total ban on the sale of a particular product such as cigarettes, pornography, alcohol or illegal drugs, can be viewed as preventing access to the market'[566]. It must be agreed that a clear distinction between selling

[562] *See:* Keck C-267/91 and C-268/9, para 16; TK-Heimdienst C-254/98, para 23; Deutscher Apothekerverband C-322/01, para 68. *Compare:* Moore S. 'Quantitative Restrictions and Measures having Equivalent Effect Re-vising the Limits of Article 30 EEC' 19(2) *E.L. Rev.* (1994) 195; Arndt H.-W. 'Warenverkehrfreiheit innerhalb der Europäischen Union: der Fall „Keck" – EuGH' *JuS* (1994) 472 *et seq*

[563] Keck C-267/91 and C-268/9, para 16

[564] *See also*: Keck C-267/91 and C-268/9, para 12

[565] *See also*: AG in: Leckerc-Siplec C-412/93; Arnull A., Dashwood A. (*et. al.*) *Wyatt and Dashwood's European Union Law* (London: Sweet & Maxwell 2006) 591-3; Craig P., de Burca G. *EU Law: Text Cases and Materials*, 3rd ed. (Oxford: Oxford University Press 2003) 653-658; Barnard C. 'Fitting the Remaining Pieces into the Goods and Persons Jigsaw' 26(1) *E.L.Rev.* (2001) 35; Pullen M. 'The Use of Articles 30 and 52 to Attack Barriers to Market Access: an Overview of the Court's Case Law' 17(7) *E.C.L. Rev.* (1996) 388; Weatherill S. 'After Keck: some Thoughts on how to clarify the Clarification' 33(5) *C.M.L. Rev.* (1996) 885; Woods L. *Free Movement of Goods and Services within the European Community* (Ashgate: Ashgate Publishing Limited 2004) 64-6; Oliver P., Roth W.-H. 'The Internal Market and the Four Freedoms' 41 *C.M.L. Rev.* (2004) 413; Keßler J. Das System der Warenverkehrfreiheit im Gemeinschaftsrecht. Zwischen Produktbezug und Verkaufsmodalitäten (Berlin: Nomos Verlagsgesellschaft 1997) 78 *et seq*

[566] Barnard C., Deakin S. 'Market Access and Regulatory Competition', in: *The Law of the Single European Market*, Barnard C., Scott J. *eds*. (Oxford and Portland, Oregon: Hart Publishing 2002) 210

arrangements and product arrangements cannot easily be drawn in all cases[567]. Marketing can also involve some 'elements of products'. In this regard, the adjudicator should on a case-by-case basis decide what elements are predominant. In light of this, it is sometimes argued that the *Keck* ruling created even more legal uncertainty than before[568]. On the other hand, the Court of Justice tried hard to establish a clear and consistent distinction between product requirements and selling arrangements in its later case law[569].

For example, the Court of Justice has, through cases over time considered the following as selling arrangements: national rules that involved regulation of the working hours as well as prohibition of work on Sundays, public holidays or other opening hours regulations[570], rules concerning the monopoly of sale of tobacco[571], prohibitions on advertising outside pharmacies[572], prohibitions on advertising on TV[573]. In general, one may list several groups of rules that should be considered selling arrangements: (i) rules of pricing, (ii) advertisement rules, (iii) restrictions relating to the working hours of business, and (iv) rules on channelling[574]. According to the so-called 'Keck formula' requirements relating to designation, packing, form, size, composition, presentation, labelling, and weight should be regarded as product requirements[575]. The country of destination is not permitted to restrict the imports of goods that have already been legally introduced into one Member State on the basis of the product requirements.

It seems that the Court of Justice tends toward expanding the category of product arrangements in some areas - so as to enhance the free flow of intra-Union trade, - where different interpretations are possible. For example, in the *Mars* case, according to German law the flash on the sweet wrappers exceeded

---

567 *See also:* Oliver P. 'Some further Reflections on the Scope of Articles 28-30, (*ex* 30-36)' 36(4) *C.M.L. Rev.* (1999); Fezer K.-H. 'Europäisierung des Wettbewerbsrechts. Gemeinschaftsrechtliche Grenzen im Recht des unlauteren Wettbewerbs – Kommentar zur jüngsten Entwicklung der Rechtsprechung des EuGH zum Warenverkehrrecht (Rechtssachen 'Yves Rocher', 'Keck und Mithouard' und 'Hünermund')' *JZ* (1994) 323; Reich N. 'Anmerkung zu EuGH' *ZIP* (1993) 1817

568 See, *e.g.*, Steindorff E. 'Unvollkommener Binnenmarkt' *ZHR* (1994) 158. About the criticism in the English literature *see e.g.* Craig P., de Burca G. *EU Law. Text, Cases and Materials*, 3rd ed. (Oxford: Oxford University Press 2003) 653

569 *See:* Punto Casa SpA C-69-258/93; Boermans C-401 and C-402/92; Criminal Proceedings v. Banchero C-387/93; Commission v. Greece C-391/92

570 *See*: Boermans C-401 and C-402/922; Semeraro C-418/93

571 *See*: Criminal Proceedings v. Banchero C-387/93

572 *See*: Hünermund C-292/92

573 Leclerc-Siplec C-412/93

574 *For the commentary see: e.g.* Oliver P., Enchelmaier S. 'Free Movement of Goods: Recent Developments in the Case Law' 44 *C.M.L. Rev.* (2007) 673

575 Keck C-267/91 and C-268/9, para 15

10% of the surface area. Thus, the importer had to change the packaging of the product and incurred additional costs on packing and advertising[576]. The Court of Justice explained that a reasonably circumspect consumer[577] would not be confused (in fact, he should be able to distinguish the actual size and effects of marketing that related to an increase in a product's quantity) in cases where companies do not abide by German packaging rules. Rules on advertisement and marketing that are indistinctly applicable were acknowledged as being able to infringe Article 34 TFEU [*ex* 28 EC], since it compels the importer to adjust the presentation of products to domestic requirements and therefore the importer will incur additional packaging and advertising costs[578]. On the other hand, the Court of Justice has persistently been unwilling to engage in an extensive economic review of the costs of complying with foreign regulations.

2.6 The Later Case Law of the Court of Justice: *De Facto* Discrimination and Substantive Market Access

Despite a great willingness to adhere to the *Keck* dichotomy, the recent case law of the Court of Justice witnesses a much wider interpretation of the market freedoms. Indeed, the Court of Justice has to a certain extent deviated from the formalistic approach established in the *Keck* case law by scrutinising selling arrangements that could under certain circumstances have an effect as prohibited trade barriers between Member States[579]. In the recent time the Court of Justice adopted a number of rulings on indirectly discriminatory rules that hinder trade.

For example, in the *De Agostini* ruling the Court of Justice established that it suffices if the measure discriminates in fact, *i.e.* an unequal burden in law and fact, while Swedish rules prohibited some forms of advertisement for children under twelve years old being broadcasted by satellite from the UK[580]. The national courts had to examine whether the rules were in fact discriminatory as the company was restrained from using certain marketing practices. Similar reasoning regarding actual discrimination that constitutes a prohibited barrier to free movement of economic factors was also restated in other cases[581].

---

[576] Mars C-470/93, para 13, *cf.* Heimdienst C-254/98, para 21 *et seq*

[577] See: Clinique C-315/92, paras 21-22

[578] Mars C-470/93, para 13; for certain deviations from the *Keck* case law as well as court's reasoning on the 'additional costs' *see e.g.* Heimdienst C-254/98

[579] For some new alternative approaches regarding interpretation of the scope of Article 28 EC *see*: AG Geelhoed in Douwe Egberts C-239/02 and AG Poiares Maduro in Alfa Vita C-158,159/04. Both opinions tend to advocate a broader interpretation of 'product requirements' in order to avoid any unjustified less favourable treatment of foreign production.

[580] De Agostini C-34/95-36/95, para 41 *et seq*

[581] *See*: *e.g.* Criminal Proceedings v. Harry Franzén C-189/95, paras 69-71; Parfums Christian

In another interesting example, the *Deutscher Apothekerverband* case, the establishment of a Dutch 'virtual pharmacy' was barred in Germany, though this prohibition was indistinctly applicable with respect to German pharmacies as well. This measure was regarded as factual discrimination against foreign enterprises wishing to gain direct access to the German market[582]. It seems that in this case the Court of Justice actually departed from its prominent '*Keck* test', whereby the restrictions on advertising would constitute selling arrangements[583], and therefore they would ordinarily have been held outside the scope of Article 34 TFEU. Here, the Court of Justice decided not just to follow the formal division of production and selling arrangements, but rather to examine measures that can actually burden foreign producers more severely than domestic ones, which distorts competition in the internal market. In this respect, *Craig* and *de Burca* argue that even if a rule is categorised as being about selling, it is still within Article 34 TFEU if the rules have a differential impact, in law and fact, for domestic traders and importers[584].

Thus, it would seem that the concept of selling arrangements is no longer relevant where the actual discrimination is noticeable. However, if so-called 'factual discrimination' is interpreted broadly, the scope of free movement of goods may be extended substantially also, as almost any national measure may actually burden a foreign supplier more heavily. Furthermore, some post-*Keck* developments imply that the Court of Justice tends to analyse non-discriminatory measures - either in law or in fact - provided they impede access to the market from other Member States[585]. Following the prominent opinion of the AG Jacobs in the *Leclerc–Siplec*, the guiding principle of the internal market should entitle all enterprises to have unimpeded access to foreign markets:

> 'A test of discrimination … seems inappropriate. The central concern of the Treaty provisions on the free movement of goods is to prevent unjustified obstacles to trade between Member States'[586].

Dior SA C-337/95, paras 52-54

[582] Deutscher Apothekerverband C-322/01, paras 74-75

[583] This was confirmed in Hünermund C-292/92, para 22; Leclerc-Siplec C-412/93, para 22

[584] Craig P., de Burca G. *EU Law. Text, Cases and Materials*, 3rd *ed.* (Oxford: Oxford University Press 2003) 650-1

[585] *See:* A-Punkt Schmuckhandels GmbH C-441/04. About the difference between partial and total prohibitions in the sense of the TFEU *see*: De Agostini C-34/95-36/95; Leclerc-Siplec C-412/93; Karner C-71/02; Gourmet C-405/98. *Cf.* Oliver P. *Free Movement of Goods in the European Community under Articles 28 to 30 of the EC Treaty* (London: Sweet & Maxwell 2003) 122-33; Oliver P., Roth W.-H. 'The Internal Market and the Four Freedoms' 41 *C.M.L. Rev.* (2004) 415; Weatherill S. 'After Keck: Some Thoughts on how to clarify the Clarification' 33(5) *C.M.L. Rev.* (1996) 885, 896-7 *etc.*; Barnard C. 'Fitting the Remaining Pieces into the Goods and Persons Jigsaw?' 26 *E.L. Rev.* (2001) 35 *et seq*

[586] Leclerc-Siplec C-412/93. *Compare:* AG Lenz in: Commission v. Greece C-391/92

AG Jacobs offered to apply a new test, whereby a non-discriminatory measure could be evaluated as a restrictive measure within the meaning of the EC Treaty provided it exerted a substantive restriction on the market. The issue, of whether traditional selling arrangements can substantially affect market access, depends on various criteria, *e.g.* the nature of restriction, *etc.* In short, *AG Jacobs* argued that the '*Keck* formula' in relation to selling arrangements was inappropriate, as enterprises exercising legitimate economic activity should have unhindered access to the market unless there are legitimate reasons for denying full access. Subsequently, the regulatory powers of Member States would be more reduced with respect to non-discriminatory selling arrangements. Nevertheless, it is difficult to state firmly to what extent the Court of Justice has agreed to follow this approach in respect of the free movement of goods and services.

In the *Gourmet International* ruling, the Court of Justice said that a non-discriminatory ban on advertisement of alcohol on radio and television could be more liable to impede access to the market of products from other Member States than domestic products, as it impedes access to domestic products with which consumers are instantly more familiar[587]. Furthermore, in the *Alpine Investment* case, the Court of Justice confirmed that a disputed measure on cold calling was non-discriminatory, but it 'directly affects access to the market in services in the other Member States[588]'. Finally, the *Schindler* case made clear that the prohibition on foreign companies to hold international lotteries was by nature non-discriminatory, though companies were denied access to the market[589]. All these rulings imply that suppliers or providers from other Member States should have the equal opportunity to compete with the domestic companies of the country of destination in the internal market.

On balance, the Court of Justice is gradually moving towards a new approach, where national authorities have reduced rights to defend national regulations that substantially hinder access to the market. However, the Court of Justice may also decide to follow its previous case law by explaining that certain regulations are 'too indirect and uncertain' to distort intra-Union trade. The application of the test of substantive access to the market may sometimes be

[587] In Gourmet C-405/98 (para 39) it was stated: '*even if the prohibition ... is non-discriminatory ... has a particular effect on the cross-border supply of advertising space, given the international nature of advertising market in the category of products to which the production relates, and thereby constitutes a restriction on the freedom to provide services within the meaning of Article 59*'. For a general comment *see e.g.* Straetmans G. 'Case C-405/98 Konsumentombudsmannen (KO) v. Gourmet International Products AB (GIP) Judgement of the Court (Sixth Chamber) of 8 March 2001' 39 *C.M.L. Rev.* (2002) 1407 *et seq*

[588] *Compare:* Pro Sieben Media C-6/98; Konsumentombudsmannen (KO) Gourmet International Products AB (GIP) C-405/98

[589] Schindler C-275/92, para 45

cumbersome since it is difficult to measure without extensive economic calculations. Finally, the Court of Justice has ordinarily refused to apply a *de minimis* rule when assessing breaches of TFEU[590]. The lack of consistency in the Court of Justice's judicature makes predicting the court's decisions difficult in ambiguous situations. It would go well beyond the scope of this study to present predictions as to the further case law of the Court of Justice[591]. On the other hand, it is also difficult to identify concrete factual disadvantages resulting from national private laws in cross-border trade that substantially reduces access to the market. In practice, this may be inferred by assessing circumstances on a case-by-case basis, and that is why it is difficult to conclude that precise national private law rules clearly breach the provisions of TFEU.

3. CONCLUSION

With the creation of the internal market, all market participants should be able to conduct business without impediment across the Union. TFEU, as well as its predecessor the EC Treaty, explicitly prohibited quantitative restrictions on imports and exports as well as all measures having equivalent effect in intra-Union trade. Having experienced decades of attempts to achieve closer economic integration, legal boundaries to the free movement of goods were set out following the famous *Dassonville, Cassis de Dijon,* and *Keck* rulings. In short, there is now a consensus in the European Union that in the absence of harmonised national regulations, Member States are permitted to decide on how goods should be sold in their jurisdictions. This means that negative integration via the market freedoms has not led to the full approximation of legal systems in the Member States. Furthermore, the case law of the Court of Justice would suggest that the court has consistently followed the principle of mutual recognition. The implementation of the principle of mutual recognition ought to enhance regulatory competition among Member States. However, at the same time, employing the concept of mandatory requirements can safeguard the legitimate essential interests of Member States and their inhabitants.

The case law on the application of Article 34 TFEU has developed differently throughout the last decades. Unfortunately, the Court of Justice has adopted different approaches in assessing breaches of TFEU, which are sometimes difficult to reconcile. It would probably be right to argue that the

---

590 This would mean that even slight prohibited distortions of trade may amount to the breach of TFEU. *See:* van de Haar C-177 & 178/82; Bluhme C-67/97. *Cf.* AG *Jacobs'* position in: Leclerc–Siplec C-412/93. According to the Commission Regulation No. 1998/2006 of 15 December 2006 '*de minimis* rule' is, however, applied in the European Union competition law.

591 About some proposals to modify the 'Keck formula' *see e.g.* Craig P., de Burca G. *EU Law: Text Cases and Materials*, 3rd ed. (Oxford: Oxford University Press 2003) 658

Court of Justice has almost never referred to cases that were explicitly overruled. Article 34 TFEU is considered not only as an outright prohibition on discrimination, but rather as a prohibition on imposing any kind of restriction that makes access to the markets of other Member States less attractive. Much uncertainty may also emanate from the so-called 'post-Keck' case law. Non-discriminatory selling arrangements are not treated as being completely immune from scrutiny nowadays, where they act as an impediment to market access or actually discriminate against foreign manufacturers. Nonetheless, one may also argue that these developments are somewhat more relevant to the free movement of services, which means that prohibitions affecting free movement of goods will be assessed more leniently than the other market freedoms.

Finally, it should not be forgotten that pure differences in legal regulation were not a sufficient basis for finding a breach of TFEU. In 1995 in the *Reisebüro Broede* case the Court of Justice explained that the fact that one Member State imposes more rigid rules than another Member State does not mean that the latter's regulations are *per se* disproportional and therefore incompatible with Union law[592]. Conversely, the existence of different jurisdictions may contribute to the promotion of competition in promoting the best regulation. It is also true that uncontrolled competition between different regulators is not necessarily a positive thing - it may result in inducing the producing of cheaper, but poorer quality goods. Given the phenomenon of the so-called 'race to the bottom', it is submitted that it is unfair if a supplier from one Member State gains a competitive advantage in the international market simply because his jurisdiction is more lightly regulated. Such special restrictive regulations may sometimes be necessary to protect a weaker contracting party and guarantee fair business arrangements.

[592] Reisebüro Broede C-3/95, para 42, *see also:* Mac Quen C-108/96, para 33; Wouters and Others C-309/99, para 108; Deutsche Paracelsus Schulen C-294/00, para 46

II. The Legitimacy of Regulations on Standard Form Contracts in Union Law

1. REMOVAL OF TRADE DISTORTIONS IN INTRA-UNION BUSINESS TRANSACTIONS

1.1 Law of Contract and the Freedoms

As outlined in Part I, regulations on standard form contracts are handled differently in different European laws. Some terms excluding contractual liability are prohibited absolutely, while similar terms in other jurisdictions are assessed in the context of reasonableness, good faith or similar criteria. In general, the basic approach on how to tackle unfair trade practices does not diverge significantly between the countries observed here; a contracting party should act honestly and not deceive the other party.

However, it may occur that the abstract criteria of proportionality or reasonableness gain a different meaning or different weight in different jurisdictions. For instance, it is possible that in some situations an English judge would consider the different bargaining power of contracting parties - or the process of contracting - through an assessment of unfair trade practices, whereas a Lithuanian or German judge would prioritise substantial fairness or review the terms the parties agreed. It must also be noted that some of the selected jurisdictions have established extensive regulations on what is presumed to be fair and what is not (*e.g.* Germany), while many other countries (*e.g.* Lithuania, France) rely more on general statutory regulations. In the author's view, less favourable provisions of national law - especially if they cannot be contracted out of - may hinder parties from accepting the most liberal legal order and thereby limiting free trade.

Assuming that an information deficit is an inherent feature of international business dealings, it would probably be reasonable to contend that a national regulator should not enact rules that restrict access to the internal market, no matter whether these rules could have been opted into or opted out of by private parties. Some commentators take a more radical approach, arguing that companies may be reluctant to enter into export business where there is a chance that terms included in their standard forms may be found unenforceable because of foreign mandatory laws[593]. For example, strict national regulations on the

[593] *For more discussion on these issues see e.g.:* Collins H. 'Good Faith in European Contract Law' 14(2) *O.J.L.S.* (1994) 230; Wolf M. 'Harmonisation of Protection against unfair Contract Terms in Private European Law', in: *European Legal Traditions and Israel*, Rabello A.M., ed. (Jerusalem: The Harry and Michael Sacher Institute for Legislative Research and Comparative Law 1994) 379 *et seq.*

exclusion clauses may discourage exporters from supplying products from other Union jurisdictions.

Thus, if we assume that divergent national regulations on standard form contracts can influence the behaviour of market participants and thereby influence intra-Union trade, the legitimacy of these rules should be assessed in the light of the market freedoms as well[594]. Following the *Dassonville* case law, MEEs should be prohibited even though they create only indirect or potential trade barriers. If they were prohibited, a vendor whose national laws did not permit the exclusion or limitation of contractual liabilities would at least theoretically be exposed to higher production and distribution costs than similar vendors from other Union jurisdictions whose national laws were more lenient, except where another neutral legal order governing the contractual relations was chosen. National regulations that are more stringent on the enforceability of standard form contracts may appear less attractive at first sight, and therefore can preliminarily be regarded as inhibiting access to a foreign market. For example, *Hesselink* submits that certain rules of contract law can indeed be said to be rules that 'lay down requirements to be met by ... goods. ... An example of this is rules on non-conformity or hidden defects in sales'[595]. Given the broad concept of product requirements, strict national rules of private law may be scrutinised under the '*Keck formula*'.

Generally speaking, European private law is based on the principle of party autonomy and the freedom of contract. Self-regulation of private relations is of paramount importance for the market freedoms as well. In essence, the market freedoms guarantee not only unhindered cross-border movement of goods, services, workers and capital across the Union, but also private autonomy for parties entering into commercial arrangements. Supply of goods, provision of services, and transfer of capital would not be possible if market participants were excessively burdened by foreign regulations and were therefore barred from entering foreign markets. Seen from this perspective, the regulation of national private law should probably be subservient to the market freedoms, rather than vice versa.

The potential conflict between private laws and Union law may occur if a foreign seller is not able to enter foreign markets due to the strict requirements of the country of destination. In the absence of the possibility of choosing a law to govern contractual relations, Article 4 of the Rome I Regulation would

---

594 It should be noted that the market freedoms ordinarily cover public measures, but not the conduct of undertakings (*for some relevant case law* see *e.g.* Vereinung van Vlaamse Reisbureaus (VVR) C-311/85, para 30). However, according to *Angonese*, some discriminatory acts of private persons may also fall under the scope of the free movement of persons and free movement of services (*see:* Angonese C-281/98, paras 37-46).

595 Hesselink M. 'Non-Mandatory Rules in European Contract Law' 1/2005 *ERCL* (2005) 74

usually be invoked in most Union jurisdictions. Ultimately, the law of the country where the seller has its habitual residence would come into play (*see*: Art. 4(1)(a)). The applicable governing law would be ascertained similarly in distribution and franchise agreements, and contracts for provision of services. In some international commercial arrangements, a contract under certain circumstances can also be governed by the Vienna Convention (CISG), unless the parties agree to contract out of the application of the Convention. However, it must also be noted that countries are normally interested in expanding export so would rarely deliberately discriminate against their own exporters. Furthermore, a strict interpretation of Article 35 TFEU would also suggest that indistinctly applicable rules of contract law in the exporting country would not contravene the market freedoms, as they do not provide any particular advantage for national production at the expense of the trade from other Member States[596]. Finally, many areas - mostly related to consumer protection, environmental protection and the regulation of labour markets - of private law have already been harmonised in the internal market on the basis of directives[597]. Preventive harmonisation has already moderated the many differences among different legal systems and thereby facilitated intra-Union trade.

Legal doctrine has so far done little to address the interrelation of Union law and national contract law[598]. In academic circles the view has often been

596 For so-called 'Groenveld formula' see C-15/79, para 7

597 *See e.g.* Directives 85/577/EEC on protection of consumers with respect of contracts negotiated away from business premises, 86/653/EEC on the coordination of the laws of the Member States relating to self-employed commercial agents, 90/314/EEC on package travel, package holidays and package tours, 93/13/EEC on unfair terms in consumer contracts, 94/47/EC on the protection of purchasers in respect of certain aspects of contracts relating to the purchase of the right to use immovable properties on a timetable share basis, 97/7/EC on the protection of consumers in respect of contract negotiated away from business premises, 99/44/EC on certain aspects of the sale of consumer goods and associated guarantees, 2000/35/EC on combating late payments in commercial transactions, 2000/31/EC on electronic commerce, 2002/65/EC on distance marketing of consumer financial products, *etc.* Currently, the Commission does *inter alia* examine how far a Member State had gone beyond the minimum standards as most of the directives relating to the consumer protection provide for the principle of minimum harmonisation.

598 *See e.g.* Roth W.-H. 'Der Einfluss des Europäischen Gemeinschaftsrechts auf das Internationale Privatrecht' 55 *RabelsZ* (1991) 623; Rott P. 'Minimum Harmonisation for the Completion of the Internal Market? The Example of Consumer Sales Law' 40 *C.M.L. Rev.* (2003); Basedow J. 'Der kollisionsrechtliche Gehalt der Produktfreiheiten im europäischen Binnenmarkt: *favor offerentis*' 59 *RabelsZ* (1995) 1 *et seq*; Rittner F. 'Die wirtschaftliche Ordnung und das Privatrecht' *JZ* (1990) 839; Schaub R. 'Die Neuregelung des Internationalen Deliktsrecht in Deutschland und das europäische Gemeinschaftsrecht' 66 *RabelsZ* (2002) 18 *et seq*; von Wilmosky P. 'EG-Vertrag und kollisionsrechtliche Rechtswahlfreiheit' 62 *RabelsZ* (1998) 1 *et seq*; Lurger B. *Regulierung und Deregulierung im europäischen Privatrecht* (Frankfurt am Main 1997) 89 *et seq*

defended that the diversity of private laws in Europe does not contravene the market freedoms[599]. For example, *Körber* stated that private law and Union law never clash[600]. Indeed, the Court of Justice deals mostly with public law regulations of that are sometimes set aside because they inhibit free trade in the internal market. However, one may also argue that legal differences are inherently linked with the impairment of competition[601]. The most decisive factor should not be just the formal attribution of norms to public or private law, but the actual and potential effect of private laws on the free movement of persons, products and capital. Given the general lack of case law on this issue, it is doubtful whether the tests developed by the Court of Justice to review national public law regulations under the market freedoms would be suitable for the regulation of contract law.

Pragmatic arguments have often been used to stop attempts at evaluating national contract laws against the benchmark of the market freedoms. National civil laws were sometimes considered to represent an acknowledged benchmark of justice within the jurisdiction in question[602]. The European regulator might end up colliding with the acknowledged principles of fairness and propriety in local jurisdictions. Finally, contract law - in particular, the French civil law - is often linked with national cultural heritage. Indeed, if one assumes that the mandatory rules of private law represent a recognised benchmark of justice and fairness in a particular jurisdiction, the possible intervention of the market freedoms would require a re-evaluation of the whole national legal system, which would be difficult for national parliaments and electorates to accept. Practically speaking, any substantial reconstruction of contract law is difficult to implement in many civil law jurisdictions. It would probably be right to assume

---

599 *For some in-depth discussion see*: Hesselink M. 'Non-Mandatory Rules in European Contract Law, *1/2005* ERCL 2005; Riesenhuber K. *Europäisches Vertragsrecht* (Berlin: de Gruyter 2003); Langner O. 'Das Kaufrecht auf dem Prüfstand der Warenverkehrsfreiheit des EG-Vertrages' 65 *RabelsZ* (2001); Bruinier S. *Der Einfluss der Grundfreiheiten auf das Internationale Privatrecht* (Frankfurt am Main 2003); Brödermann E., Iversen H. *Europäisches Gemeinschaftsrecht und Internationales Privatrecht* (Tübingen 1994)

600 Körber T. *Grundfreiheit und Privatrecht* (Tübingen: Mohr Siebeck 2004) 2. *See also*: Wurmnest W. *Grundzüge eines europäischen Haftungsrechts. Eine rechtsvergleichende Untersuchung des Gemeinschaftsrechts* (Tübingen 2003) 107 *et seq*

601 *Compare:* Rittner F. 'Die wirtschaftliche Ordnung der EG und das Privatrecht' *JZ* (1990) 842

602 Some commentaries point out that default (German 'dispositives Recht') rules provide something of a yardstick for applying tests of fairness in many areas of economic life. These rules are actually semi-compulsory. *See*: von Bar C., Lando O., Swan S. 'Communication on European Contract Law: Joint Response of the Commission on European Contract Law and the Study Group on a European Civil Code' 2 *ERPL* (2002) 201

that the 'europeanisation' of the English common law system has never been seriously considered. Assuming statutory civil laws as a benchmark of justice, the market freedoms would represent not the icon of personal freedom, but rather a major factor in demolishing national systems of private law[603].

Finally, it is worthwhile to note that most private law rules could be elected by the parties and, if not required, contracted out of. The non-existence of somewhat similar rules of contract law in statutes or civil codes, whereby the activity of companies is limited, hardly seems to be a sufficient basis for finding a breach of market freedoms. In essence, these statutory civil law rules mostly represent the framework of contractual rights and obligations proposed by a government to market participants, and private laws rarely entail straightforward prohibitions or restrictions similar to those set out in public law. These considerations would suggest that the rules of private law are not really suitable to be assessed under the market freedoms. It must also be noted that the Court of Justice has almost never given explicit guidelines as to what areas of national law are immune from the interference of the market freedoms[604]. This is probably due to the influence of common law countries, which do not draw a firm line between the rules of private and public law.

However, the rules of private law also represent the national choices of economic, political and social policy. From this perspective, the impact of private law is similar to that of public law, and no difference should be made when carrying out an assessment in relation to the market freedoms.

1.2 The Boundary between Measures hindering Access to the Market and Measures that do not impede Trade: Analysis of the Case Law

Practically speaking, the Court of Justice has been silent on the issue of whether rules of contract law may breach the market freedoms[605]. It seems that current Court of Justice's case law does not provide a completely unambiguous answer as to which national norms are completely free from scrutiny under Union law.

---

603 *Critically about effects of the market freedoms on the private law see*: Remien O. 'Illusion und Realität eines europäischen Privatrechts' *JZ* (1992) 280 *et seq*; Mülberg O. P. 'Privatrecht, die EG- Grundfreiheiten und der Binnenmarkt' 159 *ZHR* (1986) 6 *et seq*; Armbrüster Ch. 'Ein Schuldvertragsrecht für Europa? Bemerkungen zur Privatrechtsangleichung in der Europäischen Union nach „Maastricht" und „Keck"' 60 *RabelsZ* (1996) 74

604 *See also*: Wurmnest W. *Grundzüge eines europäischen Haftungsrechts. Eine rechtsvergleichende Untersuchung des Gemeinschaftsrechts* (Tübingen 2003) 107; Mülbert O. P. 'Privatrecht, die EG - Grundfreiheiten und der Binnenmarkt' 159 *ZHR* (1986) 9

605 Compare, however, the effect of taxation rules as examined in Krantz C-69/88 as well as the legitimacy of licencing rules handled in DIP SpA C-140-142/94.

Conversely, the case law of the Court of Justice on the market freedoms would suggest that all national regulations should be judged in relation to the market freedoms where they hinder access to the market[606].

For example, in the *Alpine Investments* case the Court of Justice scrutinised the Dutch prohibition of cold-calling potential clients for providing financial services[607]. The prohibition was adjudged an export restriction, as it was applicable in all cases where clients in other Member States were approached. Following *Keck*, 'cold calling' (in essence, marketing rules) could probably have been regarded as a permitted selling arrangement. The *Alpine Investments* case represents a different approach in assessing the market freedoms. The Court of Justice stressed the necessity of allowing access to the market, though the rules in question were applied indistinctly[608]. Because of its disadvantageous character the prohibition was interpreted under Article 56 TFEU (free movement of services) and later justified on the grounds of promoting the general good, in particular with regard to the need to 'maintain the good reputation of the national financial sector'[609]. Interestingly, the Court of Justice also stressed that the Dutch authorities should not be concerned with protecting consumers in other Member States[610].

In the *Buet* ruling, the Court of Justice dealt with the prohibition on selling educational material door-to-door. This prohibition could also have been regarded as a selling arrangement. In this case, one company achieved approximately 90% of its turnover in England and Belgium. Thus the Court of Justice decided that the French sales prohibition on suppliers restricted access to the market (*restriction of Euro-marketing*)[611]. Nevertheless, this prohibition was justified taking into consideration *inter alia* the proportionality of the prohibition.

---

606 For some relevant case law on the 'test of the access to the market' see: De Agostini C-34/95-36/95; Gourmet C-405/98. *Compare:* Weatherill S. 'Free Movement of Goods', 55(2) *ICLQ* 2006; Connor T. 'Accentuating the Positive: the "Selling Arrangement"; the First Decade and beyond' 54 *ICLQ* 2005

607 'Cold–calling' means that individuals are contacted by telephone to be offered various services, without their prior consent in writing. In this particular case, the individuals were offered portfolio management, investment advice and the transmission of clients' offers to brokers operating commodities futures within and outside the Union.

608 Snell J., Andenas M. 'Exploring the Outer Limits: Restrictions on Free Movement' in: *The Law of the Single European Market*, Barnard C. Scott J. *eds*. (Oxford and Portland, Oregon: Hart Publishing 2002) 107

609 Alpine Investments C-384/93, paras 42-44. *Cf.* Bosman C-415/93, para 103; Volker Graf C-190/98, paras 23-26

610 Alpine Investments C-384/93, para 43, *Cf.:*AG Trabucchi, in Dassonvile C-8/74

611 *See*: Buet C-382/87, paras 7-9. Similar to the 'Mars' ruling (C-470/93), the Court of Justice acknowledged that enterprises should have a right to the 'euro-wide marketing' unless these national restrictions are justifiable.

The legitimacy of prohibitions in respect of contract law has been examined several times before the Court of Justice. For example, some relevant issues were raised in the *Alsthom Atlantique* case. This case concerned the French company Sulzer, which had supplied defective vessel motors to the French company Alsthom Atlantique, and which were later put into vessels and sold to the Dutch company Holland & America Tours. Sulzer originally ordered the defective vessel motors from its German subsidiary. The German subsidiary excluded liability, because German law governing contractual relations permitted such exclusion[612]. However, under French law a seller is 'liable for hidden defects, even though he did not know of them unless, in such case, he had stipulated that he would not be obliged for any guarantee' (Art. 1643 Code Civil). In the end, Sulzer remained responsible for the loss suffered as a result of the defective motors. In considering this issue, the Court of Justice was *inter alia* asked whether or not strict French contract law may inhibit the free movement of goods. Indeed, for example, under the English Sale of Goods Act 1979, together with UCTA 1977, a professional vendor may limit his liability insofar as this is reasonable or exclude or limit liability as to the satisfactory quality of goods[613]. However, the Court of Justice dismissed this approach, explaining that French law neither limited nor aimed at limiting the volume of exports[614]. Breach of the market freedoms would not be established in cases where parties were permitted to choose the legal order governing their contractual relations so as to avoid unfavourable statutory norms[615]. The norms of conflicts of law entitle parties to escape the application of national rules by opting for its non-application.

The reasoning of the Court of Justice cannot be completely accepted. Still, even if parties were in theory permitted to choose the most favourable legal system, this would not mean that *per se* all trade barriers would be eliminated. Any choice of law must be *de facto* effective. In many cases, a weaker party will accept an unfavourable governing law because of the information deficit or simply because the party knows that the other party is unwilling to negotiate on the choice of the law or other contract terms. For example, many large companies from common law jurisdictions will agree only on English or New York law or the law of some other United States jurisdiction, which is often explained as a corporate policy, arguing that the board of the company would not approve any other choice of governing law.

Small contracting parties can be especially deterred, and therefore adversely affected by foreign law, because they are not familiar with foreign

---

612 *See:* AG in Alsthom Atlantique C-339/89, para 1

613 *See*: section 14(2) Sale of Goods Act 1979

614 *See*: *e.g.* Kramer C-6/76, para 56/59

615 *Compare also*: Alsthom Atlantique C-339/89, para 15

regulations[616]. Moreover, a party can only choose national regulations on standard form contracts - or other rules - in the framework of a whole national legal system. The legal order can be contracted out of only in total[617]. Finally, the choice of law can be also deficient. The fact that contracting parties are permitted to choose appropriate jurisdictions under the Rome I Regulation does not put aside national overriding mandatory provisions. Thus, the 'free' choice of applicable law is almost never free in real life.

A similar conclusion to that achieved in the *Alsthom Atlantique* with regard to the test of remoteness[618] was made in the *CMC Motor Vehicles* case. In this case, the Court of Justice explained that a pre-contractual duty to divulge information to the seller of parallel imported motorcycles imposed under German contract law, applied without exception to all contractual relationships, and that its purpose was not to regulate trade[619]. According to the Court of Justice, the restrictive effects were too uncertain and too indirect to be found to hinder trade between Member States[620].

In the view of the author, the fact patterns in both cases were not suited to finding a substantive distortion of intra-Union trade. The *CMC Motor Vehicles* case basically related to a duty to divulge information, which would contribute to fairness in contractual arrangements, while the *Alsthom Atlantique* case was more related to export restrictions that are interpreted more leniently in the case law on the application of Article 35 TFEU[621]. Thus it seems that the Court of Justice managed to avoid solving the ambivalence of fairness in contractual relations and the restrictions on intra-Union trade. It must also be borne in mind that the Court of Justice applied the test of remoteness more often in its early case law[622]. Nonetheless, it is submitted that the court's arguments about the 'unclear and indirect effect' of statutory rules of contract law are ambiguous.

---

616 Drexl J. 'Continuing Contract Law Harmonisation under the White Paper of 1985? – Between Minimum Harmonisation, Mutual Recognition, and Uniform Law', in: *An Academic Green Paper on European Contract Law* (The Hague: Kluwer Law International 2002) 114

617 Langner O. 'Das Kaufrecht auf dem Prüfstand der Warenverkehrsfreiheit des EG-Vertrages' 65 *RabelsZ* (2001) 229. *See also*: Drasch W. *Das Herkunftslandprinzip im internationalen Privatrecht: Auswirkungen des europäischen Binnenmarktes auf Vertrags- und Wettbewerbsstatut* (Baden-Baden 1997) 211

618 The test of remoteness has been fiercely criticised in the 1980s and early 1990s.

619 CMC Motor Vehicles C-93/92, para 10

620 *See also:* Kranz C-69/88, para 11; DIP SpA C-140-142/94, para 29; Peralta C-379/92, para 24.

621 *For more see:* Gkoutzinis A. 'Free Movement of Services in the EC Treaty and the Law of Contractual Obligations relating to Banking and Financial Services' 41 *C.M.L. Rev* (2004) 125

622 *See, e.g.,* Directeur Général des Impots C-148/85; BASF C-44/98; Esso Espanola C-134/94; Centro Servizi C-96/94, *etc.*

There is a lack of objective criteria - and this deficiency will remain as long as the Court of Justice does not undertake a detailed economic analysis - in evaluating the remoteness of national measures in respect of intra-Union trade. In accordance with the recent case law of the Court of Justice even *de facto* discrimination or measures hindering access to a foreign market can and should probably be considered as infringing TFEU unless these are saved by mandatory requirements developed by *Cassis de Dijon* case law or other legitimate grounds. In other words, even if the measure is 'too remote and unclear' to prevent trade, it may still amount to actual discrimination, as the Court of Justice has consistently denied the application of a *de minimis* test regarding the free movement of economic factors. In this respect, it is not completely clear what contract law rules must *per se* be excluded from oversight giving consideration to the market freedoms.

1.3 Free Choice of Law in Commercial Arrangements

The rules of contract law have traditionally been divided into mandatory and default rules[623]. Default rules of contract law ordinarily come into play unless the parties stipulate otherwise. It is nowadays the consensus in Union law that a government must enact only those rules that are in line with the Treaties. The principle of the supremacy of Union law[624] states that no national rule should contradict Union law (*inter alia* by restricting intra-Union trade and leading to distortions in the internal market), regardless of whether they can be contracted out of or not upon the will of the parties. Given the supremacy of Union law, a review of the conformity with the market freedoms compares logically with the reviews exercised in respect of the compatibility of national constitutional rights. It seems that it should be irrelevant whether these rules are attributed to public or private law. The fact that default rules can be contracted out of does not mean that they thereby lose their official nature and become exempt from such scrutiny.

By entering into commercial arrangements, parties may not only choose the desired legal order, but also contract out of unfavourable national provisions on the regulation of standard form contracts. However, in many cases, companies decide not to contract out of the default rules even where it would be possible to do so. This choice can be explained not by the fact that companies

[623] In the literature, the rules of civil law are sometimes divided into non-excludable rules, imperative rules, excludable rules and default rules. This classification is based on the grounds that not all rules that parties cannot exclude give rise to a penalty. *For more see*: Alpa G. 'Party Autonomy and Freedom of Contract Today', in: *The Politics of the Draft Common Frame of Reference*, Somma A. *ed.* (Wolters Kluwer Law and Business, The Netherlands 2009) 85-6

[624] *See*: Costa v. ENEL C-6/64

have faith in certain jurisdictions, but that the parties themselves are not able to implement the rules they most desire. However, a party may rely on statutory default rules because it is expected that a court may rectify the contract at some later stage if a dispute arises. Furthermore, the default rules of contract law would bind parties in cases where they cannot reach agreement over the law applicable. In this case, their effect on default statutory rules is the same as mandatory rules. This is relevant for cross-border trade, where parties are burdened with a lack of knowledge about the foreign law system[625].

Finally, as noted above, none of the legal systems is completely liberal. Every European legal system has at least some provisions that cannot be contracted out of[626]. Parties are bound by rules that were not initially desired, but cannot be avoided[627]. To what extent these rules represent the true will of the parties is a matter of discussion. Thus, it may be assumed that even if default laws come into play, this does not mean freedom of contract has been fully exercised. Given the existence of mandatory rules, one may also contend that national default norms should not *ab initio* remain outside the scope of control of the market freedoms. On the other hand, default rules of contract law should not ordinarily appreciably constrain the autonomy of parties. By enacting rules of private law, a government, merely offers parties a possibility of incorporating default rules in a contract if they wish to do so. Generally, the government is under no duty to enact default rules and thereby facilitate trade.

Even though the Court of Justice has consistently rejected a *de minimis* test for the free movement of economic factors, it seems that the Court of Justice would still implicitly measure to what extent parties are really affected by foreign regulations. The asymmetry of information as well as the uncertainty of foreign laws is inherent to international trade. In many cases, information received on foreign legal systems is rarely accurate in all aspects and suggests the most favourable solution[628]. Therefore, it would probably be reasonable to

---

625 Langner O. 'Das Kaufrecht auf dem Prüfstand der Warenverkehrsfreiheit des EG-Vertrages' 65 *RabelsZ* (2001) 227 *et seq*. It is sometimes contended that tackling the asymmetries of information in consumer contracts was one of the incentives for adopting Directive 93/13/EEC on Unfair Terms in Consumer Contracts. *See*: Grundmann S. 'Information, Party Autonomy and Economic Agents in European Contract Law' 39 *C.M.L. Rev.* (2002) 275

626 Union law takes priority over the rules of conflicts of law. The limitation regarding mandatory requirements should be applicable for transactions between companies in the internal market.

627 *Compare*: von Wilmowsky P. 'EG-Freiheiten und Vertragsrecht' *JZ* (1996) 596; Langner O. 'Das Kaufrecht auf dem Prüfstand der Warenverkehrsfreiheit des EG-Vertrages' 65 *RabelsZ* (2001) 227

628 *See e.g.* Staudenmayer D. 'The Commission Communication on European Contract Law and its Follow-up', in: *An Academic Green Paper on European Contract Law* (The Hague: Kluwer Law International 2002) 41

argue that before entering into international arrangements, parties should normally understand that they bear somewhat higher risks in international business dealings than in domestic transactions. These risks should not be considered a special restriction on the market freedoms in international business transactions. Therefore, in my view, these constraints do not appreciably affect international trade, and purely default rules of contract law should be deemed as being in line with TFEU.

2. THE LEGITIMACY OF NATIONAL REGULATIONS ON STANDARD FORM CONTRACTS AS A TRADE BARRIER

2.1 REGULATIONS ON STANDARD FORM CONTRACTS: MANDATORY OR DEFAULT LAWS?

As noted above, most of the statutory norms of civil law may be contracted out of. The parties are generally permitted to arrange their contractual relations as they wish. Many mandatory rules can be found in employment and consumer contracts; however, typical commercial contracts also entail some provisions that cannot be deviated from. In this respect, in legal doctrine the rules of private law are sometimes conventionally classified into three major categories: mandatory, pre-formulated and default provisions[629]. It is argued that some countries - Germany, the Netherlands - have a concept of so-called half-mandatory rules[630]. The peculiarity of so-called pre-formulated contract terms is that parties may deviate from them only if they individually agree on other terms. Indeed, regulations on standard form contracts (or pre-formulated terms) cannot be termed plain default rules. National regulations on standard form contracts are somewhere between mandatory and default rules. They may be contracted out of, but only under certain circumstances, for example where a contract is tailored individually.

However, the Member States' legal systems show no unanimous approach to what terms are absolutely unenforceable (so-called '*black lists*' of the rules) and what terms are tolerated in certain circumstances (so-called the '*grey lists*' of rules). As submitted in the previous chapter, default norms of contract law should not contravene the market freedoms, as they can be contracted out of

---

[629] Remien O. *Zwingendes Vertragsrecht und Grundfreiheiten des EG-Vertrages* (Tübingen: Mohr Siebeck 2003) 471. For more about the concept of mandatory rules see *e.g.* Sinai A. R. 'The Inclusion of Mandatory Rules in an Optimal EC Contract Law Instrument' 15(1) *EBLR* (2004) 41 *et seq*

[630] For example, unconscionability is claimed to be difficult to classify either as a mandatory or default rule. *See*: Hesselink M. 'Non-Mandatory Rules in European Contract Law, 1/2005 *ERCL* (2005) 60 *et seq*; Markesinis B. Unberath H. Johnston A. *The German Law of Contract* (Oxford and Portland, Oregon: Hart Publishing 2006) 47

according to the will of individual parties. Nonetheless, owing to the economic and intellectual power of the *proferens* proposing his standard form contracts, the counterparty may have no chance but to bargain on the basis of the stipulator's one-sided and well-drafted standard terms. Given the unequal bargaining power of many contract counterparties, national regulators prescribe that even if in theory parties have the chance to amend rules by individual agreement, the mandatory effect of regulations on standard form contracts would not thereby cease to exist. It would probably be right to assert that the mere possibility of amending terms of a standard form contract will not guarantee substantive private autonomy. In this respect, the effect of regulations on standard form contracts may actually be equivalent to those public regulations that are mandatory in nature. It is, therefore, submitted that national regulations on standard form contracts should not completely fall outside the scope of scrutiny under Article 34 TFEU.

Nevertheless, it is also possible to argue that regulations on standard form contracts can not only be considered a limitation of freedom of contract, but also as a measure protecting the legitimate interests of a weaker party. Using this line of argument, regulations on standard form contracts can be treated not as a special restriction imposed upon parties, but rather as a means of achieving the fair and legitimate expectations of the parties in commercial arrangements. Given the purpose of such rules, both regulations on standard form contracts and the market freedoms should facilitate the legitimate private autonomy of contracting parties. Therefore, these instruments should not conflict with one another. On balance, it seems that the interrelation between the market freedoms and national regulations on standard form contracts is subordinated to the perspective from which they are approached.

2.2 Relevance of the '*Keck*' Case Law to the Legitimacy of Regulations on Standard Form Contracts

The market freedoms do not deal with pure legal differences among Member States as such. Following the *Keck* case law, the market freedom of free movement of goods would not be called into question, provided national authorities enacted appropriate rules in which selling arrangements were defined indistinctly. One may tentatively assume that any prohibitions which require the stipulator's own standard contract terms to be amended should affect him restrictively. Thanks to the obligation to amend standard contract terms so that they comply with foreign statutory requirements, the seller would be burdened more than a foreign company based in that jurisdiction.

However, first of all it must be seen whether these national statutory requirements are related more to product requirements or selling arrangements.

For example referring to the *Hünermund* and *CMC Motor Vehicles* cases, *Remien* contended that advertising law is a genuine selling arrangement, and therefore the rest of civil law should be a plain selling arrangement as well[631]. Many statutory provisions of civil law can indeed be considered selling arrangements, as they do not concern material objects. Conversely, *Mülbert* explained that national laws on quality of goods in respect of their conformity with contracts are product-related arrangements, as they refer to the primary obligations of parties[632]. In the author's view, there is force in *Rott's* reasoning, which convincingly explains that Article 34 TFEU [*ex* 28 EC] catches rules that relate to product quality, while rules on liability will usually fall outside its scope[633].

It is submitted that statutory regulations on standard form contracts, as well as other rules of contract law, in particular the prohibition on excluding liability for intentional breaches of a contract under German or Lithuanian law, are neither genuine selling nor genuine product arrangement. If we consider contract law from the perspective of the contracting parties' obligations, these would probably define the way the product is sold and be more related to so-called 'selling arrangements'. On the other hand, granting some other relevant right, *e.g.* warranty terms, is probably more closely linked with the product. It seems that a longer warranty suggests a better quality of product. A warranty can also be regarded as a separate legal product, as some traders directly or indirectly charge for a longer warranty separately[634].

It must be noted that the Court of Justice has consistently applied a wide interpretation to the concept of product arrangements (*e.g.* in the *Clinique, Mars, Familiapress* rulings[635]) in order to extend protection for foreign suppliers engaged in inter-Union trade. Indeed, to a certain extent, exclusion clauses can also relate to the composition of the product. This line of reasoning is, however, not always convincing as under the concept of goods the case law of the Court of Justice only gives consideration to physical objects[636]. The separation of the main object of the contract (*i.e.* goods in question) from its warranty may seem artificial, because parties ordinarily agree on the supply of one product. In

631 Remien O. *Zwingendes Vertragsrecht und Grundfreiheiten des EG-Vertrages* (Tübingen: Mohr Siebeck 2003) 194

632 Mülbert O. P. 'Privatrecht, die EG-Grundfreiheiten und der Binnenmarkt' 159 *ZHR* (1986) 21

633 Rott P. 'Minimum Harmonisation for the Completion of the Internal Market? The Example of Consumer Sales Law' 40 *C.M.L. Rev.* (2003) 1115

634 *Compare:* Langner O. 'Das Kaufrecht auf dem Prüfstand der Warenverkehrsfreiheit des EG-Vertrages' 65 *RabelsZ* (2001) 223, *also:* Riesenhuber K. *Europäisches Vertragsrecht* (Berlin: de Gruyter 2003) 36

635 *See*: Clinique C-315/92; Mars C-470/93; Familiapress C-368/95

636 *See*: Keck C-267/91 and C-268/91

essence, the rules pertaining to the law of obligations has nothing to do with physical products. As was noted in the *Keck* case, product arrangements involve form, weight, composition, presentation, and labelling as well as the packaging of the product[637]. Given this definition, it is arguable whether granting or abrogating certain rights results in separate goods or parts of a product. On balance, it is submitted that it must be decided on a case-by-case basis what terms define the product and what terms have closer links to performance. The interrelation of product requirements and selling arrangements has evolved over the years. Numerous cases processed by the Court of Justice would suggest that the Court has faced significant difficulties in delimiting product requirements and selling arrangements. In this respect, *Dauses* must be right in submitting that the artificial separation of market elements as specified by the Court of Justice is not consistent with economic realities[638]. A more radical conclusion is drawn by *von Wilmowsky*, who expressed the view that the scrutiny of regulations restricting freedom of contract against the benchmark of market freedoms should avoid the *Keck* case law, as the separation of the arrangements defined in the *Keck* ruling creates more problems than it solves[639].

Furthermore, it should be borne in mind that in many cases the Court of Justice did not deal directly with the 'Keck dichotomy'. For example, in the *Alsthom Atlantique* case the prohibition on cold calling, *i.e.* contacting potential clients in other Member States by telephone without prior consent, was regarded as constituting a restriction on the freedom to provide services. This restriction was justified by employing the overriding objectives (more generally known as mandatory requirements) of public interest in protecting the good reputation of the financial sector[640]. Interestingly, the Court of Justice, while analysing labour laws, did not deal with the formal separation into product and selling arrangements either. In the *Graf* case, the Court of Justice dismissed *Graf's* pleas that an Austrian law contravened Article 45 TFEU (free movement of workers), as a worker who had worked for the same employer for more than three years was entitled to compensation when his employment came to an end, subject to a provision to the effect that the right would be forfeited if the employment was terminated on the worker's own initiative. The Court of Justice did not find this rule discriminatory, as 'it was not such as to preclude or deter a worker from ending his contract of employment in order to take a job with another employer … the subsequent termination of his contract without such

637 Ibid., para 15

638 Dauses A. (*ed.*) *Rechtshandbuch des EU-Wirtschaftsrechts, Loseblattsammlung* Vol. 1 (München 1997) para 130. *See also*: Remien O. 'Illusion und Realität eines europäischen Privatrechts' *JZ* (1992) 353

639 Wilmowsky P. von. 'EG-Freiheiten und Vertragsrecht' *JZ* (1996) 594

640 *See*: Alpine Investments C-384/93, para 14. Nonetheless, the 'Keck formula' was followed consistently in A-Punkt Schmuckhandels GmbH C-441/04 and many other cases.

termination being at his own initiative or attributable to him'[641]. The Court of Justice employed similar arguments in the *CMC Motor Vehicles* case. In particular, the Court of Justice decided that the measures in question were too uncertain and indirect to be capable of being regarded as liable to hinder the free movement of economic factors. On balance, it seems that previous decisions of the Court of Justice are of little use in helping draw a clear conclusion as to how mandatory contract law rules should be regarded. Following the court's reasoning, rules on 'product requirements' and 'selling arrangements' should be mutually exclusive[642], but the rules cannot easily be separated; nonetheless, the court did not specify any third group of arrangements[643].

Even though regulations on standard form contracts are more likely to be regarded as selling arrangements, they should not be left outside the scope of Article 34 TFEU. In the later case law of the Court of Justice 'selling arrangements' are not completely immune from being examined *vis-a-vis* the market freedoms, such as where they influence the cost of a product or substantially hinder access to the market[644]. National regulations on standard form contracts can equally be considered a factor increasing transactional costs. There is no doubt that the possibility of excluding or limiting liability makes products cheaper. Conversely, the longer a warranty is offered, the more valuable and therefor more expensive products would be. In this respect, warranty or exclusion terms, which should make a product cheaper, can at least indirectly influence the quality and price of goods. However, it is still difficult to measure this effect, as, as noted above, the Court of Justice is unlikely to undertake the necessary detailed economic analysis. An increase in the costs of a transaction would not always constitute a barrier to entering foreign markets.

If we follow the rulings of the *Alsthom Atlantique* and *CMC Motor Vehicles* cases, national contract law rules would probably be found to directly inhibit intra-Union trade. Generally, it is difficult to measure the exact extent to which they can hinder access to foreign markets, assuming that parties basically have the right to avoid unfavourable legal orders in international commercial arrangements. One should also take into consideration the fact that the Court of Justice has never held that the market freedoms should create a completely

---

641 Volker Graf C-190/98, paras 24-25

642 *For a similar notion see e.g.:* Snell J. *Goods and Services in EC Law. A Study of the Relationship Between the Freedoms* (Oxford: Oxford University Press 2002) 81; Oliver P. and Enchelmaier S. 'Free Movement of Goods: Recent Developments in the Case Law' 44 *C.M.L. Rev.* (2007) 673

643 *Compare*: Jickeli J. 'Der Binnenmark im Schatten des Subsidiaritätsprinzips' *JZ* (1995) 60 *et seq.* For example, the existence of the third category has been rejected by A.G. Stix-Hackl, in Deutscher Apothekerverband C-322/01.

644 *For some relevant case law see:* Mars C-470/93; De Agostini C-34/95-36/95, compare also: Karner C-71/02

unrestricted internal market. Thus restrictions arising from differences in statutory regulations where a foreign trader has to accept the unfavourable mandatory rules of foreign legal order would probably not amount to a breach of the market freedoms. Finally, to a certain extent, regulations on standard form contracts are aimed at prohibiting the exercise of harmful trade practices. In this respect, it will be examined further whether additional justification may be found for saving the application of these national statutory rules in intra-Union trade.

3. JUSTIFICATION FOR NATIONAL REGULATIONS ON STANDARD FORM CONTRACTS

Though a national measure may provisionally be deemed to be a restriction under TFEU, this does not necessarily mean that the market freedoms are violated. Following the *Cassis de Dijon* case law, all measures having equivalent effect can be justified in accordance with derogations envisaged in Article 36 TFEU or with reference to the mandatory requirements insofar as they are proportional.

3.1 DEROGATIONS FROM ARTICLE 36 TFEU

Article 36 TFEU sets out different kinds of derogations (*e.g.* public morality, public policy or public security, the protection of health and life of humans, animals and plants, the protection of national treasures possessing artistic, historic or archaeological value, *etc.*) to the extent that they do not 'constitute a means of arbitrary discrimination or a disguised restriction on trade among Member States'. These derogations are sometimes termed textual exceptions[645]. Probably the most relevant common ground to justify derogating from the rules of private law is 'public policy'. As outlined above, regulations on standard form contracts should not limit freedom of contract, but rather restore fair contractual relations. It is possible to argue that regulating standard form contracts reflects a benchmark of justice as well as public order in a particular country. Generally speaking, notions of 'public order' or 'public policy' in England and France indicate a group of rules that may not be contracted out of by the individual agreement of parties – *e.g.* mandatory rules of contract law, contracts breaching the interests of third parties, statutory requirements, *etc.* English '*public policy*' is much wider than the French concept of '*ordre public*', German '*öffentliche*

[645] Jarass D. H. 'A Unified Approach to the Fundamental Freedoms', in: *The Law of the Single European Market*, Barnard C. Scott J. eds. (Oxford and Portland, Oregon: Hart Publishing 2002) 154

Ordnung' or Lithuanian '*viešoji tvarka*'[646]. For example, in some instances the English judiciary may strike out contracts on what are essentially public policy grounds, but without making an express reference to the public policy in question[647]. On the other hand, the concept of public policy as established in TFEU has little resemblance to its common law equivalent[648]. Nowadays there is a broad consensus in the Union that the concept of public policy should be interpreted narrowly, according to the Court of Justice 'so as its scope would not be unilaterally determined by each Member State without being subject to control by the institutions of the Community'[649]. Indeed, the Court of Justice has accepted that the recourse to public policy may vary from country to country[650]. This derogation may be invoked only if the most fundamental interests of the state are at stake.[651].

Union law does not prescribe a positive list of measures that may be categorised as pertaining to public policy. Mandatory rules of contract law mostly protect the interests of a weaker contracting party. Thus this justification would not be relevant in these cases. Furthermore, according to the consistent case law of the Court of Justice on similar matters, a derogation regarding public order would not be invoked if taking into consideration objectives of a purely economic nature[652]. It is prohibited for Member States to enact rules that protect national companies or other economic participants from foreign competition. The difficulties a Member State may experience because of increased competition cannot generally be justified by Article 36 TFEU. In this regard, it would be difficult to prove that these private interests are of extraordinary importance to the Member State concerned. The other derogations set out in Article 36 TFEU (*e.g.* protection of health) may not be linked directly with the application of national regulations on standard form contracts either.

---

[646] *For some relevant Lithuanian case law see*: the Decisions of the Lithuanian Supreme Court No 3K-3-521/2006; 3K-6-641/2006; 3K-3-24/2009

[647] Treitel G. *The Law of Contract,* 11th ed. (London: Sweet & Maxwell 2003) 480

[648] Barnard C. *The Substantive Law of the EU. The Four Freedoms* (Oxford: Oxford University Press 2004) 66

[649] Van Duyn 41/74, para 18; Bouchereau C-30/77, para 34. *Compare*: Commission v. Federal Republic of Germany Case 12-74; Kohl C-177/83; Bauhuis C-46/76

[650] Omega Spielhallen C-36/02, para 31

[651] *See:* Thompson C-7/78, para 34

[652] *See also:* Commission v. Italy C-95/81, para 27; Kohll C-158/96, para 41; Campus Oil C-72/83, paras 35-36

3.2 Mandatory Requirements and Statutory Rules of Private Law

3.2.1 Fairness of Commercial Transactions

In line with the *Cassis de Dijon* case law, indistinctly applicable measures can be saved *inter alia* by mandatory requirements. It is sometimes contended that the recent case law of the Court of Justice on the application of mandatory requirements has been extended to discriminatory measures as well[653]. As a general principle, regulations on standard form contracts are applied indistinctly to all market participants in a non-discriminatory manner.

The list of mandatory requirements as presented in the *Cassis de Dijon* case is only indicative, but was subsequently expanded through the developing case law of the Court of Justice. In several rulings, the Court of Justice outlined measures dealing with the notions of 'fairness of commercial transactions[654]. This requirement *inter alia* includes a duty to provide correct information to the purchaser[655], measures aimed at combating certain deceptive practices[656], and marketing practices considered proper and fair in the importing Member State[657], *etc*. For example, according to the *Oosthoek* case, a company offered a world atlas and a dictionary as a newspaper supplement to all subscribers. On the one hand, the prohibitions against giving free gifts as an incentive to purchase products set out in the contested *Wet Beperking Cadeaustelsel* 1977 law were justified because they served 'consumer protection and fair trading' at the European Union level[658]. Pure national economic rationales are not regarded as mandatory requirements for permitting restriction on the free movement of goods. The regulation of standard form contracts serves *inter alia* to protect a weaker party from unfair disadvantage. In this regard, the prohibition on unreasonably excluding or limiting contractual liabilities ought to safeguard the fairness of business-to-business transactions. Furthermore, measures aimed at protecting a weaker contracting party can be saved as a 'political or economic choice'[659] or possibly as a choice relating to particular 'national or regional socio-cultural characteristics'[660], or 'concerns of social policy and the prevention

---

[653] *See*: Aher-Waggon C-389/96, para 26

[654] The terms of '*fairness of commercial transactions*' and '*prevention of unfair competition*' are ordinarily used interchangeably. *See*: Oliver P. *Free Movement of Goods in the European Community under Articles 28 to 30 of the EC Treaty* (London: Sweet and Maxwell 2003) 171

[655] *See*: Miro C-182/84, paras 25-27; Prantl C-16/83, para 26

[656] Commission v. Italy C-67/88, see also: Mars C-470/93

[657] Dansk Supermarked C-58/80, para 15

[658] Oosthoek C-286/81, para 18

[659] *See:* Torfaen Borough Council C-145/88, para 14

[660] *See:* B&Q C-169/91, para 11

of fraud'[661]. Given these legitimate purposes, it is submitted that regulations on standard form contracts that are aimed at protecting a weaker counterparty should be in line with the mandatory requirements developed by the Court of Justice. Moreover, certain national prohibitions relating to the application of disproportionate exclusion clauses – even if they are stipulated for standard form contracts - should contribute to the fair distribution of commercial risks between parties. The Court of Justice has stated numerous times that social and economic goals must also be considered in the light of the general purpose of regulating contracts. These goals can serve as a basis to save national measures having equivalent effect[662]. Therefore the regulator's endeavours to eradicate unfair bargaining, fraudulent practices or not divulging all essential information in business transactions and thereby passively misleading the contract counterparty can be soundly justified *inter alia* in the framework of economic and political decisions.

3.2.2 Proportionality

MEEs must be proportional; the principle of proportionality has become a general principle of law in the European Union. In accordance with the case law of the Court of Justice, measures should be proportionate insofar as they constitute a barrier that restricts the exercise of market freedoms[663].

The introduction of the principle of proportionality was of paramount importance so that the measure in question would not constitute arbitrary discrimination or a disguised restriction on trade. In theory, the principle of proportionality is two-fold: it requires that the measures employed by a national government are appropriate (suitable)[664] with regard to the objective to be attained and should not go beyond what is necessary[665] to achieve these objectives[666]. Some commentators add that the test of proportionality is three-fold. It is sometimes contended that it also includes the element of 'true proportionality'; in other words that the interests of the individual Member State should be weighed against the interests of the Union in free trade[667].

---

661 Schindler C-275/92, para 63

662 Torfän Borough Council C-145/88; B&Q C-169/91, para 15

663 Rau C-261/81, para 12; Mars C-470/93, para 15; Familiapress C- 368/95, para 19

664 *See*: ERT v. DEP C-260/89, para 25

665 Gebhard C-55/94, para 37; Centros C-212/97, para 34-5; Commission v. Germany C-205/84 para 52 *et seq*

666 *Compare:* 3 Glocken C-407/85; Commission v. Germany C-178/84; Käserei Champignon C-210/00

667 *Cf.* Snell J. Goods and Services in EC Law. A Study of the Relationship between the Freedoms (Oxford: Oxford University Press 2002) 200 *et seq*. Snell J. 'True Proportionality and Free Movement of Goods and Services' 11 *EBLR* (2000) 50 *et seq*

The burden of proving that a measure is proportionate lies with the Member State that introduced the contested measure, and national courts are often involved in assessing the proportionality of a measure that restricts intra-Union trade. In practice, the Court of Justice refers mostly to the requirement of proportionality only if the measures at stake are manifestly disproportional[668]. It may be argued that national authorities are not required to choose the most effective means, in order that their regulations meet the benchmark of proportionality[669]. On balance, the Court of Justice is rarely engaged in a more detailed economic analysis with respect to the test of proportionality[670]. In the author's view, it is very difficult to find objective criteria to measure proportionality. On the one hand, the test is often praised for its flexibility. On the other hand, at the same time it could be considered 'unsystematic' or 'vague'. It is submitted that the rules of contract law do not ordinarily have an appreciable effect on the behaviour of market participants, as most of these are default regulations. Similarly, mandatory national rules on the exclusion or limitation of liability are often drafted in the context of reasonableness or good faith. It can, therefore, be concluded that introducing national regulations altering freedom of contract should not breach the principle of proportionality. Nonetheless, this reasoning does not mean that every prohibition relating to the exclusion of liability would be justified when referring to the fairness of business transactions. The prohibitions on excluding or limiting liability should ordinarily be considered proportional insofar as they serve the better prevention of dishonest practices and thereby contribute to the fair distribution of transactional risks. Given this ambivalence, the English experience, whereby the judiciary consider which party had the better chance to indemnify against possible losses, seems to be reasonable.

It is submitted that the legitimacy of national rules on exclusion clauses should be examined on a case-by-case basis, giving consideration as to whether these measures achieve fairer business dealings and whether these aims cannot be achieved by less restrictive measures in intra-Union trade. In this respect, it is doubtful whether prohibitions applicable to a professional vendor limiting his capability to exclude liability, as developed in French case law, are proportional since they expose French exporters to significantly higher transactional costs than parties from other Member States, unless another legal order is chosen and the French seller manages to circumvent French law.

---

[668] Sam Schiffart C-248/95 and C-249/95, paras 65-70; Alliance for National Health C-154/04 and C-155/04, para 52; ABNA, Joined cases C-453/03, C-11/04, C-12/04 and C-194/04, para 69; Swedish Match C-210/03, para 48

[669] In some cases, the Court of Justice has, however, recognised that national measures were disproportional. See, *e.g.* Commission v. Germany C-178/84, para 53. *Also*: Commission v. France C-152/78, where the issue of proportionality has been explicitly handled.

[670] *See*: Safety Hi-Tech Srl. & T Srl. C-284/95, para 66

4. CONCLUSION

TFEU prohibits open and disguised discrimination, as well as other restrictions affecting intra-Union trade. Many jurisdictions have lists of 'black' and 'grey' prohibitions, and suppliers from other jurisdictions in the Union could actually be barred from adopting unified marketing and sales practices across the Union. It seems that divergent national regulations on standard form contracts can have a negative effect on competition from companies incorporated in different Member States or otherwise deter them from concluding international contracts. Given the legal differences, the transaction of business in certain Member States may become less attractive.

This chapter has analysed the question of whether regulations on standard form contracts can amount to prohibited MEEs in the sense of Article 34 TFEU. It seems that there is no general answer. Practically speaking, the interaction of the market freedoms and the norms of private law remain vague. It is highly controversial whether divergent rules of national private law systems can directly hinder international trade, as all businesses are burdened with more or less similar costs - *e.g.* information and legal costs – in whenever they do business abroad. Another important point is that all companies incorporated in the Union can choose a legal order for their international transactions using their discretion, as well as national regulations on standard form contracts. Given this choice, businesses might ordinarily able to avoid strict national regulations that may deter a foreign supplier. However, this is probably only a theoretical assumption. In practice, it is easy to envisage parties being burdened with substantial lack of information on foreign legal systems. The most appropriate legal system may not be considered, or else the parties fail to discuss the merits and shortcomings of the law chosen to govern their international contractual arrangements. Finally, parties must still abide by the mandatory rules of at least one jurisdiction. Legal uncertainly about unknown regulations increases product cost, and can deter from entering into international commercial agreements. However, it is not completely clear how to measure this effect of uncertainty or deterrence at a general level and to what extent these burdens distort intra-Union trade.

It is submitted that national regulations on standard form contracts are more likely to be found to be consistent with Union law. Even though some national regulations on standard form contracts may have a restrictive effect on the freedom of parties, these distortions are probably only 'too uncertain and too indirect' to have an appreciable (this term implies a somewhat lesser extent than 'substantial') impact on intra-Union trade. Moreover, such national regulations can be regarded as being only indistinctly applicable selling arrangements that do not substantially hinder access to the internal market, or else their application can be saved by inclusion under mandatory requirements relating to the fairness of business transactions. This does not, however, mean that every prohibition relating to exclusion clauses should be justified under the general framework of fairness of intra-Union trade. It is submitted that an absolute prohibition on the exclusion of liability in international business transactions is not absolutely necessary. There is force in the view of *Collins*, who explains that 'choice of law rules do not offer a solution to the potential deterrent to trade threatened by diversity in the laws applicable to contracts in the Member States of the European Community Union'[671].

In light of this, it is worthwhile considering whether or not there are any other viable ways in which the Union could eliminate alleged trade distortions as well as increase the transparency of trade in the internal market. The rule of mutual recognition and the approximation of national contract laws will be examined further.

---

[671] Collins H. 'Good Faith in European Contract Law' 14(2) *O.J.L.S.* (1994) 231

1. MUTUAL RECOGNITION IN INTERNATIONAL TRADE

1.1 GENERAL OBSERVATIONS

Legal restrictions on the free movement of goods, as well as other distortions of competition, can be mitigated by employing the rule of mutual recognition. This rule means that goods and services must be offered freely in a foreign jurisdiction provided they comply with product and marketing regulations as established in national laws. As a consequence, the supplier would be able to offer his product in the same manner as in the home jurisdiction. It is sometimes, therefore, argued that the rule of mutual recognition can produce diversity of legal rules in one Member State[672].

This rule originally derives from the *Cassis de Dijon* case, where the Court of Justice confirmed that in the absence of common technical or commercial rules, goods that were legally produced and marketed in one Member State cannot be refused access to other Member States. This principle was later applied in respect of other market freedoms as well. For example, the Court of Justice recognised that an enterprise legitimately incorporated in a foreign jurisdiction may act in accordance with its domestic professional rules in other Member States[673]. The principle of mutual recognition was introduced with regard to restrictive effects on foreign market participants, not only in relation to particular national norms, but also where there was a lack of sufficiently favourable rules. Thus this principle was supposed to permit the creation of different ways of offering the same products and services in the Union. At the same time, mutual recognition leads to the co-existence of different legal solutions that compete with each other in terms of efficiency. A supplier should not be forced to abstain from doing business in other Member States merely because of existing legal differences where no sound justifications to restrict intra-Union trade are found. In cases where the rule of mutual recognition is fully implemented, the norms of the country of destination would be unenforceable where they deviated from benchmarks set out by the country of origin. On the other hand, the principle of mutual recognition would not be applicable for local market participants who offered goods and services under the rules of a foreign jurisdiction.

---

672 Wolf M. 'Privates Bankvertragrecht im EG-Binnenmarkt. Auswirkung der II. EG-Bankrechts-Richtlinie auf privatrechtliche Bankgeschäfte' 47 *WM* (1990) 1942

673 Klopp C-107/83, paras 18-20; *see also* Centros C-212/97, para 19 *et seq. For an interesting contribution see*: Weatherill S. 'The Free Movement of Goods: a Survey of the Decisions of the Court of Justice in 1991: Mutual Recognition' 17(5) *E.L. Rev.* (1992) 424

To a certain extent, the principle of mutual recognition may be considered a principle of conflict of laws, offering a possibility for companies to choose the most favourable legal system[674]. However, this principle cannot fully be substituted by the rules of conflicts of law, as the free choice of law is not always permitted, *e.g.* in the areas of consumer law, property law, *etc*[675]. Insomuch as Union law offers mutual recognition, different forms of business transactions may be conducted without recourse to the law on conflict of laws.

1.2 Export by a Country of its Own National Regulations on Standard Form Contracts to other Jurisdictions in the European Union

It is submitted that the principle of mutual recognition can substantially facilitate intra-Union trade. Thus it is worth contemplating whether this principle can be transposed into the area of private law. In particular, does this mean that participants in the internal market should be permitted to apply national provisions of contract law in foreign jurisdiction provided they are more favourable than those set out in the foreign law (the so-called 'export of legal institutes')[676]?

The theoretical consideration underlying the introduction of the rule of mutual recognition was that of permitting products to be sold under the same terms across the Union. Nevertheless, it is possible to envisage that a trader (supplier) may *inter alia* require the application of his own country's regulations on standard form contracts on the ground of *favour offerentis*, arguing that the absence of such rules inhibits the free movement of goods and services. On the other hand, such need may also arise for a counterparty in cases where domestic law provides special protection against unfair standard form contracts, but not the law of *proferens* or the law of a third country. It seems that the practical implementation of the rule of mutual recognition is almost impossible to enforce in the area of private law. For example, *Weatherill* submits that 'there is no

[674] On the principle of country of origin see also: Giovannopoulos R. *Die Harmonisierung des privatrechtlichen Bankgeheimnisses im europäischen Wirtschaftsverkehr. Eine rechtsdogmatische und rechtsvergleichende Untersuchung zum deutschen, englischen, französischen und griechischen Rech unter besonderer Berücksichtigung der Europäischen Datenschutzrichtlinie, der EG-Grundfreiheiten und der Gemeinschaftsgrundrecht*e (Baden Baden 2000/2001) 325 *et seq*

[675] Wolf M. 'Privates Bankvertragrecht im EG-Binnenmarkt. Auswirkung der II. EG-Bankrechts-Richtlinie auf privatrechtliche Bankgeschäfte' 47 *WM* (1990) 1942

[676] *Compare:* Basedow J. 'Der kollisionsrechtliche Gehalt der Produktfreiheiten im europäischen Binnenmarkt: *favor offerentis*' 59 *RabelsZ* (1995) 1 *et seq*; Wolf M. 'Privates Bankvertragrecht im EG-Binnenmarkt. Auswirkung der II. EG-Bankrechts-Richtlinie auf privatrechtliche Bankgeschäfte' 47 *WM* (1990) 1942 *et seq*

mutual recognition in Union trade law: rather it is a principle of non-absolute mutual recognition'[677]. In accordance with the rules of mutual recognition, it would be reasonable to suggest that not only the *proferens*, but also the counterparty may invoke market freedoms and thereby require adequate protection in a foreign jurisdiction, as would be afforded at home[678]. For example, a French buyer acting in a foreign jurisdiction can require somewhat the stricter protection provided in French law, compared with German and Lithuanian legislation. As a consequence, both parties – vendor and buyer - may put forward similar requirements[679]. Thus the adjudicator would inevitably face the problem of what legal system should actually be applied. Indeed, the rules that are more favourable to one party would ordinarily be less favourable to the other. For instance, the prohibition on excluding liability for the product sold would adversely affect suppliers; but customers would take advantage of it. Thus, a freedom for one party would constitute a burden for another.

The question of whether a foreign supplier may require a mandatory application of his national law is linked to the more general problem of the interaction of the rules of conflict of laws and Union law. If we admit that the rule of mutual recognition is applicable in the area of private law a conflict arises between the Rome I Regulation (N.B. as noted above, it harmonised the rules of choice of law in Europe) and the principle of mutual recognition. It is difficult to envisage the practical implications of such conflict in cases where the core rules of conflict of laws (*e.g.* free choice of law) would be found to contravene TFEU. Indeed, it is not completely unambiguous what solution should be adopted if a party first voluntarily chooses to be subject to the law of a foreign jurisdiction but later seeks special protection or seeks to get rid of these restrictions via domestic law. In light of this, *Schneider* submitted that the Rome Convention - now superseded by the Rome I Regulation - was a common result of the development of European private international law, and that it therefore may not be displaced by other rules[680].

---

677 Weatherill S. 'Free Movement of Goods' 55(2) *ICLQ* (2006) 460

678 *Compare*: Remien O. *Zwingendes Vertragsrecht und Grundfreiheiten des EG-Vertrages* (Tübingen: Mohr Siebeck 2003) 493

679 *See e.g.*: Wolf M. 'Privates Bankvertragrecht im EG-Binnenmarkt. Auswirkung der II. EG- Bankrechts-Richtlinie auf privatrechtliche Bankgeschäfte' 47 *WM* (1990) 1981 *et seq*. Giovannopoulos R. *Die Harmonisierung des privatrechtlichen Bankgeheimnisses im europäischen Wirtschaftsverkehr. Eine rechtsdogmatische und rechtsvergleichende Untersuchung zum deutschen, englischen, französischen und griechischen Rech unter besonderer Berücksichtigung der Europäischen Datenschutzrichtlinie, der EG-Grundfreiheiten und der Gemeinschaftsgrundrechte* (Baden Baden 2000/2001) 329

680 Schneider U. H. 'Europäische und Internationale Harmonisierung des Bankrechts. Zugleich ein Beitrag zur Angleichung des Privatrechts in der Europäischen Gemeinschaft' *NJW* (1991) 1993

It would seem that the most logical solution in such cases is to weigh up the interests of both parties in light of Union law. In the author's view, the Court of Justice should decide on a case-by-case basis how the goals of TFEU could be achieved when applying the rule of mutual recognition. However, what particular criteria should be chosen to arrive at the conclusion that a vendor's interests are more important than buyer's or otherwise? Given this ambivalence, for some commentators the 'export' of home rules of private law to the other jurisdiction of the Union seems impossible to implement[681]. For example, *von Wilmowsky* submits that the rules of mutual recognition 'end up in constitutional stalemate' in the area of private law[682]. It seems that this rule is of little value in eliminating disparities in trade between Member States arising from divergent legislation on standard form contracts.

As observed in Part I, most legal orders of the Union mostly provide for non-absolute prohibitions regarding the application of exclusion clauses. Our comparative research yields the conclusion that the application of the test of reasonableness, or an examination of the contract using the criterion of good faith, often provides for similar general results without substantial economic disadvantages to any of the parties. It is, therefore, inferred that the rules of any country can be applied without significant damage to the interests of the Union. These arguments give additional support to the assumption that the rules of the country of destination must not necessarily be set aside where they are somewhat different from the rules of the country of origin. Finally, the implementation of the principle of mutual recognition has its own boundaries too. The mandatory application of the laws of the country of destination can still be justified pursuant to Article 36 TFEU or under the concept of mandatory requirements developed by the *Cassis de Dijon* case law[683]. Thus, the country of destination (together with local businesses) can *inter alia* rely on the fairness of commercial transactions by retaining strict national regulations on standard form contracts.

---

[681] Remien O. *Zwingendes Vertragsrecht und Grundfreiheiten des EG-Vertrages* (Tübingen: Mohr Siebeck 2003) 179

[682] von Wilmowsky P. 'EG-Vertrag und kollisionsrechtliche Rechtswahlfreiheit' 62 *RabelsZ* (1998) 19

[683] There are numerous examples that confirm that the rule of mutual recognition is not absolute. *See e.g.* Oosthoek C-286/81, paras 18-21; Buet C-382/87, paras 11-17, *etc*.

2. POSITIVE ELIMINATION OF DISTORTIONS IN INTRA-UNION TRADE

2.1 HARMONISATION OF NATIONAL REGULATIONS ON STANDARD FORM CONTRACTS

2.1.1 SHORTCOMINGS OF THE EXISTING INTERNATIONAL REGULATIONS

As analysed in the preceding chapters, the market freedoms are of little use in striking out strict national regulations on standard form contracts, even if such rules may actually deter market participants from concluding contracts in the jurisdictions of foreign Member States. These regulations may be considered as falling outside the scope of Article 34 TFEU or their application may find sound justification in assessing the fairness of business transactions. Moreover, the transfer of national laws by means of the rule of mutual recognition seems to be impossible to implement in the area of private law. Finally, further existing multilateral international treaties ratified in the Member States do not offer fully acceptable solutions on how to avoid the mandatory effect of foreign laws. Given these arguments, further ways of eliminating all trade distortions in the internal market would be welcome.

First, most of the Member States ratified the CISG, which takes priority over national laws. It was expected that this convention would supersede national legislation and unify sales laws across Europe and other regions. However, England together with Ireland and Portugal has not elected to do this[684]. On the other hand, Germany, France, and Lithuania are not members of the Hague Conventions on Uniform Law on Sale of Goods and Uniform Law on Formation of Contracts that is, for example, applicable in England. As with its position in respect of general trends towards the unification of private laws in Europe, England is also sceptical about transposing the CISG into its national legislation. The reasons for this are not completely clear; however, English lawyers are generally suspicious about the uncertainty that may emanate from broadly formulated provisions of the CISG. Moreover, lawyers have often criticised the CISG for not adequately reflecting the peculiarities of the trade in commodities, in particular documentary sales of commodities[685]. In practice,

---

[684] The relevant Hague Conventions were enacted by the UK in the Uniform Law on International Sales Act 1967. *As for the application of the CISG see, e.g.*, DiMatteo A. L. *The Law of International Contracting* (The Hague London Boston: Kluwer Law International 2000) 207; Stadler H.-J. *Allgemeine Geschäftsbedingungen im internationalen Handelsverkehr* (Heidelberg 2003) 50; Bonell M. J. 'The Need and Possibilities of a Codified European Contract Law' 5 *ERPL* (1997) 508 *et seq*

[685] *See e.g.*: Schlechtriem P. 'Interpretation, Gap-Filling and Further Development of the UN-Sales Convention' *Pace International Law Review* (2004), Paper 215

many law firms advising large businesses on international business transactions – by virtue of Article 6 CISG - opt out of the convention and rely on domestic law[686]. Thus the CISG can also be excluded on the basis of standard form contracts. Though most Member States of the European Union have ratified the CISG, pursuant to Article 2 the convention does not address all issues relating to the international supply of goods. For example, sales of shares, stocks, investment securities or financial products, sales of ships, vessels, and aircraft fall out of the scope of this convention. These questions are decided under the national law governing contractual relations[687]. The concept of standard form contracts does not appear in the CISG either.

Pursuant to Article 4 *lit. a*, the CISG does not regulate the validity of contract terms. Issues regarding the enforceability of standard terms should be decided under relevant national laws governing a contract[688]. Only the assessment of the validity of incorporation of standard contract terms would definitely fall within the scope of CISG, as Articles 14-24 CISG establish general rules for the formation of contracts. In future, issues regarding the enforceability of contractual terms may be regulated by a new convention to be drafted under the auspices of UNIDROIT. The new convention is, however, hardly likely to materialise in the foreseeable future. Furthermore, the situation is not much different if we consider the actual effect of the Rome I Regulation. True, the Rome I Regulation permits the free choice of law.

However, this choice of law is subject to some constraints. First, parties cannot derogate where the case is connected to the law of one member state only. Second, parties can derogate from the mandatory provisions of one country only. Finally, under the Rome I Regulation, similarly to its predecessor the Rome Convention, free choice of law is guaranteed only for international but not domestic transactions. Usually, parties face considerable difficulties in choosing the applicable law in practice as the prestige of both parties often precludes agreement on one or other of their national laws. As a result, a third foreign law

---

686 Basedow J. 'Codification of Private Law in the European Union: the making of a Hybrid' 1 *E.R.P.L.* (2001) 44; Ziegel S. J. 'The Future of the International Sales Convention from a Common Law Perspective' 6 *New Zealand Business Law Quarterly* (November 2000) 341-2. *Compare also*: Siehr K. in: *Kommentar zum UN-Kaufrecht. Übereinkommen der Vereinigten Nationen über Verträge über den Internationalen Warenkauf (CISG),* Honsell H., Hrsg. (Springer Heidelberg Dordrecht London New York 2010) 47-9; Bonell J. in: Bianca-Bonell *Commentary on the International Sales Law. The 1980 Vienna Sales Convention* (Giuffré Milan 1987) 53-8

687 *See more:* Müller H., Otto H.-H. *Allgemeine Geschäftsbedingungen im internationalen Wirtschaftsverkehr* (Neuwied, Kriftel, Berlin 1994) 42

688 Koch R. 'Wider den formularmäßigen Ausschluss des UN-Kaufrechts' *NJW* (2000) 910; Sieg O. 'Allgemeine Geschäftsbedingungen im grenzüberschreitenden Verkehr' *RIW* (1997) 811

is often chosen in the international transactions, which is unknown to both parties and creates additional costs[689].

Finally, in cases where the law chosen is different from the *lex fori,* the court handling the case may also face substantial difficulties in applying foreign laws. These difficulties are even greater if the forum does not share the same language as that foreign jurisdiction. For example, in many European jurisdictions (*e.g.* England, Lithuania) foreign law, as a matter of fact, must be pleaded and proved by private parties[690], which can be expensive for them. Foreign experts are required, at the expense of the parties. Despite these efforts, there are many studies that indicate that the ratio of cases where foreign law was applied wrongly is unexpectedly high[691]. Even if the forum gets accurate information on the foreign law, it is sometimes submitted that in such cases it would not be authorised to improve the existing foreign legal doctrine if that were necessary[692]. Given these difficulties, practically speaking it seems that the Rome I Regulation is not sufficient for parties hoping to avoid unfavourable foreign regulations.

It is, therefore, submitted that an international supplier doing business abroad has to check that his typical contracts would not conflict with national regulations on standard form contracts. Even though domestic law would eventually come into play, probably the safest approach would be to abide by different national regulations so as to reduce chances that a contract would be struck out at some stage. Naturally, this may burden a company substantially, as it is hindered from preparing one standard form contract to be used in any jurisdiction across the European Union. Bearing this in mind, the Commission's concern regarding possible intervention via secondary legislation is entirely understandable.

---

689 von Bar Ch., Lando O., Swan S. 'Communication on European Contract Law: Joint Response of the Commission on European Contract Law and the Study Group on a European Civil Code' 2 *ERPL* (2002) 217

690 *See*: Art. 808 of the Lithuanian Civil Procedure Code. It should be noted that the German courts in accordance with § 293 Civil Procedure Law investigate foreign law *ex officio. For more see:* Heidemann M. 'Methodology of Uniform Contract Law – The Unidroit Principles as a Source of Law' 18(4) *EBLR* (2007) 736

691 For instance, in the legal literature one may find that *Max Rheinstein's* survey is reported, according to which in forty American cases of applying foreign law, it was wrongly applied in thirty two of the cases. *See*: Lord Mance J. 'Is Europe Aiming to civilise the Common Law?' *EBRD* (2007) 98

692 Wagner G. 'The Economics of Harmonisation: the Case of Contract Law' 39 *C.M.L. Rev.* (2002) 1011

2.1.2 *Legitimacy of Harmonisation of the Laws of Contract under TFEU*

In the report on 'Completing the Internal Market' of 1985 the Commission took the position that harmonisation should be used to eliminate those barriers that passed the *Cassis de Dijon* mutual recognition test[693]. Pursuant to Article 114(1) TFEU [*ex* 95(1) EC], the term 'harmonisation' refers to the 'measures for the approximation of the provisions laid down by law, regulation, administrative action in Member States which have as their object the establishment and functioning of the internal market'.

The harmonisation of national laws is somewhat different from the negative integration that is achieved by ensuring the free movement of economic factors. The Court of Justice has said that:

> 'Fundamental principle of a unified market and its corollary, the free movement of goods, many not under any circumstances be made subject to the condition that there should first be an approximation of national laws for if that condition has to be fulfilled the principle would be reduced to a mere cipher. Moreover it is apparent that the purposes of Articles 30 and 100 are different. The purpose of Article 30, save for certain specific exceptions, to abolish in the immediate future all quantitative restrictions on the imports of goods and all measures having an equivalent effect, whereas the general purpose of Article 100, is by approximating the laws, regulations and administrative provisions of the member states, to enable obstacles of whatever kind arising from disparities between them to be reduced.'[694]

Thus, according to the Court of Justice, the harmonisation of European laws would not eliminate all restrictions arising from divergent legal systems in intra-Union trade, but rather mitigate them. Both the market freedoms and secondary legislation can be applied concurrently. The dismantling of trade restrictions in the internal market must not be implemented exclusively through harmonisation. Probably the foremost issue regarding possible harmonisation of the laws of contract in Europe is whether or not the Union has the competence to act in this area at all, as the Union can introduce new legislation only insofar as the

---

693 *See*: European Communities, Commission, Completing the Internal Market. White Paper from the Commission to the European Council (Milan, 28-29 June 1985) COM (85) 310 final, 14 June 1985, para 65

694 Commission of the European Communities v. Italian Republic C-193/80, para 17. *Compare also:* van Gerven W. 'Harmonisation of Private Law: do we need it?' 41(2) *C.M.L. Rev.* (2004) 507 *et seq*

Member States confer competence upon it (*see*: 5(2) TEU). Currently, areas of law that must remain free from Union intervention are not entirely clear.

The harmonisation of the laws of contract is not explicitly stipulated in TFEU. It is, therefore, questionable whether the TFEU provides sufficient legal basis for the implementation of such harmonisation[695]. Article 81, 114 and 352 TFEU may provide possible legal grounds for adopting new legislation; however it seems that there are no general competences for the enactment of fundamental and comprehensive new legislation such as a European Civil Code. According to the case law of the Court of Justice, legal grounds must be free of any ambiguities as 'the choice of the legal basis does not depend on the institution's conviction, but rather must be based on objective factors which are amenable to judicial review'[696].

The application of Article 81 TFEU is basically limited to private international law and civil procedure law, while Article 352 TFEU would not be applicable unless specific action by the institutions of the Union cannot be justified using the other legal grounds. For example, the Court of Justice noted in its Opinion 2/94 that 'Article 352 TFEU [*ex* 308 EC] is designed to fill the gap where no specific provisions in the Treaty confers on the Community institutions expressed or implied powers to act if such powers appear none the less to be necessary to entitle the Community to carry out its functions with a view to attaining one of the objectives laid down by the Treaty'[697]. Thus the legal grounds as established in Article 352 TFEU and Article 114 TFEU are mutually exclusive. Moreover, the Council must adopt the measures introduced under Article 352 TFEU by unanimity, which is difficult to achieve in practice. In this regard, it would seem that the specific provisions of Article 114 TFEU would currently be the most appropriate legal basis[698].

---

[695] *For more disucussion see*: Davies G. 'Can Selling Arrangements be harmonised?' 30(3) *E. L. Rev.* (2005) 371-385; Rutgers J. W. European Competence and a European Civil Code, a Common Frame of Reference or an Optimal Instrument. Downloaded on 1 March 2010 from <http://papers.ssrn.com>; Gerven van W. 'Codifying European Private Law: Top down and Bottom up', in: *An Academic Green Paper on European Contract Law* Grundmann S., Stuyck J. eds. (The Hague: Kluwer Law International 2002) 432

[696] Commission v. Council ('Titanium Dioxide') C-300/89, para 10

[697] Opinion 2/94 of the Court 28 March 1996 (Accession by the Community to the European Convention for Protection of Human Rights and Fundamental Freedoms) para 29. *See some relevant case law about the effect of Article 352 TFEU [ex 308 EC] as a proper legal basis see*: Netherlands v. European Parliament and Council C-377/98, paras 24-25; European Parliament v. Council C-436/03, paras 36-37

[698] *For some discussions see*: Staudenmayer D. 'The Commission Communication on European Contract Law and its Follow-up', in: *An Academic Green Paper on European Contract Law* (The Hague: Kluwer Law International 2002) 47; Basedow J. 'Codification of Private Law in the European Union: the Making of a Hybrid' 1 *E.R.P.L.* (2001) 44 *et seq.*

Article 114 TFEU [*ex* 95 EC] was included in the EC Treaty by the Single European Act with effect from 1987. This article was used as a legal basis for adopting the majority of directives in recent decades. It empowered the Community to adopt measures under the procedure laid down in Article 294 TFEU [*ex* 251 EC] for the approximation of laws of the Member States in order to maintain the establishment and functioning of the internal market. In earlier case law, the Court of Justice showed a notably relaxed approach towards the harmonisation of laws across the Union. For example, in the *Titanium Dioxide* case the Court of Justice explained that the Union is permitted to legislate in cases where 'harmonising measures are necessary to deal with disparities between the laws of Member States in areas where such disparities are liable to create or maintain distorted conditions of competition …'[699]. Given the above analysis, measures aimed at harmonisation of national regulations on standard form contracts in business-to-business contracts would probably pass this test. However, in more recent rulings the legal boundaries of the Union's competences with respect to the harmonisation of national laws were defined anew.

In the prominent case of *Germany v. European Parliament and Council* the Court of Justice confirmed that the Union cannot increase the power conferred upon the Community by TFEU, and it does not possess general competences with regard to the harmonisation of the internal market, but rather should contribute to measures that are intended to eliminate obstacles to the free movement of goods and freedom to provide services, or to the removal of distortions of competition[700]. These considerations were restated functionally in

[699] Commission v. Council ('Titanium Dioxide') C-300/89, para 15

[700] 'Tobacco Advertising' C-376/98, para 83. *See also*: Arnold André GmbH & Co. C-434/02, paras 31-34; Swedish Match C-210/03, para 33; Federal Republic of Germany v. European Parliament and Council of the European Union C-380/03, para 95. United Kingdom v. European Parliament and Council C-66/04, para 41. *For more discussions about the ramifications of this ruling 'Tobacco Advertising ruling' see*, *e.g.*, Weatherill S. 'Constitutional issues – how much is Best Left unsaid?' in: *The Harmonisation of European Contract Law. Implications for European Private Laws, Business and Legal Practice,* Vogenauer S., Weatherill S. eds. (Oxford and Portland, Oregon: Hart Publishing 2006) 93 *et seq.*; Weatherill S. 'European Contract Law: Taking the Heat out of Questions Competence' 15(1) *EBLR* (2004) 23 *et seq.*; Usher A. J. 'C-376/98 Germany v. European Parliament and Council ('Tobacco advertising'). Judgement of the Full Court of 5 October 2000 [2000] ECR I-8419', 38 *C.M.L. Rev.* (2001)1519 *et seq.*; Davies G. 'Can Selling Arrangements be Harmonised?' 30(3) *E.L.Rev.* 2005, 371-385; Blair W. QC, Brent R. 'A Single European Law of Contract' 15(1) *EBLR* (2004) 13-15; Strese J. *Die Kompetenzen der Europäischen Gemeinschaft zur* Privatrechtsangleichung *im Binnenmarkt. Eine Untersuchung zur vertikalen Kompetenzenverteilung im Bereich des Gemeinschaftsprivatrechts und zu den Folgen komptenzüberschreitenden Handels* (Nomos Verlagsgesellschaft Baden Baden 2006) 24-31, *etc.*

the *British American Tobacco and Imperial Tobacco* case[701]. According to the rationale from this case, Article 114 TFEU [*ex* 95 EC] can be used to improve the functioning of the internal market, thereby eliminating obstacles to the free movement of goods and to the freedom to provide services. In addition, such distortion of competition must be *appreciable* to be able to justify harmonisation[702]. The existence of legal differences between national private laws as such would not be a sufficient ground *per se* to justify the harmonisation of trade laws or to create unified European laws. On the other hand, the legal ramifications of this case are not unambiguous. For instance, *Basedow* submits that 'the contested directive prohibiting the effective advertising of tobacco products impaired the functioning of the internal market itself. The prohibition of advertisement effectively prevents the integration of internal markets. Therefore, factual background should be considered before referring to this case'[703]. In this regard, another interesting example is *the Netherlands v. European Parliament and Council of the European Union*, where the Court of Justice concluded that Article 114 TFEU [*ex* 95 EC] could be used as a legal basis for harmonising laws if, due to the differing interpretation of the national laws, 'the aim is to prevent the emergence of future obstacles to trade resulting from multifarious development of national laws provided that the emergence of such obstacles is likely, and the measure in question is designed to prevent them'[704]. Finally, Article 114 TFEU may be employed as a measure harmonising or approximating laws of the Member States, but not for the introduction of any additional legal instruments to national legislation.

It is difficult to answer to what extent the unification of contract laws would eliminate trade obstacles. Different interpretations are possible. *Remien* is right in submitting that it is more a question of political influence as to whether contract law and other areas of private law should be unified[705]. Interestingly, the Commission has consistently devoted more attention – as *Weatherill* outlines - to the question of what technical steps are to be taken in developing European contract law than what is to be done constitutionally[706]. For the Commission the issue of legal grounds is tied to legal form, content and scope[707].

---

701 British American Tobacco C-491/01, para 60

702 'Tobacco Advertising' C-376/98, para 106

703 Basedow J. 'The Case for A European Contract Act' in: *An Academic Green Paper on European Contract Law* (The Hague: Kluwer Law International 2002) 155-6

704 Netherlands v. European Parliament and Council C-377/98, para 18. *Compare also:* Swedish Match C-210/03; Alliance for National Health C-154/04 and C-155/04

705 Remien O. *Zwingendes Vertragsrecht und Grundfreiheiten des EG-Vertrages* (Tübingen: Mohr Siebeck 2003) 578

706 Weatherill S. 'Reflections on the EC's Competence to develop a 'European Contract Law' 3 *ERPL* (2005) 406

707 Ibid., p. 415

In conclusion, the regulatory competences of the Union are prevented from enacting comprehensive new legislation to harmonise national regulations on standard form contracts. TFEU, as along with the former EC Treaty, does not contain sufficient legal grounds for future harmonisation of national regulations on standard form contracts in business-to-business contracts. Moreover, even if such harmonisation took place, a Member State that still tried to maintain national provisions would have to notify the Commission of these provisions as well as of the grounds for maintaining them. The list of legitimate exclusions whereby national countries may maintain national provisions is exhaustive: they basically include the basis of major needs referred to in Article 36 TFEU and additionally as relates to the protection of environment and the working environment. Though this provision has been criticised fiercely, as *Craig* indicates, many fears about the exception established in Article 114(4) TFEU [*ex* 95(4) EC] 'have not been borne out by state practice'[708]. It is true that this exception largely diminishes the effects of harmonisation, as the legal differences are likely to continue in existence. On the other hand, Article 114(4) TFEU stipulates that this exception only be invoked in order to retain the existing provisions, and not to introduce new rules that are not in line with harmonised secondary legislation.

2.1.3 PRACTICAL OBSTACLES TO INTRA-UNION TRADE

It is a commonplace that harmonisation would simplify inter-state business dealings as well as make them less costly[709]. A domestic supplier could gain a competitive advantage against foreign companies that are exposed to unknown regulations. As outlined earlier, businesses are usually ignorant of foreign legal systems unless they have previously gathered relevant experience. This asymmetry of information can have a deterrent effect. In particular, genuinely

---

708 Craig P. 'The Evolution of the Single Market', in: *The Law of the Single European Market*, Barnard C., Scott J. *eds*. (Oxford and Portland, Oregon: Hart Publishing 2002) 19. *Compare also*: de Sadeleer N. 'Procedures for Derogations from the Principle of Approximation Laws under Article 95 EC' 40 *C.M.L. Rev* (2003) 891 *et seq*

709 *For a sceptical view see:* Wagner G. 'The Economics of Harmonisation: the Case of Contract Law' 39 *C.M.L. Rev.* (2002) 995-1023; Weatherill S. 'Why object to the Harmonisation of Private Law by the EC?' 12 *ERPL* (2004) 633. *Compare also*: Drobnig U. A 'Subsidiary Plea: A European Contract Law for Intra-European Border-Crossing Contracts', in: *An Academic Green Paper on European Contract Law* (The Hague: Kluwer Law International 2002) 343 *et seq.*; Smits J. 'Diversity of Contract Law and the European Internal Market', in: *The Need of a European Contract Law. Empirical and Legal Perspectives*, Smits J. *ed.* (Groningen: Europa Law Publishing 2005) 166 *et seq.*; Mattei U. 'A Transaction Costs Approach to the European Code' 5 *ERPL* (1997) 537

small companies can face problems entering foreign markets because of little-known foreign regulations or because it is too costly to get advice on foreign legal systems[710]. Such companies would have more faith in harmonised legal orders, even though the actual legal results of applying different rules may be more or less the same.

Indeed, it is also true that companies face not only legal, but also linguistic and cultural problems if they decide to do business in a foreign jurisdiction. In this respect, *Wagner* convincingly argued that the co-existence of different legal systems at the level of the Union is a kind of tax on European businesses[711]. It may be questioned whether the existence of additional costs relating to familiarisation with foreign legal systems *per se* constitutes the '*appreciable*' distortion of competition to pass the test developed by the *Tobacco Advertising* case, and therefore is a sufficient legal basis to justify harmonisation under Article 114 TFEU [*ex* 95 EC]. As noted earlier, the links between Article 114 TFEU and European contract law seem to be too indirect to find a sound legal basis for any harmonisation under TFEU. Somewhat higher transactional costs of doing business abroad are inherent to every transaction, and therefore they should not constitute a special restriction on the exercise of the market freedoms[712]. Moreover, the harmonisation of laws *per se* will not solve the issue of unfamiliarity with foreign laws unless this harmonisation is accomplished *in toto*. Another important point is that the obstacles mentioned above are more apparent in theory than in practice. The practical evidence as to what extent parties are actually burdened by foreign laws when entering these markets is difficult to gather, if it is available at all[713].

Interestingly, *Posner* stresses that 'the hypotheses [of contract law] are either so general that they cannot be tested empirically or they can be tested, but

---

710 *See also*: Basedow J. 'A Common Contract Law for the Common Market' 33 *C.M.L. Rev.* (1996) 1184 *et seq;* Beale H. 'Finding the Remaining Traps Instead of Unifying Contract Law', in: *An Academic Green Paper on European Contract Law* (The Hague: Kluwer Law International 2002) 68; Staudenmayer D. 'The Commission Communication on European Contract Law: What Future for European Contract Law?' 2 *ERPL* (2002) 255; Wagner G. 'The Project of Harmonizing European Tort Law' 42 *C.M.L. Rev.* (2005) 1271-2

711 Wagner G. 'The Project of Harmonizing European Tort Law' 42 *C.M.L. Rev.* (2005) 1272

712 *See also:* Drexl J. 'Continuing Contract Law Harmonisation under the White Paper of 1985? – Between Minimum Harmonisation, Mutual Recognition, and Uniform Law in: *An Academic Green Paper on European Contract Law* (The Hague: Kluwer Law International 2002) 115; Basedow J. 'The Case for a European Contract Act', in: *An Academic Green Paper on European Contract Law* (The Hague: Kluwer Law International 2002) 152

713 *Cf.* Schwartze A. 'Design for an Empirical Data Investigation in to the Impact of Existing Law Harmonisation under the White Paper of 1985', in: *An Academic Green Paper on European Contract Law* (The Hague: Kluwer Law International 2002) 59 *et seq.*

their implications are so specific that they do not reach the minimum level of generality which is necessary for manageable legislation'[714]. For example, English lawyers emphasise pragmatic solution, stating that legal authorities should deal with practical problems and intervene only if these practical problems cannot be solved in another way. The institutions of the Union, in particular the Commission, put considerable effort into collecting empirical data about the deterrent effect of foreign laws, yet the reliability of these data is difficult to prove as laws are continuously changing[715]. Responses from legal practitioners and other businesses about the effect of foreign legislation are mixed and the feedback is somewhat inconclusive[716]. For example, *Vogenauer* and *Weatherill* submit that roughly a quarter of all businesses are effectively deterred from cross-border trade[717]. Some other surveys indicate that many businesses consider foreign laws obstacles to cross-border trade; however, a much smaller percentage (14%) considered them large[718]. For example, according to *Smits*:

> 'It seems impossible to calculate either the cost of legal diversity or the costs of uniform law: a quantitative analysis cannot provide the answer to the question raised'[719].

It is submitted by way of conclusion that the extent to which a company is actually deterred by a foreign legal system should be determined on a case-by-case basis. Many companies may be adversely affected by legal diversity; however, this is not necessarily a case for them all. Nonetheless, even if this

---

714 Posner R. 'Economic Analysis of Contract Law after three Decades: Success or Failure?' 112 *Yale L. J.* (2003) 829

715 *See also:* Oliver P. *Free Movement of Goods in the European Community under Articles 28 to 30 of the EC Treaty* (London: Sweet and Maxwell 2003) 129

716 Vogenauer S., Weatherill S. 'The EC's Competence to Pursue Harmonisation', in: *The Harmonisation of European Contract Law. Implications for European Private Laws, Business and Legal Practice*, Vogenauer S., Weatherill S. eds. (Oxford and Portland, Oregon: Hart Publishing 2006) 116. Different responses to the Commission's Communication on European Contract law (COM (2001) Final) are published under: <ec.europa.eu/consumers/cons_int/safe_shop/fair_bus_pract/cont_law/comments>

717 Vogenauer S., Weatherill S. 'The EC's Competence to Pursue Harmonisation', in: *The Harmonisation of European Contract Law. Implications for European Private Laws, Business and Legal Practice*, Vogenauer S., Weatherill S. eds. (Oxford and Portland, Oregon: Hart Publishing 2006) 136

718 *See*: Mance, Lord Jonathan 'Is Europe Aiming to Civilise the Common Law?' *EBRD* (2007) 98

719 Smits J. 'Diversity of Contract Law and the European Internal Market', in: *The Need for a European Contract Law. Empirical and Legal Perspectives*, Smits J. ed. (Groningen: Europa Law Publishing 2005) 178-9

were relevant for some of them, it would still be worthwhile to pursue the harmonisation of national laws further. By way of a thought experiment: some consumers are rich, have sufficient knowledge on foreign laws and are therefore actually hardly affected by legal diversity either. However, this issue did not inhibit the Union from enacting a number of directives relating to the protection of consumers. It would seem that some additional legal protection should be provided for genuinely small companies even though it is difficult to establish which exact companies really need this protection.

In practice, a court would examine all issues on a case-by-case basis, in particular whether the company really lacked special knowledge or had weak bargaining power, and therefore accepted derisory standard contract terms. According to some surveys conducted on behalf of the Commission, the problems of complying with different national regulations on consumer protection were highlighted as the most crucial factor causing difficulty in the development of sales abroad. Given these difficulties, the harmonisation of divergent national regulations was seen as an effective measure in making the development of sales throughout the Union easier[720]. One may suggest that the harmonisation or at least preparation of sectorial subject–specific guidelines on regulations on standard contract terms would be viewed positively by representatives of different entrepreneurs and other non-governmental organisations (*e.g.* Chartered Institute of Purchasing and Supply, United Parcel Service, General Electric, representatives of the International Chamber of Commerce). Nevertheless, significant difficulties were faced when identifying best practices in the usage of standard terms.

It should be stressed that some scholars have reached the conclusion that harmonisation leading to unified European contract law is not necessary, at least at this stage. For example, *Wagner* argues that there are many small and medium sized companies in southern Germany that remain undeterred by legal diversity[721]. Many companies engaged in international business decide to opt out of ordinary judicial systems, and are therefore often subject to the kind of customary business law that is commonly known as *lex mercatoria.* Thus, in practice, formal legal rules - along with formal dispute settlement mechanisms, legal sanctions - are not as important to business as might seem. Businesses also often rely on trust, business understanding or simply the pressure they can exert

---

[720] Vogenauer S., Weatherill S. 'The EC's Competence to Pursue Harmonisation', in: *The Harmonisation of European Contract Law. Implications for European Private Laws, Business and Legal Practice*, Vogenauer S., Weatherill S. *eds*. (Oxford and Portland, Oregon: Hart Publishing 2006) 114-5

[721] Wagner G. 'The Economics of Harmonisation: the Case of Contract Law' 39 *C.M.L. Rev.* (2002) 1015. *Contra*: Lando O. 'Principles of European Contract Law: An Alternative to or a Precursor of European Legislation?' 40(3) *Am. J. Com. L* (1992) 573 *et seq*

by threatening loss of future business[722]. For instance, retailers may replace goods merely because the contract counterparty or consumer does not like them, which creates confidence in further business relations. This factor probably explains why businesses often consider what is commercially reasonable, and not what the formal legal stipulations of contract are. The reality is that businesses often agree contracts even though lawyers advise them that the contracts would be unenforceable or that there are other legal problems, for instance, issues relating to the incorporation of terms into a contract, exclusion clauses, etc. Surprisingly, many such contracts are often enforceable and do not create any issues for the contracting parties in practice. These examples show that businesses are probably less affected by foreign regulations than legal theory would lead us to expect.

Finally, cultural differences should also be considered. For instance, it is sometimes argued that Germans are more likely to rely on a contract that can be seen as building trust, whereas commentators believe that in England contract and trust are seen as mutually exclusive. References to contractual arrangements are more likely to destroy business relations in England[723]. In light of these attitudes, cultural peculiarities relating to the conduct of business abroad may sometimes be even more important than differences in the law of contract between various jurisdictions in the Union. As for different legal systems co-existing in one country, an interesting example is the United Kingdom. The issue of legal differences as a barrier to trade is often exaggerated if one considers the example of England and Scotland. It is claimed that the existing legal differences between England and Scotland do not impede trade between these two jurisdictions[724]. However, it cannot be denied that the common language shared by the jurisdictions is enough to overcome legal differences. Arguably it is for this reason that an English or Irish lawyer trained in common law would be able to find a proper answer to a question of Scottish law more quickly than a

---

[722] Beale H. 'Finding the Remaining Traps Instead of Unifying Contract Law', in: *An Academic Green Paper on European Contract Law* (The Hague: Kluwer Law International 2002) 70-1. *See also:* Macaulay S. 'An Empirical View of Contract' *Wisconsin Law Review* (1985) 465; Wilhelmsson T. 'The Legal, the Cultural and the Political – Conclusions from Different Perspectives on Harmonisation of European Contract Law' 13 *EBLR* (2002) 543; Collins H. 'Formalism and Efficiency: Designing European Commercial Contract Law' 1 *ERPL* (2000) 218

[723] Beale H. 'Finding the Remaining Traps instead of Unifying Contract Law' in: *An Academic Green Paper on European Contract Law* (The Hague: Kluwer Law International 2002) 71

[724] *See*: McKendrick E. 'Harmonisation of European Contract Law: the State we are in', in: *The Harmonisation of European Contract Law. Implications for European Private Laws, Business and Legal Practice*, Vogenauer S., Weatherill S. eds. (Oxford and Portland, Oregon: Hart Publishing 2006) 15. Similar examples of legal diversity within one country could be Spain as well, where Catalanian law exists besides the Spanish law.

lawyer from continental Europe. Hence one should give consideration not only to differences in law, but also in the actual ability of parties to become familiarised with foreign laws. In light of the foregoing discussion, it is sometimes argued that the European regulator would prefer to encourage competition rather than strive for unity[725]. However, it is unlikely that a company would move to a foreign jurisdiction just because its legal system seemed to be more favourable.

As outlined at the beginning of the book, there is almost no competition between large companies in offering the most favourable standard form contracts. In practice, 'auxiliary' contract terms are more or less the same for all companies in the same sector. Thus even though the Commission's proposals are difficult to implement, any other initiatives intended to seek an approximation in this area or aimed at enhancing the awareness of businesses are welcome. In the author's view, it is difficult to support *Wagner's* position that companies do not face substantial obstacles regarding their unfamiliarity with foreign legal systems. Though it is difficult to collect much empirical evidence, it is simply hard to believe that companies from, for example, Eastern and Central Europe (*e.g.* associations of farmers exporting dairy products to other jurisdictions) that desperately want to save money on legal advice in domestic transactions could afford advice from foreign law firms on all possible legal risks in relation to conducting business in a foreign jurisdiction. Thus the conclusion must be drawn that large companies would gain a competitive advantage against smaller ones with regard to entering into foreign markets where legal diversity continues to exist. Similarly, enterprises incorporated in smaller jurisdictions in the Union ordinarily deal more often with companies from other countries, and are therefore more affected by legal diversity than companies from large jurisdictions. Finally, it must be noted that intra-Union commercial trade has not been left completely out of the scope of regulation. In fact, several European Union directives are also relevant for commercial arrangements[726]. Thus, even if an appropriate legal basis for the further approximation of laws is found under TFEU, the legal ramifications should not be over-estimated. It would probably be too ambitious to expect that secondary rules - *e.g.* directives - would set aside legal differences between Member States regarding rules on standard form contracts in business-to-business transactions entirely. Union-wide standard contract terms have come in for fierce criticism, as trade associations or

[725] Hesselink M. 'The European Commission's Action Plan: towards a more Coherent European Contract Law?' 4 *ERPL* (2004) 418

[726] See, *e.g.*, the Directive 97/5/EC on cross-border credit transfers, the Directive 2000/35/EC on combating late payment in commercial transactions, the Directive 2000/31/EC on electronic commerce, the Directive 2006/114/EC concerning misleading and comparative advertising, *etc.*

professional societies normally undertake the drafting of these terms. It is doubtful whether the Commission would be able to prepare sufficiently specific guidelines as an appropriate means of enhancing intra-Union trade[727]. For example, some directives have defined the consumer slightly differently[728]. Moreover, the directives still need to be implemented in national legal systems. Discrepancies can also arise owing to the divergent adaptation of domestic laws.

In this respect, a good example is the concept of good faith that was included in Directive 93/13/EEC on Unfair Terms in Consumer Contracts. It is sometimes contended that 'it is not impossible that the concept means something different to a common lawyer when it comes to be applied to individual cases'[729]. Indeed, different interpretations of the same terms in various jurisdictions may lead to confusion, or they else may increase transactional costs. Finally, owing to the fact that national authorities are left with the choice of form and method for achieving the objectives established by the directive, a foreign lawyer would be inherently unable to research the law or understand the specifics of national terminology without special training and good language skills[730]. In this context, it must be agreed with *von Bar* and *Swann* that a directive would be the least appropriate instrument for harmonising European Union contract law[731]. A regulation would seem to be a more suitable tool for these purposes. However, considering the fundamental differences between Member States on this issue, this would be very difficult to achieve.

---

727 *See*: von Bar Ch., Swan S. 'Response to the Action Plan on European Contract Law: a more Coherent European Contract Law (COM (2003) 63)' 3 *ERPL* (2003) 606-7

728 Compare, for example, the notion of 'consumer' as defined in the Directive 99/44/EC on certain aspects of the sale of consumer goods and associated guarantees and in the Directive 93/13/EC on unfair terms in consumer contracts.

729 *See*: Markesinis B., Unberath H., Johnston A. *The German Law of Contract* (Oxford and Portland, Oregon: Hart Publishing 2006) 168, *see also*: Unberath H., Johnston A. 'Law at, to or from the Centre? The European Court of Justice and the Harmonisation of Private Law in the European Union', in: *The Institutional Framework of European Private Law*, Cafaggi F., *ed.* (Oxford: Oxford University Press 2006) 190-1. For some more criticism on this issue see *e.g.* von Bar Ch., Lando O., Swan S. 'Communication on European Contract Law: Joint Response of the Commission on European Contract Law and the Study Group on a European Civil Code' 2 *ERPL* (2002) 232-3

730 *Compare*: Basedow J. 'A Common Contract Law for the Common Market' 33 *C.M.L. Rev.* (1996) 1189

731 von Bar C., Swann S. 'Response to the Action Plan on European Contract Law: a More Coherent European Contract Law (COM (2003) 63) 5 *ERPL* (2003) 613. As for the strict compliance with the requirements established by the Directive 93/13/EEC on unfair contract terms in consumer contract see: Commission v. the Netherlands C-144/99, para 17; Commission v. Spain C-70/03, para 15

2.2 Alternative Avenues to the Unification of Rules on Standard Form Contracts for European Business Transactions

Consumer law currently remains the most harmonised area of private law in the European Union[732]. As noted previously in this book, along with legal differences other important barriers persist which actually inhibit intra-Union trade (*e.g.* language, different cultures, traditions, communication)[733]. Thus it is clear that the harmonisation of laws will not eliminate trade barriers in Europe. On the basis of this assumption, the Commission's position that any approximation of civil laws should avoid radical interventions and instead contain gradual approximations, should be supported. At the same time, the other factors inhibiting intra-Union trade would be mitigated. A decade ago, *Wolf* persuasively advocated the use of an appropriate temporary solution pending the full harmonisation of private laws:

> 'In view of the differences in methodological and cultural backgrounds and perceptions of the law and its functions by the member States, uniform results are hard to imagine ... In a short time it may be useful to create precise rules that prohibit certain clauses'[734].

In 1989, and again in 1994, 2001, and 2006, the European Parliament called for common rules in the area of private law[735]. A number of communications from

---

[732] *About the approximation of consumer law in the Union see also*: Rott P. 'Minimum Harmonisation for the Completion of the Internal Market? The Example of Consumer Sales Law' 40 *C.M.L. Rev.* (2003) 1107; Reich N., Micklitz H.-W. *Europäisches Verbraucherrecht* (Baden-Baden 2003); Nebbia P. *Unfair Contract Terms in European Law. A Study in Comparative and EC Law* (Oxford and Portland, Oregon: Hart Publishing 2007)

[733] *For more about the harmonisation of legal terminology see, e.g.,* Pozzo B. 'Harmonisation of European Contract Law and the Need of Creating Common Terminology' 6 *ERPL* (2003) 754 *et seq*

[734] Wolf M. Harmonisation of Protection against Unfair Contract Terms in Private European Law, in: *European Legal Traditions and Israel*, Rabello A. M., *ed.* (Jerusalem: The Harry and Michael Sacher Institute for Legislative Research and Comparative Law 1994) 384

[735] OJ C 158/400 1989. The Resolution proposing harmonisation of certain parts of private law has been reiterated in several later resolutions *see*: OJ C205/518 1994, OJ C377/323 2000, OJ C140/538 2002, OJ C76E/95 2004, text adopted P6_TA (2006) 0109. *For some general comment on this issue and historical discourse see also:* Schwarz I. E. 'Perspektiven der Angleichung des Privatrechts in der Europäischen Gemeinschaft' *ZEuP* (1994) 570 *et seq*; Alpa G. 'Harmonisation of Contract Law and the Plan for a European Civil Code' 15(1) *EBLR* (2004) 33 *et seq*; Ciacchi A. C. 'An Optional Instrument for Consumer Contracts in the EU: Conflict of Laws and Conflict of Policies', in: *The Politics of the Draft Common Frame of Reference*, Somma A. *ed.* (Wolters Kluwer Law and Business, The Netherlands 2009) 3 *et seq*

the Commission on European contract law have also stressed the necessity of enacting unified rules for business transactions in the European Union in. In this respect, the most important one is the response by the Commission published on 11 June 2001, whereby the Commission invited the Parliament, Council and stakeholders, including businesses, legal practitioners, academics, and consumer groups to express their views on further developments in European contract law[736]. The Commission conceded *inter alia* that legal diversity increased the transactions costs of cross-border contracting, and therefore discouraged SMEs from engaging in such transactions[737]. Thus beyond those measures already planned, it was expected that harmonised regulations on standard contracts would be adopted. However, the possible scenarios stretch from doing nothing, to developing common contract law principles leading to the actual convergence of national laws, improving the quality of legislation already available, or adopting comprehensive new legislation at an European Union level[738]. Unfortunately, the idea of adopting comprehensive private law at the Union level received little support from national governments and legal practitioners[739]. Summarising the feedback received from various stakeholders regarding the anticipated harmonisation of civil laws in Europe, the Commission suggested supporting the second option and preparing a CFR, which would make European contract law more coherent. According to the Commission, the CFR should

---

736 Communication from the Commission to the European Parliament and the Council 'A more Coherent European Contract Law: An Action Plan' COM (2003) 68 final, OJ, 2003 C 63/01. *For the commentary see, e.g.:* Grundmann S., Stuyck J. 'An Academic Green Paper on European Contract Law – Scope, Common Ground and Debated Issues', in: *An Academic Green Paper on European Contract Law* (The Hague: Kluwer Law International 2002) 3-4; Hesselink M. 'The European Commission's Action Plan: Towards a more Coherent European Contract Law?" 4 *ERPL* (2004) 397 *et seq*

737 Communication from the Commission to the Council and the European Parliament 'On European Contract Law', Brussels 11.07.2001 Com (2001) 398 final

738 *See*: COM (2001) 398 final, para 16-20. About different public responses see *e.g.*: Staudenmayer D. 'The Commission Action Plan on European Contract Law' 2 *ERPL* (2003) 117-8

739 van Gerven W. 'Harmonisation of Private Law: do we need It?' 41(2) *C.M.L. Rev.* (2004) 528. *See also:* McKendrick E. 'Harmonisation of European Contract Law: the state we are in', in: *The Harmonisation of European Contract Law. Implications for European Private Laws, Business and Legal Practice*, Vogenauer S., Weatherill S. eds. (Oxford and Portland, Oregon: Hart Publishing 2006) 21-25; British Communication on European Contract Law. A Position on behalf of the Law Reform Committee of the General Bar Council of England and Wales. 21 October 2001; Beale H. 'The Development of European Private Law and European Commission's Action Plan on Contract Law', *X Juridica International* (2005) 7 *et seq. More about the attitude of the Commission see*: Report from the Commission. First Annual Progress on European Contract Law and the Acquis Review, 23.9.2005, COM (2005) 456 final; Report from the Commission. Second Progress Report on the Common Frame of Reference, 25.7.2007, COM (2007) 447 final

'provide for the best solutions in terms of common terminology and rules, *i.e.* the definition of fundamental concepts and abstract terms like 'contracts'[740]. In addition, the Action Plan has *inter alia* called for promotion of Union-wide standard contract terms for cases where 'a single contracting party possesses sufficient bargaining power to impose its contract terms'[741].

Preparatory work started in 2005 and the Academic Research Network produced the draft CFR in December 2007. Though the draft was declared to be an academic codification, it was prepared as a set of model rules that were intended to serve as a basis for an ultimate Community instrument[742]. Unfortunately, the draft was criticised by scholars across Europe as lacking political authority[743] and a coherent structure, inadequately addressing social justice[744], not being suitable use either as 'tool-box' or as an 'optional

---

740 *See*: Communication from the Commission to the European Parliament and the Council '*A more Coherent European Contract Law: An Action Plan*', COM (2003) 68 final, OJ, 2003 C 63/01; Communication from the Commission to the European Parliament and the Council 'European Contract Law and the revision of the *acquis:* the way forward' COM (2004) 651 final. *For academic discussions about the draft of the CFR see*: Lando O. The Structure and the Legal Values of the Common Frame of Reference (CFR) 3 *ERPL* (2007) 245; Somma A. Towards a European Private Law? The Common Frame of Reference in the Conflict between EC Law and National Laws, in: *European Private Law after the Common Frame of Reference*, Micklitz H.-W., Cafaggi F. eds. (Edward Elgar 2010) 1; Smits J. The Draft Common Frame of Reference: how to improve it?, in: *European Private Law after the Common Frame of Reference*, Micklitz H.-W., Cafaggi F. eds. (Edward Elgar 2010) 90; Whitettaker S. 'Draft Common Frame of Reference'. An Assessment (Commissioned by the Ministry of Justice, United Kingdom. November 2008); Grundmann S. 'Grand European Code Napoléon or Concise Uniform Contract Law? Defining the Scope of a Common Frame of Reference', in: *The Politics of the Draft Common Frame of Reference*, Somma A. ed. (Wolters Kluwer Law and Business, The Netherlands 2009) 19, etc.

741 OJ 2003, C63/1, para 83

742 Sefton-Green R. 'The DCFR: A Technical or Political Toolbox?', in: *The Politics of the Draft Common Frame of Reference*, Somma A. ed. (Wolters Kluwer Law and Business, The Netherlands 2009) 40

743 See, *e.g.,* Jansen N. The Authority of an Academic 'Draft Common Frame of Reference', in: *European Private Law after the Common Frame of Reference*, Micklitz H.-W., Cafaggi F. eds. (Edward Elgar 2010) 148-9; Rutgers J. W. European Competence and a European Civil Code, a Common Frame of Reference or an Optimal Instrument. Downloaded on 1 March 2010 from <http://papers.ssrn.com>

744 *Cf.* Grundmann S. The Role of Competition in the European Codification Process, in: European Private Law after the Common Frame of Reference, Micklitz H.-W., Cafaggi F. eds. (Edward Elgar 2010) 36; Alpa G. 'Party Autonomy and Freedom of Contract Today', in: *The Politics of the Draft Common Frame of Reference*, Somma A. *ed.* (Wolters Kluwer Law and Business, The Netherlands 2009) 90

instrument'[745], being too abstract and at times obscure[746], *etc.* In any case, the draft did not contain special rules for SMEs, which, as discussed earlier in this book, can be exploited in contractual relations by a larger company. Currently, the future of this draft as 'a toolbox for the Commission when reviewing *acquis*[747]' and preparing proposals is uncertain. Even if the draft gains more support later, as with the PECL, the CFR may not be chosen as a governing law of contract, since in accordance with the Rome I Regulation a contract must be governed by at least one national law. It seems that the CFR would rather serve the purposes of legal innovation, not as a tool replacing national civil laws or creating a uniform European Civil Code.

In the author's view, at a general level the idea of enacting a unified European instrument for cross-border transactions should be supported. It is submitted that the European regulator should issue something similar to the Restatements drawn up by the American Law Institute[748]. These would serve as non-binding guidelines for Member States to be able to implement those positive practices that are endorsed by the Union. The optional code or guidelines could also be prepared for transactions, so as, for example, to force Member States to eliminate traps to unsuspecting foreign enterprises conducting business in that state. It seems that the implementation of the optional guidelines would be in line with the requirements of Article 352 TFEU[749]. This could be an interim path towards further convergence of legal systems.

At the moment the UNIDROIT Principles or the PECL could provide a possible stepping-stone for the further approximation of national civil laws. In particular, the PECL - despite the fact that the Lando-Group that drafted this document lacked an explicit mandate from European institutions to harmonise private law systems in Europe - represents a suitable framework for further

---

[745] Whitettaker S. 'Draft Common Frame of Reference'. An Assessment (Commissioned by the Ministry of Justice, United Kingdom. November 2008) 11

[746] Sefton-Green R. 'The DCFR: A Technical or Political Toolbox?', in: *The Politics of the Draft Common Frame of Reference*, Somma A. ed. (Wolters Kluwer Law and Business, The Netherlands 2009) 47

[747] *See*: Communication from the Commission to the European Parliament and the Council 'European Contract Law and the revision of the *acquis:* the way forward' COM (2004) 651 final; Communication from the Commission to the Council and the European Parliament '*The Hague Programme: Ten Priorities for the next five years. The Partnership for European renewal in the field of Freedom, Security and Justice*' COM (2005) 184 final

[748] *For criticism see e.g.* Müller – Graf P.-Ch. 'EC Directives as a Means of Private Law Unification', in: *Towards a European Civil Code*. Hartkamp A., Hesselink M. [*et. al.*] ed. (Ars Aequi Libri – Nijmegen Kluwer Law International 2004) 86

[749] It must be noted that Article 352 TFEU [*ex* 308 EC] has been used to introduce the European Company (SE), the European Cooperative Society, the Community Trade Mark, *etc.*

drawing up regulations on standard form contracts, while the UNIDROIT Principles do not pursue any specific 'European' purposes[750]. Both UNIDROIT Principles and the PECL overlap in many aspects with regard to rules on the regulation of standard form contracts[751], except that the PECL *inter alia* contains notes explaining the origin of certain rules.

The PECL includes special provisions (Art. 4:110 (1)) that deal with the validity of non-individually negotiated contract terms: a party may avoid these terms if, contrary to the requirements of good faith and fair dealing, they cause a significant imbalance in the parties' rights and obligations. This means that the Principles exercise a form of judicial review of non-individually negotiated contract terms. In essence, Article 4:110 PECL provides somewhat stricter requirements than Article 8:109 PECL - exclusion and limitation of remedies - as a significant imbalance in the parties' rights and obligations should also be assessed when evaluating the validity of non-individually negotiated terms. According to the PECL, remedies in respect of the taking of unfair advantage and the right to avoid unfair contract terms which have been individually negotiated cannot be excluded or otherwise restricted (Art 4:118(1) PECL). In common with the German BGB and Lithuanian Civil Code, the PECL fixes somewhat stricter requirements for the enforceability of standard form contracts. In cases where parties deal on the basis of standard form contracts, they should consider not only principles of good faith, but also the fairness of business transactions and the balance of contractual rights and obligations between parties. As to content, this Article largely replicates the provisions of Directive 93/13/EEC on Unfair Terms in Consumer Contracts, whereby, provided the term is in plain and intelligent language, both the subject matter of contracts and the adequacy in value of one party's obligations compared to the value of the obligations of the other party are excluded from the scope of the rule.

---

750 *See also*: Zimmermann R. 'Konturen eines Europäischen Vertragsrechts' *JZ* (1995) 477; Heidemann M. 'Methodology of Uniform Contract Law – The Unidroit Principles as a Source of Law' 18(4) *EBLR* (2007) 709 *et seq. For the critical view see*: Rield K. 'The Work of the Lando Commission from an Alternative Viewpoint' 1 *ERPL* (2000) 76

751 *Compare also*: Remien O. *Zwingendes Vertragsrecht und Grundfreiheiten des EG-Vertrages* (Tübingen: Mohr Siebeck 2003) 94; Pfeiffer T. 'Auf dem Weg zu einem Europäischen Vertragsrecht', *in: Privat- und Wirtschaftsrecht im Zeichen der Europäischen Integration,* Kieninger E. M., Remien O. Hrsg. (Baden Baden 2004) 127; Bonell M. J., Peleggi R. 'UNIDROIT Principles of International Commercial Contracts and Principles of European Contract Law: A Synoptical Table' *Uniform Law Review* (2004) 315-96; Hesselink W. M. *The New European Private Law. Essays on the Future of Private Law in Europe* (Kluwer Law International The Hague/ London/ New York 2002) 81 *et seq.*; Zimmermann R. 'Ius Commune and the Principles of European Contract Law: Contemporary Renewal of an Old Idea', in: *European Contract Law: Scots and South African Perspectives* MacQueen H. L., Zimmermann R. eds. (Edinburgh University Press 2005) 7

On the other hand, the PECL may be applicable to business-to-business contracts as well. Finally, it must be noted that Directive 93/13/EEC (similar to the German BGB) contains an Annex with a list of terms that are presumed to be unfair. There is no similar list in the PECL, since the drawing of a precise list of cases covering disparities between contractual rights and obligations is assumed to be impossible. This seems to be a reasonable outcome, as most business-to-business contracts should be assessed on a case-by-case basis, and therefore flexible rules seem to be absolutely necessary. As already noted, most European legal orders do not contain explicit prohibitions on business-to-business contracts.

The rules established in the PECL may be criticised, as being too general to further approximate national laws. Moreover, the PECL is a relatively new set of rules. In the absence of any comprehensive practice of applying the Principles, it could be difficult to foresee an outcome in more complicated cases. Probably therefore the national reforms of private law conducted over recent years do not rely heavily on the PECL. However, the creation of somewhat more specific rules may be wholly rejected by national governments, as, according to *Markesinis*, 'achieving harmonisation is difficult because control of standard terms is interwoven with the function of the specific term within the framework of national law'[752]. Finally, the PECL scarcely touches on the development of the *acquis communautaire,* consumer protection, and many other issues.

In any case, it is difficult to invoke the PECL or UNIDROIT Principles before a national forum directly. None of these documents were originally deemed to be applied compulsorily. As noted in previous chapters, Article 3 of the Rome I Regulation, like its predecessor the Rome Convention, explicitly refers to the law chosen by the parties. The PECL and UNIDROIT principles are not ratified laws and therefore do not have force in any European country[753].

In fact, both sets of rules represent the modernised rules of merchant practices[754], and therefore cannot be chosen directly as the law governing contractual relations, nor in litigation before ordinary state courts. For these

752 Markesinis B. Unberath H. Johnston A. *The German Law of Contract* (Oxford and Portland, Oregon: Hart Publishing 2006) 168

753 *See also:* Heutger V. 'UNIDROIT Principles of International Commercial Contracts 2004' 1 *ERPL* (2005) 89; Berger K. P. 'European Private Law, Lex Mercatoria and Globalisation', in: *Towards a European Civil Code*. Hartkamp A. Hesselink M. (*et. al.*) *eds*. (Ars Aequi Libri – Nijmegen Kluwer Law International 2004) 43 *et seq*

754 *Cf.* McKendrick E. 'Harmonisation of European Contract Law: the State we are in', in: The Harmonisation of European Contract Law. Implications for European Private Laws, Business and Legal Practice, Vogenauer S., Weatherill S. eds. (Oxford and Portland, Oregon: Hart Publishing 2006) 9; Hesselink M. *The New European Private Law. Essays on the Future of Private Law in Europe* (The Hague, London New York: Kluwer Law International 2002) 87

reasons, a specific set of European regulations would be desirable. At the same time, common rules on the regulation of standard form contracts would be an additional European instrument for closer integration between Member States. It is submitted that these rules might cover at least 'black-letter' rules, in order to prevent traders from including terms that are absolutely prohibited in other jurisdictions.

Another interesting option to pursue would be only to enact those general principles applicable in respect of exclusion clauses - both for standard form and individually tailored contracts - instead of adopting exhaustive regulations on standard form contracts. Again, the rules elaborated in the PECL may be taken as a starting point for achieving further consensus in negotiations between Member States. The Principles *inter alia* permit the exclusion and limitation of remedies unless exclusion is contrary to good faith and fair dealing (Art. 8:109 PECL). This provision reflects the attitude of most European countries, where the exclusion of liability is normally permitted for business-to-business contracts. However, this provision is subject to a general exception, whereby the exclusion or limitation of liability for intentional as well as grossly negligent infringements of contractual duties is not permitted. This prohibition is also applicable for individually negotiated contracts.

It is easier to implement such legislation if it is not mandatory in nature. Indeed, it is feasible that enhancing consistency of national laws, in particular mandatory rules of contract law, can be achieved by developing a non-binding legal document that might later be adopted voluntarily by Member States[755]. Many Member States from Central and Northern Europe have recently enacted new civil laws, having considered major international developments in private law. Such guidelines for cross-border business transactions on standard form contracts could also be applied where a special agreement is concluded between parties (so-called 'opt-in' rules), or their application may similarly be opted out of as provided for in Article 6 of the CISG.

[755] *For some discussion on this issue see:* van Gerven W. *Codifying European Private Law: Top Down and Bottom Up*, in: *An Academic Green Paper on European Contract Law*, Grundmann S., Stuyck J. eds. (The Hague: Kluwer Law International 2002); Grundmann S., Kerber W. *European System of Contract Laws – a Map of Combining the Advantages of Centralised and Decentralised Rule-Making*, in: *An Academic Green Paper on European Contract Law*, Grundmann S., Stuyck J. eds. (The Hague: Kluwer Law International 2002); Chamboredon A. 'The Debate on a European Civil Code: for an 'Open Texture,' in: *The Harmonisation of European Private Law*, van Hoecke M., Ost F. eds. (Oxford and Portland, Oregon: Hart Publishing 2000); Tillmann W. 'Zweiter Kodifikationsbeschluss des Europäischen Parlaments' *ZEuP* (1995); Möslein F. Legal Innovation in European Contract Law: within and Beyond the (Draft) Common Frame of Reference, in: *European Private Law after the Common Frame of Reference*, Micklitz H.-W., Cafaggi F. *eds.* (Edward Elgar 2010) 173

In theory, the contracting parties would be able to exclude the undesired legal system if they so wished. However, the drawback of such directly applicable, but non-mandatory legislation, is that businesses may decide to avoid mandatory national rules safeguarding fair business transactions. Eventually, this may reduce social protection and enable a stronger party to force the weaker one to accept such optional laws. So such optional laws should not be overtly liberal, but must also give due consideration to the fair distribution of business risks as well.

3. AN INTERIM SOLUTION: PURPOSIVE INTERPRETATION OF DIVERGENT NATIONAL RULES

As outlined above, the European regulator has limited competence to enact new rules on the enforceability of standard contract terms in business-to-business contracts. Moreover, apart from the non-binding *Lando Principles,* there are no clear guidelines at the Union level on this issue.

It is possible to envisage the Court of Justice playing a somewhat bigger role through the procedure established in Article 267 TFEU[756]. However, under Article 267 TFEU the court may give rulings concerning 'the validity and interpretation of acts of the institutions, bodies, offices or agencies of the Union'. It is important to note that the Court of Justice decides on the interpretation of primary and secondary Union law where its meaning is in doubt, but not on purely national law. As long as there are no harmonised rules on business-to-business contracts, the role of the Court of Justice is limited to interpreting TFEU. Moreover, even if we consider such harmonised areas as consumer protection, the case law of the Court of Justice implies that the court usually does not want to confront national regulators, since the ruling of the Court of Justice would not be directly applicable in most national private law cases. Thus, national courts decide on their own initiative the effectiveness of standard contract terms, including in consumer transactions.

For instance, the *Océano Grupo* case, which was referred to the Court of Justice for a preliminary ruling under Article 267 TFEU [*ex* 234 EC], concerned a consumer who bought an encyclopaedia and paid in instalments. The contract in question included a term conferring exclusive jurisdiction on a Barcelona district court. This was too remote from the defendant consumer's place of residence, and thus the buyer did not attend the court's hearing. The court of First Instance in Barcelona applied to the Court of Justice for a preliminary

---

[756] *For further discussions see:* Gerven W. van 'The ECJ Case-Law as a Means of Unification of Private Law?', in: *Towards a European Civil Code.* Hartkamp A., Hesselink M. (et. al.) eds. (Ars Aequi Libri–Nijmegen Kluwer Law International 2004) 101 *et seq*

ruling, requesting advice on whether a contract term stipulating that the location of the court must be that of the incorporation of the company must be regarded as a discriminatory term[757]. In particular, the Spanish court was interested in whether, pursuant to Article 3 of Directive 93/13/EEC on Unfair Terms in Consumer Contracts, it should declare the terms void on its own initiative or rather at a consumer's request. The Court of Justice considered this provision unfair because it prevented a consumer from taking legal action[758]. Indeed, in this case the provision included in the contract was undoubtedly unfair, as it served solely to benefit the supplier. However, the case was important as the Court of Justice *inter alia* confirmed that a national court should ensure effective consumer protection using its discretion. Though the Court of Justice expressed its opinion after assessing the contract terms in question, it did not insist further on developing a comprehensive system of European consumer law[759] and instead shifted this duty to national courts.

In the case of *Freiburger Kommunalbauten*, spouses Mr and Mrs Hofstetter sold a parking space for private use in a multi-storey car park. Under the contract, the full price was due to be paid immediately, irrespective of progress in construction work. A German court applied to the Court of Justice for a preliminary ruling on whether the term could be considered unfair with respect to Article 3(1) of the Directive 93/13/EEC, as the full price was charged separately from the progress of construction work[760]. The reason for applying to the Court of Justice was that these provisions would probably not be considered unfair in all Member States. The Court of Justice did not deliver a definitive answer to this issue, as it did not know the peculiarities of national law and was not aware of all the circumstances of the case. According to the Court of Justice, insofar as there are no totally harmonised rules, national courts should regulate the fairness of contractual relations[761].

One positive development is that the Court of Justice has confirmed its competence in interpreting Directive 93/13/EEC on Unfair Terms in Consumer Contracts, and admitted that a consumer needs additional protection with regard to his bargaining power and level of experience. The Court of Justice could also have clarified the concept of unfair contract terms in the wider context of Union

---

757 Océano Grupo C-240-244/98, para 22

758 Ibid., para 22 *et seq*. *See also:* Markwardt K. 'Inhaltskontrolle von AGB-Klauseln durch den EuGH' 4 *ZIP* (2005) 153; Stuyck J. 'Case Law. Joined cases C-240/98 to C-244/98, Océano Grupo Editorial SA *v*. Rocio Murciano Quintero and Salvat Editore SA v. José M. Sanchez Alcon Prades *et. al*. Judgement of the Full Court of 27 June 2000' 38 *C.M.L. Rev.* (2001)

759 *For some further case law see also*: Mostaza Claro C-168/05 (para 28), where the Court of Justice has called to ensure the effective consumer protection.

760 Freiburger Kommunalbauten C-237/02, para 14

761 Ibid., para 25

law. However, the court remained reluctant to present exhaustive guidelines on what terms should be considered unfair in all Member States. *Rott* is probably right in submitting that the 'ECJ [the Court of Justice] cannot give countless judgements on the unfairness of standard contract terms... This would overburden the ECJ [the Court of Justice]'[762].

It would seem that national courts should take a proactive role by interpreting national laws on unfair contract terms in the light of European developments. It would be welcome if in the absence of the harmonisation national courts safeguarded the consistency of different European laws. As far as possible, national laws must be construed correctly, while taking into consideration Union law and provide effective protection for a weaker party. In the author's view, a forum should not hesitate to set national rules aside in cases where they are not in line with the market freedoms. However, this does not mean that national courts should act *ultra vires* or otherwise breach the requirements of national law. Furthermore, the national courts in applying local laws should develop common methods for the purposive interpretation of divergent national rules of contract law. At the same time, these laws would be applied taking into consideration developments in other European countries (even without explicit reference to their case law). In other words, the national courts should use their discretion to achieve the gradual approximation of European contract laws.

It is submitted that a purposive interpretation of the enforceability of standard form contracts would moderate legal differences between the Member States, as well as create more legal certainty without directly importing legal rules from the country of origin or amending national laws. Still, such a purposive interpretation of Union law remains a big challenge for national courts, as they are ordinarily unfamiliar with foreign law; many relevant judgments are only publicly available in national languages; they are predicated upon different moral values and apply different legal reasoning.

4. CONCLUSION

Both buyer and seller face disadvantages and inconvenience if the laws governing their contractual relations differ from their domestic laws. Even if a party considers that a foreign legal system could be substantially more favourable than that of its own nation of origin, the legal uncertainty of selecting foreign governing law, as well as higher costs of obtaining necessary legal

[762] Rott P. 'What is the Role of the ECJ in EC Private Law? A Comment on the ECJ Judgements in Oceano Grupo, Freiburger Kommunalbauter, Leitner and Veedfald' 1(1) *Hanse L. Rev.* (2005) 15; *compare also*: Weatherill S. 'Harmonisation: How much, how little?' 16 *EBLR* (2005) 536

advice, reduces the perceived advantage. It is submitted that genuinely small businesses are more vulnerable in this respect, as they lack sufficient resources to seek competent legal assistance and to evaluate business risks when choosing a foreign governing law. Thus, full mutual recognition of foreign laws, as well as uniform international regulations – though not necessarily via mandatory harmonisation - appears more valuable for both parties than the legal diversity currently prevalent. Practically speaking, implementing the rule of mutual recognition is difficult in private law. For example, it is highly debatable whether one party can require a mandatory application of its own regulations on standard form contracts by invoking the rule of mutual recognition. In that case, both parties could invoke the market freedoms. Given this ambivalence, the Court of Justice should start weighing up the interests of both parties and the Union itself, but it would be difficult to justify why only one party should benefit from the rule of mutual recognition.

Some further codification of European regulations on standard form contracts is worth considering. However, unified regulations on business-to-business contracts should not be overly restrictive and should not disadvantage those suppliers who come from more lenient jurisdictions. The PECL may represent a possible model - or at least a starting point for further negotiations – as regards unified regulations on standard form contracts in the internal market. However, the adoption of any new regulations is not an advantage *per se*, but should rather deal with practical obstacles arising out of different national regulations. Beyond the difficulties in finding a proper legal basis for harmonisation under TFEU, it is still difficult to agree on specific legal rules that would be acceptable to all Member States. For these reasons, a European regulator should seek voluntary approximation and informally push national authorities to improve existing legislation and enhance actual convergence of legal systems. In the meantime, European countries should endeavour to achieve at least a consistent interpretation of different regulations on standard form contracts. Consistent interpretation would mitigate the legal differences and thereby achieve similar legal results in various jurisdictions without substantive interference with national laws. This may be possible because, as shown in this book, at a fundamental level English, German, French and Lithuanian laws show a high degree of similarity, without being exactly the same.

FINAL REMARKS

The analysis conducted in this book proves the initial hypothesis that unfairness in contractual relations is not just a hypothetical assumption. In many reported cases, the courts have acknowledged that a party adhering to a standard form contract was forced to accept derisory or otherwise unfair terms not because he receives different advantages under a contract, but because there was no choice to conduct business except on the terms offered. Greater social solidarity and social justice can be achieved by instating judicial review to deal with unfairness in contractual relations and inhibit the exploitation of a weaker party. It seems that this attitude is in line with contemporary tendencies towards constitutionalisation of the law of contract as well as with the Treaty of Lisbon, which amended the Treaty of European Union and the Treaty establishing European Community[763]. Given this political background, it is submitted that judicial intervention in contracts that are intended to protect a weaker party from unfair standard form contracts is advisable. From an economic point of view, regulated social markets should achieve a fairer balance of contractual obligations and thereby produce a better economic outcome for both contracting parties. Where the regulator permits judicial review of flawed contractual obligations, a counterparty may rely less on legal advice in the final phase of negotiations, bearing in mind that grossly unfair contract terms would be struck out in cases where they were not in line with mandatory statutory requirements. Tighter regulation of standard form contracts should, thus, enable both parties to avoid unfair surprises as well as disguised or otherwise grossly unfavourable contract terms. On the other hand, it is also true that judicial intervention may create a certain degree of uncertainty as to the enforceability of standard terms incorporated in a contract. Such a statutory framework may induce a dishonest party to challenge contract terms that were at the time of signing a contract explicitly accepted but later rejected when the whole contract appeared less commercially attractive.

In general, the same advantages to regulating unfair transactions are apparent both in business-to-consumer and business-to-business transactions. Modern contract law must respond adequately to economic realities and acknowledge the need to protect not only consumers, but also genuinely small businesses in their dealings with more powerful companies. The comparative analysis conducted in this book confirms that businesses are more likely to challenge possibly unfair contracts - or the misuse of strong bargaining power - before courts in those jurisdictions where special laws tackling unfair trade

763 'The Union shall establish an internal market that works for the sustainable development of Europe based *inter alia* on 'highly competitive social market economy' – see: Art. 3(3) TEU

practices have been enacted. These arguments support the hypothesis that detailed laws that stipulate wholly or partly prohibited transactions and afford legislative protection represent a desirable solution for countries seeking to create an effective review system for unfair commercial arrangements.

It is submitted that special regulation relating to the enforceability of standard form contracts seems especially useful for small companies, as the latter may not invest time in negotiating and avoiding grossly unfavourable terms. However, a proper balance between certainty and flexibility should be maintained in all cases. The government and not the judiciary should consider the relevant issues of social and economic policy in deciding what kind of transactions should be prohibited. The enactment of particular prohibitions for business-to-business contracts is a very complicated matter, as businesses vary according to size, capital, influence in the market and many other important factors. On balance, it is submitted that over-regulation of business dealings may also deter businesses from entering into strictly regulated markets because of the increased costs of business transactions and the risks that signed contracts would be invalidated by national adjudicators.

The level of protection afforded to businesses against unfair standard form contracts in business-to-business transactions is stipulated differently in many Member States. Generally speaking, prohibitions on excluding liability for intentional or grossly negligent infringements are a fact of the law in many continental jurisdictions of the Union, either explicitly established in the civil statutes or derived from case law. From a practical point of view, it is clear that by incorporating such grossly unfavourable exclusions or limitations a stronger party would take advantage to reduce its business costs at the expense of the weaker party, unless there were special circumstances showing that such distribution of transactional risks was fair and reasonable. Exclusion of liability for minor negligent infringements in standard form contracts only is, therefore, permitted in most civil law jurisdictions.

The analysis conducted in this book confirms that the approaches to tackling unfair trade practices in standard form contracts are not exactly the same in all jurisdictions. It is, therefore, still difficult to foresee the outcome of disputes entered into in different legal systems. In fact, much depends on the perspective of the forum when it starts to examine the circumstances of the case. English judges tend to pay more attention to procedural fairness or the equality of bargaining power between parties. The reasonableness of contractual terms is assessed on a case-by-case basis assessing the actual interests of parties in the particular situation in that country. At the same time, many civil law judges tend to pay more attention to the contents of a contract, assessing contractual rights and duties in the light of abstract statutory provisions that fully or partly prohibit such allegedly illegal transactions. Ultimately, the enforceability of particular provisions in cross-border commercial contracts can be assessed differently in cases where the contract is governed by different European laws. For example, the English courts tend to enforce signed contracts containing standard terms. It must be also borne in mind that the English UCTA is not intended to control international business transactions, while the strict French professional vendor's case law applies both to domestic and international commercial contracts. In general, English law is traditionally more lenient than other European legal orders with respect to international business transactions.

Given these differences, a contracting party whose national contract law is more stringent would ordinarily take more risks than a contracting party from another Union jurisdiction. On the one hand, strict national regulations would provide better protection for the weaker party. Stringent laws do increase operating costs and reduce the competitive advantage of a business in that jurisdiction. For example, one may suggest that a French exporter is exposed to somewhat stricter controls than exporters from other Member States, unless a more favourable jurisdiction is chosen. In this regard, different regulations relating to the enforceability of standard form contracts - though at the basic level the English, German, French and Lithuanian laws are consistent - can tentatively be seen as a limitation of trade in the sense of Articles 34 and 35 TFEU, which set out prohibitions with respect to quantitative restrictions on imports, exports and all measures having equivalent effect. Indeed, it is an established fact that every unknown legal system levies more legal costs on foreign market participants. In that context this research examined whether the somewhat stricter rules of one Member State, that does not have similar rules, can lead to the distortion of competition as well as being of detriment to foreign companies.

As has been made clear in this book, European private law permits parties to choose the legal order they wish for international business dealings. The contracting parties may avoid undesired national regulations by concluding an agreement on the choice of governing law. Moreover, strict national regulations on standard form contracts can be justified by the imperative requirements of common interest, by substantiating the restrictions as emanating from the fairness of trade. These arguments lead to the conclusion that discrepancies in national regulations on the effectiveness of standard form contracts should not be considered to be a breach of the free movement of economic factors. However, practically speaking, owing to information deficits and mandatory laws in different jurisdictions, contracting parties cannot ordinarily choose the most favourable rules. Moreover, in cases where a business supplies products to different countries, it would be easier to abide by common harmonised rules and avoid lengthy negotiations on the choice of law. Even slight distortions or potential uncertainty arising out of foreign laws can adversely affect enterprises and their trade volumes. However, the fact that some countries provide for more favourable rules is not a sufficient basis to repeal somewhat stricter rules in other Member States. Currently, neither the free movement of economic factors guaranteed by the TFEU, nor current international instruments that offer a free choice of law (*e.g.* the Rome I Regulation) are sufficient means of overcoming trade distortions arising from different national regulations. This path will continue to fragment Union legislation, and does not guarantee the consistency of private law. In this context, the intervention of the Union in harmonising national rules across the Member States would be an appropriate decision and make contracting easier in the internal market.

It is submitted that the scope of Directive 93/13/EEC on Unfair Terms in Consumer Contracts should be expanded or an alternative legal instrument across Europe created, so as to afford similar protection to genuinely small businesses from derisory contract terms proposed by a stronger party. These small businesses are normally no less vulnerable than ordinary consumers, and, as a rule, do not have sufficient resources to research the intricacies of foreign legal systems. The experience of the different European countries studied in this book confirms that national courts tend not to distinguish between commercial or consumer contracts in assessing unfair contract terms.

The approximation of national regulations on standard form contracts in Europe can also be judged from a broader perspective. It is submitted that even common guidelines at the Union level would provide uniform protection of businesses active in intra-Union trade, as well as approximate the conditions of competition in across the internal market. Otherwise, a stronger proferens would always seek to have a contract governed under a more liberal system in international business transactions, which would not correspond to the legitimate expectations of the counterparty. The approximation of European private laws should create more certainty and security for both contracting parties. Nevertheless, it is desirable that a degree of flexibility be reserved for the contracting parties to shape their business relations and the risks of a transaction as they see fit. There is no need to subject the contracting parties to a large number of absolute prohibitions in international business. Commercial contract terms should be treated as being enforceable insofar as they are not obviously unreasonable for both parties. In view of this, it seems reasonable to distribute transactional risks so that the party in breach takes more risks by accepting liability for intentional and grossly negligent infringements.

Finally, though at Union level initiatives seeking to approximate national regulations on standard form contracts are endorsed, it is currently difficult to foresee what further shape such approximation will take. Most crucial of all is political consensus among the Member States. Member States should finally discard national ambitions for the sake of a common European perspective. On the basis of the foregoing analysis, it is submitted that a welfare state model that permits a forum to intervene in contract law matters with the intention of securing fair contractual relations, is right and necessary. In the meantime, it is recommended that courts should *inter alia* pay attention to the consistent interpretation of national laws, which would help to achieve homogenous legal results without directly setting aside significant national rules.

BIBLIOGRAPHY

1. ACIERNO, SILVIA: The Carpenter Judgement: Fundamental Rights and Limits of the Community Legal Order, 28 E.L. Rev. 2003, 398
2. ADAMS, JOHN, N., BROWNSWORD R.: The Unfair Contract Terms Act: a Decade of Discretion, 104 L.Q.R., 1988, 94
3. ADAMS, JOHN, N.: Unconscionability and the Standard Form Contract, in: Brownsword R., Howells G. and Wilhelmsson T. (eds.) Welfarism in Contract Law, Darthmouth Publishing Company Limited 1994
4. ALISCH, HERBERT: Zur Kontrolle von Allgemeinen Geschäftsbedingungen im rein kaufmännischen Geschäftsverkehr, JZ, 1982, 706
5. ALPA, GUIDO: European Community Resolutions and the Codification of Private Law, 2 ERPL, 2000, 321
6. ALPA, GUIDO: Harmonisation of Contract Law and the Plan for a European Civil Code, 15(1) EBLR, 2004, 33
7. ALPA, GUIDO: Party Autonomy and Freedom of Contract Today, in: The Politics of the Draft Common Frame of Reference, Somma A. (ed.) Wolters Kluwer Law and Business, The Netherlands 2009, 71
8. AQUARO, GIOVANNI: Enhancing the Legal Protection of the European Consumer. Beyond the Wording of the E.U. Directive 93/13, 14(4) EBLR, 2003, 405
9. ARMBRÜSTER, CHRISTIAN: Ein Schuldvertragsrecht für Europa? Bemerkungen zur Privatrechtsangleichung in der Europäischen Union nach „Maastricht“ und „Keck“, 60 RabelsZ, 1996, 72
10. ARNDT, HANS-WOLFGANG: Warenverkehrfreiheit innerhalb der Europäischen Union: der Fall „Keck“ – EuGH, JuS, 1994, 469
11. ARNULL, ANTHONY, DASHWOOD, ALAN (et. al.) Wyatt and Dashwood's European Union Law, London: Sweet & Maxwell 2006
12. ATIYAH, PATRIC SELIM, SMITH, STEPHEN: Atiyah's Introduction to the Law of Contract, Oxford: Clarendon Press 2005
13. ATIYAH, PATRIC SELIM: The Rise and Fall of Freedom of Contract, Oxford: Oxford University Press 1979
14. BAR, CHRISTIAN, VON; SWANN, STEPHEN: Response to the Action Plan on European Contract Law, 11 ERPL, 2003, 595
15. BARNARD, CATHERINE, DEAKIN, SIMON: Market Access and Regulatory Competition, in: The Law of the Single European Market, Barnard C. Scott J. (ed.) Oxford and Portland, Oregon: Hart Publishing 2002
16. BARNARD, CATHERINE: Fitting the Remaining Pieces into the Goods and Persons Jigsaw, 26(1) E.L. Rev., 2001, 35
17. BARNARD, CATHERINE: The Substantive Law of the EU. The Four Freedoms, Oxford: Oxford University Press 2004

18. BARONESS ASHTON OF UPHOLLAND: Harmonisation of European Contract Law – The United Kingdom Government's Thinking, in: The Harmonization of European Contract Law. Implications for European Private Laws, Business and Legal Practice, Vogenauer S. Weatherill S. (eds.) Oxford and Portland, Oregon: Hart Publishing 2006
19. BARRY, NICHOLAS: Introduction to the French Law of Contract, in: Contract Law Today, Donald Harris, Denis Tollan (eds.) Oxford: Clarendon Press 1989
20. BARRY, NICHOLAS: The French Law of Contract, 2nd ed., Oxford: Clarendon Press 1992
21. BASEDOW, JÜRGEN: A Common Contract Law for the Common Market, 33 C.M.L. Rev., 1996, 1169
22. BASEDOW, JÜRGEN: Codification of Private Law in the European Union: the making of a Hybrid, 9(1) ERPL, 2001, 35
23. BASEDOW, JÜRGEN: Das BGB im künftigen europäischen Privatrecht, der hybride Kodex – Systemsuche zwischen nationaler Kodifikation und Rechtsvergleichung, 200 AcP, 2000, 445
24. BASEDOW, JÜRGEN: Der kollisionsrechtliche Gehalt der Produktfreiheiten im europäischen Binnenmarkt: *favor offerentis*, 59 RabelsZ, 1995, 1
25. BASEDOW, JÜRGEN: Grundlagen des europäischen Privatrechts, in: Privat- und Wirtschaftsrecht im Zeichen der Europäischen Integration, Kieninger E.-M., Remien O. (Hrsg.) Baden Baden 2004
26. BASEDOW, JÜRGEN: Handelsbräuche und AGB-Gesetz, 150 ZHR, 1986, 469
27. BASEDOW, JÜRGEN: The Case for A European Contract Act, in: An Academic Green Paper on European Contract Law, Grundmann S., Stuyck J. (eds.) The Hague: Kluwer Law International, 2002
28. BASTIAN, GÜNTHER, BÖHM, KLAUS: Schutz der Kaufleute vor Allgemeinen Geschäftsbedingungen, BB, 1974, 100
29. BAUDENBACHER, CARL: Zur Bedeutung der Klauselkataloge des AGB-Gesetzes für den kaufmännischen Verkehr, JA, 1987, 217
30. BAYREUTHER, FRANK: Wirtschaftlich-existenziell abhängige Unternehmen im Konzern-, Kartell- und Arbeitsrecht. Duncker & Humblot Berlin 2001
31. BEALE HUGH: Finding the Remaining Traps Instead of Unifying Contract Law, in: An Academic Green Paper on European Contract Law Grundmann S., Stuyck J. (eds.) The Hague: Kluwer Law International, 2002
32. BEALE HUGH: Inequality of Bargaining Power, 6 O.J.L.S., 1986, 123
33. BEALE HUGH: Legislative Control of Fairness: the Directive on Unfair Terms in Consumer Directive on Unfair Terms in Consumer Contracts, in:

Good Faith and Fault in Contract Law, Beatson, J. and Friedmann, D. (ed.) Oxford: Clarendon Press 1994
34. BEALE HUGH: The Development of European Private Law and European Commission's Action Plan on Contract Law, X Juridica International, 2005, 4
35. BEALE HUGH: The European Civil Code Movement and the European Union's Common Frame of Reference, Legal Information Management, Legal information Management, 2006, 4
36. BEALE HUGH: Unfair Contract in Britain and Europe, 42 C.L.P., 1989, 197
37. BEALE HUGH: Unfair Contract Terms Act 1977, 5(1) British Journal of Law and Society, 1978, 114
38. BEALE, HUGH, GORIELY, TAMARA: An Unfairly Complex Law, 155 N.J.L. 2005, 318
39. BEALE, HUGH, HARTKAMP, ARTHUR, KÖTZ, HEIN, TALLON, DENIS: Casebooks on the Common Law of Europe: Contract, Oxford: Hart Publishing 2002
40. BEATSON, FRIEDMAN D.: Introduction: From 'Classical to Modern Contract Law', Oxford: Clarendon Press 1994
41. BECKER, ULRICH: Voraussetzungen und Grenzen der Dienstleistungsfreiheit, NJW, 1996, 179
42. BEHRENS, PETER: Die Konvergenz der wirtschaftlichen Freiheiten im Europäischen Gemeinschaftsrecht, EuR, 1992, 145
43. BELL, JOHN, BOYRON, SOPHIE, WHITTAKER SIMON: Principles of French Law, Oxford: Oxford University Press 1998
44. BELL, JOHN: French Legal Cultures, London, Edinburgh, Dublin: Butterworths 2001
45. BERGER, KLAUS PETER: European Private Law, Lex Mercatoria and Globalisation, in: Towards a European Civil Code. Hartkamp A. Hesselink M. (ed.) Ars Aequi Libri – Nijmegen Kluwer Law International 2004
46. BIANCA C. M., BONELL M. J.: Commentary on the International Sales Law. The 1980 Vienna Sales Convention. Giuffré Milan 1987
47. BLAIR, WILLIAM QC, BRENT, RICHARD A.: Single European Law of Contract, 15(1) EBLR, 2004, 5
48. BLECKMANN, ALBERT: Europarecht. Das Recht der Europäischen Union und der Europäischen Gemeinschaften, 6. Neubearbeitete und erweitertete Auflage. Carl Heymanns Verlag KS 1997
49. BOEMKE-ALBRECHT, BURKHARD: Rechtsfolgen unangemessener Bestimmungen in Allgemeinen Geschäftsbedingungen, DZWiR, 1992, 77

50. BONELL M. J., PELEGGI R. UNIDROIT Principles of International Commercial Contracts and Principles of European Contract Law: A Synoptical Table, Uniform Law Review 2004, 315
51. BONELL MICHAEL JOACHIM: An International Restatement of Contract Law. The UNIDROIT Principles of International Commercial Contracts. 3rd ed. Transnational Publishers Inc. Ardsley, New York USA 2005
52. BONELL MICHAEL JOACHIM: The Need and Possibilities of a Codified European Contract Law, 5 ERPL 1997, 505
53. BOUCOCK CARY: In the Grip of Freedom Law and Modernity in Max Weber, University of Toronto Press Toronto Buffalo London 2000
54. BRADGATE, ROBERT: Unreasonable Standard Terms, 60(4) M.L.R. 1997, 582
55. BRAINSWORD R., ADAMS N., JOHN: The Unfair Contract Terms Act: A Decade of Discretion, 104 L.Q.R. 1988, 94
56. BRANDNER, ERICH HANS: Kaufmännische Vertragsgestaltung unter den Zwängen des Rechts der Allgemeinen Geschäftsbedingungen, DZWiR, 1992, 177
57. BRIGOLA, ALEXANDER: Das System der EG – Grundfreiheiten: vom Diskriminierungsverbot zum spezifischen Beschränkungsverbot. Verlag V. H. Beck München 2004
58. BRÖDERMANN, ECKHART, IVERSEN, HOLGER: Europäisches Gemeinschaftsrecht und Internationales Privatrecht, Tübingen 1994
59. BROTHERS, STUART, HERINGTON, MICHAEL: Unfair Terms and Consumer Contracts Regulation, 3(8) International Insurance Law Review 1995, 262
60. BROWN, IAN: Business and Consumer Contracts, Sep., J.B.L. 1988, 388
61. BROWNSWORD ROGER: The Philosophy of Welfarism, in: Welfarism in Contract Law Brownsword R., Howells G. and Wilhelmsson T. (eds.) Darthmouth Publishing Company Limited 1994
62. BROWNSWORD, ROGER, HOWELLS GERAINT, WILHELMSSON THOMAS: Between Market and Welfare: Some Reflections on Art. 3 of the EC Directive on Unfair Terms in Consumer Contracts', in: Aspects of Fairness in Contract, Willet C. (ed.) Blackstone Press Limited 1996
63. BROWNSWORD, ROGER: Contract Law: Themes for the Twenty-First Century, London: Butterworths 2001
64. BRUINIER, STEFAN: Der Einfluss der Grundfreiheiten auf das Internationale Privatrecht, Frankfurt am Main 2003
65. BRUNNER, ALEXANDER: Allgemeine Geschäftsbedingungen im internationalen Privatrecht, Grüsch 1985

66. BUNTE, HERMANN-JOSEF; HINRICHS, HELMUT: Aktuelle Rechtsfragen zur Freizeichnung nach dem AGB-Gesetz, Köln 1985
67. BURROWS F.: Free Movement in European Community Law, Clarendon Press Oxford 1987
68. BUSSANI, MAURO, MATTEI, UGO: The Common Approach of to European Private Law, 3 Col. L.R., 1997, 339
69. BUSSANI, MAURO; MATTEI, UGO (ed.): The Common Core of European Private Law, The Hague/London/New York: Kluwer Law International 2002
70. BUTTERWORTHS COMMON LAW SERIES: The Law of Contract, London, Dublin, Edinburgh: Butterworths 1999
71. CAREY, STEVEN: Exclusion Clauses – What is Reasonable? 12(6) Cons. Law 2001, 18
72. CHAMBOREDON ANTHONY: The Debate on a European Civil Code: for an 'Open Texture', in: The Harmonisation of European Private Law, van Hoecke M., Ost F. (eds.) Oxford and Portland, Oregon: Hart Publishing 2000
73. CHANDLER, ADRIAN; BROWN, IAN: Unreasonableness and the Unfair Contract Terms Act, 109 L.Q.R. 1993, 41
74. CHEN-WISHART, MINDY: Contract Law, Oxford: Oxford University Press 2005
75. CHEREDNYCHENKO OLHA: Fundamental Rights, Contract Law and the Protection of the Weaker Party: a Comparative Analysis of the Constitutionalisation of Contract Law, with Emphasis on Risky Financial Transactions, Sellier: European Law Publishers 2007
76. CHRIS, WILLET: Unfair Terms in Consumer Contracts, 4(12) I.C.C.L.R. 1993, 454
77. CIACCHI, AURELIA, COLOMBI: Non-Legislative Harmonisation: Protection from Unfair Suretyships, in: The Harmonization of European Contract Law. Implications for European Private Laws, Business and Legal Practice, Vogenauer S., Weatherill S. (eds.) Hart Publishing 2006
78. CIACCHI, AURELIA, COLOMBI: An Optional Instrument for Consumer Contracts in the EU: Conflict of Laws and Conflict of Policies, in: The Politics of the Draft Common Frame of Reference, Somma A. (ed.) Wolters Kluwer Law and Business, The Netherlands 2009, 3
79. CLARKSON C.M.V., HILL JONATHAN: The Conflicts of Law, 3rd ed. Oxford: Oxford University Press 2006
80. COLLIER, JOHN GREENWOOD: Conflict of Laws 3rd ed. Cambridge: Cambridge University Press 2001
81. COLLINS, HUGH: European Private Law and the Cultural Identity of States, 3(2) ERPL 1995, 353

82. COLLINS, HUGH: Formalism and Efficiency: Designing European Commercial Contract Law, 8 ERPL 2000, 211
83. COLLINS, HUGH: Good Faith in European Contract Law, 14(2) O.J.L.S. 1994, 229
84. COLLINS, HUGH: Methods and Aims of Comparative Contract Law, 11(3) O.J.L.S. 1991, 398
85. CONNOR, TIM: Accentuating the Positive: the 'Selling Arrangement' the First Decade and Beyond, 54 I.C.L.Q, 2005, 127
86. CRAIG, PAUL, DE BURCA, GRAINNE: EU Law: Text Cases and Materials, 3rd ed., Oxford: Oxford University Press 2003
87. CRAIG, PAUL: The Evolution of the Single Market, in: The Law of the Single European Market, Barnard C. Scott J. (eds.) Oxford and Portland, Oregon: Hart Publishing 2002
88. DALHUISEN JAN H.: Domestic Contract Laws, Uniform International Contract Law and International Contract Law Principles. International Sales and Contractual Agency, 11 EBLR, 2000, 200
89. DAUSES A. (ed.) Rechtshandbuch des EU-Wirtschaftsrechts, Loseblattsammlung München 1997
90. DAVIES GARETH: Can Selling Arrangements be Harmonised? 30(3) E. L. Rev., 2005, 371
91. DAVIES GARETH: EU Internal Market Law 2th ed. Cavendish Publishing Limited London Sydney Portland Oregon 2003
92. DAVIES GARETH: Subsidiarity: the Wrong Idea in the Wrong Place at the Wrong Time, 43 C.M.L. Rev. 2006, 63
93. DE SADELEER, NICOLAS: Procedures for Derogations from the Principle of Approximation Laws under Article 95 EC, 40 C.M.L. Rev., 2003, 889
94. DEAKIN F. SIMON, MICHIE JONATHAN (eds.): Contracts, Co-operation, and Competition, Oxford: Oxford University Press 1997
95. DiMATTEO A. LARRY: The Law of International Contracting. The Hague London Boston: Kluwer Law International 2000
96. DRASCH, WOLFGANG Das Herkunftslandprinzip im internationalen Privatrecht: Auswirkungen des europäischen Binnenmarktes auf Vertrags- und Wettbewerbsstatut, Baden-Baden 1997
97. DREXL, JOSEF: Community Legislation Continued: Complete Harmonisation, Framework Legislation or Non-Binding Measures – Alternative Approaches to European Contract Law, Consumer Protection and Unfair Trade Practices? 13 EBLR, 2002, 557
98. DREXL, JOSEF: Continuing Contract Law Harmonisation under the White Paper of 1985? – Between Minimum Harmonisation, Mutual Recognition, and Uniform Law, in: An Academic Green Paper on European Contract

Law Grundmann S., Stuyck J. (eds.) The Hague: Kluwer Law International 2002
99. DROBNIG, ULRICH, ZIMMERMANN, REINCHARD, WICKE, HARTMUT: Grundregeln des Europäischen Vertragsrechts, ZEuP, 2000, 675
100. DROBNIG, ULRICH: Subsidiary Plea: A European Contract Law for Intra-European Border-Crossing Contracts, in: An Academic Green Paper on European Contract Law Grundmann S., Stuyck J. (eds.) The Hague: Kluwer Law International 2002
101. DUFFY, PETER: Unfair Contract Terms and the EC Directive, (Jan) J.B.L.1993, 67
102. DUGAN, ROBERT: Good Faith and the Enforceability of Standardized Terms, 22 William and Mary Law Review 1980, 1
103. DYLLA–KREBS, CORINNA: Schranken der Inhaltskontrolle Allgemeiner Geschäftsbedingungen, Baden-Baden 1990
104. EBERSTEIN, HANS HERMAN: Allgemeine Geschäftsbedingungen und Kaufleute, BB, 1974, 1185
105. EICKMEIER, FRANK: Rechtsweite und Grenzen der Haftungsfreizeichnung gemäß § 41a ADSp unter dem Einfluss der neugefaßten Speditionsversicherungsbedingungen, Hamburg 1993
106. EITH, WOLFGANG: Zum Schutzbedürfnis gegenüber Allgemeinen Geschäftsbedingungen, NJW, 1974, 16
107. ELLINGHAUS M. P.: In Defence of Unconscionability, 78 Yale L.J., 1969, 757
108. EPPIG, VOLKER, LENZ, SEBASTIAN, LEYDECKER, PHILLIP: Grundrechte, Springer 2005
109. FEHL, NORBERT: Systematik des Rechts der Allgemeinen Geschäftsbedingungen, ZIP, 1987, 690
110. FEZER, KARL-HEINZ: Europäisierung des Wettbewerbsrechts. Gemeinschaftsrechtliche Grenzen im Recht des unlauteren Wettbewerbs – Kommentar zur jüngsten Entwicklung der Rechtsprechung des EuGH zum Warenverkehrrecht (Rechtssachen "Yves Rocher', 'Keck und Mithouard' und 'Hünermund'), JZ, 1994, 317
111. FISCHER, FRANK O.: Praktische Probleme der Einbeziehung von AGB unter Kaufleuten insbesondere bei laufenden Geschäftsbedingungen, BB, 1995, 2491
112. FRANZEN, MARTIN: Privatrechtsangleichung durch die Europäische Gemeinschaft, Berlin New York 1999
113. FURMSTON, MICHAEL, PHILIP: Cheshire, Fifoot & Furmston's Law of Contract, Oxford: Oxford University Press 2007

114. GARDETTE, JEAN–MARIE: Die Behandlung der „unangemessenen“ Klauseln nach dem französischen „AGB“ – Gesetz, Verlag Versicherungswirtschaft GmbH, Karlsruhe 2005
115. GAY TREVOR (ed.) Zum Recht der Allgemeinen Geschäftsbedingungen in westeuropäischen Ländern: Entscheidungshilfen, Informationsdienste für Unternehmer und Führungskräfte VDMA. (ORGALIME). Abteilung Recht und Wettbewerbsordnung, Verband Deutscher Maschinen- Anlagebau e. V. Frankfurt am Main 1991
116. GAZZANIGA, GIOVANNI, CRISCIONE PAOLO: The Italian Implementation of the EU Directive on Unfair Contract Terms in Consumer Contracts, 7(9) I.C.C.L.R. 1996, 338
117. GERVEN, WALTER VAN: Codifying European Private Law: Top down and Bottom up, in: An Academic Green Paper on European Contract Law Grundmann S., Stuyck J. (eds.) The Hague: Kluwer Law International, 2002
118. GERVEN, WALTER VAN: Harmonisation of Private Law: Do We Need It? 41(2) C.M.L. Rev., 2004, 505
119. GERVEN, WALTER, VAN: The ECJ Case-Law as a Means of Unification of Private Law?, in: Towards a European Civil Code. Hartkamp A., Hesselink M. (et. al.) (eds.) Ars Aequi Libri–Nijmegen Kluwer Law International 2004
120. GIOVANNOPOULOS, RIGAS: Die Harmonisierung des privatrechtlichen Bankgeheimnisses im europäischen Wirtschaftsverkehr. Eine rechtsdogmatische und rechtsvergleichende Untersuchung zum deutschen, englischen, französischen und griechischen Rech unter besonderer Berücksichtigung der Europäischen Datenschutzrichtlinie, der EG-Grundfreiheiten und der Gemeinschaftsgrundrechte, Baden Baden 2000/2001
121. GKOUTZINIS, APOSTOLOS: Free Movement of Services in the EC Treaty and the Law of Contractual Obligations relating to Banking and Financial Services, 41 C.M.L. Rev. 2004, 125
122. GORDLEY, JAMES, VON MEHREN; ARTHUR, TAYLOR: An Introduction to the Comparative Study of Private Law. Readings, Cases, Materials, Cambridge: Cambridge University Press 2006
123. GORDLEY, JAMES: Equality in Exchange, 69 Cal. L. Rev., 1981, 1589
124. GRAF VON WESTPHALEN, FRIEDRICH: Die Wirksamkeitsgrenze von Haftungsfreizeichnungs- und Haftungsbegrenzungsklauseln bei leichter Fahrlässigkeit gem. § 9 AGBG, WM, 1983, 974
125. GRAF VON WESTPHALEN, FRIEDRICH: Fallstricke bei Verträgen und Prozessen mit Auslandsberührung, NJW, 1994, 2113

126. GRAF VON WESTPHALEN, FRIEDRICH (ed.): Vertragsrecht und AGB-Klauselwerke, Verlag C. H. Beck München 2007
127. GRAZEDEI, MICHAEL: The Functional Heritage, in: Comparative Legal Studies: Traditions and Transitions, Legrand P., Munday R. (eds.) Cambridge: Cambridge University Press 2003
128. GRUNDMANN, STEFAN, KERBER, WOLFGANG: European System of Contract Laws – a Map of Combining the Advantages of Centralised and Decentralised Rule-Making, in: An Academic Green Paper on European Contract Law Grundmann S., Stuyck J. (eds.), The Hague: Kluwer Law International, 2002
129. GRUNDMANN, STEFAN, MAZEAUD, DENIS: General Clauses and Standards, in: European Contract Law. Comparative Law, EC Law and Contract Law Codification. The Hague: Kluwer Law International 2006
130. GRUNDMANN, STEFAN: EG-Richtlinie und nationales Privatrecht, JZ, 1996, 274
131. GRUNDMANN, STEFAN: European Contract Law(s) of what Colour? 1 ERPL, 2005, 184
132. GRUNDMANN, STEFAN: Information, Party Autonomy and Economic Agents in European Contract Law, 39 C.M.L. Rev., 2002, 269
133. GRUNDMANN, STEFAN: Privatautonomie im Binnenmarkt, JZ, 2000, 1133
134. GRUNDMANN, STEFAN: Structural Elements in the Contract Law Parts of the German Civil Code, in: The Architecture of European Codes and Contract Law, Grundmann S., Schaue M. (eds.) The Hague/London/ New York: Kluwer Law International 2006
135. GRUNDMANN, STEFAN: Grand European Code Napoléon or Concise Uniform Contract Law? Defining the Scope of a Common Frame of Reference, in: The Politics of the Draft Common Frame of Reference, Somma A. (ed.) Wolters Kluwer Law and Business, The Netherlands 2009, 19
136. GRUNDMANN, STEFAN: The Role of Competition in the European Codification Process, in: European Private Law after the Common Frame of Reference, Micklitz Hans-W., Cafaggi F. (eds.), Cheltenham UK, Northampton, MA, USA: Edward Elgar 2010, 36
137. GULLIANI M., FREDERICO: Italy: Contract Terms-Unfair Terms and Conditions, 8(9) I.C.C.L.R. 1997, 150
138. HAAS, MATTHIAS: Haftungsfreizeichnungsklauseln in Allgemeinen Geschäftsbedingungen. Eine rechtsdogmatische und ökonomische Analyse, Frankfurt am Main 1991
139. HAKENBERG, WALTRAUD: Grundzüge des Europäischen Gemeinschaftsrechts, 3. Aufl. München 2003

140. HALSBURY'S LAWS OF ENGLAND: Sale of Goods and Supply of Services, Vol. 41, Lexis Nexis Butterworths 2005
141. HANDELSGESETZBUCH. Großkommentar. Dritter Band, 1. Halbband §§ 343-351, Walter de Gruyter Berlin New York 1978
142. HARBACEVICA SOLVITA, REICH NORBERT: Citizenship and Family on Trial: A Fairly Optimistic Overview of Recent Court Practice with Regard to Free Movement of Persons, 39 C.M.L. Rev. 2002, 615
143. HARRIS DONALD, TALLON, DENIS (eds.) Contract Law Today. Anglo-French Comparisons, Oxford: Clarendon Press 1989
144. HARTKAMP S. ARTHUR, HESSELINK MARTIJN *(et. al.)* (eds.): Towards a European Civil Code, Nijmegen: Kluwer Law International 2004
145. HARTLEY C. TREVOR: International Commercial Litigation. Text, Cases and Materials on Private International Law, Cambridge: Cambridge University Press 2009
146. HARTWELL, NICKY: The Application of the Reasonableness Test under UCTA 1977: a Schism between Certainty and Fairness, 3(2) Hertfordshire Law Journal, 2005, 55
147. HATZIS, ARISTIDES N.: Civil Contract Law and Economic Reasoning – An Unlikely Pair, in: The Architecture of European Codes and Contract Law, Grundmann S., Schaue M. (eds.) The Hague/London/ New York: Kluwer Law International 2006
148. HATZIS, ARISTIDES N., ZERVOGIANNI, ELENI: Judge-Made Contracts Reconstructing Unconscionable Contracts (the working paper downloaded from <http://papers.ssrn.com/sol3/papers.cfm?abstract_id=953669> on 25 August 2009)
149. HATZOPOULOS VASSILIS, DO, THIEN UYEN: The Case Law of the ECJ concerning the Free Provision of Services: 2000-2005, 43 C.M.L. Rev., 2006, 92
150. HATZOPOULOS, VASSILIS: Recent Developments of the Case Law of the ECJ in the Field of Services, 37 C.M.L. Rev., 2000, 43
151. HÄYHÄ, JUHA: Scandinavian Techniques for Controlling Fairness in Contracts in: Brownsword R., Howells G. and Wilhelmsson T. (eds.) Welfarism in Contract Law, Darthmouth Publishing Company Limited, 1994
152. HEIDEMANN, MAREN: Methodology of Uniform Contract Law – The Unidroit Principles as a Source of Law, 18(4) EBLR 2007, 709
153. HEINRICHS, HELMUT: Die Entwicklung des Rechts der Allgemeinen Geschäftsbedingungen im Jahre 1988, NJW, 1998, 1604

154. HEINRICHS, HELMUT: Maßstäbe und Anwendungsbereich der Inhaltskontrolle, in: Zehn Jahre AGB-Gesetz, Heinrichs H., Löwe W., Ulmer P. (Hrsg.), Köln 1987
155. HELM, JOHANN GEORG: Zur Inhaltskontrolle von Allgemeinen Geschäftsbedingungen bei Verwendung gegenüber Kaufleuten, BB, 1977, 1109
156. HELLWEGE PHILLIP: Allgemeine Geschäftsbedingungen, einseitig gestellte Vertragsbedingungen und die allgemeine Rechtsgeschäftslehre, Tübingen: Mohr Siebeck 2010
157. HENNEMANN, MARC SAMUEL: AGB-Kontrolle im UN–Kaufrecht aus deutscher und französischer Sicht, Tübingen 2001
158. HENSELER, PETER: Beispiele zur Haftung und Haftungsbegrenzung im kaufmännischen Geschäftsverkehr - § 24 AGB-Gesetz, DZWiR, 1992, 192
159. HENSEN, HORST-DIETHER: Die Auswirkung des AGB-Gesetzes auf den kaufmännischen Verkehr, NJW, 1987, 1986
160. HERMANN, HANS: Allgemeine Geschäftsbedingungen und Kaufleute, BB, 1974, 1185
161. HERTEL, BERND, OHLENDORF-VON: Kontrolle von allgemeinen Geschäftsbedingungen im kaufmännischen Geschäftsverkehr gemäß § 24 AGB-Gesetz, Heidelberg, 1986
162. HESSELINK, MARTIJN (ed.): The Politics of a European Civil Code, The Hague: Kluwer Law International 2006
163. HESSELINK, MARTIJN: Non-Mandatory Rules in European Contract Law, 1 ERCL, 2005, 44
164. HESSELINK, MARTIJN: Special Issue on Critical Legal Theory and European Private Law, ERPL 2000, 3
165. HESSELINK, MARTIJN: The European Commission's Action Plan: towards a More Coherent European Contract Law? 12 ERPL, 2004, 397
166. HESSELINK, MARTIJN: The CFR and Social Justice, in: The Politics of the Draft Common Frame of Reference, Somma A. (ed.) Wolters Kluwer Law and Business, The Netherlands 2009, 96
167. HESSELINK, MARTIJN: The New European Private Law. Essays on the Future of Private Law in Europe, The Hague, London New York: Kluwer Law International 2002
168. HESSELINK, MARTIJN: The Politics of a European Civil Code, 10 European Law Journal 2004, 675
169. HESSELINK, MARTIJN: SMEs in European Contract Law. Background note for the European Parliament on the position of small and medium-sized enterprises (SMEs) in a future Common Frame of Reference (CFR) and in the review of the consumer law acquis. – 5 July 2007. Centre for the Study of European Contract Law. Working Paper Series No 2007/03

170. HESSELINK, MARTIJN: The Politics of European Contract Law: Who has an Interest in What Kind of Contract Law for Europe? 2 Global Jurist Frontiers, Issue 1, 2002
171. HEUTGER, VIOLA: UNIDROIT Principles of International Commercial Contracts 2004, 1 ERPL, 2005, 89
172. HEYBROCK, HASSO: Zur Dogmatik der Kardinalpflichte, Frankfurt am Main, 1990
173. HILL, JONATHAN: International Commercial Disputes, 2nd ed. LLP: London Hong Kong 1998
174. HILLMAN, ROBERT A.: Debunking Some Myth about Unconscionability: a New Framework for UCC § 2-302, 67 Cornell L. R., 1981, 1
175. HIPPEL, VON, EIKE: Zur Kontrolle Allgemeiner Geschäftsbedingungen, BB, 1985, 1629
176. HOFFMANN VON, BERND: Über den Schutz des schwächeren bei internationalen Schuldverträgen, 38 RabelsZ 1974, 396
177. HOMMELHOFF, PETER: Zivilrecht unter dem europäischer Rechtsangleichung, 192 AcP 1992, 71
178. HOMMELHOFF, PETER; WIEDERMANN, KAI-UDO: Allgemeine Geschäftsbedingungen gegenüber Kaufleuten und unausgehandelte Klauseln in Verbraucherverträgen: Grundsätzliches zur Transformation der EG- Klauselrichtlinie ins deutsche Recht, ZIP, 1993, 562
179. HONDIUS EWOUD: European Private Law–Survey 2002-2004, 6 ERPL 2004, 855
180. HONDIUS EWOUD: Unfair Contract Terms: Towards a European Law. Introduction, 5 ERPL 1997, 121
181. HONDIUS, EWOUD: European Approaches to Fairness in Contract Law, in: Aspects of Fairness in Contract, Willet C. (eds.) Blackstone Press Limited 1996
182. HONDIUS, EWOUD: Protection of the Weaker party in Dutch Contract Law, in: Brownsword R., Howells G. and Wilhelmsson T. (eds.) Welfarism in Contract Law, Darthmouth Publishing Company Limited, 1994
183. HÜBNER, ULRICH: Allgemeine Geschäftsbedingungen und Internationales Privatrecht, NJW, 1980, 2601
184. HUNT, ALAN: The Sociological Movement in London. Maxmillian London 1978
185. JANSEN, NILS: The Authority of an Academic “Draft Common Frame of Reference”, in: European Private Law after the Common Frame of Reference, Micklitz Hans-W., Cafaggi F. (eds.), Cheltenham UK, Northampton, MA, USA: Edward Elgar 2010, 147

186. JARASS, HANS D.: A Unified Approach to the Fundamental Freedoms in: The Law of the Single European Market, Barnard C. Scott J. (eds.) Oxford and Portland, Oregon: Hart Publishing 2002
187. JARASS, HANS D.: Elemente einer Dogmatik der Grundfreiheiten, EuR, 1995, 200
188. JAYME, ERIK: Allgemeine Geschäftsbedingungen und internationales Privatrecht, 142 ZHR, 1978, 103
189. JICKELI, JOACHIM: Der Binnenmark im Schatten des Subsidiaritätsprinzips, JZ, 1995, 57
190. JOERGES, CHRISTIAN: Die Europäisierung des Privatrechts als Rationalisierungsprozess und als Streit der Disziplinen, ZEuP, 1995, 181
191. JOERGES, CHRISTIAN: The Impact of European Integration on Private Law: Reductionist Perceptions, True Conflicts and a New Constitutional Perspective, E.L.R., 1997, 378
192. JOOST, DETLEV: Der Ausschluss der Inhaltskontrolle bei Entgeltregelungen in allgemeinen Geschäftsbedingungen, ZIP, 1996, 1685
193. KESSLER, FRIEDRICH: Contracts of Adhesion – Some Thoughts about Freedom of Contract, 43 Colum. L. Rev., 1943, 629
194. KESSLER JUTTA: Das System der Warenverkehrsfreiheit im Gemeinschaftsrecht. Zwischen Produktbezug und Verkaufsmodalitäten. Berlin: Nomos Verlagsgesellschaft 1997
195. KLEINWÄCHER, KARIN: Möglichkeiten einer Haftungsbeschränkung im französischen Recht, RIW, 1984, 690
196. KLIMA, PETER: Missbräuchliche Klauseln in Verträgen, RIW, 1992, 98
197. KOCH, ROBERT: Wider den formularmäßigen Ausschluss des UN-Kaufrechts, NJW, 2000, 910
198. KOENIG, CHRISTIAN, HARATSCH, ANDREAS: Europarecht, 3. Aufl. Tübingen: Mohr Siebeck 2004
199. KOOPMANS, THIJMEN: Towards a European Civil Code?', 5 ERPL (1997) 542
200. KÖRBER, TORSTEN: Grundfreiheit und Privatrecht. Tübingen: Mohr Siebeck 2004
201. KÖTZ, HEIN: European Contract Law, Oxford: Oxford University Press 1997
202. KÖTZ, HEIN: Zur Wirksamkeit der Freizeichnungsklauseln, NJW, 1984, 2447
203. KÖTZ, HEIN; FLESSNER, AXEL: Europäisches Vertragsrecht Band I: Abschluss, Gültigkeit und Inhalt des Vertrages. Die Beteiligung Dritter am Vertrag, Tübingen: Mohr Siebeck 199
204. KRAJEWSKI, MARKUS: The New German Law of Obligations, 14 EBLR 2003, 201

205. KREIENBAUM, BIRGIT: Transparenz und AGB-Gesetz. Eine Untersuchung des Inhalts und der Schranken des Transparenzgebotes. Berlin: Duncker & Humblot 1997
206. KROPHOLLER, JAN: Internationales Privatrecht. Tübingen: Mohr Siebeck 2004
207. LAJOS VÉKÁS: Models in Central-Eastern European Codes, in: The Architecture of European Codes and Contract Law, Grundmann S., Schaue M. (eds.) The Hague/London/ New York: Kluwer Law International 2006
208. LANDO OLE, BEALE HUGH (eds.): Principles of European Contract Law Parts I and II, The Hague: Kluwer 2000
209. LANDO OLE: Principles of European Contract Law: An Alternative to or a Precursor of European Legislation? 40(3) Am. J. Com. L. 1992, 573
210. LANDO OLE: Optional or Mandatory Europeanisation of Contract Law, 1 ERPL 2000, 59
211. LANDO, OLE: Liberal, Social and 'Ethical' Justice in European Contract Law', 43 C.M.L. Rev. 2006, 828
212. LANDO, OLE: On Legislative Style and Structure, 14(4) ERPL 2006, 475
213. LANDO, OLE: The Structure and the Legal Values of the Common Frame of Reference (CFR), 3 ERPL 2007, 245
214. LANDO, OLE; BEALE, HUGH: Grundregeln des Europäischen Vertragsrechts, Teile I und II. Kommission für Europäisches Vertragsrecht (Deutsche Übersetzung von Christian von Bar, Reinhard Zimmermann), München 2002
215. LANG, THOMAS: Die Anwendung des AGB-Gesetzes auf Formularmietverträge und deren Inhaltskontrolle eine Bestandaufnahme und kritische Würdigung der Rechtsprechung. Stuttgart 1999
216. LANGNER, OLAF: Das Kaufrecht auf dem Prüfstand der Warenverkehrsfreiheit des EG-Vertrages, 65 RabelsZ, 2001, 222
217. LANGNER, OLAF: Der Europäische Gerichtshof als Rechtsmittelgericht. Der Prüfungsumfang im europäischen Rechtsmittelverfahren, Frankfurt am Main 2003
218. LAWSON RICHARD: Exclusion Clauses and Unfair Contract Terms, 8th ed, Thomson Sweet & Maxwell 2005
219. LEAKE, STEPHEN MARTIN: The Elements of the Law of Contracts London: Stevens and Sons, 26 Bell Yard 1867
220. LEFF, ARTHUR ALLEN: Unconscionability in the Code, the Emperor's New Clause, 115 U. Pa. L. R., 1967, 485
221. LEGRAND, PIERE: Against a European Civil Code', 60 M. L. R. 1997, 44
222. LEGRAND, PIERE: European Legal Systems are not Converging, 45 ICLQ, 1996, 52

223. LEGRAND, PIERE: The Same and the Different in: Comparative Legal Studies: Traditions and Transitions, Legrand P., Munday R. (eds.) Cambridge: Cambridge University Press 2003
224. LEHRBERG, BERT: Renegotiation Clauses, the Doctrine of Assumptions and Unfair Contract Terms, 3 ERPL, 1998, 272
225. LENA S. JEFFREY, MATTEI, UGO: Introduction to Italian Law, The Hague, London, New York: Kluwer Law International 2002
226. LEPPAULE, PIERRE: The Function of Comparative Law. With a Critique of Sociological Jurisprudence. XXXV Harv. L. Rev., 1922, 838
227. LEWISON, KIM: The Interpretation of Contracts, London: Sweet & Maxwell 2004
228. LORD COLLINS LAWRENCE OF MAPESBURY (ed.): Dicey, Morris & Collins The Conflicts of Law, London: Sweet & Maxwell 2006 (and up-to-date to October 2009)
229. LÖWE, WALTER, GRAF VON WESTPHALEN, FRIEDRICH, TRINKNER, REINHOLD: Großkommentar zum AGBG, Bd. (II) 1983, Bd. III (1985), 2 Aufl. Heidelberg
230. LÖWE, WALTER; GRAF VON WESTPHALEN, FRIEDRICH VON; TRINKNER, REINHOLD: Kommentar zum Gesetz zur Regelung des Rechts der Allgemeinen Geschäftsbedingungen. Heidelberg 1977
231. LURGER, BRIGITTA: Regulierung und Deregulierung im europäischen Privatrecht, Frankfurt am Main 1997
232. LÜTKENHAUS, ALTFRIED M: Unfair Contract Terms Act 1977 und AGB-Gesetz 1976: Rechtsregeln zu Allgemeinen Geschäftsbedingungen im Vergleich Frankfurt am Main [u. a.] 1987
233. LUTZ REINHARD: AGB-Kontrolle im Handelsverkehr unter Berücksichtigung der Klauselverbote, München 1991
234. MACAULAY, STIUART: An Empirical View of Contract, Wisconsin L.R. 1985, 465
235. MACDONALD, ELISABETH: A Particular Problem for E-Commerce: Section 3 of the Unfair Contract Terms Act 1977, Web Journal of Current Legal issue, 2000, 3 Web JCLI (the paper downloaded from <http://webjcli.ncl.ac.uk/2000/issue3/macdonald3.html> on 10 September 2007)
236. MACDONALD, ELISABETH: Exemption Clauses and Unfair Terms, London Edinburgh Dublin: Butterworths 1999
237. MACDONALD, ELISABETH: Mapping the Unfair Contract Terms Act 1977 and the Directive on Unfair Terms in Consumer Contracts, Journal of Business Law 1994

238. MACDONALD, ELISABETH: Watford v Sanderson: The Requirement of Reasonableness in System Supply Contracts and More Generally, Web Journal of Current Legal issues Ltd. 2001
239. MACDONALD, ELISABETH: Y2K and Contractual Exemption Clauses, (2) The Journal of Information, Law and Technology 1999
240. MANCE, LORD JONATHAN: Is Europe Aiming to Civilise the Common Law?, 18 EBRD 2007, 77
241. MARKESINIS, SIR, BASIL; UNBERATH HANNES; JOHNSTON ANGUS: The German Law of Contract, Oxford and Portland, Oregon: Hart Publishing 2006
242. MARKESINIS, SIR, BASIL: Why a Code is Not the Best Way to Advance the Cause of European Legal Unity', 5(4) ERPL, 1997, 519
243. MATTEI, UGO: A Transaction Costs Approach to the European Code', 5 ERPL, 1997, 537
244. MEYER, JUSTUS: Auf dem Weg zu einem Europäischen Zivilgesetzbuch. Der Aktionsplan der EG-Kommission für ein kohärentes europäisches Vertragsrecht, BB, 1994, 1285
245. McKENDRICK, EWAN: Contract Law: Text, Cases and Materials, 2nd ed., Oxford: Oxford University Press 2005
246. McKENDRICK, EWAN: Harmonization of European Contract Law: the State we are, in: The Harmonization of European Contract Law. Implications for European Private Laws, Business and Legal Practice, Vogenauer S., Weatherill S. (eds.) Hart Publishing 2006
247. MELI, MARISA: Unfair Terms and Unfairness Test in Contracts between Businesses and Consumers, in: The Politics of the Draft Common Frame of Reference, Somma A. (ed.) Wolters Kluwer Law and Business, The Netherlands 2009, 151
248. MENSKI WERNER: Comparative Law in a Global Context, Cambridge: Cambridge University Press 2006
249. MEYER-SPARENBERG, WOLFGANG: Rechtswahlvereinbarungen in Allgemeine Geschäftsbedingungen, RIW, 1989, 347
250. MICHAELS RALF: The Functional Method of Comparative Law, 2005
251. MICHEALS RALF, JANSEN, NILS: Private Law beyond the State? Europeanisation, Globalisation, Privatisation, 54 Am. J. Com. L. 2006, 843
252. MIKELĖNAS, VALENTINAS: Lietuvos Respublikos Civilinio kodekso komentaras. Šeštoji knyga prievolių teisė (1) Vilnius 2003
253. MIKELĖNAS, VALENTINAS: Unification and Harmonisation of Law at the Turn of the Millennium: the Lithuanian Experience, 2 Uniform Law Review, 2000, 253
254. MILOŠ VEC: Recht und Normierung in der Industriellen Revolution. Neue Strukturen der Normsetzung in Völkerrecht, staatlicher Gesetzgebung und

gesellschaftlicher Selbstnormierung. Frankfurt am Main: Vittorio Klostermann 2006
255. MOJZESOWIZC, KAROLINA: Möglichkeit und Grenzen einer einheitlichen Dogmatik der Grundfreiheiten, Baden Baden 2001
256. MÖLLERS, A. THOMAS: European Directives on Civil Law. The German Approach: Towards the Re-codification and New Foundation of Civil Law Principles', 6 ERPL 2002, 777
257. MÖSLEIN, FLORIAN: Legal Innovation in European Contract Law: within and Beyond the (Draft) Common Frame of Reference, in: European Private Law after the Common Frame of Reference, Micklitz Hans- W., Cafaggi F. (eds.), Cheltenham UK, Northampton, MA, USA: Edward Elgar 2010, 173
258. MOORE, SARAH: Quantitative Restrictions and Measures having Equivalent Effect Re-vising the Limits of Article 30 EEC, 19(2) E.L.Rev., 1994, 195
259. MORTELMANS, KAMIEL: The Common Market, the Internal Market and the Single Market, What's in a Market?, 35 C.M.L. Rev. 1998, 101
260. MUIR WATT, HORATIA, SEFTON – GREEN, RUTH: Fitting the Frame: an Optional Instrument, Party Choice and Mandatory / Default Rules, in: European Private Law after the Common Frame of Reference, Micklitz Hans- W., Cafaggi F. (eds.), Cheltenham UK, Northampton, MA, USA: Edward Elgar 2010, 201
261. MÜLBERG, O. PETER: Privatrecht, die EG-Grundfreiheiten und der Binnenmarkt, 159 ZHR 1986, 2
262. MÜLHANS, CHRISTINA: Die Umsetzung der Klausel-Richtlinie und ihre Auswirkung auf den Binnenmarkt. Eine Untersuchung anhand der Umsetzungsgesetze zur Richtlinie 93/13 EWG in Deutschland, Frankreich und im Vereinigten Königreich, Frankfurt am Main 2004
263. MÜLLER, HOLGER, OTTO, HANS-HERMAN: Allgemeine Geschäftsbedingungen im internationalen Wirtschaftsverkehr, Neuwied, Kriftel, Berlin 1994
264. MÜLLER-GRAFF PETER-CHRISTIAN: EC Directives as a Means of Private Law Unification in: Towards a European Civil Code. Hartkam A. Hesselink M. (*et. al.*) (eds.) Ars Aequi Libri – Nijmegen Kluwer Law International 2004
265. MÜLLER-GRAFF PETER-CHRISTIAN: Privatrecht und Europäisches Gemeinschaftsrecht, 1991
266. MÜLLER-GRAFF, PETER-CHRISTIAN (Hrsg.): Gemeinsames Privatrecht in der Europäischen Gemeinschaft, 2 Aufl. 1999

267. MÜNCHENER KOMMENTAR: Münchener Kommentar zum Bürgerlichen Gesetzbuch. Schuldrecht Allgemeiner Teil §§ 241-432, München 2003 (cited: Author, in: MünchKomm)
268. MUNZ, MARTIN: Allgemeine Geschäftsbedingungen in den USA und Deutschland im Handelsverkehr, Heidelberg 1992
269. NEBBIA, PAOLISA: Standard Form Contracts between Unfair Terms Control and Competition Law, 31(1) E.L. Rev. 2006, 102
270. NEBBIA, PAOLISA: Unfair Contract Terms in European Law. A Study in Comparative and EC Law, Oxford and Portland, Oregon: Hart Publishing 2007
271. NICKLISCH, FRITZ.: Zum Anwendungsbereich der Inhaltskontrolle Allgemeiner Geschäftsbedingungen, BB, 1974, 941
272. NIGLIA, LEONE: The Transformation of Contract in Europe The Hague: Kluwer Law International 2003
273. NEUMANN, JOHANNES: Geltungserhaltende Reduktion und ergänzende Auslegung von Allgemeinen Geschäftsbedingungen. Nomos Verlagsgesellschaft Baden Baden 1988
274. NORTH, PETER, FAWCETT J.: Cheshire and North's Private International Law, 13th ed. Butterworths: London, Edinburgh, Dublin 1999
275. NORTH, PETER: Essays in Private International Law, Clarendon Press Oxford 1993
276. OLENDORF-VON HERTEL, BERND: Kontrolle von Allgemeinen Geschäftsbedingungen im kaufmännischen Geschäftsverkehr gemäß § 24 AGB- Gesetz, Heidelberg 1988
277. OLIVER, PETER AND ENCHELMAIER, STEFAN: Free Movement of Goods: Recent Developments in the Case Law, 44 C.M.L. Rev. 2007, 673
278. OLIVER, PETER, ROTH, WULF-HENNIG: The Internal Market and the Four Freedoms, 41 C.M.L. Rev., 2004, 407
279. OLIVER, PETER: Free Movement of Goods in the European Community under Articles 28 to 30 of the EC Treaty, London: Sweet and Maxwell 2003
280. OLIVER, PETER: Some further Reflections on the Scope of Articles 28-30, (ex 30-36), 36(4) C.M.L. Rev. 1999, 783
281. ÖRÜCÜ, ESIN: The Enigma of Comparative Law. Variations on a Theme for the Twenty-first Century Martinus Nijhoff Publishers: Leiden/ Boston 2004
282. OTTO, HANS-HERMANN: Allgemeine Geschäftsbedingungen und internationales Privatrecht Göttingen, 1984
283. PADFIELD, ALISON: The Impact of English Contract Law of the EC Directive on Unfair Terms in Consumer Contracts, 10(5) J.I.B.L. 1995, 175
284. PALAND, OTTO: KOMMENTAR ZUM BGB, 64. neubearbeitete Auflage. München 2005 (cited: Author, in: Paland)

285. PAULUSCH, BERND-ARTHUR: Haftung und Haftungsbegrenzung im kaufmännischen Geschäftsverkehr, DZWiR, 1992, 182
286. PAULY, HANS-JOACHIM: Anwendung des AGB - Gesetzes auch auf Kaufleute, BB, 1976, 534
287. PEEL, EDWIN: Making More Use of the Unfair Contract Terms Act 1977: Steward Gill Ltd. v Horation Myer & Co Ltd., 56 M.L.R., 1993, 98
288. PEEL, EDWIN: Reasonable Exemption Clauses, 117 L.Q.R. 2001, 545
289. PETERS, ANNE; SCHWENKE, HEINER: Comparative beyond Post-Modernism, 49 ICLQ, 2000, 800
290. PFEIFFER, THOMAS: Auf dem Weg zu einem Europäischen Vertragsrecht, in: Privat- und Wirtschaftsrecht im Zeichen der Europäischen Integration, Kieninger E.-M., Remien O. (Hrsg.) Baden Baden 2004
291. PFEIFFER, THOMAS: Vom kaufmännischen Verkehr zum Unternehmensverkehr, NJW, 1999, 169
292. PFEIL, WERNER: Historische Vorbilder und Entwicklung des Rechtsbegriffs der „Vier Grundfreiheiten" im Europäischen Gemeinschaftsrecht, Frankfurt am Main 1998
293. PISKE, PEER INGO: Die Kontrolle der Allgemeinen Geschäftsbedingungen in Spanien, Frankfurt am Main 2002
294. PLENDER, RICHARD, WILDERSPIN MICHAEL: The European Contracts Convention. The Rome Convention on the Choice of Law for Contracts London: Sweet & Maxwell 2001
295. POHLHAUSEN, ROBERT: Zum Recht der allgemeinen Geschäftsbedingungen im 19. Jahrhundert, Ebelsbach 1978
296. POOLE JILL: Textbook on Contract Law, Oxford: Oxford University Press 2003
297. POSNER RICHARD: Economic Analysis of Contract Law After Three Decades: Success or Failure? 112 Yale L. J., 2003, 829
298. POZZO, BARBARA: Harmonisation of European Contract Law and the Need of Creating Common Terminology', 6 ERPL, 2003, 754
299. PRAUSNITZ O.: The Standardization of Commercial Contracts in English and Continental Law. London: Sweet & Maxwell 1937
300. PRINZ ZU LÖWENSTEIN, MICHAEL: AGB–Probleme beim Ein- und Verkauf von Computersoftware, BB, 1985, 1696
301. PULLEN, MIKE: The Use of Articles 30 and 52 to Attack Barriers to Market Access: an Overview of the ECJ's case Law, 17(7) ECLR, 1996, 388
302. RABE, DIETER: Die Auswirkung des AGB-Gesetzes auf den kaufmännischen Verkehr, NJW, 1987, 1978

303. RADLEY-GARDNER, OLIVER; BEALE, HUGH; ZIMMERMANN, REINHARD; SCHULZE, REINER: Fundamental Texts on European Private Law. Oxford and Portland, Oregon: Hart Publishing 2003
304. RAISER, LUDWIG: Das Recht der Allgemeinen Geschäftsbedingungen, Gentner, Nachdruck Bad Homburg 1961
305. RAKOFF, TODD: Contracts of Adhesion: An Essay in Reconstruction, 96 Harv. L. Rev., 1983, 1173
306. REH, HERALD JÜRGEN: Einbeziehung und Inhaltskontrolle Allgemeiner Geschäftsbedingungen im kaufmännischen Verkehr, Nürnberg 1990
307. REICH, NORBERT: Anmerkung zu EuGH, ZIP, 1993, 1815
308. REICH, NORBERT: Bürgerrechte in der Europäischen Union: subjektive Rechte von Unionsbürger und Drittstaatsangehörigen unter besonderer Berücksichtigung der Rechtslage nach der Rechtsprechung des EuGH und dem Vertrag von Amsterdam, Baden-Baden, 1999
309. REICH, NORBERT; MICKLITZ, HANS-WOLFGANG: Europäisches Verbraucherrecht, 4. Aufl. Baden-Baden, 2003
310. REIMANN, MATHIAS, ZEKOLL JOACHIM (eds.): Introduction to German Law, Kluwer Law International 2005
311. REINELT, EKKEHART: AGB-Klausel oder Individualvereinbarung? Zum Begriff Aushandeln. downloaded on 20 August 2009 from <http://www.reinelt-bghanwalt.de/veroeffentlichungen/vo_r45_c.htm>
312. REINER R.: Crime, Law, Deviance: the Durkheim Legacy, in: Durkheim and Modern Sociology, Fenton S., ed., Cambridge: Cambridge University Press 1984
313. REMIEN, OLIVER: Grenzen der gerichtlichen Privatrechtsangleichung mittels der Grundfreiheiten des EG-Vertrages. Bemerkungen zu den Urteil des EuGH vom 24.11.1993 (Keck und Mithouard) und 15.12.1993 Hünermund u.a., JZ, 1994, 349
314. REMIEN, OLIVER: Illusion und Realität eines europäischen Privatrechts, JZ, 1992, 277
315. REMIEN, OLIVER: Zwingendes Vertragsrecht und Grundfreiheiten des EG-Vertrages, Tübingen: Mohr Siebeck 2003
316. RENÉ, DAVID; BRIERLEY, JOHN: Major Legal Systems in the World Today. An Introduction to the Comparative Study of Law. London: Stevens 1985
317. RIEDL, KRISTINA: The Work of the Lando Commission from an Alternative Viewpoint, 1 ERPL 2000, 75
318. RIESENHUBER, KARL: Europäisches Vertragsrecht. Berlin: de Gruyter 2003
319. RIESENHUBER, KARL: System und Prinzipien des Europäischen Vertragsrechts, Berlin: de Gruyter 2003

320. RITTER, CYRIL: Purely Internal Situations, Reverse Discrimination, Guiomnt, Dzodzi and Article 234, 31 E.L.R., 2006, 1617
321. RITTNER, FRITZ: Die wirtschaftliche Ordnung der EG und das Privatrecht, JZ, 1990, 838
322. ROTH, WULF-HENNIG: Der Einfluss des Europäischen Gemeinschaftsrechts auf das Internationale Privatrecht, 55 RabelsZ, 1991, 623
323. ROTH, WULF-HENNIG: Die Freiheit des EG-Vertrages und das nationale Privatrecht, ZEuP, 1994, 5
324. ROTH, WULF-HENNING: Transposing Puintillist' EC Guidelines into Systematic Codes – Problems and Consequences, 10 ERPL, 2002, 761
325. ROTT, PETER: Minimum Harmonisation for the Completion of the Internal Market? The Example of Consumer Sales Law, 40 C.M.L. Rev. 2003
326. ROTT, PETER: What is the Role of the ECJ in EC Private Law? A Comment on the ECJ Judgements in Oceano Grupo, Freiburger Kommunalbauter, Leitner and Veedfald, 1(1) Hanse L.R., 2005, 17
327. ROUTHETTE, GEORGES: The Obligatory Force of Contract in French Law, in: Contract Law Today. Anglo-French Comparisons, Harris D., Tallon D. (eds.) Oxford: Clarendon Press 1991
328. RÜHL, CHRISTIANE: Rechtswahlfreiheit und Rechtswahlklauseln in Allgemeinen Geschäftsbedingungen, Baden-Baden 1999
329. RUTGERS, JACOBIEN W.: The DCFR, Public Policy, Mandatory Rules, and the Welfare State, in: The Politics of the Draft Common Frame of Reference, Somma A. (ed.) Wolters Kluwer Law and Business, The Netherlands 2009, 117
330. RUTGERS, JACOBIEN W: European Competence and a European Civil Code, a Common Frame of Reference or an Optimal Instrument. Downloaded on 1 March 2010 from <http://papers.ssrn.com>
331. SACCO RODOLFO: Legal Formants: A Dynamic Approach to Comparative Law, 39 Am. J. Com. L. 1991, 1
332. SCHAUB, RENATE: Die Neuregelung des Internationalen Deliktsrecht in Deutschland und das europäische Gemeinschaftsrecht, 66 RabelsZ, 2002
333. SCHÄFFER, JÜRGEN: Das Transparenzgebot im Recht der Allgemeinen Geschäftsbedingungen. Verlag Peter Lang GmbH Frankfurt am Main 1992
334. SCHILLER, K. VOLLER: Gerichtsstandsklauseln in AGB zwischen Vollkaufleuten und das AGB-Gesetz, NJW, 1979, 636
335. SCHLECHTRIEM, PETER: Interpretation, Gap-Filling and Further Development of the UN Sales Convention, *Pace International Law Review* (2004), Paper 215

336. SCHLOSSER, PETER: Freizeichnungsklauseln im kaufmännischen Verkehr, in: Zehn Jahre AGB-Gesetz, Heinrichs H., Löwe W., Ulmer P. (Hrsg.), Köln 1987, 121
337. SCHLOSSER, PETER; COESTER-WALTJEN, DAGMAR; GRABE, HANS-ULRICH: Kommentar zum Gesetz zur Regelung des Rechts der allgemeinen Geschäftsbedingungen, Bielefeld 1977
338. SCHMIDT–RIMPLER, WALTER: Das Gesetz zur Regelung des Rechts der Allgemeinen Geschäftsbedingungen, NJW, 1977, 135
339. SCHMITTHOFF M. The Science of Comparative Law, 7 Cambridge L.J., 1939, 94
340. SCHMITTHOFF, CLIVE: The Unification and Harmonisation of Law by Means of Standard Contract and General Conditions, 17 ICLQ, 1968, 551
341. SCHNEIDER, UWE H.: Europäische und Internationale Harmonisierung des Bankrechts. Zugleich ein Beitrag zur Angleichung des Privatrechts in der Europäischen Gemeinschaft, NJW, 1991, 1985
342. SCHNITZER F., ADOLF: Vergleichende Rechtslehre, Bd. I, Verlag für Recht und Gesellschaft AG. Basel 1961
343. SCHULTZE RAINER: European Private Law and the Existing EC Law, 1 ERPL 2005
344. SCHULZE, REINER, ZIMMERMANN, REINHARD: Basistexte zum Europäischen Privatrecht, Baden Baden 2002
345. SCHWARTZ BERNARD (ed.): The Code Napoleon and the Common-Law World, New York: New York University Press 1956
346. SCHWARTZE A.: Design for an Empirical Data Investigation in to the Impact of Existing Law Harmonization under the White Paper of 1985, in: An Academic Green Paper on European Contract Law Grundmann S., Stuyck J. (eds.), The Hague: Kluwer Law International, 2002
347. SCHWARZ ALAN; WILDE L. LOUIS P.: Intervening in Markets on the Basis of Imperfect Information: A Legal and Economic Analysis, 127 U. Pa. L.R. 1979, 682
348. SCHWARZ, ALAN: A Re-examination of non-substantive Unconscionability, 63 Va. L.Rev., 1977, 1053
349. SCHWARZ, IVO E.: Perspektiven der Angleichung des Privatrechts in der Europäischen Gemeinschaft, ZEuP, 1994, 559
350. SCHWENZER INGEBORG: Das UN-Übereinkommen zum internationalen Warenkauf, NJW, 1990, 602
351. SEFTON–GREEN, RUTH: The DCFR: A Technical or Political Toolbox?, in: The Politics of the Draft Common Frame of Reference, Somma A. (ed.) Wolters Kluwer Law and Business, The Netherlands 2009, 39
352. SIEG, OLIVER: Allgemeine Geschäftsbedingungen im grenzüberschreitenden Verkehr, RIW, 1997, 811

353. SINAI, ALI R.: The Inclusion of Mandatory Rules in an Optimal EC Contract Law Instrument, 15(1) EBLR, 2004, 41
354. SLAWSON W DAVID: Standard Form Contracts and Democratic Control of Lawmaking Power, 84 Harv. L. Rev., 1971, 529
355. SLOT, PIET JAN: Harmonisation, 21(5) E.L. Rev. 1996, 378
356. SMITH, STEPHEN A.: In Defence of Substantive Fairness, 112 L.Q.R., 1996, 138
357. SMITS, JAN: Diversity of Contract Law and the European Internal Market, in: The Need to a European Contract Law. Empirical and Legal Perspectives. Smits J. (ed.) Groningen: Europa Law Publishing 2005
358. SMITS, JAN: The Making of European Private Law. Towards ius Commune Europeum as a mixed Legal System, Intersentia 2002
359. SMITS, JAN: The Draft Common Frame of Reference: how to improve it?, in: European Private Law after the Common Frame of Reference, Micklitz Hans- W., Cafaggi F. (eds.), Cheltenham UK, Northampton, MA, USA: Edward Elgar 2010, 90
360. SNELL, JUKKA; ANDENAS, MADS: Exploring the Outer Limits: Restrictions on Free Movement in: The Law of the Single European Market, Barnard C. Scott J. (eds.) Oxford and Portland, Oregon: Hart Publishing 2002
361. SNELL, JUKKA: Goods and Services in EC Law. A Study of the Relationship between the Freedoms Oxford: Oxford University Press 2002
362. SNELL, JUKKA: True Proportionality and Free Movement of Goods and Services, 11 EBLR, 2000, 55
363. SOBICH, CHRISTOPHER PHILIP: Die verfahrensrechtliche Kontrolle 'unfairer' Allgemeiner Geschäftsbedingungen in England. Zur praktischen Wirksamkeit von AGB – Kontrollverfahren im Vergleich zum deutschen Recht. Frankfurt am Main [u. a.] 1997
364. SOMMA, ALESSANDRO: Towards a European Private Law? The Common Frame of Reference in the Conflict between EC law and National Laws, in: European Private Law after the Common Frame of Reference, Micklitz Hans- W., Cafaggi F. (eds.), Cheltenham UK, Northampton, MA, USA: Edward Elgar 2010, 1
365. SONNENBERGER, HANS JÜRGEN: Das französische Recht der allgemeiner Geschäftsbedingungen (*conditions générales*), RIW, 1990, 167
366. SONNENBERGER, HANS JÜRGEN; SCHWEINBERGER, EUGEN: Einführung in das französische Recht, zweite, völlig neu bearbeitete Aufl., Darmstadt 1986
367. STADLER, HANS-JÖRG: Allgemeine Geschäftsbedingungen im internationalen Handelsverkehr. Heidelberg 2003

368. STAUB, HERMANN (BEGR.): Großkommentar zum HGB, Dritter Band, 1 Halbband §§ 343-351, Berlin New York 1978 (cited: author, in: Staub)
369. STAUDENMAYER, DIRK: Die Mitteilung der Kommission zum Europäischen Vertragsrecht, EuZW, 2001, 485
370. STAUDENMAYER, DIRK: The Commission Action Plan on European Contract Law, 2 ERPL 2003, 113
371. STAUDENMAYER, DIRK: The Commission Communication on European Contract Law and its Follow-up: in: An Academic Green Paper on European Contract Law Grundmann S., Stuyck J. (eds.), The Hague: Kluwer Law International, 2002
372. STAUDENMAYER, DIRK: The Way Forward in European Contract, 13 ERPL, 2005, 95
373. STEFAN GRUNDMANN, STUYCK JULES: An Academic Green Paper on European Contract Law – Scope, Common Ground and Debated Issues, in: An Academic Green Paper on European Contract Law Grundmann S., Stuyck J. (eds.), The Hague: Kluwer Law International 2002
374. STEIN, AXEL: Gesetz zur Regelung des Rechts der Allgemeinen Geschäftsbedingungen, Stuttgart, 1977
375. STEIN, GÜNTER: Inhaltskontrolle vorformulierter Verträge, Berlin 1982
376. STEINDORFF, ERNST: Anmerkung zur EuGH Rechtsprechung, JZ, 1994, 95
377. STEINDORFF, ERNST: EG-Vertrag und Privatrecht, Baden-Baden 1996
378. STEINDORFF, ERNST: Unvollkommener Binnenmarkt, 158 ZHR, 1994, 149
379. STOFFELS, MARKUS: AGB-Recht, Heidelberg 2003
380. STONE RICHARD: The Modern Law of Contract, London Sydney Portland Oregon: Cavendish Publishing Limited 2005
381. STORME, E. MATTHIAS: Freedom of Contract: Mandatory and Non-Mandatory Rules in European Contract Law. Working paper, Conference European Legal Harmony: Goals and Milestones, 10th Anniversary Juridica International, Tartu, December 6th, 2005
382. STRAETMANS, GERT: 'Case C-405/98 Konsumentombudsmannen (KO) v. Gourmet International Products AB (GIP), Judgement of the Court (Sixth Chamber) of 8 March 2001', 39 C.M.L. Rev. 2002, 1407
383. STRESE JULIA: Die Kompetenzen der Europäischen Gemeinschaft zur Privatrechtsangleichung im Binnenmarkt. Eine Untersuchung zur vertikalen Kompetenzenverteilung im Bereich des Gemeinschaftsprivatrechts und zu den Folgen kompetenzüberschreitenden Handels. Baden Baden 2006
384. STRUMPF, HERBERT: Sand in Getriebe unternehmerischen Handeln, BB, 1985, 963

385. SUNSTEIN, R. CASS: Paradoxes of the Regulatory State, 57 U. Chicago L. Rev., 1990, 407
386. TESKE, WOLFGANG: Schriftformklauseln in allgemeinen Geschäftsbedingungen. Köln Berlin Bonn München 1990
387. THALMAIR, PETER: Von Postulat der Überraschungsfreiheit von AGB-Klauseln zu ihrer Transparenskontrolle, München 1999
388. TILLMANN, WINFRIED: Das AGB – Gesetz und die Einheit des Privatrechts, 142, ZHR, 1978, 52
389. TILLMANN, WINFRIED: Towards a European Civil Code, ZEuP, 1997, 595
390. TILLMANN, WINFRIED: Zweiter Kodifikationsbeschluss des Europäischen Parlaments, ZEuP, 1995, 535
391. TINBERGER, JAN: International Economic Integration, Elsevier Amsterdam 1965
392. TREBILCOCK, J. MICHAEL: The Limits of Freedom of Contract, Cambridge, Massachusetts,, and London: Harvard University Press 1993
393. TREITEL, GUENTER SIR: The Law of Contract, 11th ed., London: Sweet & Maxwell 2003
394. ULMER, PETER, BRANDNER, HANS-ERICH, HENSEN, HORST-DIETER (Hrsg.): AGB Gesetz 9. Aufl. Köln 1991 (cited: author, in: Ulmer/Brandner/Hensen)
395. ULMER, PETER: Erfahrungen mit dem AGB-Gesetz, BB, 1982, 584
396. ULMER, PETER: Von deutschen zum europäischen Privatrecht, JZ, 1992, 1
397. ULMER, PETER: Zehn Jahre AGB–Gesetz–Rückblick und Ausblick, in: Zehn Jahre AGB-Gesetz, Heinrichs H., Löwe W., Ulmer P. (Hrsg.), Köln 1987
398. UNBERATH, HANNES; JOHNSTON, ANGUS: Law at, to or from the Centre? The European Court of Justice and the Harmonisation of Private Law in the European Union', in: The Institutional Framework of European Private Law, Cafaggi F. (ed.), Oxford: Oxford University Press 2006, 149
399. USHER, A. JOHN: C-376/98 Germany v. European Parliament and Council (Tobacco Advertising). Judgement of the Full Court of 5 October 2000, [2000] ECR I-8419, 38 C.M.L. Rev. 2001, 1519
400. VAN BAR, CHRISTIAN: Internationales Privatrecht. Zweiter Bd. Besonderer Teil. C. H. Beck'sche Verlagsbuchhandlung München 1991
401. VAN DEN BERGH, VISSCHER LOUIS: The Principles of European Tort Law: The Right Path to Harmonisation? 4 ERPL, 2006, 514
402. VERHAGEN, HENDRIK: The Tension between Party Autonomy and European Union Law: Some Observations on Ingmar GB LTD v Eaton Leonard Technologies Inc., 51 ICLQ, 2002, 135

403. VOGENAUER, STEPHEN; WEATHERILL, STEPHEN: The EC's Competence to Pursue Harmonisation, in: The Harmonization of European Contract Law. Implications for European Private Laws, Business and Legal Practice, Vogenauer S., Weatherill S. (eds.) Oxford and Portland, Oregon: Hart Publishing 2006
404. VOLTAIRE: Oeuvres de Voltaire. Dialogues. Backquenois, éditeur Paris 1838
405. VON BAR, CHRISTIAN, LANDO, OLE, SWAN, STEPHEN: Communication on European Contract Law: Joint Response of the Commission on European Contract Law and the Study Group on a European Civil Code, 2 ERPL, 2002, 183
406. VON BAR, CHRISTIAN, SWAN STEPHEN: Response to the Action Plan on European Contract Law: A More Coherent European Contract Law (COM (2003) 63), 5 ERPL 2003, 595
407. VON STAUDINGER, JULIUS; BECKMANN, ROLAND, MICHAEL; MARTINEK, MICHAEL: J. von Staudingers Kommentar zum Bürgerlichen Gesetzbuch mit Einführungsgesetz und Nebengesetzen, 12 Ed. Walter de Gruyter, 2005 (cited: author, in: von Staudingers Kommentar)
408. VON WILMOWSKY, PETER: EG - Freiheiten und Vertragsrecht, JZ, 1996, 590
409. VON WILMOWSKY, PETER: EG - Vertrag und kollisionsrechtliche Rechtsfreiheit, 62 RabelsZ, 1998, 1
410. WAGNER, GERHARD: The Economics of Harmonisation: the Case of Contract Law, 39 C.M.L. Rev., 2002, 995
411. WAGNER, GERHARD: The Project of Harmonizing European Tort Law, 42 C.M.L. Rev., 2005, 1269
412. WATSON, ALAN: Legal Transplants: an Approach to Comparative law. 2nd ed. Athens and London: The University of Georgia Press 1993
413. WEATHERILL, STEPHEN: Constitutional Issues – How much is best Left unsaid? in: The Harmonization of European Contract Law. Implications for European Private Laws, Business and Legal Practice, Vogenauer S., Weatherill S. (eds.) Oxford and Portland, Oregon: Hart Publishing 2006
414. WEATHERILL, STEPHEN: After Keck: Some Thoughts on How to clarify the Clarification, 33(5) C.M.L. Rev., 1996, 885
415. WEATHERILL, STEPHEN: European Contract Law: Taking the Heat out of Question of Competence, 15(1) EBLR, 2004, 23
416. WEATHERILL, STEPHEN: Free Movement of Goods, 52(4) ICLQ, 2003, 1021
417. WEATHERILL, STEPHEN: Free Movement of Goods, 55(2) ICLQ 2006, 457

418. WEATHERILL, STEPHEN: Harmonisation: How Much, How Little?, 16 EBLR 2005, 533
419. WEATHERILL, STEPHEN: Reflections on the EC's Competence to develop 'European Contract Law', 13(3) ERPL, 2005, 405
420. WEATHERILL, STEPHEN: The Free Movement of Goods: a Survey of the Decisions of the Court of Justice in 1991: Mutual Recognition, 17(5) ERPL, 1992, 424
421. WEATHERILL, STEPHEN: Why object to the Harmonisation of Private Law by the EC? 12 ERPL 2004, 633
422. WEBER, MAX: Economy and Society, Roth G., Wittich C. (eds.) New York, Bedminster Press 1968
423. WEICK, GÜNTER: Unfair Contract Terms Act und AGB-Gesetz, 145, ZHR 1981, 68
424. WEIR, TONY: All or Nothing, 78 Tul. L. R. 2004, 511
425. WESTERMANN, HARM PETER: Abgrenzung von Neben- und Hauptleistungspflichten im Hinblick auf die Inhaltskontrolle, in: Zehn Jahre AGB-Gesetz, Heinrichs H., Löwe W., Ulmer P. (Hrsg.), Köln 1987
426. WHINCUP, H. MICHAEL (ed.): Contract Law and Practice. The English System and Continental Comparisons, The Hague London Boston: Kluwer Law International 2001
427. WHITTAKER, SIMON: The 'Draft Common Frame of Reference'. An Assessment. Commissioned by the Ministry of Justice, United Kingdom. November 2008
428. WHITTAKER, SIMON; ZIMMERMANN, REINHARD: Good Faith in European Contract Law, in: Good Faith in European Contract Law, Zimmermann R., Whittaker S. (eds.) Cambridge: Cambridge University Press 2000
429. WILHELMSSON, THOMAS: Social Contract Law and European Integration. Dartmouth: Publishing Company 1995
430. WILHELMSSON, THOMAS: Standard Form Conditions in: Towards a European Civil Code. A. Hesselink M. (*et. al.*) (ed.) Ars Aequi Libri – Nijmegen Kluwer Law International 2004
431. WILHELMSSON, THOMAS: The European Civil Code, European Legal Traditions and Neo-Positivism, 4 ERPL 1998, 351
432. WILHELMSSON, THOMAS: The Legal, the Cultural and the Political – Conclusions from Different Perspectives on Harmonisation of European Contract Law, 13, EBLR 2002, 541
433. WILKE, PETER JOSEF: Inhaltskontrolle und deren Rechtsfolgen im System der Überprüfung Allgemeiner Geschäftsbedingungen. München 1983

434. WILLET, CHRIS (ed.): Aspects of Fairness in Contract, Blackstone Press Limited 1996
435. WILLISTON, SAMUEL: Freedom of Contract, 6 Corn. L.Q., 1921, 365
436. WOLF, DIETRICH: Vorschläge für eine gesetzliche Regelung der Allgemeinen Geschäftsbedingungen, JZ, 1974, 41
437. WOLF, MANFRED: Auslegung und Inhaltskontrolle von AGB im internationalen kaufmännischen Verkehr, 153 ZHR, 1989, 300
438. WOLF, MANFRED: Preisanpassungsklauseln im Allgemeinen Geschäftsbedingungen unter Kaufleuten, ZIP, 1987, 341
439. WOLF, MANFRED: Gesetz und Richterrecht bei AGB, JZ, 1974, 465
440. WOLF, MANFRED: Harmonisation of Protection against unfair Contract Terms in Private European Law, in: European Legal Traditions and Israel, Rabello A. M. (ed.) Jerusalem: The Harry and Michael Sacher Institute for Legislative Research and Comparative Law 1994
441. WOLF, MANFRED: Privates Bankvertragrecht im EG-Binnenmarkt. Auswirkung der II. EG- Bankrechts-Richtlinie auf privatrechtliche Bankgeschäfte, 47 WM, 1990, 1941
442. WOLF, MANFRED; HORN, NORBERT; LINDACHER, WALTER F.: AGB-Gesetz, Kommentar, 4. Auf. 1999 (cited: author, in: Wolf/Horn/Lindacher)
443. WOOD, PHILIP: Law and Practice of International Finance. London: Sweet & Maxwell 2008
444. WOODS, LORNA: Free Movement of Goods and Services within the European Community. Ashgate: Ashgate Publishing Limited 2004
445. WURMNEST, WOLFGANG: Grundzüge eines europäischen Haftungsrechts. Eine rechtsvergleichende Untersuchung des Gemeinschaftsrechts, Tübingen 2003
446. YATES, DAVID: Exclusion Clauses in Contract, 2nd ed. London: Sweet & Maxwell 1982
447. YATES, DAVID; HAWKINS, A. J.: Standard Business Contracts: Exclusion and Related Devices, London: Sweet & Maxwell 1986
448. ZIEGEL S. JACOB: The Future of the International Sales Convention from a Common Law Perspective, 6 New Zealand Business Law Quarterly, November 2000, 336
449. ZIMMERMANN, REINHARD: Codification: History and Present Significance of an Idea, 3 ERPL, 1995, 95
450. ZIMMERMANN, REINHARD: Contract Law Reform: The German Experience, in: The Harmonization of European Contract Law. Implications for European Private Laws, Business and Legal Practice, Vogenauer S., Weatherill S. (eds.) Oxford and Portland, Oregon: Hart Publishing 2006

451. ZIMMERMANN, REINHARD: Ius Commune and the Principles of European Contract Law: Contemporary of an Old Idea, in: European Contract Law: Scots and South African Perspectives, MacQueen H. L., Zimmermann R. (eds.) Edinburgh University Press 1996
452. ZIMMERMANN, REINHARD: Konturen eines Europäischen Vertragsrechts, JZ, 1995, 477
453. ZIMMERMANN, REINHARD: The Law of Obligations Roman Foundations of the Civilian Tradition. Oxford: Oxford University Press 1990
454. ZWEIGERD, KONRAD, KÖTZ, HEIN: Introduction to Comparative Law. Translated by Weird T. Oxford: Clarendon Press 1998

Studien zum europäischen Privat- und Prozessrecht

Herausgegeben von Marina Wellenhofer
Begründet von Manfred Wolf

Band 1 Axel Pajunk: Die Bedeutung und Reichweite der Kapitalverkehrs- und Dienstleistungsfreiheit des EG-Vertrages. Die gegenseitige Anerkennung von Privatrechtsinstituten am Beispiel der englischen Mobiliarkreditsicherheiten. 1999.

Band 2 Kerstin Pudor: Die Wirkungsweise verbraucherschützender Widerrufsrechte. Zur Wirksamkeit des Verbrauchervertrages bei bestehendem Widerrufsrecht nach den §§ 1 HWiG, 7 VerbrKrG und 5 TzWrG. 2000.

Band 3 Michael Brück: Das Vorabentscheidungsverfahren vor dem Europäischen Gerichtshof als Bestandteil des deutschen Zivilprozesses. Rechtsschutzhemmendes Integrationsproblem oder kohärente Rechtsschutzerweiterung. 2001.

Band 4 Christine Steven: Immobiliarsicherheiten im englischen und deutschen Recht. Eine rechtsvergleichende Untersuchung unter besonderer Berücksichtigung der Insolvenz des Sicherheitengebers. 2002.

Band 5 Jochen Kaiser: Schutzrechtsfremde Wettbewerbsverbote in immaterialgüterrechtlichen Lizenzverträgen. 2002.

Band 6 Nikolaj Fischer: Das allgemeine verbraucherschützende Widerrufsrecht gemäß § 355 BGB. Ein Beitrag zur Dogmatik der Wirkungsweise von Widerrufsrechten im Privatrecht. 2003.

Band 7 Markus Dinnes: Softwareentwicklung im Vertragsverhältnis. Die Zuordnung von Nutzungsrechten bei fehlender vertraglicher Vereinbarung. 2003.

Band 8 Jan Roth: Interessenwiderstreit im Insolvenzeröffnungsverfahren. Eine Untersuchung des Insolvenzeröffnungsverfahrens unter verfahrens- und verfassungsrechtlichen Gesichtspunkten. 2004.

Band 9 Cengiz Kulaksiz: Die Teilklage im deutschen und türkischen Zivilprozessrecht. 2004.

Band 10 Franc Zimmermann: Mobiliar- und Unternehmenshypotheken in Europa. Auswirkungen der Grundfreiheiten des EG-Vertrages auf das nationale Sachrecht. 2005.

Band 11 Erik Hintz: Die Unternehmensbeleihung im europäischen Binnenmarkt. Die grenzüberschreitende Bestellung von Unternehmenshypotheken nach französischem, englischem und schwedischem Recht im Kontext der Kapitalverkehrsfreiheit. 2007.

Band 12 Carsten Fischer: Die Investmentaktiengesellschaft aus aufsichtsrechtlicher und gesellschaftsrechtlicher Perspektive. 2008.

Band 13 Niels Höra: Haftung für fehlerhafte Informationen gegenüber Nichtvertragspartnern. 2008.

Band 14 Gintautas Šulija: Standard Contract Terms in Cross-Border Business Transactions. A Comparative Study from the Perspective of European Union Law. 2011.

www.peterlang.de